TEACHER GUIDE

Includes Worksheets

7th – 8th Grade | Math | Quizzes

PRINCIPLES OF MATHEMATICS BOOK 2

Author: Katherine A. Loop

Master Books Creative Team:

Editor: Craig Froman

Design: Jennifer Bauer

Cover Design: Diana Bogardus

Copy Editors:
Judy Lewis
Willow Meek

Curriculum Review:
Kristen Pratt
Laura Welch
Diana Bogardus

First printing: March 2016
Sixth printing: March 2021

Copyright © 2016 by Katherine A. Loop. All rights reserved. No part of this book may be reproduced, copied, broadcast, stored, or shared in any form whatsoever without written permission from the publisher, except in the case of brief quotations in articles and reviews. For information write:

Master Books®, P.O. Box 726, Green Forest, AR 72638

Master Books® is a division of the New Leaf Publishing Group, Inc.

ISBN: 978-0-89051-907-3
ISBN: 978-1-61458-491-9 (digital)

Unless otherwise noted, Scripture quotations are from the King James Version of the Bible.

Based on and designed to go with *Principles of Mathematics Student Textbook* (Book 2). Please see the *Student Textbook* for further information and sources.

For the most part, units are based on the official standards given in Tina Butcher, Linda Crown, Rick Harshman, and Juana Williams, eds. NIST Handbook 44: 97th National Conference on Weights and Measures 2012, 2013 ed. (Washington: U. S. Department of Commerce, 2012), Appendix C. Found on http://www.nist.gov/pml/wmd/pubs/ h44-13.cfm, accessed 10/6/2014.

Printed in the United States of America

Please visit our website for other great titles:
www.masterbooks.com

Permission is granted for copies of reproducible pages from this text to be made for use with immediate family members living in the same household. However, no part of this book may be reproduced, copied, broadcast, stored, or shared in any form beyond this use. Permission for any other use of the material must be requested by email from the publisher at info@nlpg.com.

Problems from the Early 1900s

History…in math? Why not! Throughout the text, we've sprinkled in some math problems from early 1900 math textbooks, often with significant adaptation. The sources are listed here for your reference.

The following problems were adapted from Eugene Henry Barker, *Applied Mathematics for Junior High Schools and High Schools* (Boston: Allyn and Bacon, 1920). Available on Google Books.

Worksheet 2.3, problem 3c; Quiz 1, problems 3a and 5c; Worksheet 5.4, problems 2a and 2b; Quiz 4, problems 1a–1b; Test 1, problem 1a–1b; Worksheet 6.1, problem 2; Worksheet 6.3A, problems 1 and 2; Worksheet 6.3B, problems 1a and 1c; Quiz 5, problem 1c; Worksheet 7.1, problems 4c and 4d; Worksheet 7.2, problem 5; Worksheet 7.3, problem 3; Quiz 6, problem 3; Worksheet 11.6, problems 1a and 1c; Test 2, problem 3d; Worksheet 17.5, problem 4; Worksheet 20.3, problem 5a; Worksheet 21.3C, problem 3

The following problems were adapted from John C. Stone and James F. Millis, *A Secondary Arithmetic: Commercial and Industrial for High, Industrial, Commercial, Normal Schools, and Academies* (Boston: Benj. H. Sanborn & Co., 1908). Available on Google Books.

Worksheet 1.4, problem 3; Worksheet 3.7, problem 5; Worksheet 5.2, problem 3; Worksheet 5.3, problem 3; Worksheet 5.5, problem 1a; Worksheet 11.6, problem 9; Worksheet 12.1, problem 5; Worksheet 13.4, problems 3b–3c; Worksheet 14.7, problem 2, Quiz 16, problem 4; Worksheet 18.4, problem 6; Worksheet 20.4, problem 3; Worksheet 21.3C, problem 2

This problems were adapted from Joseph Victor Collins, *Practical Algebra: First Year Course* (New York: American Book Co. 1910). Available on Google Books.

Worksheet 3.2, problem 5b; Worksheet 5.6, problems 6a–6c; Worksheet 7.4, problem 5; Worksheet 9.4, problem 1; Worksheet 10.1, problem 4; Worksheet 10.3, problem 3; Worksheet 11.3, problem 3b–3d; Worksheet 11.4, problem 5c; Worksheet 12.3, Problems 3 and 4

Table of Contents

Using This Teacher Guide 4

Course Description 4

Course Objectives 5

Supplies Needed 5

Suggested Daily Schedule 6

Suggested Accelerated Daily Schedule 14

Worksheets 19

Quizzes 307

Tests 347

Answer Key 361

Reference Sheets 423

Preparing to Use the Curriculum

We've tried to streamline everything to make this curriculum as easy to use as possible. Rather than long instructions on how to teach each lesson, the *Student Textbook* contains all the explanation of the material. Important terms are bolded in the textbook so you can easily spot them. Examples you can work through with the student if needed are all included there.

Here are two different suggestions for how to prep the information in this *Teacher Guide*:

- Tear out the schedule, answer key, quizzes, and tests and put them in a binder for you to use as needed, and then hand the student the rest of the guide to work from when instructed.

- Tear out each worksheet as you assign it and hand it to the student, and have them store the completed pages in a binder.

Either way, all the pages are already hole punched for you and ready to go.

The schedule on page 6 explains what to assign each day. This schedule can be adapted to fit your needs. For example, in a classroom setting, several days could be taught at once, with the assignments due at the next class.

Katherine Loop is a homeschool graduate from northern Virginia. Understanding the biblical worldview in math made a tremendous difference in her life and started her on a journey of researching and sharing on the topic. For over a decade now, she's been researching, writing, and speaking on math, along with other topics. Her books on math and a biblical worldview have been used by various Christian colleges, homeschool groups, and individuals. You can connect with her at www.ChristianPerspective.net.

Using This Teacher Guide

Features: The suggested weekly schedule enclosed has easy-to-manage lessons that guide the reading, worksheets, and all assessments. The pages of this guide are perforated and three-hole punched so materials are easy to tear out, hand out, grade, and store. Teachers are encouraged to adjust the schedule and materials as needed in order to best work within their unique educational program.

Lesson Scheduling: Students are instructed to read the pages in their book and then complete the corresponding section provided by the teacher. Assessments that may include worksheets, activities, quizzes, and tests are given at regular intervals, with space to record each grade. Space is provided on the weekly schedule for assignment dates, and flexibility in scheduling is encouraged. Teachers may adapt the scheduled days per each unique student situation. As the student completes each assignment, this can be marked with an "X" in the box.

🕐	Approximately 30 to 45 minutes per lesson, four to five days a week
🔑	Includes answer keys for worksheets, quizzes, and tests.
📝	Worksheets for each section
🔄	Quizzes and tests are included to help reinforce learning and provide assessment opportunities.
📄	Designed for grades 7 to 8 to complete in a one-year course or for older students to use at an accellerated speed.

Course Description

This a Book 2 of a two-book math course designed to give students a firm mathematical foundation, both academically and spiritually. Not only does the curriculum build mathematical thinking and problem-solving skills, it also shows student how a biblical worldview affects our approach to math's various concepts. Students learn to see math, not as an academic exercise, but as a way of exploring and describing consistencies God created and sustains. The worldview is not just an addition to the curriculum, but is the starting point. Science, history, and real life are integrated throughout.

Course Objectives

Students completing this course will:

- Discover how a biblical worldview affects how we view and use math, and how math's very existence points us to a faithful Creator we can trust

- Be equipped to use the math they learn as a useful tool in a wide range of settings, learning to see math as much more than a textbook exercise

- Have a solid foundation for algebra, understanding the core concepts of working with unknowns, equalities, inequalities, functions, and graphing relationships

- Grasp core concepts in statistics and probability, including line graphs and trends, scatter graphs and correlation, stem-and-leaf plots, averages, independent events, dependent events, and the fundamental counting principle

- Work with exponents and square roots, including negative exponents, scientific notation, finding square roots, and the Pythagorean theorem

- Get a glimpse of how math applies in other areas, including trigonometry, sets, and consumer math

Supplies Needed

- *Principles of Mathematics Student Textbook (Book 2)*

- **Binder with Lined Paper** — Students will need to tear out the reference section from this book and put it in the binder, as well as add notes to the binder during the course. They can also use their binder to store their completed worksheets, if desired.

- **Calculator** — Students need a calculator that is able to handle scientific notation; has at least a 10-digit display; and has exponent (y^x), square root ($\sqrt{}$), sine (SIN), cosine (COS), and tangent (TAN) buttons. Graphing calculators should not be used in this course.

- **Graph Paper** — Students will need graph paper to draw coordinate graphs.

- **Ruler** — Students will need a ruler to draw straight lines when graphing.

- **Additional Paper** (if needed) — Students should have extra paper available in case they need more room to complete a problem.

- **Index Cards** (optional) — Making flashcards of definitions or formulas can be a helpful way to learn and review the material. Students are encouraged to use index cards to make flashcards as needed.

Additional Resources and Course Notes

- Please see http://www.christianperspective.net/math/pom2 for links to helpful online resources, along with additional notes and information related to this course. There is also a way to ask questions there.

Suggested Daily Schedule
(to complete Book 2 in a school year)

Date	Day	Assignment	Due Date	✓	Grade
		First Semester—First Quarter			
Week 1	Day 1	Lesson 1.1 (*Student Textbook*, pages 13–18) Worksheet 1.1 (*Teacher Guide*, pages 21–22)			
	Day 2	Lesson 1.2 (*Student Textbook*, pages 18–22) Worksheet 1.2 (*Teacher Guide*, pages 23–24)			
	Day 3	Lesson 1.3 (*Student Textbook*, pages 22–24) Worksheet 1.3 (*Teacher Guide*, pages 25–26)			
	Day 4	Lesson 1.4 (*Student Textbook*, pages 24–26) Worksheet 1.4 (*Teacher Guide*, pages 27–28)			
	Day 5	Lesson 1.5–1.6 (*Student Textbook*, pages 27–31) Worksheet 1.5 (*Teacher Guide*, pages 29–30)			
Week 2	Day 6	Lesson 2.1 (*Student Textbook*, pages 33–35) Worksheet 2.1 (*Teacher Guide*, page 31)			
	Day 7	Lesson 2.2 (*Student Textbook*, pages 36–38) Worksheet 2.2 (*Teacher Guide*, pages 33–34)			
	Day 8	Lesson 2.3 (*Student Textbook*, pages 38–41) Worksheet 2.3 (*Teacher Guide*, pages 35–36)			
	Day 9	Lesson 2.4 (*Student Textbook*, pages 41–46) Worksheet 2.4 (*Teacher Guide*, pages 37–38)			
	Day 10	Lesson 2.5 (*Student Textbook*, pages 46–52) Worksheet 2.5 (*Teacher Guide*, pages 39–40)			
Week 3	Day 11	Lesson 2.6 (*Student Textbook*, pages 53–57) Worksheet 2.6 (*Teacher Guide*, pages 41–42)			
	Day 12	Lesson 2.7 (*Student Textbook*, page 58) Study Day			
	Day 13	**Quiz 1** (*Teacher Guide*, pages 309–310)			
	Day 14	Study Day*			
	Day 15	Study Day*			
Week 4	Day 16	Lesson 3.1 (*Student Textbook*, pages 59–61) Worksheet 3.1 (*Teacher Guide*, pages 43–44)			
	Day 17	Lesson 3.2 (*Student Textbook*, pages 61–64) Worksheet 3.2 (*Teacher Guide*, pages 45–46)			
	Day 18	Lesson 3.3 (*Student Textbook*, pages 64–68) Worksheet 3.3 (*Teacher Guide*, pages 47–48)			
	Day 19	Lesson 3.4 (*Student Textbook*, pages 68–70) Worksheet 3.4 (*Teacher Guide*, pages 49–50)			
	Day 20	Lesson 3.5 (*Student Textbook*, pages 70–72) Worksheet 3.5 (*Teacher Guide*, pages 51–52)			

* Use these study days to spend extra time reviewing any concepts covered in the first two chapters that need more review. The first two chapters reviewed many foundational concepts; it's important to be comfortable with them before continuing.

Suggested Daily Schedule
(to complete Book 2 in a school year)

Date	Day	Assignment	Due Date	✓	Grade
Week 5	Day 21	Lesson 3.6 (*Student Textbook*, pages 72–75) Worksheet 3.6 (*Teacher Guide*, pages 53–54)			
	Day 22	Lesson 3.7 (*Student Textbook*, pages 75–79) Worksheet 3.7 (*Teacher Guide*, pages 55–56)			
	Day 23	Lesson 3.8 (*Student Textbook*, pages 79–80) Study Day			
	Day 24	**Quiz 2** (*Teacher Guide*, pages 311–312)			
	Day 25				
Week 6	Day 26	Lesson 4.1 (*Student Textbook*, pages 81–83) Worksheet 4.1 (*Teacher Guide*, pages 57–58)			
	Day 27	Lesson 4.2 (*Student Textbook*, pages 83–86) Worksheet 4.2 (*Teacher Guide*, pages 59–60)			
	Day 28	Lesson 4.3 (*Student Textbook*, pages 86–88) Worksheet 4.3 (*Teacher Guide*, pages 61–62)			
	Day 29	Lesson 4.4 (*Student Textbook*, pages 89–90) Worksheet 4.4 (*Teacher Guide*, pages 63–64)			
	Day 30				
Week 7	Day 31	Lesson 4.5 (*Student Textbook*, pages 91–93) Worksheet 4.5 (*Teacher Guide*, pages 65–66)			
	Day 32	Lesson 4.6 (*Student Textbook*, pages 93–94) Study Day			
	Day 33	**Quiz 3** (*Teacher Guide*, pages 313–314)			
	Day 34	Lesson 5.1 (*Student Textbook*, pages 95–101) Worksheet 5.1A (*Teacher Guide*, pages 67–68)			
	Day 35	Worksheet 5.1B (*Teacher Guide*, pages 69–70)			
Week 8	Day 36	Lesson 5.2 (*Student Textbook*, pages 101–105) Worksheet 5.2 (*Teacher Guide*, pages 71–72)			
	Day 37	Lesson 5.3 (*Student Textbook*, pages 106–108) Worksheet 5.3A (*Teacher Guide*, pages 73–74)			
	Day 38	Worksheet 5.3B (*Teacher Guide*, pages 75–76)			
	Day 39	Lesson 5.4 (*Student Textbook*, pages 108–110) Worksheet 5.4 (*Teacher Guide*, pages 77–78)			
	Day 40	Lesson 5.5 (*Student Textbook*, pages 111–115) Worksheet 5.5 (*Teacher Guide*, pages 79–80)			
Week 9	Day 41	Lesson 5.6 (*Student Textbook*, pages 115–116) Study Day			
	Day 42	**Quiz 4** (*Teacher Guide*, pages 315–316)			
	Day 43	Worksheet 5.6 (*Teacher Guide*, pages 81–84)			
	Day 44	Study Day			
	Day 45	**Test 1** (*Teacher Guide*, pages 347–348)			

Suggested Daily Schedule
(to complete Book 2 in a school year)

Date	Day	Assignment	Due Date	✓	Grade
		First Semester—Second Quarter			
Week 1	Day 46	Lesson 6.1 (*Student Textbook*, pages 117–120) Worksheet 6.1 (*Teacher Guide*, pages 85–86)			
	Day 47	Lesson 6.2 (*Student Textbook*, pages 121–124) Worksheet 6.2A (*Teacher Guide*, pages 87–88)			
	Day 48	Worksheet 6.2B (*Teacher Guide*, pages 89–90)			
	Day 49	Lesson 6.3 (*Student Textbook*, pages 124–128) Worksheet 6.3A (*Teacher Guide*, pages 91–92)			
	Day 50	Worksheet 6.3B (*Teacher Guide*, pages 93–94)			
Week 2	Day 51	Lesson 6.4 (*Student Textbook*, pages 128–130) Worksheet 6.4 (*Teacher Guide*, pages 95–96)			
	Day 52	Lesson 6.5 (*Student Textbook*, pages 130–132) Study Day			
	Day 53	**Quiz 5** (*Teacher Guide*, pages 317–318)			
	Day 54	Lesson 7.1 (*Student Textbook*, pages 133–136) Worksheet 7.1 (*Teacher Guide*, pages 97–98)			
	Day 55	Lesson 7.2 (*Student Textbook*, pages 136–139) Worksheet 7.2 (*Teacher Guide*, pages 99–100)			
Week 3	Day 56	Lesson 7.3 (*Student Textbook*, pages 140–141) Worksheet 7.3 (*Teacher Guide*, pages 101–102)			
	Day 57	Lesson 7.4 (*Student Textbook*, pages 141–143) Worksheet 7.4 (*Teacher Guide*, pages 103–104)			
	Day 58	Lesson 7.5 (*Student Textbook*, pages 143–145) Worksheet 7.5 (*Teacher Guide*, pages 105–106)			
	Day 59	**Quiz 6** (*Teacher Guide*, page 319)			
	Day 60	Lesson 8.1 (*Student Textbook*, pages 147–149) Worksheet 8.1 (*Teacher Guide*, pages 107)			
Week 4	Day 61	Lesson 8.2 (*Student Textbook*, pages 149–150) Worksheet 8.2 (*Teacher Guide*, pages 109–110)			
	Day 62	Lesson 8.3 (*Student Textbook*, page 151–153) Worksheet 8.3 (*Teacher Guide*, pages 111–112)			
	Day 63	Lesson 8.4 (*Student Textbook*, pages 153–155) Worksheet 8.4 (*Teacher Guide*, pages 113–114)			
	Day 64	Lesson 8.5 (*Student Textbook*, pages 156–157) Worksheet 8.5 (*Teacher Guide*, pages 115–116)			
	Day 65	Lesson 8.6 (*Student Textbook*, page 157) Study Day			

Suggested Daily Schedule
(to complete Book 2 in a school year)

Date	Day	Assignment	Due Date	✓	Grade
Week 5	Day 66	**Quiz 7** (*Teacher Guide*, page 321)			
	Day 67	Lesson 9.1 (*Student Textbook*, pages 159–162) Worksheet 9.1 (*Teacher Guide*, pages 117–118)			
	Day 68	Lesson 9.2 (*Student Textbook*, pages 162–167) Worksheet 9.2 (*Teacher Guide*, pages 119–120)			
	Day 69	Lesson 9.3 (*Student Textbook*, pages 167–169) Worksheet 9.3 (*Teacher Guide*, pages 121–122)			
	Day 70				
Week 6	Day 71	Lesson 9.4 (*Student Textbook*, pages 169–172) Worksheet 9.4 (*Teacher Guide*, pages 123–124)			
	Day 72	Lesson 9.5 (*Student Textbook*, pages 172–175) Worksheet 9.5 (*Teacher Guide*, pages 125–126)			
	Day 73	Lesson 9.6 (*Student Textbook*, page 176) Study Day			
	Day 74	**Quiz 8** (*Teacher Guide*, pages 323–324)			
	Day 75	Lesson 10.1 (*Student Textbook*, pages 177–179) Worksheet 10.1 (*Teacher Guide*, pages 127–128)			
Week 7	Day 76	Lesson 10.2 (*Student Textbook*, pages 179–180) Worksheet 10.2 (*Teacher Guide*, pages 129–130)			
	Day 77	Lesson 10.3 (*Student Textbook*, pages 180–182) Worksheet 10.3 (*Teacher Guide*, pages 131–132)			
	Day 78	Lesson 10.4 (*Student Textbook*, pages 182–186) Worksheet 10.4 (*Teacher Guide*, pages 133–134)			
	Day 79	Lesson 10.5 (*Student Textbook*, pages 186–189) Worksheet 10.5 (*Teacher Guide*, pages 135)			
	Day 80	**Quiz 9** (*Teacher Guide*, pages 325–326)			
Week 8	Day 81	Lesson 11.1 (*Student Textbook*, pages 189–194) Worksheet 11.1 (*Teacher Guide*, pages 137–138)			
	Day 82	Lesson 11.2 (*Student Textbook*, pages 194–199) Worksheet 11.2 (*Teacher Guide*, page 139–140)			
	Day 83	Lesson 11.3 (*Student Textbook*, pages 199–201) Worksheet 11.3 (*Teacher Guide*, pages 141–142)			
	Day 84	Lesson 11.4 (*Student Textbook*, pages 201–203) Worksheet 11.4 (*Teacher Guide*, pages 143–144)			
	Day 85	Lesson 11.5 (*Student Textbook*, pages 204–208) Worksheet 11.5 (*Teacher Guide*, pages 145–148)			
Week 9	Day 86	Lesson 11.6 (*Student Textbook*, pages 208–209) Study Day			
	Day 87	**Quiz 10** (*Teacher Guide*, page 327)*			
	Day 88	Worksheet 11.6 (*Teacher Guide*, pages 149–152)			
	Day 89	Study Day			
	Day 90	**Test 2** (*Teacher Guide*, pages 349–350)			
		Midterm Grade			

Quiz 10 gives students the assignment to write a one to three paragraph analysis of a real-life use of statistics.

Suggested Daily Schedule
(to complete Book 2 in a school year)

Date	Day	Assignment	Due Date	✓	Grade
		Second Semester—Third Quarter			
Week 1	Day 91	Lesson 12.1 (*Student Textbook*, pages 211–213) Worksheet 12.1* (*Teacher Guide*, pages 153–154)			
	Day 92	Lesson 12.2 (*Student Textbook*, pages 213–216) Worksheet 12.2 (*Teacher Guide*, pages 155–156)			
	Day 93	Lesson 12.3 (*Student Textbook*, pages 216–218) Worksheet 12.3 (*Teacher Guide*, pages 157–158)			
	Day 94	Lesson 12.4 (*Student Textbook*, pages 218–222) Worksheet 12.4 (*Teacher Guide*, pages 159–160)			
	Day 95	Lesson 12.5 (*Student Textbook*, pages 222–225) Worksheet 12.5 (*Teacher Guide*, pages 161–162)			
Week 2	Day 96	Lesson 12.6 (*Student Textbook*, pages 225–227) Worksheet 12.6 (*Teacher Guide*, pages 163–164)			
	Day 97	Lesson 12.7 (*Student Textbook*, pages 228–232) Worksheet 12.7 (*Teacher Guide*, pages 165–166)*			
	Day 98	Lesson 12.8 (*Student Textbook*, pages 233–234) Study Day			
	Day 99	**Quiz 11** (*Student Textbook*, pages 329–330)			
	Day 100	Lesson 13.1 (*Student Textbook*, pages 235–238) Worksheet 13.1 (*Teacher Guide*, pages 167–168)			
Week 3	Day 101	Lesson 13.2 (*Student Textbook*, pages 238–241) Worksheet 13.2 (*Teacher Guide*, pages 169–171)			
	Day 102	Lesson 13.3 (*Student Textbook*, pages 241–243) Worksheet 13.3 (*Teacher Guide*, pages 173–174)			
	Day 103	Lesson 13.4 (*Student Textbook*, pages 243–245) Worksheet 13.4 (*Teacher Guide*, pages 175–178)			
	Day 104	Lesson 13.5 (*Student Textbook*, pages 245–247) Worksheet 13.5 (*Teacher Guide*, pages 179–180)			
	Day 105	Lesson 13.6 (*Student Textbook*, page 247) Study Day			
Week 4	Day 106	**Quiz 12** (*Teacher Guide*, pages 331–332)			
	Day 107	Lesson 14.1 (*Student Textbook*, pages 249–254) Worksheet 14.1 (*Teacher Guide*, pages 181–183)			
	Day 108	Lesson 14.2 (*Student Textbook*, pages 254–257) Worksheet 14.2 (*Teacher Guide*, pages 185–186)			
	Day 109	Lesson 14.3 (*Student Textbook*, pages 258–260) Worksheet 14.3 (*Teacher Guide*, pages 187–190)			
	Day 110	Lesson 14.4 (*Student Textbook*, pages 260–265) Worksheet 14.4 (*Teacher Guide*, pages 191–192)			

* Worksheet 12.1 includes assignment to toss a coin and roll a die.
* Worksheet 12.7 includes assignment to read or watch one of the suggested videos on genetics and write a paragraph summary.

Suggested Daily Schedule
(to complete Book 2 in a school year)

Date	Day	Assignment	Due Date	✓	Grade
Week 5	Day 111	Lesson 14.5 (*Student Textbook*, pages 265–270) Worksheet 14.5 (*Teacher Guide*, pages 193–195)			
	Day 112	Lesson 14.6 (*Student Textbook*, pages 270–275) Worksheet 14.6 (*Teacher Guide*, pages 197–200)			
	Day 113	Lesson 14.7 (*Student Textbook*, pages 275–278) Worksheet 14.7 (*Teacher Guide*, pages 201–204)			
	Day 114	Lesson 14.8 (*Student Textbook*, pages 279–280) **Quiz 13** (*Teacher Guide*, pages 333–334)			
	Day 115				
Week 6	Day 116	Lesson 15.1 (*Student Textbook*, pages 281–285) Worksheet 15.1 (*Teacher Guide*, pages 205–206)			
	Day 117	Lesson 15.2 (*Student Textbook*, pages 285–287) Worksheet 15.2 (*Teacher Guide*, pages 207–208)			
	Day 118	Lesson 15.3 (*Student Textbook*, pages 287–291) Worksheet 15.3 (*Teacher Guide*, pages 209–210)			
	Day 119	Lesson 15.4 (*Student Textbook*, pages 291–292) Worksheet 15.4 (*Teacher Guide*, pages 211–212)			
	Day 120	Lesson 15.5 (*Student Textbook*, pages 292–295) Worksheet 15.5 (*Teacher Guide*, pages 213–214)			
Week 7	Day 121	Lesson 15.6 (*Student Textbook*, pages 296–298) Worksheet 15.6 (*Teacher Guide*, pages 215–216)			
	Day 122	Lesson 15.7 (*Student Textbook*, pages 298–301) Worksheet 15.7 (*Teacher Guide*, pages 217–218)*			
	Day 123	Lesson 15.8 (*Student Textbook*, pages 302–303) **Quiz 14** (*Teacher Guide*, pages 335–336)			
	Day 124	Lesson 16.1 (*Student Textbook*, pages 305–306) Worksheet 16.1 (*Teacher Guide*, pages 219–220)			
	Day 125	Lesson 16.2 (*Student Textbook*, pages 306–308) Worksheet 16.2A (*Teacher Guide*, pages 221–222)			
Week 8	Day 126	Worksheet 16.2B (*Teacher Guide*, pages 223–224)			
	Day 127	Lesson 16.3 (*Student Textbook*, pages 308–312) Worksheet 16.3A (*Teacher Guide*, page 225)			
	Day 128	Worksheet 16.3B (*Teacher Guide*, pages 227–228)			
	Day 129	Lesson 16.4 (*Student Textbook*, pages 313–314) Worksheet 16.4 (*Teacher Guide*, pages 229–330)			
	Day 130	Lesson 16.5 (*Student Textbook*, pages 314–316) Worksheet 16.5 (*Teacher Guide*, pages 331–332)			
Week 9	Day 131	Lesson 16.6 (*Student Textbook*, pages 316–319) Worksheet 16.6 (*Teacher Guide*, pages 233–234)			
	Day 132	Lesson 16.7 (*Student Textbook*, pages 319–320) **Quiz 15** (*Teacher Guide*, page 337)			
	Day 133	Worksheet 16.7 (*Teacher Guide*, pages 235–240)			
	Day 134	Study Day			
	Day 135	**Test 3** (*Teacher Guide*, pages 351–353)			

Worksheet 15.7 includes assignment to watch suggested video or read suggested article on radiometric dating.

Suggested Daily Schedule
(to complete Book 2 in a school year)

Date	Day	Assignment	Due Date	✓	Grade
		Second Semester—Fourth Quarter			
Week 1	Day 136	Lesson 17.1 (*Student Textbook*, pages 321–323) Worksheet 17.1 (*Teacher Guide*, page 241)			
	Day 137	Lesson 17.2 (*Student Textbook*, pages 323–325) Worksheet 17.2 (*Teacher Guide*, pages 243–244)			
	Day 138	Lesson 17.3 (*Student Textbook*, pages 325–327) Worksheet 17.3 (*Teacher Guide*, pages 245)			
	Day 139	Lesson 17.4 (*Student Textbook*, pages 327–328) Worksheet 17.4 (*Teacher Guide*, pages 247–248)*			
	Day 140				
Week 2	Day 141	Lesson 17.5 (*Student Textbook*, pages 328–332) Worksheet 17.5 (*Teacher Guide*, pages 249–250)			
	Day 142	Lesson 17.6 (*Student Textbook*, pages 333–334) Worksheet 17.6 (*Teacher Guide*, pages 251–252)			
	Day 143	Lesson 17.7 (*Student Textbook*, pages 334–336) Worksheet 17.7 (*Teacher Guide*, pages 253–254)			
	Day 144	Lesson 17.8 (*Student Textbook*, pages 336–339) Worksheet 17.8 (*Teacher Guide*, pages 255–256)			
	Day 145				
Week 3	Day 146	Lesson 17.9 (*Student Textbook*, pages 339–341) Study Day			
	Day 147	**Quiz 16** (*Teacher Guide*, pages 339–340)			
	Day 148	Lesson 18.1 (*Student Textbook*, pages 343–347) Worksheet 18.1 (*Teacher Guide*, pages 257–260)			
	Day 149	Lesson 18.2 (*Student Textbook*, pages 347–352) Worksheet 18.2 (*Teacher Guide*, pages 261–262)			
	Day 150				
Week 4	Day 151	Lesson 18.3 (*Student Textbook*, pages 352–354) Worksheet 18.3 (*Teacher Guide*, pages 263–265)			
	Day 152	Lesson 18.4 (*Student Textbook*, pages 354–357) Worksheet 18.4 (*Teacher Guide*, pages 267–268)			
	Day 153	Lesson 18.5 (*Student Textbook*, pages 357–363) Worksheet 18.5 (*Teacher Guide*, pages 269)			
	Day 154	**Quiz 17** (*Teacher Guide*, page 341)			
	Day 155	Lesson 19.1 (*Student Textbook*, pages 365–367) Worksheet 19.1 (*Teacher Guide*, pages 271–272)			

* Worksheet 17.4 includes assignment to research the history of a calculator.

Suggested Daily Schedule
(to complete Book 2 in a school year)

Date	Day	Assignment	Due Date	✓	Grade
Week 5	Day 156	Lesson 19.2 (*Student Textbook*, pages 367–369) Worksheet 19.2 (*Teacher Guide*, pages 273–274)			
	Day 157	Lesson 19.3 (*Student Textbook*, pages 369–371) Worksheet 19.3 (*Teacher Guide*, pages 275–276)*			
	Day 158	Lesson 19.4 (*Student Textbook*, pages 371–374) Worksheet 19.4 (*Teacher Guide*, pages 277–278)*			
	Day 159	Lesson 19.5 (*Student Textbook*, pages 374–375) Worksheet 19.5* (*Teacher Guide*, page 279)			
	Day 160	**Quiz 18** (*Teacher Guide*, page 343)			
Week 6	Day 161	Lesson 20.1 (*Student Textbook*, pages 377–380) Worksheet 20.1 (*Teacher Guide*, pages 281–282)			
	Day 162	Lesson 20.2 (*Student Textbook*, pages 380–383) Worksheet 20.2 (*Teacher Guide*, pages 283–284)			
	Day 163	Lesson 20.3 (*Student Textbook*, pages 383–385) Worksheet 20.3 (*Teacher Guide*, pages 285–286)			
	Day 164	Lesson 20.4 (*Student Textbook*, pages 385–388) Worksheet 20.4 (*Teacher Guide*, pages 287–288)			
	Day 165				
Week 7	Day 166	Lesson 20.5 (*Student Textbook*, page 388) Study Day			
	Day 167	**Quiz 19** (*Teacher Guide*, page 345)			
	Day 168	Worksheet 20.5 (*Teacher Guide*, pages 289–292)			
	Day 169	Study Day			
	Day 170	**Test 4** (*Teacher Guide*, pages 355–356)			
Week 8	Day 171	Lesson 21.1 (*Student Textbook*, pages 389–390) Worksheet 21.1 (*Teacher Guide*, pages 293–294)* (Project Assigned)			
	Day 172	Lesson 21.2 (*Student Textbook*, pages 390–391) Worksheet 21.2 (*Teacher Guide*, pages 295–296)			
	Day 173	Lesson 21.3 (*Student Textbook*, pages 391–392) Worksheet 21.3A (*Teacher Guide*, pages 297–298)			
	Day 174	Work on Project			
	Day 175	Worksheet 21.3B (*Teacher Guide*, pages 299–300)			
Week 9	Day 176	Work on Project			
	Day 177	Worksheet 21.3C (*Teacher Guide*, pages 301–302)			
	Day 178	Study Day			
	Day 179	Study Day			
	Day 180	**Test 5** (Final) (*Teacher Guide*, pages 357–360) Project Due			
		Final Grade			

Worksheet 19.3 includes optional assignment to play notes on a piano.
Worksheet 19.5 includes assignment involving an Internet search.
End-of-the-year project includes hands-on assignment to either put together a budget for a vacation or explore different savings accounts.

Suggested Accelerated Daily Schedule
(to complete Book 2 in a semester)

This schedule assumes students finished the material covered in Book 1 in the previous semester. Many lessons in the first two chapters that review those foundational concepts have been skipped. If your student has not recently finished Book 1, you will need to have them read the entire first two chapters before beginning, as an understanding of the concepts covered there is crucial.

On days students are completing multiple worksheets, you may wish to assign students only some of each type of problem (especially if the problems are mainly review), assigning additional problems only if the student gets problems incorrect.

Date	Day	Assignment	Due Date	✓	Grade
		First Semester—First Quarter			
Week 1	Day 1	Lessons 1.1, 2.1, 2.4 (*Student Textbook*, pages 13–18, 33–35, 41–46) Worksheets 1.1, 2.1, 2.4 (*Teacher Guide*, pages 21–22, 31, 37–38)			
	Day 2	Lessons 2.5–2.7 (*Student Textbook*, pages 46–58) Worksheets 2.5–2.6 (*Teacher Guide*, pages 39–42)			
	Day 3	**Quiz 1** (*Teacher Guide*, pages 309–310) Study Day*			
	Day 4	Lessons 3.1–3.2 (*Student Textbook*, pages 59–64) Worksheets 3.1–3.2 (*Teacher Guide*, pages 43–46)			
	Day 5	Lessons 3.3–3.4 (*Student Textbook*, pages 64–70) Worksheets 3.3–3.4 (*Teacher Guide*, pages 47–50)			
Week 2	Day 6	Lessons 3.5–3.6 (*Student Textbook*, pages 70–75) Worksheets 3.5–3.6 (*Teacher Guide*, pages 51–54)			
	Day 7	Lessons 3.7–3.8 (*Student Textbook*, pages 75–80) Worksheet 3.7 (*Teacher Guide*, pages 55–56) **Quiz 2** (*Teacher Guide*, pages 311–312)			
	Day 8	Lessons 4.1–4.2 (*Student Textbook*, pages 81–86) Worksheets 4.1–4.2 (*Teacher Guide*, pages 57–60)			
	Day 9	Lesson 4.3 (*Student Textbook*, pages 86–88) Worksheet 4.3 (*Teacher Guide*, pages 61–62)			
	Day 10	Lesson 4.4 (*Student Textbook*, pages 89–90) Worksheet 4.4 (*Teacher Guide*, pages 63–64)			

* Use this study day to spend extra time reviewing any concepts covered in the first two chapters that need more review. The first two chapters reviewed many foundational concepts; it's important to be comfortable with them before continuing.

Suggested Accelerated Daily Schedule
(to complete Book 2 in a semester)

Date	Day	Assignment	Due Date	✓	Grade
Week 3	Day 11	Lessons 4.5–4.6 (*Student Textbook*, pages 91–94) Worksheet 4.5 (*Teacher Guide*, pages 65–66) **Quiz 3** (*Teacher Guide*, pages 313–314)			
	Day 12	Lesson 5.1 (*Student Textbook*, pages 95–101) Worksheets 5.1A–5.1B (*Teacher Guide*, pages 67–70)			
	Day 13	Lesson 5.2 (*Student Textbook*, pages 101–105) Worksheet 5.2 (*Teacher Guide*, pages 71–72)*			
	Day 14	Lesson 5.3 (*Student Textbook*, pages 106–108) Worksheets 5.3A–5.3B (*Teacher Guide*, pages 73–76)			
	Day 15	Lessons 5.4–5.5 (*Student Textbook*, pages 108–115) Worksheets 5.4–5.5 (*Teacher Guide*, pages 77–80)			
Week 4	Day 16	Lesson 5.6 (*Student Textbook*, pages 115–116) **Quiz 4** (*Teacher Guide*, pages 315–316)			
	Day 17	Worksheet 5.6 (*Student Textbook*, page 81–84) Study Day			
	Day 18	**Test 1** (*Teacher Guide*, pages 347–348)			
	Day 19	Lessons 6.1–6.2 (*Student Textbook*, page 117–124) Worksheets 6.1–6.2B (*Teacher Guide*, pages 85–90)			
	Day 20	Lesson 6.3 (*Student Textbook*, pages 124–128) Worksheet 6.3A (*Teacher Guide*, pages 91–92)			
Week 5	Day 21	Lesson 6.4 (*Student Textbook*, pages 128–130) Worksheets 6.3B–6.4 (*Teacher Guide*, pages 93–96)			
	Day 22	Lesson 6.5 (*Student Textbook*, pages 130–132) **Quiz 5** (*Teacher Guide*, pages 317–318)			
	Day 23	Lesson 7.1 (*Student Textbook*, pages 133–136) Worksheet 7.1 (*Teacher Guide*, pages 97–98)			
	Day 24	Lessons 7.2–7.3 (*Student Textbook*, pages 136–141) Worksheets 7.2–7.3 (*Teacher Guide*, pages 99–102)			
	Day 25	Lessons 7.4–7.5 (*Student Textbook*, pages 141–145) Worksheets 7.4–7.5 (*Teacher Guide*, pages 103–106)			
Week 6	Day 26	**Quiz 6** (*Teacher Guide*, page 319) Lessons 8.1–8.2 (*Student Textbook*, pages 147–150) Worksheets 8.1–8.2 (*Teacher Guide*, pages 107–110)			
	Day 27	Lesson 8.3 (*Student Textbook*, pages 151–153) Worksheet 8.3 (*Teacher Guide*, pages 111–112)			
	Day 28	Lessons 8.4–8.5 (*Student Textbook*, pages 153–157) Worksheets 8.4–8.5 (*Teacher Guide*, pages 113–116)			
	Day 29	Lesson 8.6 (*Student Textbook*, page 157) **Quiz 7** (*Teacher Guide*, page 321)			
	Day 30	Lessons 9.1–9.2 (*Student Textbook*, pages 159–167) Worksheets 9.1–9.2 (*Teacher Guide*, pages 117–120)			

Suggested Accelerated Daily Schedule
(to complete Book 2 in a semester)

Date	Day	Assignment	Due Date	✓	Grade
Week 7	Day 31	Lessons 9.3–9.4 (*Student Textbook*, pages 167–172) Worksheets 9.3–9.4 (*Teacher Guide*, pages 121–124)			
	Day 32	Lessons 9.5–9.6 (*Student Textbook*, pages 172–176) Worksheet 9.5 (*Teacher Guide*, pages 125–126) **Quiz 8** (*Teacher Guide*, pages 323–324)			
	Day 33	Lessons 10.1–10.2 (*Student Textbook*, pages 177–180) Worksheets 10.1–10.2 (*Teacher Guide*, pages 127–130)			
	Day 34	Lessons 10.3–10.4 (*Student Textbook*, pages 180–186) Worksheets 10.3–10.4 (*Teacher Guide*, pages 131–134)			
	Day 35	**Quiz 9** (*Teacher Guide*, pages 325–326) Lessons 10.5–11.1 (*Student Textbook*, pages 186–194) Worksheets 10.5 (optional)–11.1 (*Teacher Guide*, pages 135–138)			
Week 8	Day 36	Lessons 11.2–11.3 (*Student Textbook*, pages 194–201) Worksheets 11.2–11.3 (*Teacher Guide*, pages 139–142)			
	Day 37	Lessons 11.4–11.5 (*Student Textbook*, pages 201–208) Worksheets 11.4–11.5 (*Teacher Guide*, pages 143–148)			
	Day 38	Lesson 11.6 (*Student Textbook*, pages 208–209) **Quiz 10** (*Teacher Guide*, page 327)*			
	Day 39	Worksheet 11.6 (*Teacher Guide*, pages 149–152) Study Day			
	Day 40	**Test 2** (*Teacher Guide*, pages 349–350)			
Week 9	Day 41	Lessons 12.1–12.2 (*Student Textbook*, pages 211–216) Worksheets 12.1–12.2 (*Teacher Guide*, pages 153–156)*			
	Day 42	Lessons 12.3–12.4 (*Student Textbook*, pages 216–222) Worksheets 12.3–12.4 (*Teacher Guide*, pages 157–160)			
	Day 43	Lesson 12.5 (*Student Textbook*, pages 222–225) Worksheet 12.5 (*Teacher Guide*, pages 161–162)			
	Day 44	Lesson 12.6 (*Student Textbook*, pages 225–227) Worksheet 12.6 (*Teacher Guide*, pages 163–164)			
	Day 45	Lessons 12.7–12.8 (*Student Textbook*, pages 228–234) Worksheet 12.7 (*Teacher Guide*, pages 165–166)* **Quiz 11** (*Teacher Guide*, pages 329–330)			
		First Semester—Second Quarter			
Week 1	Day 46	Lesson 13.1 (*Student Textbook*, pages 235–238) Worksheet 13.1 (*Teacher Guide*, pages 167–168)			
	Day 47	Lessons 13.2–13.3 (*Student Textbook*, pages 238–243) Worksheets 13.2–13.3 (*Teacher Guide*, pages 169–174)			
	Day 48	Lesson 13.4 (*Student Textbook*, pages 243–245) Worksheet 13.4 (*Teacher Guide*, pages 175–178)			
	Day 49	Lessons 13.5–13.6 (*Student Textbook*, pages 245–247) Worksheet 13.5 (*Teacher Guide*, pages 179–180) **Quiz 12** (*Teacher Guide*, pages 331–332)			
	Day 50	Lessons 14.1–14.2 (*Student Textbook*, pages 249–257) Worksheets 14.1–14.2 (*Teacher Guide*, pages 181–186)			

* Quiz 10 gives students the assignment to write a one to three paragraph analysis of a real-life use of statistics.
* Worksheet 12.1 includes assignment to toss a coin and roll a die.
* Worksheet 12.7 includes assignment to read or watch one of the suggested videos on genetics and write a paragraph summa

Suggested Accelerated Daily Schedule
(to complete Book 2 in a semester)

Date	Day	Assignment	Due Date	✓	Grade
Week 2	Day 51	Lessons 14.3–14.4 (*Student Textbook*, pages 258–265) Worksheets 14.3–14.4 (*Teacher Guide*, pages 187–192)			
	Day 52	Lesson 14.5 (*Student Textbook*, pages 265–270) Worksheet 14.5 (*Teacher Guide*, pages 193–195)			
	Day 53	Lesson 14.6 (*Student Textbook*, pages 270–275) Worksheet 14.6 (*Teacher Guide*, pages 197–200)			
	Day 54	Lessons 14.7–14.8 (*Student Textbook*, pages 275–280) Worksheet 14.7 (*Teacher Guide*, pages 201–204) **Quiz 13** (*Teacher Guide*, pages 333–334)			
	Day 55	Lessons 15.1–15.2 (*Student Textbook*, pages 281–287) Worksheets 15.1–15.2 (*Teacher Guide*, pages 205–208)			
Week 3	Day 56	Lessons 15.3–15.4 (*Student Textbook*, pages 287–292) Worksheets 15.3–15.4 (*Teacher Guide*, pages 209–212)			
	Day 57	Lessons 15.5–15.6 (*Student Textbook*, pages 292–298) Worksheets 15.5–15.6 (*Teacher Guide*, pages 213–216)			
	Day 58	Lessons 15.7–15.8 (*Student Textbook*, pages 298–303) Worksheet 15.7 (*Teacher Guide*, pages 217–218)*			
	Day 59	**Quiz 14** (*Teacher Guide*, pages 335–336); Lesson 16.1 (*Student Textbook*, pages 305–306) Worksheet 16.1 (*Teacher Guide*, pages 219–220)			
	Day 60	Lesson 16.2 (*Student Textbook*, pages 306–308) Worksheets 16.2A–16.2B (*Teacher Guide*, pages 221–224)			
Week 4	Day 61	Lesson 16.3 (*Student Textbook*, pages 308–312) Worksheets 16.3A–16.3B (*Teacher Guide*, pages 225–228)			
	Day 62	Lessons 16.4–16.5 (*Student Textbook*, pages 313–316) Worksheets 16.4–16.5 (*Teacher Guide*, pages 229–332)			
	Day 63	Lessons 16.6–16.7 (*Student Textbook*, pages 316–320) Worksheet 16.6 (*Teacher Guide*, pages 233–234)			
	Day 64	**Quiz 15** (*Teacher Guide*, page 337) Worksheet 16.7 (*Teacher Guide*, pages 235–240)			
	Day 65	**Test 3** (*Teacher Guide*, pages 351–353)			
Week 5	Day 66	Lessons 17.1–17.2 (*Student Textbook*, pages 321–325) Worksheets 17.1–17.2 (*Teacher Guide*, pages 241–244)			
	Day 67	Lessons 17.3–17.4 (*Student Textbook*, pages 325–328) Worksheets 17.3–17.4 (*Teacher Guide*, pages 245–248)*			
	Day 68	Lesson 17.5 (*Student Textbook*, pages 328–332) Worksheet 17.5 (*Teacher Guide*, pages 249–250)			
	Day 69	Lesson 17.6 (*Student Textbook*, pages 333–334) Worksheet 17.6 (*Teacher Guide*, pages 251–252)			
	Day 70	Lesson 17.7 (*Student Textbook*, pages 334–336) Worksheet 17.7 (*Teacher Guide*, pages 253–254)			

* Worksheet 15.7 includes assignment to watch suggested video or read suggested article on radiometric dating.
* Worksheet 17.4 includes assignment to research the history of a calculator.

Suggested Accelerated Daily Schedule
(to complete Book 2 in a semester)

Date	Day	Assignment	Due Date	✓	Grade
Week 6	Day 71	Lesson 17.8 (*Student Textbook*, pages 336–339) Worksheet 17.8 (*Teacher Guide*, pages 255–256)			
	Day 72	Lesson 17.9 (*Student Textbook*, pages 339–341) **Quiz 16** (*Teacher Guide*, pages 339–340)			
	Day 73	Lesson 18.1 (*Student Textbook*, page 343–347) Worksheet 18.1 (*Teacher Guide*, pages 257–260)			
	Day 74	Lesson 18.2 (*Student Textbook*, pages 347–352) Worksheet 18.2 (*Teacher Guide*, pages 261–262)			
	Day 75	Lesson 18.3 (*Student Textbook*, pages 352–354) Worksheet 18.3 (*Teacher Guide*, pages 263–265)			
Week 7	Day 76	Lessons 18.4–18.5 (*Student Textbook*, pages 354–363) Worksheets 18.4–18.5 (*Teacher Guide*, pages 267–269)			
	Day 77	**Quiz 17** (*Teacher Guide*, page 341) Lesson 19.1 (*Student Textbook*, pages 365–367) Worksheet 19.1 (*Teacher Guide*, pages 271–272)			
	Day 78	Lesson 19.2 (*Student Textbook*, pages 367–369) Worksheet 19.2 (*Teacher Guide*, pages 273-274)			
	Day 79	Lessons 19.3–19.5 (*Student Textbook*, pages 369–375) Worksheets 19.3–19.5 (*Teacher Guide*, pages 275–279)*			
	Day 80	**Quiz 18** (*Teacher Guide*, page 343) Lesson 20.1 (*Student Textbook*, pages 377–380) Worksheet 20.1 (*Teacher Guide*, pages 281–282)			
Week 8	Day 81	Lesson 20.2 (*Student Textbook*, pages 380–383) Worksheet 20.2 (*Teacher Guide*, pages 283–284)			
	Day 82	Lesson 20.3 (*Student Textbook*, pages 383–385) Worksheet 20.3 (*Teacher Guide*, pages 285–286)			
	Day 83	Lessons 20.4–20.5 (*Student Textbook*, pages 385–388) Worksheet 20.4 (*Teacher Guide*, pages 287–288) **Quiz 19** (*Teacher Guide*, page 345)			
	Day 84	Worksheet 20.5 (*Teacher Guide*, pages 289–292)			
	Day 85	**Test 4** (*Teacher Guide*, pages 355–356)			
Week 9	Day 86	Lesson 21.1 (*Student Textbook*, pages 389–390) Worksheet 21.1 (*Teacher Guide*, page 293–294)* (Project Assigned)			
	Day 87	Lesson 21.2 (*Student Textbook*, pages 390–391) Worksheet 21.2 (*Teacher Guide*, pages 295–296) Work on Project			
	Day 88	Lesson 21.3 (*Student Textbook*, pages 391–392) Worksheet 21.3A (*Teacher Guide*, pages 297–298) Work on Project			
	Day 89	Worksheets 21.3B–21.3C (*Teacher Guide*, pages 299–302) Work on Project			
	Day 90	**Test 5** (Final) (*Teacher Guide*, pages 357–360) Project Due			
		Final Grade			

* Worksheet 19.3 includes optional assignment to play notes on a piano.
* Worksheet 19.5 includes assignment involving an Internet search.
* End-of-the-year project includes hands-on assignment to either put together a budget for a vacation or explore different savings accounts.

Principles of Mathematics 2 Worksheets

PRINCIPLES OF MATHEMATICS 2 | Overview of Mathematics Pages 13–18 | Day 1 | Worksheet 1.1 | Name

1. **Notebook and Flashcard Preparation** — Place a copy of the reference sheets (pages 421–436) inside a three-ring binder. Use this "notebook" to **take additional notes as you study** (make sure you have some extra lined paper inside), as well as to store your completed worksheets. Keeping a notebook of key information as you go can help you remember the information and find it easily when needed. You may also find it helpful to use index cards to make flashcards of new terms or concepts, so make sure you have some blank index cards in the front of your binder that you can use.

2. **Flashcard and Notebook Use** — Now that your notebook is prepped, add the definitions for *expression*, *equation*, and *simplify* to it. You may also wish to make flashcards for the terms using index cards. We will not include a reminder about writing in your notebook or making flashcards; however, you'll save yourself a lot of frustration if you use the notebook, flashcards, or whatever other method works for you to keep track of terms and concepts.

3. **Math in Action** — Name 10 ways math applies outside of a textbook.

    a.

    b.

    c.

    d.

    e.

    f.

    g.

    h.

    i.

    j.

4. **Worldview Thinking**

    a. What is a worldview?

    b. Summarize what math is and why it works.

    c. As we use math, why do we find both evidence of God's wisdom and care and evidence of suffering and death?

5. **Term Time**

   a. Is 5 + 9 an expression or an equation?

   b. Simplify 5 + 9

6. **General Instructions** — Be sure to read the "General Instructions for Students" section (p. 421–422).

   a. When are you allowed to use a calculator in this course?

   b. Round 0.5432 the way it should be rounded if it's the answer to a problem.

   c. Round 0.8975 the way it should be rounded if it's the answer to a problem.

   d. Should you round 0.8975 if it's a number you need to input into your calculator in order to solve a problem?

   e. When should you include a unit of measure in your answer?

   f. List one suggestion given for how to study on study days.

| PRINCIPLES OF MATHEMATICS 2 | The Language of Mathematics — Symbols and Conventions Pages 18–22 | Day 2 | Worksheet 1.2 | Name |

These next few worksheets include a lot of practice performing operations with both whole and decimal numbers. Hopefully, these operations are all quite familiar to you — if not, stop and review the appropriate sections of Book 1.

1. **Questions**

    a. We use symbols to _____ quantities, _____, and _____.

    b. Write down the mathematical symbols for minus, plus, equals, and does not equal.

    c. Represent the multiplication of "20 times 6" three different ways.

    d. What is a convention?

2. **Place Value**

    Example: What does the 4 in 0.4 represent? *Answer:* 4 tenths or $\frac{4}{10}$

    a. What does the 8 in 83 represent?

    b. What does the 8 in 0.08 represent?

3. **Representing Multiplication** — Rewrite each multiplication using parentheses and simplify.

    Example: 4 x 5 = 4(5) = 20

    a. 5 x 6

    Example Meaning: 5 tickets at $6 each

    b. 2 x 105

    Example Meaning: 2 tickets at $105 each

4. **Representing Multiplication** — Rewrite each multiplication using a • and simplify.

    Example: 4 x 5 = 4 • 5 = 20

    a. 8 x 9   b. 7 x 218

5. **The Order of Operations** — Simplify.

   a. 8 − 3 + 2

   b. (8 − 2)10 ÷ 2

   c. 7.5(0.23 + 0.96) − 1.8

   d. $4\overline{)4 + 9 + 7}$

   e. 2.5 + 4.1(5.6 − 3) ÷ 2

6. **Term Review**

   a. Is 8.5 ÷ 2 an expression or an equation?

   b. Simplify: 8.5 ÷ 2

| PRINCIPLES OF MATHEMATICS 2 | The Consistency of Mathematics — Operations and Properties Pages 22–24 | Day 3 | Worksheet 1.3 | Name |

1. **Reviewing Properties**

   a. Insert either = or ≠ in between these expressions:

      5 + 2 + 6   5 + 2 + 5

   b. Insert either = or ≠ in between these expressions:

      (17 + 5) + 2   17 + (5 + 2)

   c. What property describes the fact that the expressions in 1b were/were not equal?

   d. Insert either = or ≠ in between these expressions:

      15 ÷ 5 ÷ 1   5 ÷ 15 ÷ 1

   e. Insert either = or ≠ in between these expressions:

      2 • 1   2

   f. What is the property that describes the fact that multiplying by 1 doesn't change the value of a number?

   g. Insert either = or ≠ in between these expressions:

      2 + 0   2

   h. What is the property that describes the fact that adding 0 doesn't change the value of a number?

   i. Insert either = or ≠ in between these expressions:

      36 ÷ 36   1

   j. Insert either = or ≠ in between these expressions:

      36 ÷ 1   36

2. **Reviewing the Distributive Property** — Simplify using the distributive property; show your work.

   a. 9(15 + 22)

   Example Meaning: If one package contains 15 plates and another 22, and I decide to buy 9 of each package, how many plates will I get altogether?

   b. 5($8.45 + $3.99)

   Example Meaning: If it costs $8.45 for admission and $3.99 for food per person, what is the total cost for 5 people?

3. **Operations Review**

   a. Simplify: 80 + 93 + 83

   Example Meaning: Your scores on three tests so far are 80, 93, and 83. What is the total of all three scores?

   b. Divide the sum from problem 3a by 3.

   Example Meaning: What is the average score of all three tests?

   c. Simplify: $23.15 – $11.79

   Example Meaning: You spend $23.15 and then return $11.79. How much did you spend after the return?

   d. Simplify: 42($69.49)

   Example Meaning: If it costs $69.49 to attend a conference and 42 people attend, how much did the conference receive in admission fees?

   As we study math, we see evidence everywhere of God's faithfulness in holding the universe together. Take a moment to praise God for being the faithful Creator and Sustainer of all.

1. **Bonuses** — Suppose you're trying to give gifts to the employees of your small business. One gift option (Option A) costs $32.50 an employee, while another (Option B) costs $5.50 + $25.30 per employee, plus a $50 initial charge. Which option is less expensive for 50 employees, and by how much less per employee is it?

2. **Cell Phone Plan** — Suppose you're trying to choose a cell phone plan. One plan (Plan A) offers you unlimited minutes for $76.45 a month for two phones, plus $19.99 a month for each additional phone. Another plan (Plan B) charges $23.45 a month for each phone, plus $35.40 per phone for service. If the phones themselves are free in both plans, what is the difference in total monthly cost if you need 4 phones?

3. **Cow Profits** — If a cow eats pasture worth $6 per year, 3.5 tons of hay worth $6.50 per ton, and 1,200 pounds of chopped feed worth $0.75 per 100 pounds, gives birth to a calf worth $6, gives 3 quarts of milk per day for 280 days in the year which is worth $0.05 a quart, and produces manure annually worth $12, how much money per year does the farm make off the cow after you deduct the expenses from the income? *Note*: As you might have guessed from the prices, this problem was adapted from an early 1900s book.

4. **Skill Sharpening** — Simplify.

   a. $8 + (82 \cdot 2)5 + 5$

   b. $88 \cdot 1 + 0$

   c. $8 + 5 - 3 + 2$

1. **Name That Shape** — What two-dimensional shape best describes these pictures? Choose the most descriptive name you can.

a. _____ b. _____ c. _____ d. _____ e. _____

2. **Reviewing Measuring Shapes**

    a. If the outline of the snowflake shown has sides that are 0.5 cm, what is its perimeter?

    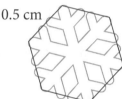

    b. What is the area of a square garden with 8-ft sides?

    c. What is the volume of a rectangular fish tank (a rectangular prism) that's 36 in long, 13 in wide, and 24 in tall?

    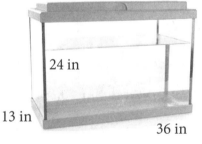

    d. What is the area of a rectangle with a length of 9.5 in and a width of 3.3 in?

3. **Term Time**

    a. What is an exponent?

    b. Rewrite 8^2 as a multiplication.

    c. Rewrite ft^2 as a multiplication.

4. **Formulas**

    a. What is a formula?

    b. Given that the power equals the voltage times the current ($P = V \cdot I$), what is the power (P) coming from an outlet with a voltage (V) of 120 volts and a current (I) of 25 amps? List your answer in a unit called watts (which is the result of multiplying volts by amps).

    c. In the formula for finding the area of a rectangle ($A = \ell \cdot w$), what does the ℓ stand for?

    d. If one month you made $62.54 in addition to your $587.89 monthly salary, how much did you make that month?

    e. If you started with $56.15 and ended with $19.29, what is the difference between your starting and ending dollars?

5. **Understanding Check** — What does geometry mean?

PRINCIPLES OF MATHEMATICS 2 | Fractions as Division, Pages 33–35 | Day 6 | Worksheet 2.1 | Name

You may use a calculator on this worksheet whenever you see this symbol (🖩).

1. **Understanding Fractions** — You do not need to include units of measure in your answers for this problem.

   a. Express as an improper fraction: 58 tasks divided by 3 people

   b. Rewrite problem 1a as a mixed number.

   c. Express as an improper fraction: 4 cups water divided by 3 cups sugar

   d. Express as an improper fraction: 45 divided by 5

   e. What is the numerator in $\frac{3}{5}$?

   f. What is the denominator in $\frac{6}{11}$?

   g. Give an example meaning for $\frac{50}{6}$.

   h. If $\frac{3}{5}$ of a project has been completed, express the amount of the project that has been completed as a decimal number.

   i. Express $1\frac{1}{3}$ yards of fabric as a decimal number.

   j. Express $\frac{4+5+7}{2}$ as a whole number. *Hint*: Notice the assumed grouping in the numerator — we have to add to find the number we need to divide by 2, just as if $\frac{4+5+7}{2}$ were written like this: $2\overline{)4+5+7}$.

2. **Geometry Time** (🖩) — How much will it cost to carpet a rectangular room if the dimensions are 6 ft by 8 ft, and carpet costs $23.50 a square foot installed?

| PRINCIPLES OF MATHEMATICS 2 | Factoring and Simplifying Fractions Pages 36–38 | Day 7 | Worksheet 2.2 | Name |

You may use a calculator on this worksheet whenever you see this symbol (▦).

Factoring (▦) — Use a factor tree to factor the following numbers; circle all the prime factors.

   a. 26

   b. 54

Equivalent Fractions (▦) — *Hint*: To decide if the two fractions are equivalent, simplify them both as much as possible or convert them both to a decimal. If they are equivalent, you'll get the same answer for both.

   a. Are $\frac{4}{8}$ and $\frac{1}{2}$ equivalent fractions? Why or why not?

   b. Are $\frac{1}{2}$ and $\frac{2}{3}$ equivalent fractions? Why or why not?

Greatest Common Factor (▦)

   a. What is the greatest common factor of 56 and 36?

   b. Use your answer to 3a to help simplify $\frac{36}{56}$.

   c. What is the greatest common factor of 60 and 40?

   d. Use your answer to 3c to simplify $\frac{40}{60}$.

Simplifying with Units (▦) — Simplify these fractions.

   a. $\frac{2 \text{ m}}{64 \text{ m}}$

   Example Meaning: the ratio (a comparison via division) between a model with a length of 2 m and the original building with a length of 64 m

   b. $\frac{132 \text{ ft}^2}{6 \text{ ft}}$

   Example Meaning: The area of a 136 ft² room divided by the length of one of its sides (6 ft).

5. **Exploring $\frac{564}{1,000}$** (🖩)

   a. Rewrite $\frac{564}{1,000}$ as a fraction of just its prime factors. *Hint*: Use a factor tree to help if you need to. You'll find it easiest to spot common factors if you list them all in order from least to greatest.

   Example: $\frac{6}{12} = \frac{2 \cdot 3}{2 \cdot 2 \cdot 3}$

   b. In your answer to 5a, circle any common factors the numerator and denominator have.

   c. What is the greatest common factor of 564 and 1,000? *Hint*: Use your answer in 5b to help you.

   d. Simplify $\frac{564}{1,000}$ by dividing the numerator and the denominator by the greatest common factor (which you found in 5c).

6. **Fractions as Division** (🖩)

   a. Express 60 ft² divided by 7 ft as an improper fraction.

   Example Meaning: The area of a 60 ft² room divided by the length of one of its sides if that side measures 7 ft.

   b. Simplify your answer to 6a, giving your answer as a mixed number.

   c. Simplify your answer to 6a, giving your answer as a decimal.

Adding and Subtracting Fractions and Mixed Numbers — Perform the requested addition or subtraction.

a. $\dfrac{7}{10} + \dfrac{2}{5}$

b. $5\dfrac{1}{2} + 6\dfrac{2}{3}$

c. $\dfrac{8}{9} - \dfrac{3}{6}$

d. $1\dfrac{1}{3} - \dfrac{2}{7}$

2. **Multiplying and Dividing Fractions and Mixed Numbers** — Perform the requested multiplication or division. Be sure to simplify as you go when you can.

a. $4 \cdot \dfrac{2}{3}$

b. $\dfrac{8}{7} \cdot \dfrac{14}{24}$

c. $5\dfrac{1}{7} \cdot \dfrac{8}{9}$

d. $2 \div \dfrac{2}{3}$

e. $\dfrac{\dfrac{9}{12}}{\dfrac{6}{18}}$

f. $\dfrac{\dfrac{7}{8}}{1\dfrac{1}{2}}$

3. **Fractions Applied** (🖩)

a. If a recipe calls for $\dfrac{3}{4}$ c. of sugar and you want to triple the recipe but half the sugar, how much sugar should you put in?

b. If a shelf requires $56\frac{1}{2}$ inches of plastic, how much plastic will 5 shelves require?

c. If railroad cars carried $24\frac{1}{2}$, $18\frac{2}{5}$, $15\frac{2}{5}$, 28, $17\frac{4}{5}$, $32\frac{3}{5}$, and $27\frac{2}{3}$ tons of coal, how many tons of coal did they carry altogether?

4. **Fractions as Division**

   a. Write 700 divided by 3 as an improper fraction.

   b. Rewrite your answer to 4a as a decimal number.

   c. Complete the division to give a decimal answer: $\dfrac{52.4}{12.56}$

Negative Numbers Representing Data

a. How would you describe the lowest point in the sound wave shown?

b. If you use positive numbers to describe temperatures above zero and negative numbers to describe temperatures below 0, represent a temperature that, in Celcius, is 9 degrees below 0.

c. If you represent east with positive numbers and west with negative numbers, represent 80 miles west.

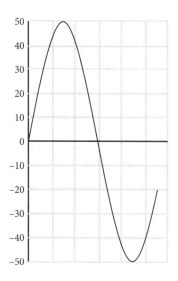

Number Line — Draw each of these numbers on a number line.

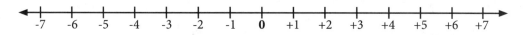

a. −2.5

b. 5

c. $-\dfrac{1}{2}$

d. 3.5

Different Types of Numbers — Circle all the names listed that can be used to describe the number given.

a. $-\dfrac{1}{2}$ Integers   Negative Numbers   Rational Numbers

b. 7   Integers   Prime Numbers   Irrational Numbers

c. 6   Rational Numbers   Prime Numbers   Whole Numbers

d. π   Integers   Irrational Numbers   Rational Numbers

Hint: Remember that π, while in this course we use 3.14 as its value, is a number that goes on and on.

Additive Inverse — Write the additive inverse of each number listed.

a. 5 mi

b. −6 mi

c. $\dfrac{2}{5}$ ft

d. $-\dfrac{5}{9}$ ft

5. **Viewing Subtraction as Addition of Negative Numbers**

    a. Simplify using the order of operations: 5 – 3 – 1

    b. Rewrite the expression as an *addition* of negative numbers and simplify from right to left (show your work): 5 – 3 – 1

    c. Simplify using the order of operations: 23 – 6 – 2

    d. Rewrite the expression as an *addition* of negative numbers and simplify from right to left (show your work): 23 – 6 – 2

6. **Temperature** — If a solution starts at 30° F, and you cool it 50° F, what will its ending temperature be?

7. **Working with Opposites** — Simplify.

    a. 5 + –68

    b. –5 – –9

    c. –5 – – – –9

    d. $\dfrac{-8 \text{ mi}}{2 \text{ mi}}$

    e. $\dfrac{-12}{-2}$

    f. $\dfrac{-40}{4}$

    g. 7 • –30 mi

    h. –5 • –12

    i. –5 • –1 • –1

    j. $50\dfrac{1}{3}$ pounds + $698\dfrac{2}{3}$ pounds

Absolute Value — Simplify.

a. $|-9|$

b. $|-6.89|$

c. $|\frac{2}{3}|$

d. $|-\frac{2}{3}|$

Longitude and Latitude

a. If Los Angeles is at 118.24° W (−118.24°) longitude, while Boston is at 71.06° W (−71.06°), how far apart are the two cities in longitude?

b. If we start at Boston, do we have to travel in the positive or the negative longitudinal direction to get to Los Angeles?

Distance Between Cities

a. Using a negative number to represent south, rewrite the latitude of Lima, Peru, which is at approximately 12.09° S.

b. If Dallas, Texas, is at 32.80° N and Lima, Peru, is at 12.09° S, how many degrees apart are the two cities in latitude? *Hint*: Rewrite these locations using positive (for north) and negative (for south). Then find the difference.

Miraflores Park, Lima, Peru

Dallas, TX

c. If Toronto, Canada, has a longitude of 79.38° W, while Quebec City, Canada, has a longitude of 71.24° W, how many degrees apart are the two cities in longitude?

Toronto, Canada

Quebec City, Canada

4. **Skill Sharpening** — Unless otherwise instructed, simplify these expressions.

   a. $\dfrac{16}{-8}$

   b. $\dfrac{-16}{-8}$

   c. $7 - 5(2 + \dfrac{1}{2})$

   d. $\dfrac{1}{6} \div \dfrac{3}{4}$

   e. Rewrite as a fraction (simplify your answer): $2 \div 16$

5. **Geometry Time** — If a seed packet says that each plant needs 18 inches (1.5 ft) in every direction, how many plants can you fit in a 6 ft by 6 ft section? *Hint*: We've drawn the problem out for you. This problem requires more than simply substituting numbers into a formula — you need to think through how many plants can fit down the length and across the width.

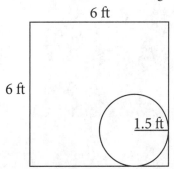

Longitude and latitude values vary slightly depending on where in the city they are describing. For this worksheet and others in this course, we used the values listed on David B. Zwiefelhofer, "Find Latitude and Longitude," www.findlatitudeandlongitude.com, accessed 10/2015, rounded to the nearest hundredth.

| PRINCIPLES OF MATHEMATICS 2 | Time Zones Pages 52–57 | Day 11 | Worksheet 2.6 | Name |

1. **Global Time Zones** — Use the information given and the time zone map in your refernce sheets (p. 433) to solve the problems.

    a. If Kansas City is at UTC−06:00 and Berlin, Germany, is at UTC+01:00, what is the difference in time between the two cities?

    b. What time is it in Kansas City when it's 8 a.m. in Berlin? Use the difference you found in problem 1a.

    c. If it's 1 p.m. in Boston and it's 4 hours later in London than in Boston, what time is it in London?

    d. If it's 9 p.m. on August 5 in Richmond, Virginia, and Tokyo, Japan is 13 hours *ahead* of Richmond (meaning it's 13 hours later in Tokyo), what day and time is it in Tokyo?

    e. If Los Angeles is at UTC−07:00 and Berlin, Germany, is at UTC+01:00, what day and time is it in Berlin when it's 5 p.m. on October 29 in Los Angeles? *Hint*: First find the time difference between the two cities, and then use that to find the time in Berlin.

2. **Temperature** — What temperature is shown on the thermometer to the right? Give your answer in degrees Fahrenheit.

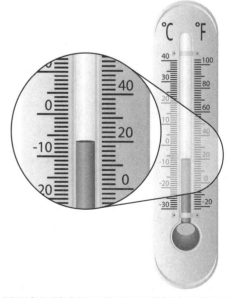

3. **Latitude and Longitude** — Buffalo is at a latitude of approximately 42.89°; Buenos Aires, Argentina, is a a latitude of approximately −34.61°. What is the *difference* in these latitudes (i.e., how many degrees apart are they)?

4. **Skill Sharpening** — Simplify.

   a. $\dfrac{7}{8} \div \dfrac{2}{3}$

   b. $\dfrac{\frac{1}{5}}{8}$

   c. $8 \div -2$

   d. $-4 \cdot -6 \cdot -1 \cdot -1$

   e. $-1 \cdot 6 \cdot -7$

Finding Unknowns — List the number the question mark is standing for in each equation.

Example: 5 – ? = 2 *Answer:* 3

a. 9 – ? = 7

Example Meaning: If we had 9 cookies on a plate, and only 7 are left now, how many were eaten?

b. 1 + ? = 7

Example Meaning: If we've finished 1 page of a book, how many more pages do we have left to finish 7 pages total?

c. 6 – ? = 6

Example Meaning: If we start with $6 and end with $6, how much did we spend?

d. 5 • ? = 30

Example Meaning: If we have 5 problems to solve, how long can we spend on each problem if we have 30 minutes in which to solve them all?

e. ? ÷ 5 = 9

Example Meaning: If we can't remember how long it took us altogether to complete all 9 problems, but we know we spent 5 minutes on each problem, how long did it take us altogether?

More Finding Unknowns — List the number *x* is standing for in each equation.

a. 2 + *x* = 11

Example Meaning: If we put together 2 flower bouquets for a wedding, how many more bouquets are needed if we need 11 total?

b. 20 – *x* = 14

Example Meaning: If we start a trip with $20, how much can we spend if we need to end the trip with $14?

c. 6 • x = 54

Example Meaning: If we need 6 packages of party invitations, how much can we afford to spend on each package if we can spend a total of $54 on all the invitations?

d. 28 ÷ x = 7

Example Meaning: If we can spend $28 buying pizza, how many pizzas can we buy if each pizza costs $7?

e. x + 3 = 8

Example Meaning: If in a board game, we started a certain number of spaces from start, moved 3 spaces away from start, and ended 8 spaces from start, how many spaces from start were we before we moved 3 additional spaces?

f. x ÷ 9 = 3

Example Meaning: How much was the total cost if it was divided evenly amongst 9 people and each person spent $3?

3. **Understanding the Meaning** — Go back and look at the example meanings for the requested problems. If we were using the equation to solve that example meaning, what would the *x* represent?

   Example: Problem 2e *Answer*: The *x* represents how many spaces from start we were before we moved 3 additional spaces.

   a. Problem 2a

   b. Problem 2b

   c. Problem 2c

   d. Problem 2d

4. **True or False** — Specify if the statement below is true or false.

   We always have to use the letter *x* to stand for an unknown.

5. **Questions**

   a. What letters do math books often use to represent unknowns?

   b. We use letters as well as numerals to _____, _____, and _____

PRINCIPLES OF MATHEMATICS 2 | Understanding Equality Pages 61–64 | Day 17 | Worksheet 3.2 | Name

Equality — Insert the equals sign (=) in between equal quantities or expressions, and the does not equal sign (≠) between unequal quantities or expressions.

a. 8   8   b. 8 + 2   8 + 2

c. 8 + 3   8 + 2   d. 8 • 2   8 • 2

e. 8 ÷ 2   8   f. 8 ÷ 2   8 ÷ 2

g. 8 − 3   8 − 3   h. 2 + 5   2 + 5

i. 2 + 5 − 2   2 + 5 − 3

Swapping Sides — Rewrite each equation so that the *entire* left side is on the right side, and vice versa.

Example: 47 − 5 = 42
42 = 47 − 5

a. 23 = 3 + 20   b. 5 ÷ 2 = 2.5

c. 6 • 9 = 54   d. $x − 6 = 15$

Finding Unknowns — List the value for x that would make these equations true.

a. $7 + x = 30$

Example Meaning: If we have $7, how many more dollars do we need to have $30?

b. $9 • x = 81$

Example Meaning: If we need 9 sheets of paper per person attending, how many attendees will 81 sheets supply?

Representing Relationships — Remember to consult the reference sheets (p. 423–428) if needed.

a. In $C = 2 • π • r$ (finding the circumference of a circle), what does r stand for?

b. Look back at the general instructions on page 421. What value should you use for π in this course?

c. Find the circumference of a circle with a radius of 8 ft.

d. What is the formula for finding the area of a circle?

e. Find the area of a circle with a radius of 8 ft.

f. If the total costs to attend an event consists of the ticket price plus the food price, use letters to show the relationship between the total cost, ticket price, and food price. You can use whatever letters you like.

5. **Miscellaneous Problems**

    a. If a concert charges $29.99 per ticket, how much will it cost for 5 people to go?

    b. What is the difference in latitude between two ships, the first at a latitude of 43° and the other at a latitude of –17°?

    c. If on December 1, Miami, Florida, is at UTC–5:00 and Jerusalem, Israel, is at UTC+2:00, how many hours apart are the two cities?

    Jerusalem

    d. At 9 p.m. in Miami on December 1, what time is it in Jerusalem? Use the information in problem 5c and the map in your reference sheets (p. 433) to help find the answer.

    e. Solve using the distributive property, showing your work: $2(10 + 3 + \frac{1}{4})$

| PRINCIPLES OF MATHEMATICS 2 | Equalities and Unknowns Pages 64–68 | Day 18 | Worksheet 3.3 | Name |

You may use a calculator on this worksheet whenever you see this symbol (🖩).

1. **Finding Unknowns** — Solve each equation for x (that is, isolate x on a side by itself so as to find its value). Show how you added or subtracted (i.e., added a negative number) the same amount to both sides to isolate x on a side by itself.

   Example: $x - 3 = 10$
   $x - 3 + 3 = 10 + 3$
   $x = 13$

   a. $x - 7 = 20$

   Example Meaning: How many brownies were there before dinner if your family ate 7 brownies after dinner and you have 20 brownies left?

   b. $x + 7 = 38$

   Example Meaning: How much more do you have to save if you've saved $7 and your goal is to save $38?

   c. $x + 8 = 26$

   d. $x - 98 = 113$

   e. $78 + x = 240$

   f. $15 + x = 121$

2. **Checking Your Work** — Go back and check each of the answers you obtained in problem 1 by substituting the value you found for x into the original equation. Does it hold true? Show your work.

   For example, we can check the example we showed for problem 1 by substituting the value for x we obtained into the original equation:

   $x - 3 = 10$
   $13 - 3 = 10$
   $10 = 10$

   a.

   b.

   c.

   d.

   e.

   f.

PRINCIPLES OF MATHEMATICS 2 | PAGE 47

3. **Understanding the Meaning**

    a. If we were using the equation in problem 1a to solve the example meaning given, what would the x represent?

    b. If we were using the equation in problem 1b to solve the example meaning given, what would the x represent?

    c. Write your own example meaning for the problem in 1c.

4. **Challenge Problem** — Solve: $-8 + x = 10$ *Hint*: It doesn't matter that the negative number comes first. This problem means the exact same as $x - 8 = 10$, which we could think of as $x + -8 = 10$.

5. **Skill Sharpening** — Simplify.

    a. $-23 \cdot -45 \cdot -1$

    b. $\dfrac{45}{-5}$

    c. $\dfrac{72}{-8}$

    d. $82.5 \cdot -6$

    e. $\dfrac{2}{3} \cdot -\dfrac{6}{7}$

    f. $\dfrac{5}{3} \div \dfrac{2}{3}$

    g. $\dfrac{6}{\frac{2}{3}}$

    h. $\dfrac{60 \text{ m}^2}{10 \text{ m}}$

6. **Miscellaneous Review** (🖩)

    a. In order to earn $55,670 a year, how much do you need to earn on average each month?

    b. If you spend $32.56 on a phone a month, how much do you spend a year?

7. **Fill in the Blanks** — Look at the box on page 65 of your *Student Textbook* to fill in the blanks.

    To find an unknown in an equation, _____
    _____. Do this by performing the _____ operation using the
    _____ to _____ of the equation.

| PRINCIPLES OF MATHEMATICS 2 | More with Equalities and Unknowns Pages 68–70 | Day 19 | Worksheet 3.4 | Name |

Finding Unknowns — Solve each equation for x (that is, isolate x on a side by itself so as to find its value). Show how you added, subtracted (i.e., added a negative number), multiplied, or divided both sides by the same amount to find the value of x.

a. $7 \cdot x = 21$

Example Meaning: If you need to buy 7 gifts for people who supported you on your mission's trip, how much can you spend per gift if you can only spend $21 total?

b. $4 \cdot x = 24$

c. $x \cdot 8 = 64$

d. $\dfrac{x}{8} = 7$

Example Meaning: You know that if you divide the total cost of an event by 8 people the cost per person will be $7. What is the total cost of the event?

e. $\dfrac{x}{9} = 9$

f. $x - 91 = 80$

g. $x - 108 = 25$

h. $87 + x = 234$

i. $x + 36 = 104$

Checking Your Work — Go back and check problems 1a–1d by substituting the value you found for x into the original equation. Show your work.

a.

b.

c.

d.

3. **Understanding the Meaning**

   a. If we were using the equation in problem 1a to solve the example meaning given, what would the x represent?

   b. If we were using the equation in problem 1d to solve the example meaning given, what would the x represent?

   c. Write your own example meaning for the problem in 1b.

4. **Skill Sharpening** — Unless otherwise instructed, simplify these expressions.

   a. $\dfrac{-80}{10}$

   b. $-8 \cdot -2 \cdot -5$

   c. $\dfrac{2}{3} \cdot \dfrac{9}{4}$

   d. $5\text{ m} \cdot 15\text{ m}$

   e. $\dfrac{30\text{ m}}{3\text{ m}}$

   f. Rewrite this equation so that the expression on the left side is on the right side, and the right side is on the left side: $10 = \dfrac{50}{10}$

| PRINCIPLES OF MATHEMATICS 2 | Applying Unknowns Pages 70–72 | Day 20 | Worksheet 3.5 | Name |

You may use a calculator on this worksheet whenever you see this symbol (🖩).

Finding Unknowns — Solve each equation for x (that is, isolate x on a side by itself so as to find its value). Show how you added, subtracted (i.e., added a negative number), multiplied, or divided both sides by the same amount to find the value of x.

a. $8 \cdot x = 72$

b. $x - 408 = 503$

c. $12 + x = 140$

d. $x \cdot 9 = 63$

e. $\dfrac{x}{8} = 48$

f. $30 \cdot x = \$80$

   Example Meaning: Suppose you buy party gifts for 30 people. How much did you spend on each gift if it cost you $80 total?

Understanding the Meaning

a. If we were using the equation in problem 1f to solve the example meaning given, what would the x represent?

b. Write your own example meaning for $4 \cdot x = \$2.50$

3. **Unit Fun**

   a. Do $\frac{15 \text{ mi}}{\text{hr}}$ and $\frac{15 \text{ mi}}{1 \text{ hr}}$ mean the same thing?

   b. Do $15\frac{\text{mi}}{\text{hr}}$ and $\frac{15 \text{ mi}}{\text{hr}}$ mean the same thing?

   c. Rewrite 30 mi *per* hour using a fraction.

   d. Rewrite 15 meters *per* second using a fraction, using m as the abbreviation for meters and s as the abbreviation for seconds. *Note*: The m and s in this situation are units of measure, *not* unknowns. Meters per second is a unit of measure that can be used to measure speed.

   e. Rewrite 2 lb *per* 1 in² using a fraction.

4. **Time and Distance** (🖩) — Use the distance formula from Lesson 3.5 to solve. (The formula is also included on p. 431 of your reference sheets for easy reference.) Show your work. Don't forget the units.

   a. If you're training for a marathon and decide you need to run 16 miles but only have 2 hours in which to run, how fast do you have to go?

   b. If it takes you 5 hours to go 200 miles, how fast are you traveling on average?

   c. If it takes you 3 hours to go 40 miles, how fast are you traveling on average?

5. **Geometry Time** (🖩) — Find the volume of the cylinder portion of this silo if its base is a circle with a radius of 4 ft and it is 28 ft tall.

| PRINCIPLES OF MATHEMATICS 2 | Finding Missing Sides Pages 72–75 | Day 21 | Worksheet 3.6 | Name |

You may use a calculator on this worksheet whenever you see this symbol (📱).

Perimeter (📱) — Find the missing sides of these polygons. The letter P stands for the perimeter.

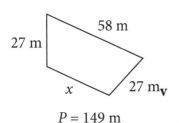
$P = 149$ m

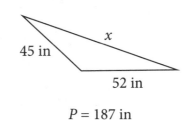
$P = 187$ in

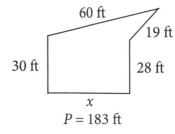
$P = 183$ ft

a. _____ b. _____ c. _____

Find the Missing Sides (📱)

a. Find the height of this rectangular prism if its volume is 200 cm³.

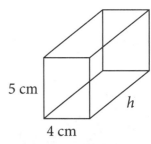

b. Suppose you're designing a railroad car. You need it to have a volume of 1,600 ft³, a width of 10 ft, and a height of 8 ft. What length does the car need to be?

Example Meaning — Write an example meaning for $18 + x = 20$

Swapping Sides — Rewrite this equation so that the expression on the left side is on the right side, and the right side is on the left side: $10 \div 2 = 5$

5. **Unit Fun**

   a. Do $\dfrac{3 \text{ km}}{\text{hr}}$, $\dfrac{3 \text{ km}}{1 \text{ hr}}$, and $3\dfrac{\text{km}}{\text{hr}}$ mean the same thing?

   b. Rewrite 100 lb *per* ft (i.e., 100 pounds per foot) using a fraction.

PRINCIPLES OF MATHEMATICS 2 | Unknowns and Altitude, Pages 75–79 | Day 22 | Worksheet 3.7 | Name

You may use a calculator on this worksheet whenever you see this symbol (📟).

Finding Unknowns — Solve each equation for the unknown (that is, isolate the unknown on a side by itself so as to find its value). Show what you added, subtracted (i.e., added a negative number), multiplied, or divided to both sides.

a. $5 \cdot r = -25$

Example Meaning: If we traveled for 5 min, what was our average rate if we started at sea level and ended at an altitude of –25 feet?

b. $605 + x = 210$

Example Meaning: If after making $605 and paying our bills, we end with $210, how much did we pay in bills?

c. $15 + x = -29$

Example Meaning: If we start a height of 15 m and then change height an unknown amount, ending at a height of –29 m, what was our change in height?

d. $\dfrac{x}{6} = -36$

Example Meaning: What was the final altitude after 6 minutes if the rate at which we changed altitude was $-36 \, \dfrac{\text{ft}}{\text{min}}$ and we started at sea level?

Altitude (📟) — Use the altitude formula given in Lesson 3.7 to solve these problems. (The formula is also included on p. 431 of your reference sheets for easy reference.) Remember that whenever you see the word *altitude*, we're measuring relative to sea level. So sea level would have an altitude of 0.

a. If a helicopter starting at sea level ascends to an altitude of 12,000 ft in 15 minutes, at what rate does it change altitude?

b. The Prospect Express ski lift at Telluride Ski Resort has a vertical rise of 1,050 ft and takes 5 minutes.[1] Another way of saying this is that the lift goes from a height of 0 ft (the reference level) to 1,050 ft in 5 minutes. At what rate is the height changing on this lift?

According to Telluride Tourism Board, Telluride Colorado, http://www.visittelluride.com/uploads/1435266720296dbc9229c.pdf?1435267440, accessed 02/10/16.

c. If a diver starting at sea level descends to an altitude of −100 ft in 30 min, what was the rate of altitude change?

d. If a WWII submarine starting at sea level changes to an altitude of −45 m in 15 seconds, what was the rate of altitude change?

e. If it takes someone riding an escalator 1.5 minutes to go from a ground floor (our reference point, s 0 ft) to the basement floor which is 70 ft below the ground floor (so a height of −70 ft), at what rate the escalator changing height?

3. **Understanding Letters** — What does h represent in the formula for finding the area of a triangle, $A = \frac{1}{2} \cdot b \cdot h$?

4. **Skill Sharpening** — Simplify, except where otherwise instructed.

   a. 5 − 8

   b. 5 − −8

   c. 5 − − − 8

   d. 5 • −2

   e. −5 • −2 • −1

   f. $\frac{10}{-2}$

   g. $-\frac{2}{3} \cdot \frac{6}{8}$

   h. Rewrite this equation so that the expression on the left side is on the right side, and the right side is on the left side: 7 = 5 − 2

5. **Corn** (🖩)

   a. A field of corn is planted in hills 44 in apart each way. If a square field has an area of 1 acre (which is 6,272,640 in²), how many hills could be planted in the square field? *Hint*: If each hill takes 44 in each way, then it takes up a circle with a 44 in radius. However, we won't be able to use some space i between each of those circles, so in reality it will take up the area of a square that can contain a circle with a 44 in radius. Find the area of the *square* shown, and then divide the total square inches in an acre by it.

   b. For the field described in 5a, what should the yield in bushels be if the average hill produces 3 ears of a size such that 120 make a bushel?

44 in

Principles of Mathematics 2
Solving Problems with Fractions and Unknowns (Addition and Subtraction) — Day 26
Worksheet 4.1

Fractions and Unknowns — Solve for x.

a. $\frac{2}{3} + x = 4$

Example Meaning: If you have added $\frac{2}{3}$ cup of flour to the mixer and need to add enough additional flour to make 4 cups altogether, how many more cups do you still need to add to the mixer?

b. $x - 4\frac{2}{3}$ lb $= 300$ lb

Example Meaning: If a machine exerts a certain amount of pressure, but, by some modifications, can have its pressure reduced by $4\frac{2}{3}$ pounds of pressure, bringing its total down to 300 pounds of pressure, how much pressure does the machine exert?

c. $5\frac{1}{2}$ lb $+ -6\frac{1}{4}$ lb $= x$

Example Meaning: If a machine exerts $5\frac{1}{2}$ pounds of pressure in the positive direction, and then the pressure is increased by $6\frac{1}{4}$ pounds of pressure in the negative direction, what pressure will the machine exert?

d. $x - \frac{3}{4} = 5\frac{1}{3}$

Example Meaning: If after you cut $\frac{3}{4}$ ft off a piece of wood there's still $5\frac{1}{3}$ ft of wood left, how long was the piece of wood in the beginning?

2. **Fractions and Unknowns** — Use the example meaning in problem 1b to help you solve these word problems.

   a. If a machine exerts a certain amount of pressure, but, by some modifications, can have its pressure increased by $70\frac{4}{13}$ pounds of pressure, bringing its total up to $650\frac{1}{3}$ pounds of pressure, how much pressure did the machine originally exert?

   b. If a machine exerts a certain amount of pressure, but, by some modifications, can have its pressure reduced by $10\frac{1}{10}$ pounds of pressure, bringing its total down to $400\frac{4}{5}$ pounds of pressure, how much pressure did the machine originally exert?

3. **Skill Sharpening**

   a. If you walked on a trail that started at sea level and headed into a valley, at what rate did you change altitude if after 1.5 hr of walking you reached an altitude of –40 ft?

   b. Write 200 kilometers *per* hour using a fraction.

PRINCIPLES OF MATHEMATICS 2
Solving Problems with Fractions and Unknowns (Multiplication and Division)
Pages 83–86 — Day 27 — Worksheet 4.2

You may use a calculator on this worksheet whenever you see this symbol (🖩).

Solving for Unknowns — Solve.

a. $\frac{2}{3} \cdot x = 30$

   Example Meaning: $\frac{2}{3}$ of the people who filled out a survey equals 30.

b. $\frac{4}{5} \cdot x = 60$

   Example Meaning: $\frac{4}{5}$ of a distance equals 60.

c. $\dfrac{x}{2\frac{1}{2}} = 49$

   Example Meaning: How many supplies do you need if you want to give $2\frac{1}{2}$ each to 49 people?

Fractions in Action

a. If $\frac{4}{9}$ of the people in a group like red, and $\frac{2}{3}$ of those people are girls, what fraction of the entire group are girls who like red?

   Hint: Find $\frac{2}{3} \cdot \frac{4}{9}$

b. If you need $\frac{1}{3}$ a yard of ribbon to trim each hat, how many hats can you trim with $5\frac{1}{2}$ yards?

3. **Pyramid Puzzles** (🖩) — Below are some actual dimensions from the Tour Egypt website[1] regarding pyramids in Egypt. Use the information given to find the requested information. Round your answers to the nearest whole number.

   a. Find the volume of the Great Pyramid of Khufu. Its height is 146.5 m, and its base has an area of 53,074.94 m².

   b. Find the volume of the main pyramid in the Pyramid Complex of Userkaf. The original height was 163 ft, and the base is a square with 240.5 ft sides. *Hint*: This time, you're not given the area of the base, so you'll have to find it using what you know about finding the area of a square (*Area of a square = side • side*).

4. **Applying Unknowns** (🖩)

   a. If the circumference of (distance around) a circular whirlpool is 45 ft, what must its diameter be?

   b. Show how you would write this problem using an unknown to stand for the starting yardage:

   If you started with an unknown yardage of fabric, used $\frac{3}{4}$ of a yard of the fabric, and have $4\frac{2}{3}$ yard left, how many yards of the fabric did you start with?

   c. Solve the problem in 4b.

   d. If a dolphin descends from sea level to an altitude of −36 ft in 4 seconds, at what rate was the dolphin changing altitude?

---

[1] Dimensions based on Jimmy Dunn (writing as Alan Winston), "The Pyramid of Khufu at Giza in Egypt" and "The Pyramid Complex of Userkaf at Saqqara in Egypt" (Tour Egypt), http://www.touregypt.net, accessed 10/12/15.

Principles of Mathematics 2 — Worksheet 4.3
Viewing Division as Multiplication (Pages 86–88) — Day 28

You may use a calculator on this worksheet whenever you see this symbol (🖩).

Division as Multiplication — Use these problems to practice dividing using the "shortcut" of multiplying by the multiplicative inverse. In addition to writing the answer, show how you multiplied both sides by the same quantity to obtain the answer.

a. $4 \cdot x = 20$

b. $6 \cdot x = 36$

c. $5 \cdot x = 200$

d. $\frac{1}{3} \cdot x = 21$

   Example Meaning: If $\frac{1}{3}$ of our total cost is $21, what is our total cost?

e. $\frac{3}{9} \cdot x = 30$

   Example Meaning: If $\frac{3}{9}$ of our total cost equals $30, what is our total cost?

f. $\frac{3}{4} \cdot x = 1$

   Example Meaning: If $\frac{3}{4}$ a pound of potatoes cost $1, how much do potatoes cost per pound?

g. $\frac{2}{3} \cdot x = \$50$

   Example Meaning: If $\frac{2}{3}$ of our total cost is $50, what is our total cost?

h. $4 \cdot x = \$60$

   Example Meaning: If 4 times our total cost is $60, what is our total cost?

2. **Check Your Work** — Substitute the value you found in problem 1d for *x*, showing your work. Did you find the correct value for *x*?

3. **Fractions in Action** (🔢) — Find the area of this triangle.

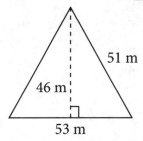

4. **Skill Sharpening** — Simplify each problem.

   a. $-\dfrac{2}{5} \cdot 5 \cdot -1$

   b. $-\dfrac{4}{5} - \dfrac{2}{5}$

   c. $1\dfrac{3}{4} - 5\dfrac{1}{4}$

5. **Pyramid Puzzle** (🔢) — The Pepi I Pyramid has a height of 52 m and its base is a square with 78 m sides.[1] Find its volume.

6. **Time and Distance** — If it takes you 4 hours to run 24 miles, how fast do you run?

---

[1] Dimensions based on Jimmy Dunn (writing as Alan Winston), "The Pyramid of Pepi 1 at South Saqqara in Egypt" (Tour Egypt), http://www.touregypt.net, accessed 10/12/15.

| PRINCIPLES OF MATHEMATICS 2 | Fractions with an Unknown in the Denominator Pages 89–90 | Day 29 | Worksheet 4.4 | Name |

You may use a calculator on this worksheet whenever you see this symbol (🖩).

Learning the Language — Rewrite each of these expressions as a fraction.

a. $8 \div x$

b. $x \div 70$

c. $100 \div x$

Understanding Fractions as Division — Express as a fraction. Do not simplify. Include units.

a. 70 miles divided by 1 hour

Example Meaning: how far a car traveled in 1 hour

b. 250 miles divided by an unknown number of hours

Example Meaning: how far a car traveled in an unknown number of hours

c. 1 day divided by 31 days

Example Meaning: what portion of a 31-day month is a day

d. an unknown dollar amount divided by 4.33 weeks

Example Meaning: the cost per week of an unknown monthly amount

Finding Unknowns with Fractions — Solve by isolating the unknown on a side of the equation by itself; show your work. Notice from the example meanings how these are really the same sort of problems you've been solving for years.

a. $\dfrac{x}{8} = 9$

Example Meaning: What quantity did we start with if, when we divided it evenly amoung 8 friends, each friend ended up with 9?

b. $\dfrac{\$54}{x} = \$9$

Example Meaning: If we have $54, how many people can we divide it among in order to give each person $9?

c. $\dfrac{\$80}{x} = \$20$

   Example Meaning: $80 divided by what number of people would give each person $20?

d. $\dfrac{-40}{x} = -20$

   Example Meaning: –40 feet divided by what number of seconds would result in changing altitude at an average rate of –20 $\dfrac{ft}{sec}$, if the starting altitude was sea level?

e. Go back and check your work in 3d by substituting the value you found for x into the equation. Did you find the correct value? Show your work.

4. **Understanding the Meaning**

   a. Write an example meaning for $\dfrac{24}{x} = 8$. Solve.

   b. Write an example meaning for $\dfrac{30}{x} = 15$. Solve.

5. **Skill Sharpening** — Simplify.

   a. $\dfrac{-88}{8}$ 　　　　　　　　　　　　 b. $\dfrac{12}{-3}$

   c. $\dfrac{-72}{-9}$ 　　　　　　　　　　　　 d. $\dfrac{\frac{2}{1}}{3}$

6. **Area Time** (🖩) — Suppose you want to plant a garden that has an area of 84 square feet. Because of the layout of your yard, the width of the garden has to be 6 feet. If you make the garden a rectangle, how long would the length be?

PAGE 64 | PRINCIPLES OF MATHEMATICS 2

Negative Numbers and Fractions — Simplify 1a and 1b; solve 1c–1g. Leave all answers as either whole numbers, mixed numbers, or proper fractions.

a. $\dfrac{-80}{40}$

Example Meaning: 80 pounds of force in a negative direction distributed over (divided by) 40 square inches

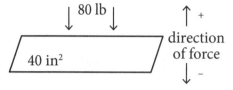

b. $40 - \dfrac{-16}{-8}$

c. $70 - \dfrac{-39}{40} = x$

d. $60 - \dfrac{25}{-10} = x$

e. $x + \dfrac{-2}{21} = 10$

f. $x - \dfrac{-40}{2} = 50$

g. $x - \dfrac{39}{-2} = 80$

Checking Your Work — Go back and check your work for problem 1g by substituting the value you found for *x* into the equation. Did you find the correct value? Show your work. Be sure to also check any of the other problems you're unsure of.

3. **Pyramid Puzzle** (🖩) — While the Egyptian pyramids had squares for bases, pyramid shapes can have different types of polygons for bases. If a pyramid has a base made of the hexagon below and a height of 54 ft, what is its volume? You can still use the same $V = \frac{1}{3} \cdot B \cdot h$ formula.

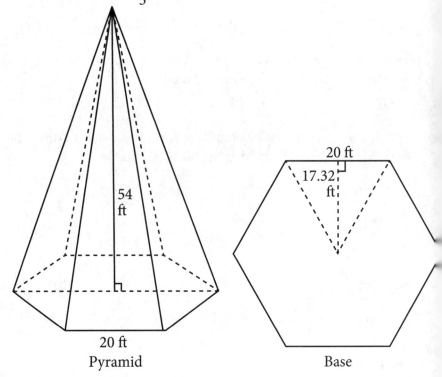

Pyramid

Base

4. **Skill Sharpening**

   a. Solve: $\frac{64}{x} = 8$

   b. Solve: $\frac{200}{x} = 10$

   c. Simplify: $\dfrac{56}{\frac{2}{4}}$

| PRINCIPLES OF MATHEMATICS 2 | Ratios and Proportions Revisited Pages 95–101 | Day 34 | Worksheet 5.1A | Name |

You may use a calculator on this worksheet whenever you see this symbol (🖩).

Reminder: See your reference sheets (p.429–430) for conversion ratios.

You've already been dealing with ratios when working with miles *per* hour ($\frac{mi}{hr}$) for several chapters now.

Remember that writing a 1 in front of a unit is optional. $4 *per* gal could be written $\frac{\$4}{1 \text{ gal}}$ or $\frac{\$4}{\text{gal}}$.

Understanding Check — A ratio is _____.

Recording Ratios — Record each ratio as a fraction.

a. $20 per 3 bushels of apples

b. 30 ounces of nitrogen per 10 ounces of phosphate (such as in a fertilizer)

c. 45 miles per 5 hours

d. 60 minutes divided by 1 hour

e. 1 hour divided by 60 minutes

f. $60 divided by an unknown amount

g. an unknown number of miles divided by 6 hours

3. **Ratios and Decimals** (🖩) — Express the ratio in 1a as a decimal number. Your answer will be the price per bushel.

4. **Proportions** (🖩) — Find the unknown in these proportions.

    a. $\dfrac{4\text{ c}}{1\text{ qt}} = \dfrac{80\text{ c}}{x}$

    b. $\dfrac{8\text{ pt}}{1\text{ gal}} = \dfrac{x}{24\text{ gal}}$

5. **Proportions Applied** (🖩) — If a solution calls for 3 cups per gallon, and you want to make 7 gallons, how many cups do you need?

6. **Term Time** — The following questions refer to this proportion: $\dfrac{1}{2} = \dfrac{5}{10}$

    a. Which two numbers are the means?

    b. Which two numbers are the extremes?

7. **Conversions** (🖩) — Use the ratio shortcut method to solve.

    a. Convert 67.8 miles to kilometers.

    b. Convert 58.3 mi² to square kilometers

    c. Suppose an inflatable pool has a volume of 60 ft³. How many cubic inches is that?

    d. How many gallons can the pool in 7c hold?

Worksheet 5.1B

You may use a calculator on this worksheet whenever you see this symbol (📱).

Conversions (📱) — Use the ratio shortcut method to solve.

a. How many hours is 345 minutes?

b. How many pounds is 5 tons?

Conversions of Different Units (📱) — You can apply your unit conversion skills to any unit. For example, graphic designers sometimes deal in a unit of measure called picas. There are 6 picas per inch. Use this information to complete the following conversions.

a. Convert 52 picas to inches.

b. Convert 28 inches to picas.

Similar Parallelograms (📱) — These two parallelograms are similar; what is the length of the side marked x?

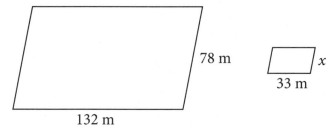

Similar Triangles (📱) — These two triangles are similar; what is the length of the side marked x?

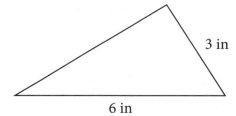
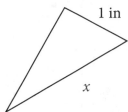

5. **Skill Sharpening**

   a. Solve: $\frac{1}{2} \cdot x = 400$

   b. If $\frac{1}{3}$ of your expenses equals $500, how much are your expenses? *Hint*: This problem is similar to 11a.

   c. Simplify: $\dfrac{8}{\frac{2}{3}}$

PRINCIPLES OF MATHEMATICS 2
Cross Multiplication — Pages 101–105 — Day 36 — Worksheet **5.2** — Name

You may use a calculator on this worksheet whenever you see this symbol (🖩).

1. **Finding the Missing Number in a Proportion** (🖩) — Use cross multiplication to solve these problems for the unknown/requested information. Show your work.

   a. $\dfrac{5\ c}{3\ gal} = \dfrac{x}{15\ gal}$

   b. $\dfrac{5\ mi}{20\ hr} = \dfrac{25\ mi}{x}$

   c. If a solution tells you to mix 2 cups of the concentrate per 4 gallons of desired solution, how many cups should you put in if you want 18 gallons of the solution?

   d. If you are traveling at 15 miles per hour, how far can you go in 14 hours?

2. **Similar Shape Review** (🖩) — These two irregular hexagons are similar. Use cross multiplication to find s. Show your work.

   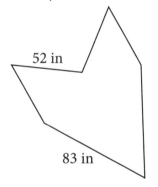

3. **More Similar Shapes** (🖩)

   a. The room of a house is 16 ft wide by 18 ft long. If, in the plan, the house's width is represented by a line 0.8 feet long, how long should the line be that represents the length of the house?

   b. If, on a map, the distance between two cities 250 miles apart is represented by a distance of 2.5 inches, what should represent the distance between two cities that are 372 miles apart?

4. **Unit Conversion** (🖩) — Graphic designers sometimes work in a unit called points. There are 72 points per inch. Use this information to complete the following conversions.

   a. Convert 780 points to inches.

   b. Convert 50 points to centimeters. *Hint*: First convert to inches and then convert to centimeters. You can do this all with one expression if you use the ratio shortcut method.

5. **Tiling a Room** (🖩)) — If a room has an area of 65 square feet and you want to tile it with tile that costs $4.50 a square yard installed, how much will it cost you if you can only buy complete yards (you can't purchase a portion of a yard)? *Hint*: First find the total square yards of the room (round up to the next square yard since you can't buy a portion of a yard), and then find the cost.

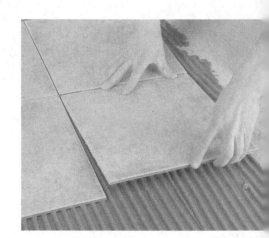

6. **Skill Sharpening**

   a. Solve: $\frac{x}{5} = 30$

   b. Suppose you know parents divided a monetary gift they received evenly among each of their 5 children. If each child got $50, how much was the gift? *Hint*: Use x to represent the amount of the gift.

   c. Simplify: $\dfrac{\frac{6}{4}}{3}$

   d. Solve: $\frac{33}{x} = 11$

| PRINCIPLES OF MATHEMATICS 2 | More with Time Pages 106–108 | Day 37 | Worksheet 5.3A | Name |

You may use a calculator on this worksheet whenever you see this symbol (🖩).

Unit Time — Multiply each unit by its inverse so as to get an answer of 1.

Example: $4\frac{mi}{hr}$ Answer: $\cancel{4}\frac{\cancel{mi}}{\cancel{hr}} \cdot \frac{\cancel{hr}}{\cancel{4}\cancel{mi}} = 1$

a. $8\frac{mi}{hr}$

b. $\frac{60\ m}{s}$ Hint: $\frac{m}{s}$ means meters *per* second

c. $\frac{1\ gal}{231\ in^2}$

Time for Time (🖩) — Use the relationship $d = s \cdot t$ (*distance = speed • time*) to solve these problems. In problems 2b–2d, give your answer in minutes.

a. How far can you travel in 20 minutes at 40 miles per hour?

b. How long will it take to travel 20 miles at 60 miles per hour?

c. How long will it take to travel 20 miles at 40 miles per hour?

d. How long will it take you to travel 10 miles at 40 miles per hour?

3. **Word Problems and Units** (🖩) — The same principles of canceling units we've been applying to geometry and time problems apply to other types of problems as well. The problems below illustrate this.

    a. Fill in the blanks and cross out any units that cancel:

    $$400 \text{ barrels} \cdot \frac{\$1.75}{\text{barrel}} = \underline{\hspace{2cm}}$$

    b. A merchant bought 400 barrels of apples at $1.75 per barrel. He sold $\frac{3}{4}$ of them at $2.50 a barrel and kept the rest. Assuming he can't sell the remaining $\frac{1}{4}$, how much did he make? *Hint*: You found the total *cost* of all the apples in problem 3a. Now find the total sales and compare the two.

    c. Fill in the blanks and cross out any units that cancel:

    $$\frac{3 \text{ quarts}}{\text{day}} \cdot \frac{280 \text{ days}}{\text{year}} = \underline{\hspace{2cm}}$$

    d. If a cow produces 3 quarts of milk per day for 280 days out of the year, how much income is obtained each year from selling the cow's milk if all the quarts are sold for $2 per quart? *Hint*: You found the total quarts this cow produces per year in problem 3c.

4. **Same Skill, Different Applications** — Just as we can solve to find the time in the $d = s \cdot t$ equation, we can also solve to find the time in other equations, such as the altitude (or height) equation we looked at back in Lesson 3.7:

    $$a = r \cdot t + a_i$$
    altitude (or height) = rate of change in altitude (or height) • time + initial altitude (or height)

    Give it a try with these problems.

    a. If an elevator changes height at a rate of 400 feet per minute, how long would it to take to go from the ground floor to a floor 900 feet above ground level, assuming it doesn't stop along the way?

    b. If an elevator changed height at a rate of 70 feet per minute, how long would it take to go from the ground floor to a floor 900 feet above ground level, assuming it didn't stop along the way?

1. **Conversion Time** (🖩) — Use whatever conversion method you like to solve these problems.

    a. If a vehicle weighs 7,000 pounds, how many tons is that?

    b. If a vehicle weighs 2.5 tons, how many pounds is that?

    c. If someone weighs 130 pounds, how many ounces do they weigh?

    d. How much do you weigh in ounces?

2. **Looking at Proportions** (🖩) — Use cross multiplication to find the unknown or requested information in these proportions. Show your work.

    a. $\dfrac{8}{12} = \dfrac{54}{x}$

    b. $\dfrac{25}{x} = \dfrac{450}{500}$

    c. Suppose you want to draw a scaled-down version of a basketball court. A basketball court is 94 feet long and 50 feet wide. If the length of your scale drawing is 9.4 inches, how many inches should you make the width of the scale drawing?

3. **Time for Time** (🖩) — Solve. Give your answer in minutes.

   a. How long will it take you to travel 15 miles at 35 miles per hour?

   b. How long will it take you to travel 15 miles at 20 miles per hour?

4. **Skill Sharpening**

   a. Solve: $\frac{2}{3} \cdot x = 50$

   b. If, in a certain city, $\frac{15}{16}$ of the days of the year are above freezing, how many days a year are below freezing? Use 365 days in a year; round to the nearest day.

   c. If someone tells you they are $\frac{1}{3}$ of the way done a book and they've read 66 pages, how many pages long is the book?

   d. Solve: $x + \frac{4}{-5} = 11\frac{1}{3}$

   e. If the difference found by subtracting $\frac{-8}{-9}$ from your starting amount is 25, how much was your starting amount?

   f. Simplify: $\dfrac{3}{\frac{2}{5}}$

PAGE 76 | PRINCIPLES OF MATHEMATICS 2

PRINCIPLES OF MATHEMATICS 2 | Proportions and the Pressure and Volume of a Gas Pages 108–110 | Day 39 | Worksheet 5.4 | Name

You may use a calculator on this worksheet whenever you see this symbol (🖩).

1. **Under Pressure** (🖩) — Use the proportion $\frac{P_1}{P_2} = \frac{V_2}{V_1}$ and cross multiplication to solve these problems.

   a. 24 cubic inches (V_1) of air under a pressure of 40 pounds (P_1) will have what volume when the pressure is increased to 100 pounds (P_2), assuming the temperature remains the same?

   b. 15 cubic yards (V_1) of air under a pressure of 35 pounds (P_1) will have what volume when the pressure is decreased to 10 pounds (P_2), assuming the temperature remains the same?

2. **Looking at Proportions** (🖩)

   a. If the fall in a barometer (device for measuring atmospheric pressure) is 0.1 inch for every 100 feet of elevation, what will the fall due to elevation be if the elevation is increased by 2,600 feet?

   b. If 1 acre of alfalfa produces 1.5 tons of alfalfa each time the alfalfa is cut, and the alfalfa is cut 7 times each growing season, how much alfalfa can you cut in one season on 12 acres? *Hint:* First find the alfalfa per time cut, and then find the alfalfa per season.

   c. Solve: $\frac{50 \text{ ft}}{20 \text{ sec}} = \frac{20 \text{ ft}}{x}$

   d. If you want to draw a scale drawing where every inch represents 11 feet of a building that is 75 feet tall, how tall will your drawing be?

PRINCIPLES OF MATHEMATICS 2 | PAGE 77

3. **Similar Figures** (🧮) — If you have two similar right triangles, one of which has a base of 4 in and a height of 8 in, and the other of which has a base of 3 in, what is the height of the second triangle? *Hint*: Draw the right triangles if you need to.

4. **Time and Distance** (🧮) — Solve.

    a. How fast do you have to travel to go 400 miles in 5 hours?

    b. If you're traveling at $65 \frac{mi}{hr}$, how much less time will it take you to go 400 miles than if you travel at $55 \frac{mi}{hr}$? Give your final answer in hours and minutes, rounded to the nearest minute.

    Example: If your final answer is 1.33 hr, convert the 0.33 portion to minutes.

    $0.33 \text{ hr} \cdot \frac{60 \text{ min}}{1 \text{ hr}} = 19.8$ min, which rounds to 20 min

    A final answer of 1.33 hr should be listed as 1 hr, 20 min

5. **Skill Sharpening**

    a. Solve: $x - \frac{-3}{7} = 5\frac{1}{3}$

    b. Solve: $x + \frac{-2}{-7} = 2\frac{1}{4}$

    c. Say $\frac{7}{9}$ of your total land is planted with tomatoes; how many acres total do you have if you have 6 acres of tomatoes?

    d. Solve: $x \cdot \frac{8}{7} = 12$

    e. Simplify: $\frac{5}{\frac{5}{6}}$

    f. If a field is 26 m long, how many feet long is it?

Levers and Proportions (📱) — Use the relationship $\frac{F_1}{F_2} = \frac{d_2}{d_1}$, the picture shown, and cross multiplication to solve these problems.

a. What force is required to lift a weight of 800 pounds (F_2) by means of a lever of which the weight is 0.5 feet (d_2) from the pivot point and the force is applied 4 feet (d_1) from the pivot point?

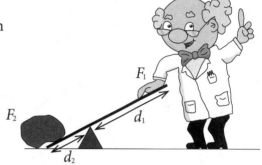

b. How much weight (force) could you lift applying 50 pounds (F_1) to a lever whose pivot point is 5 feet (d_1) from the force applied and 2 feet (d_2) from the weight (force) you're lifting?

c. If you can apply 100 pounds of force (F_1), what distance between the force you apply and the pivot point would you need in order to move 5,000 pounds (F_2) that is 1 foot (d_2) from the pivot point?

Time and Distance (📱)) — Give your final answer in hours and minutes, rounding to the nearest minute.

a. How long will it take you to go 300 miles at $65 \frac{\text{mi}}{\text{hr}}$?

b. How long will it take you to go 300 miles at $45 \frac{\text{mi}}{\text{hr}}$?

3. **Skill Sharpening**

a. Simplify: $\dfrac{4}{\frac{1}{5}}$

b. Solve: $x + \dfrac{4}{5} = 65$

c. Solve: $x + \dfrac{-4}{5} = 65$

d. If you want to make $\dfrac{2}{3}$ of a recipe, and the recipe calls for 2 cups of flour, how much flour do you need?

e. If a diver dives 10 m, how many feet is that?

| PRINCIPLES OF MATHEMATICS 2 | Review of Chapters 1–5 | Day 43 | Worksheet 5.6 | Name |

You may use a calculator on this worksheet whenever you see this symbol (🖩).

Operations and Properties (🖩)

a. Solve using the order of operations: 7.8(1.2 + 0.8) (Lesson 1.3)

b. Solve using the distributive property (show your work): 7.8(1.2 + 0.8) (Lesson 1.3)

Skill Review (Lessons 2.1–2.5) — Simplify.

a. $\dfrac{24}{-3}$

b. $\dfrac{7}{\frac{2}{3}}$

c. $\dfrac{84}{42}$

d. $-\dfrac{2}{5} \cdot 5$

e. $|-6|$

More Skill Review (🖩) — Solve.

a. $x + 9 = 25$ (Lesson 3.3)

b. $5 \cdot x = 60$ (Lesson 3.4)

c. $\dfrac{2}{3} \cdot x = 56$ (Lesson 4.2)

d. $x - \dfrac{7}{8} = 89$ (Lesson 4.1)

e. $x - \frac{-1}{-2} = 6$ (Lesson 4.5)

f. $\frac{55.6}{x} = 5$ (Lesson 4.4)

4. **Factoring** — Find the prime factors of 76. (Lesson 2.2)

5. **Understanding Check**
   a. Each negative sign means the _____. (Lesson 2.4)

   b. We use letters as _____ to stand for numbers. (Lesson 3.1)

   c. If two expressions are equal and you add the same amount to both sides, will they remain equal? (Lesson 3.2)

6. **Fraction Fun** (🖩)

   a. If an elevator starts on the ground floor and goes up $30\frac{1}{3}$ ft, then down $15\frac{1}{2}$ ft, then up $45\frac{1}{6}$ ft, then up 18 ft, and last of all down 33 ft, where is it then, in relation to the ground floor? (Lessons 2.3 and 2.4)

   b. A man is rowing at $5\frac{2}{3}$ miles per hour. If he is rowing downstream on a river that has a current of $3\frac{7}{8}$ miles an hour, how many miles an hour total will he travel downstream? *Hint*: He'll travel the rate he can row plus the rate of the current. (Lessons 2.3 and 2.4)

Continue to Next Page

c. Now suppose the same man is traveling upstream instead. He's rowing at an even 6 miles per hour, and the current is pulling him downstream at $3\frac{7}{8}$ miles an hour. How fast is he traveling upstream? *Hint*: Use negative numbers to represent the current's pull downstream, and positive numbers to represent his travel upstream. (Lessons 2.3 and 2.4)

d. $\frac{4}{5} \cdot x = 92$ (Lesson 4.2)

   Example Meaning: If $\frac{4}{5}$ of the survey results came back in favor of Candidate A, how many people were surveyed if 92 people voted for Candidate A on the survey?

e. In the previous problem, what does the *x* represent in the example meaning?

Geometry Time (🖩)

a. Find the height of this triangle. (Lesson 3.6)

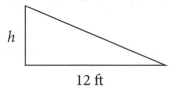

   12 ft

   Area = 30 ft²

b. If the base of a pyramid is a square with 43 ft sides, and its height is 60 ft, what is its volume? (Lesson 4.2)

c. If an area of a room is 75 square meters, what is the area in square feet? (Lesson 5.1)

d. If each shipping crate[1] is a rectangular prism 232.5 in long by 92.5 in wide by 93.9 in high, what volume in cubic feet can 6 crates hold? (Lessons 1.4 and 1.5)

8. **Time and Altitude**

   a. If we travel 40 miles in 2.25 hours, what is our speed? (Lesson 3.5)

   b. How long would it take to go from an altitude of sea level to −500 ft if you change altitude at a rate of $-25 \frac{\text{ft}}{\text{sec}}$? (Lessons 3.7 and 5.3)

9. **More Levers and Proportions (Lesson 5.2, 5.5)** — Use the relationship $\frac{F_1}{F_2} = \frac{d_2}{d_1}$ and cross multiplication to solve.

   a. How much force would it take to move a 500 pound object (F_2) if you use a lever with a pivot point 1 foot (d_2) from the object and 8 feet (d_1) from where the force is applied?

   b. How much force would it take to move the same 500 pound object (F_2) if you apply the force 20 feet (d_1) from the object instead, assuming the object is still 1 foot (d_2) from the pivot point?

10. **Making a Tree House (Lessons 5.1 and 5.2)** — Suppose you're trying to make a tree house. The instructions you have are for a house 2.5 feet wide and 4 feet long, but you want your house to be 3 feet wide instead. How long should you make it if you want the house to be proportional to the one in the instructions? Show how you used cross multiplication to find the answer.

Revisiting Percents — Worksheet 6.1

You may use a calculator on this worksheet whenever you see this symbol (▦).
Remember, percents should be rounded to the second decimal (example: 45.23%).

Reviewing Percents (▦)

a. Simplify: 20% + 60%

b. Simplify: 100% − 15%

c. Convert 56% to a fraction; simplify.

d. Convert 56% to a decimal.

e. Convert 57.85% to a decimal. Do not round.

f. Convert $\frac{8}{9}$ to a percent.

g. Convert $1\frac{1}{3}$ to a percent.

h. Convert 0.4235 to a percent.

i. Convert 0.872 to a percent.

j. Simplify: 12.53 ÷ 20%

k. Simplify: 5% • $800

Finding the Percentage Amount (▦) — Use the relationship $Rate = \frac{Percentage}{Base}$ to solve.

a. What is 20% of 156.24?

b. Find 12% of 46.

c. If iron ore yields 62% of pure metal, how much iron can be obtained from 40 tons of iron ore?

d. A gardener planted 1,000 avocado seeds and expected 10% to not survive due to frost and 15% to not survive due to not germinating. How many seeds does he expect to not survive altogether? *Hint*: Find the total percent that expected to not survive, and then set up a proportion.

e. How many avocado seeds does the gardener in problem 2d expect to survive?

3. **Skill Sharpening**

   a. Given that *distance = speed • time* ($d = s \cdot t$), how long will it take you to travel 400 miles at 60 miles per hour? Give your final answer in hours and minutes, rounded to the nearest minute.

   b. These two irregular pentagons are similar; find s.

   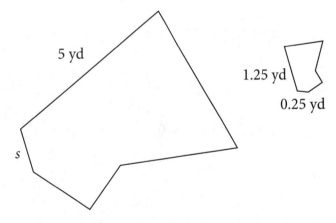

   c. Solve: $x + \$96.50 = \$425.25$

   d. Solve: $x - \dfrac{3}{-5} = 7$

   e. Simplify: $-2 \cdot \dfrac{-4}{5}$

| PRINCIPLES OF MATHEMATICS 2 | Rearranging Formulas Pages 121–124 | Day 47 | Worksheet 6.2A | Name |

You may use a calculator on this worksheet whenever you see this symbol (🖩).

Swapping Sides — Rewrite each equation so that the expression on the left side is on the right side, and the right side is on the left side.

    Example: $47 - x = 42$ *Answer:* $42 = 47 - x$

a. $45 = x + 10$

b. $6 - x = 3$

c. $s \bullet t = d$

Rearranging Formulas (🖩)

a. Rearrange the formula for the volume of a prism ($V = B \bullet h$) so the area of the base (B) is on a side by itself. *Hint:* Divide both sides by h.

b. Swap the entire sides of your answer to 2a so that B is on the left side (it is simpler to read a formula when the unknown we want to find is on the left).

c. Use your answer to 2b to find the area of the base of a prism whose volume is 70 m³ and whose height is 7 m.

d. Rearrange the formula for the volume of a prism ($V = B \bullet h$) so the height of the prism (h) is on a side by itself.

e. Swap the entire sides of your answer to 2d so that h is on the left side (it is simpler to read a formula when the unknown we want to find is on the left).

f. Use your answer to 2e to find the height of a prism that has a base area of 9 ft² and which has a volume of 60 ft³.

g. Rearrange the formula for the circumference of a circle so the radius (r) is on a side by itself: $C = 2 \cdot \pi \cdot r$. *Hint*: Divide both sides by $2 \cdot \pi$.

h. Swap the entire sides of your answer to 2g so that r is on the left side (it is simpler to read a formula when the unknown we want to find is on the left).

i. Use your answer to 2h to find the radius of a circle whose circumference is 6 cm.

3. **Finding the Percentage** (🔢) — Show how you obtained your answer using the $R \cdot B = P$ formula.
   a. 6% of $450
   b. 20% of $75.67

4. **Skill Sharpening**

   a. If a machine exerts a certain amount of pressure, but, by some modifications, can have its pressure reduced by $\frac{1}{5}$ a pound, bringing its total down to 300 pounds, how much pressure did the machine originally exert?

   b. If you use 30 gallons of water every 3 weeks, how much will you use in 72 weeks? Use a proportion and cross multiplication to solve; show your work.

Principles of Mathematics 2

Rearranging Formulas — Pages 121–124 — Day 48 — Worksheet 6.2B — Name _____

You may use a calculator on this worksheet whenever you see this symbol (🧮).

Finding the Percentage (🧮) — Solve. Show how you obtained your answer using the $R \cdot B = P$ formula.

a. 5% of 85

b. 30% of 180

Nutritional Labels (🧮) — Most processed foods list the percent of the daily value (DV) of the vitamins they contain.[1] So just how much of the vitamins do the percents represent? You can use math to find out! Use this cereal label to answer the questions. When finding a percentage, use the $R \cdot B = P$ formula.

a. If the daily value (DV) of vitamin A is 5,000 IUs, how many IUs of vitamin A does 1 cup of this cereal contain?

b. How much vitamin A would $\frac{1}{4}$ cup of the cereal contain? Give your answer as a decimal.

Nutrition Facts
Serving Size 1 cup (110g)
Servings Per Container About 6

Amount Per Serving	
Calories 250	Calories from Fat 30

	% Daily Value*
Total Fat 7g	11%
Saturated Fat 3g	16%
Trans Fat 0g	
Cholesterol 4mg	2%
Sodium 300mg	13%
Total Carbohydrate 30g	10%
Dietary Fiber 3g	14%
Sugars 2g	
Protein 5g	
Vitamin A	7%
Vitamin C	15%
Calcium	20%
Iron	32%

* Percent Daily Values are based on a 2,000 calorie diet. Your daily value may be higher or lower depending on your calorie needs.

	Calories:	2,000	2,500
Total Fat	Less than	55g	75g
Saturated Fat	Less than	10g	12g
Cholesterol	Less than	1,500mg	1,700mg
Total Carbohydrate		250mg	300mg
Dietary Fiber		22mg	31mg

c. If the daily value (DV) of vitamin C is 60 mg, how many milligrams of vitamin C does 1 cup of this cereal contain?

d. If you eat 2 cups of this cereal, how much calcium are you eating if the daily value (DV) of calcium is 1,000 mg?

e. Suppose you ate 1 cup of this cereal. How much additional iron would you need to intake 65 mg of iron, if the daily value (DV) for iron is 18 mg?

Daily values based on FDA, *Guidance for Industry: A Food Labeling Guide (14. Appendix F: Calculate the Percent Daily Value for the Appropriate Nutrients)* (January 2013), http://www.fda.gov/Food/GuidanceRegulation/GuidanceDocumentsRegulatoryInformation/LabelingNutrition/ucm064928.htm, update date: 08/20/15.

3. **Skill Sharpening**

   a. Solve: $x + \frac{1}{5} = 3$

   b. Simplify: $-2 \cdot \frac{4}{5}$

   c. Simplify: $\frac{20}{-4}$

   d. Simplify: $2\frac{1}{3} - 5\frac{1}{4}$

   e. Solve: $x - 3\frac{1}{2} = 6\frac{1}{7}$

| PRINCIPLES OF MATHEMATICS 2 | Finding Rates and Bases Pages 124–128 | Day 49 | Worksheet 6.3A | Name |

You may use a calculator on this worksheet whenever you see this symbol (🖩).

When you're finding a rate, your answer should be given as a percent. For example, a result of 0.0356 should be expressed as 3.56%.

Finding the Rate (🖩) — Use the knowledge that the *Rate* • *Base* = *Percentage* ($R \cdot B = P$) to find these rates. When you're trying to find a rate, the problems can often be thought of in terms of "what percent." This is because the rate is typically a percent — that is, a portion of a 100.

a. 30 is what percent of 60?

b. From a farm of 160 acres, 30 acres were sold. What percent was sold?

c. A gardener planted 120 trees, of which 14 died. What percent died?

d. What percent of the trees in the previous problem survived?

Finding the Base (🖩) — Use the knowledge that the *Rate* • *Base* = *Percentage* ($R \cdot B = P$) to find these percents. Remember, think in terms of "the rate *of* the base equals the percentage" and see which number fits as the base.

a. 12 is (or equals) 15% of what number?

b. A farmer received 40% of a crop as rent for his land. If his share of the crop amounted to 4,000 bushels, what was the amount of the entire crop?

c. Two men form a partnership. One agrees to furnish 40% of the start-up costs, contributing $2,500. What were the total start-up costs?

3. **Skill Sharpening**

   a. Simplify: $24 \cdot -3$

   b. Solve: $-\frac{-8}{4} + x = 20$

   c. Solve: $\frac{1}{5} \cdot x = 15$

   Example Meaning: $\frac{1}{5}$ of the 15 people on the ride were from Arizona. How many people were from Arizona?

   d. If the news announces that $\frac{5}{8}$ of the residents of a city vote for a certain candidate, and if 11,565 people in that city voted for that candidate, how many residents are in the city?

   e. A food source claims to offer 52% of the daily value (DV) of vitamin A. If the daily value (DV)[1] is 5,000 IUs, how much vitamin A does that food source contain?

   f. Solve: $5 = \frac{75}{x}$

---

[1] Based on FDA, *Guidance for Industry: A Food Labeling Guide (14. Appendix F: Calculate the Percent Daily Value for the Appropriate Nutrients)* (January 2013), http://www.fda.gov/Food/GuidanceRegulation/GuidanceDocumentsRegulatoryInformation/LabelingNutrition/ucm064928.htm, update date: 08/20/15.

| PRINCIPLES OF MATHEMATICS 2 | Finding Rates and Bases Pages 124–128 | Day 50 | Worksheet 6.3B | Name |

You may use a calculator on this worksheet whenever you see this symbol (🖩).

Mixed Percents (🖩) — These problems could require finding the rate, base, or percentage, so be sure to think carefully about what you're being asked to find. Remember that *Rate • Base = Percentage* ($R \cdot B = P$).

a. If 217 words out of 250 are spelled correctly, what is the percent of correctly spelled words?

b. If a salesman receives 2% commission on his sales for the month, and he gets $400 in commission one month, how much did he sell that month?

c. If one partner gives 60% of the start-up costs, and the total costs are $75,000, how much will he contribute?

d. If 45 out of 200 employees voted for the new insurance plan, what percent of the people voted for the new insurance plan?

e. If road maintenance was the most important issue for 800 people, and those 800 people represented 16% of the people surveyed, how many people were surveyed?

f. If you need to set a selling price that is 8 times your cost (800% of your cost), how much would you need to sell an item for that cost you $1.56?

g. If you're told the tires on a car can only last another 10,000 miles, and they were 60,000-mile tires, what percent of their total mileage do they have left?

2. **Solving for Letters** — Another way to express rearranging a problem so one letter is on a side by itself is to say we're *solving* for that letter. For example, if you solve for x, you rearrange the equation until x is on a side by itself. If you solve for B, you rearrange the equation so that B is on a side by itself.

   a. Solve $d = s \cdot t$ (*distance = speed • time*) for t. Also swap the entire sides so that t is on the left side of the equation.

   b. How long would it take you to drive 300 miles at a speed of $50 \frac{\text{mi}}{\text{hr}}$?

3. **Skill Sharpening**

   a. Solve: $\frac{\$50}{x} = \$5$

   Example Meaning: If we have $50 and want to make it so everyone ends up with $5, how many people can we divide it by?

   b. Write this problem using x to stand for the party favors and solve: If we started with an unknown number of party favors, divided them among 5 people, and ended up giving each person 7, how many did we start with?

   c. If the base of a pyramid is a square with 60 m sides and its height is 20 m, what is the volume of the pyramid?

   d. Solve: $\frac{8.5 \text{ mi}}{7 \text{ min}} = \frac{25.5 \text{ mi}}{x}$

Force and Motion — Worksheet 6.4

You may use a calculator on this worksheet whenever you see this symbol (🖩).

Dealing with Force — We've left units off these problems purposefully, since you've not learned about the units used for acceleration or force yet. Do not round your answers.

a. $F = 20 \cdot -2$

   Example Meaning: What force would it take to get a mass of 20 to accelerate negative 2 (that is, 2 units in the negative direction)?

b. Solve $F = m \cdot a$ for a (i.e., rearrange $F = m \cdot a$ so a is on a side by itself). Also swap the entire sides so that a is on the left side.

c. What would the acceleration (a) be of a mass (m) of 40 under a force of 5?

d. $7 = m \cdot 40$

   Example Meaning: What mass, if put under a force of 7, would accelerate 40 in the positive direction?

Mixed Percents (🖩)

a. If you end up saving $135 on a bike that normally costs $300, what percent did you save off the normal price?

b. If you make 15% commission on every sale and took home $560 in commission one month, how much did you sell that month?

c. If you sell items for 425% above your cost, how much would you sell an item that costs you $0.50?

d. If 125 people signed up for an event but only 70 actually came, what percent of those who signed up came?

e. In the previous scenario, what percent of those who signed up did not come?

3. **Geometry Review** (🖩) — *Hint*: Watch your units.
   a. What is the volume in cubic feet of a model pyramid whose base is a square with 7-foot sides and whose height is 8 meters? Round to the nearest whole number.

   b. What is the area of a rectangle that is 8 inches by 9 inches?

   c. What is the perimeter of a rectangle that is 8 inches by 9 inches?

4. **Mechanical Advantage** (🖩) — In the last chapter, we took a brief look at levers. Sometimes it's helpful to look at what we call the mechanical advantage of a lever. The mechanical advantage can be found using this formula, where M stands for the mechanical advantage.

$$M \cdot F_1 = F_2$$

If a lever can help you lift 100 lb by applying only 20 lb, then it's mechanical advantage is 5, as $5 \cdot 20 \text{ lb} = 100 \text{ lb}$. In other words, with the lever you were able to move 5 times the force you applied.

   a. Rearrange $M \cdot F_1 = F_2$ so M is on a side by itself (i.e., solve for M). You will usually find the mechanical advantage formula written so that mechanical advantage (which we've used M to represent) is on a side by itself.

   b. If, using a certain lever, you can move a 300-pound object (F_2) by applying 20 pounds of force (F_1), what is the lever's mechanical advantage?

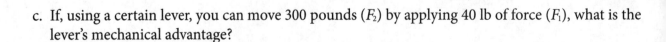

   c. If, using a certain lever, you can move 300 pounds (F_2) by applying 40 lb of force (F_1), what is the lever's mechanical advantage?

   d. If a lever has a mechanical advantage of 4, how much can you move if you apply 50 lb of force?

| PRINCIPLES OF MATHEMATICS 2 | Simplifying Multiplication Pages 133–136 | Day 54 | Worksheet 7.1 | Name |

You may use a calculator on this worksheet whenever you see this symbol (🖩).

A More Concise Representation — Rewrite the following multiplications by putting the numeral directly before the unknown.

Example: $5 \cdot x = 5x$

a. $8 \cdot x$

b. $x \cdot 6$

c. $24(x)$

d. $7 \cdot y$

Repeated Additions — Rewrite these repeated additions as multiplication. When there's an unknown, show the multiplication by putting the numeral directly before the unknown.

Example: $x + x = 2x$

a. $\$6 + \$6 + \$6$

Example Meaning: 3 packages at $6 each

b. $s + s + s + s + s$

Example Meaning: perimeter of a regular pentagon

c. 7 times an unknown distance (Use d to represent the unknown distance.)

d. 3 CDs at an unknown price (Use x to represent the unknown price.)

Evaluate — Evaluate (i.e., find the value of) these expressions for the given value of x.

Example: $3x$, when $x = 2$ *Answer:* $3(2) = 6$

a. $4x$, when x is $5

Example Meaning: 4 items that cost $5 each

b. $3x$, when x is -2

Example Meaning: sailing south (which we're viewing as the negative direction) at 2 miles an hour for 3 hours

c. 2x, when x is –8

  Example Meaning: traveling 8 miles an hour south (which we're viewing as the negative direction) for 2 hours

d. 4x, when x is 10 $\frac{mi}{hr}$

  Example Meaning: a specific horse's top galloping speed if that speed is 4 times faster than the 10 $\frac{mi}{hr}$ its owner can sprint

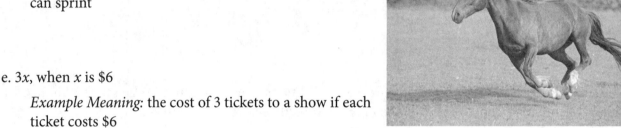

e. 3x, when x is $6

  Example Meaning: the cost of 3 tickets to a show if each ticket costs $6

4. **Skill Sharpening** (🖩)

  a. Rearrange $A = lw$ to solve for l. To make the equation easier to read, also swap the sides so that l is on the left side of the equation. *Hint*: Notice that we omitted the multiplication sign when writing the formula. $A = lw$ means the same thing as $A = l \cdot w$

  b. If you paid $14.32 in sales tax at a tax rate of 5%, what was the amount on which the tax was calculated?

  c. If wages are increased 15%, what is the new wage of a man who had been getting $620 a week? *Hint*: If the wages were increased by 15%, then the new wage would be the old wage (100% of $620) plus 15% of $620—that is, 115% of $620.

  d. In Room A are 33 pupils, 31 of whom have been present every day; in Room B are 42 pupils, 39 of whom have been present every day; in Room C are 26 pupils, 24 of whom have been present every day. What room has the highest percentage of attendance?

PRINCIPLES OF MATHEMATICS 2 | Combining Like Terms Pages 136–139 | Day 55 | Worksheet 7.2 | Name

You may use a calculator on this worksheet whenever you see this symbol (🖩).

Term Time

a. When we use the term "coefficient" in this course, to what are we referring?

b. What is the coefficient in $8y$?

c. What is the coefficient in $45x$?

d. Are $4x$ and $4y$ like terms?

Combining Like Terms — Simplify these expressions by combining like terms. If there are no like terms to combine, write, "already simplified."

a. $8x + 5x$

b. $4x + 7x$

c. $5y + 2x$

Combining Like Terms to Find Unknowns — Solve.

a. $8x + 5x = \$65$

Example Meaning: Say you have a small business selling birdhouses. You sold one birdhouse for 8 times the cost, and sold another identical birdhouse at a sale price of 5 times the cost. If the total you received for each birdhouse was $65 and both birdhouses cost the same to make, what was the cost of each birdhouse?

b. $4x + 2x = 18$

c. Check your work in problem 3b by substituting the value you found for x back into the original equation. Show how you found the correct value.

4. **Combining Like Terms in Word Problems**

   a. You are starting a woodworking business. You buy 7 pine boards, then later buy 2 more pine boards, all of which were purchased at the same price. If you spend $81 altogether, how much did each pine board cost?

   b. If Sally read 72 pages ahead in her literature course by reading 3 times the required number of pages on the first day, and 6 times the required number of pages on the second day, how many pages a day was Sally required to read? *Hint*: Use x to represent the number of pages Sally was required to read each day.

5. **Butterfat** ()

   a. If each day a cow produces an average of 3 gallons of milk, and one gallon of milk weighs about 8.5 lb, how many pounds of milk does the cow produce per year (365.25 days)?

   b. If, when measured by weight, the cow's milk is 4% butterfat, how many pounds of butterfat does the cow in 5a produce per year?

   c. If 1 pound of butterfat will make about 1.17 pounds of butter, how much butter could be made from the cow in 5a each year? Use your answer to 5b to help you solve.

   Notice how all of the questions in problem 5 built off one another (you had to use the answer from the previous question to answer the next one). We could have worded the question as a single question that you would have had to break down yourself (i.e., we could have asked right away how much butter could be made from the cow each year, giving only the numbers from all of the problems and not the intermediate questions). When you encounter challenging questions, remember to look for ways to break them down into steps.

| PRINCIPLES OF MATHEMATICS 2 | Combining Like Terms with Coefficients of 1 Pages 140–141 | Day 56 | Worksheet 7.3 | Name |

You may use a calculator on this worksheet whenever you see this symbol (🖩).

Coefficients of 1 — Add a 1 in front of each of these letters to show that they can be thought of as having a coefficient of 1. Remember that $1x$ means $1 \cdot x$.

   Example: $x = 1x$

a. s

b. t

c. x

d. d

Combining Like Terms — Combine like terms and solve.

a. $x + 3x = 28$

b. $x + 2x + 5x = 32$

   Example Meaning: Say you have three animals; the first animal eats a certain poundage of grain a day, the second eats twice that amount, and the third eats 5 times the first animal's amount. How many pounds of grain does the first animal eat if the three together eat 32 pounds of grain a day? Notice that we used x to stand for the pounds the first animal eats and have written the pounds the other animals eat in terms of how they relate to what the first animal eats.

c. If a man's salary, plus 15% of his salary, equals $250, what is salary? *Hint:* This is $x + 0.15x = \$250$

Skill Sharpening (🖩)

a. An orchardist planted 120 apple trees and lost 14; he planted 70 raspberry bushes and lost none; he planted 1,000 grapevines and lost 35. What percent of each kind planted were lost?

b. In problem 3a, what percent of the entire number of plants planted did not survive?

c. A merchant insures his stock of goods for $4,000. He pays 1% of $4,000 a year in premiums (a premium is the sum paid by the insured for his insurance). What is his premium per year?

d. By how much would the premium of the merchant in problem 3c be reduced if he only insured his goods for $2,500, making his new premium 1% of $2,500?

| PRINCIPLES OF MATHEMATICS 2 | Combining Like Terms with Fractional Coefficients Pages 141–143 | Day 57 | Worksheet 7.4 | Name |

You may use a calculator on this worksheet whenever you see this symbol (🖩).

Fractional Coefficients — Find the value of these expressions given the values for *x*.

a. $\frac{1}{4}x$, when *x* is $200

   Example Meaning: $\frac{1}{4}$ of a $200 weekly salary

b. $\frac{1}{4}x$, when *x* is –$500

   Example Meaning: $\frac{1}{4}$ of a $500 monthly mortgage payment, which is shown here as a negative since it's owed

c. $\frac{5}{3}x$, when *x* is 5

   Example Meaning: $\frac{5}{3}$ times the 5 hours someone normally works

d. $\frac{2}{3}x$, when *x* is –10 lb

   Example Meaning: $\frac{2}{3}$ of a force of –10 pounds

PRINCIPLES OF MATHEMATICS 2 | PAGE 103

2. **Combining Like Terms** — Combine these like terms. In your answers, leave any improper fractions as improper fractions.

   a. $\frac{1}{3}x + \frac{1}{2}x$

   Example Meaning: $\frac{1}{3}$ of a batch of cookies plus $\frac{1}{2}$ of the same batch of cookies

   b. $x + \frac{3}{5}x$

   Example Meaning: a weekly salary plus a bonus of $\frac{3}{5}$ of the weekly salary

3. **Putting It All Together** (🖩) — Solve.

   a. $\frac{1}{3}x + \frac{1}{2}x = 40$ b. $x + \frac{3}{5}x = 350$

4. **Checking Your Work** (🖩) — Check your work in problem 3a by substituting the value you found for x back into the original equation. Show how you found the correct value.

5. **Problem from Antiquity** (🖩) — It's time to solve a math problem first written thousands of years ago! The problem is written in words, and then using our modern symbols.

   "Heap, its seventh, its whole, it makes 19," that is, find a number such that the number and one seventh of the number equals 19.

   Written using our modern symbols: $x + \frac{1}{7}x = 19$

   Can you find the answer?

6. **Term Time** — What is the coefficient of x in $\frac{2}{3}x$

You may use a calculator on this worksheet whenever you see this symbol (🖩).

Finding Unknowns — Solve. *Hint*: While these problems may initially appear more complicated, they are quite simple if you take them step by step.

a. $2x + \$5 = \$50$

Example Meaning: If twice the cost of a ticket plus $5 equals $50, what is the cost of the ticket?

b. $4x + 5{,}000 \text{ m} = 6{,}600 \text{ m}$ *Hint*: the m in the problem is an abbreviation for meters.

Example Meaning: If walking four times the distance around a track plus the 5,000 meters from the track back to your house equals 6,600 meters, what is the distance around the track?

c. $9x + \$25 + \$3 = \$75$

Example Meaning: If 9 packages of meat plus $25 shipping plus $3 handling cost 75 dollars, how much did each package of meat cost?

d. Betty has $90 to spend on a party. If she needs to buy 12 gifts, plus $5 worth of decorating supplies, plus $20 worth of food, how much can she afford to spend on each of the 12 gifts?

e. $x + x - 11 = 50$

f. $x + 9x - 12 = 24$

g. $x + \frac{1}{3}x = 28$

h. $x + \frac{4}{5}x = 25$

2. **Remembering the Convention**

   a. Rewrite as multiplication by putting the coefficient directly before the unknown: $x + x + x + x$

   b. Rewrite by putting the coefficient directly before the unknown: $x \cdot 40$

3. **Exploring the Volume of a Pyramid** — The formula for finding the volume of a pyramid is $V = \frac{1}{3} \cdot B \cdot h$. Rewrite this formula so all the factors are next to each other without a multiplication sign.

| PRINCIPLES OF MATHEMATICS 2 | Negative Signs and Unknowns Pages 147–149 | Day 60 | Worksheet 8.1 | Name |

Simplify — Review negative numbers by simplifying these expressions.

a. 2 – –5

b. 3 – – –8

c. 5 • –9 • –1

d. –5 • –9 • –1

e. $\dfrac{-9}{-3}$

f. $\dfrac{-9}{3}$

Evaluate — Evaluate (i.e., find the value of) these expressions for the given value of x.

a. 7 – x, when x is 5

b. 7 – x, when x is –5

c. 15 – –x, when x is 2

d. 15 – –x, when x is –2

Understanding Check — A negative sign means the _____ of.

Skill Sharpening

a. $2x = 10$

b. $2a + 6a = 18$

c. $\dfrac{1}{8}x + 4x = 6$

d. If James works $\dfrac{1}{2}$ his normal hours one week and 3 times his normal hours the next week, for a total of 35 hours, how many hours does he normally work?

Revisiting the Additive Inverse
Worksheet 8.2 — Day 61 — Pages 149–150

You may use a calculator on this worksheet whenever you see this symbol (🖩).

Additive Inverse — Write the additive inverse (i.e., write what you'd have to add to equal 0).

  Example: x *Answer:* $-x$

a. 8

b. –6

c. y

d. $-s$

e. t

f. $-v$

Applying the Additive Inverse — In Lesson 8.2 of your *Student Textbook*, we walked through rearranging $n = g - w$ (*net salary = gross salary – withholdings*) to $g = n + w$. To illustrate that both $n = g - w$ and $g = n + w$ do indeed represent the same relationship, let's explore this relationship.

a. Let's say our net salary (n) equals $15,000 and our withholdings (w) equal $5,000. Show how you could find the gross salary (g) starting with this equation: $n = g - w$.

b. Let's say once again that our net salary (n) equals $15,000 and our withholdings (w) equal $5,000. This time, though, show how you could find the gross salary (g) starting with this equation: $g = n + w$. You should obtain the same value for the gross salary (g) as you did in 2a—both $g = n + w$ and $n = g - w$ represent the same relationship, only arranged differently.

More Applying the Additive Inverse

a. Solve $a + b = c$ for a (i.e., rewrite the equation so a is on a side by itself).

b. Solve $v + v_0 = 56$ for v.

c. Suppose we want the length of a garden minus the width to equal 10 ft. We'd have this relationship: $\ell - w = 10$ ft. Rewrite this relationship to solve for the length.

d. The hours in a day equal the hours you're awake plus the hours you're asleep: $t = a + s$ (*total hours = hours awake + hours asleep*). Rearrange $t = a + s$ to solve for s (the hours you're asleep). Also, swap the sides so that s is on the left side of the equation.

4. **Skill Sharpening**

    a. Solve: $\frac{2}{3}x + x = 1{,}820$

    Example Meaning: If $\frac{2}{3}$ of the weekly budget for a company plus the weekly budget equals 1,820, how much is the weekly budget?

    b. Solve: $\frac{1}{6}x + \frac{2}{5}x = 85$

    Example Meaning: $\frac{1}{6}$ of the population voted one way; $\frac{2}{5}$ of the population voted another way. If the sum of the votes they both cast is 85, what is the total population?

    c. Simplify: $-5 \cdot -26.52 \cdot -1$

PRINCIPLES OF MATHEMATICS 2
Combining Like Terms with Negative Coefficients
Pages 151–153
Day 62 — Worksheet 8.3

1. **Simplifying Multiplication** — Rewrite the following by putting the coefficient directly before the unknown. Put the negative sign in front of the coefficient, as it will apply to the product. If there's only one negative sign in the multiplication, we'll need to take *the opposite of* the product, whatever it ends up being.

    Example: $-5 \cdot x = -5x$

    a. $-2 \cdot s$

    b. $-1 \cdot x$

    c. $\frac{-2}{5} \cdot y$

    d. $\frac{1}{3} \cdot x$

    e. $8 \cdot -x$

    f. $7 \cdot -x$

2. **Simplifying Repeated Additions** — Rewrite these repeated additions as multiplication.

    Example: $-x + -x = 2(-x) = -2x$

    a. $-p + -p$

    Example Meaning: two items that were returned

    b. $-a + -a + -a + -a$

    Example Meaning: decreasing altitude by the same amount four times

    c. $-s + -s + -s$

    Example Meaning: moving back the same number of spaces in a board game three turns in a row

3. **Evaluate** — Evaluate (i.e., find the value of) these expressions for the given value of the unknown.

    a. $-5x$, when x is $6

    b. $-4x$, when x is 4

    c. $-2F$, when F is 5 lb

    d. $-x$, when x is -9

4. **Combining Like Terms** — Simplify these expressions by combining like terms. In your answers, leave improper fractions as improper fractions.

    a. $8x - 3x$

    b. $5x + 3x - 4x$

    c. $2x - 7x$

    d. $2x - 5x$

    e. $x - \frac{1}{3}x$

    f. $3x - \frac{2}{5}x$

5. **Combining Like Terms in Equations**

   a. $7x - 4x = 21$

   Example Meaning: 7 books were purchased at the same price, of which 4 were returned. If after the return the cost of the books was $21 altogether, how much did each book cost?

   b. $x - \frac{1}{3}x = 24$

   Example Meaning: We baked one batch of cookies; we then gave away $\frac{1}{3}$ of that batch. If we have 24 cookies left, how many cookies were in the batch?

   c. $7a - 5a = 6$

   d. Check your work in problem 4c by substituting the value you found for *a* back into the original equation. Show how you found the correct value.

6. **Even More Combining Like Terms** — Solve these word problems using the skills you just learned.

   a. Suppose your home business is making picture frames. You buy 9 feet of wood at a certain price per foot, but then later return 3 feet. The total you've spent on wood after your return is $96. How much does the wood cost per foot?

   b. Suppose you're cooking. You bake a batch of brownies. You then give away $\frac{1}{4}$ of that batch. If in the end you have 15 brownies, how many brownies did the batch make?

7. **Understanding Check** — True or false: $-y$ and $-1y$ mean the same thing

| PRINCIPLES OF MATHEMATICS 2 | Surprised by Negatives Pages 153–155 | Day 63 | Worksheet 8.4 | Name |

You may use a calculator on this worksheet whenever you see this symbol (🧮).

Surprised by Negatives (🧮) — Don't let the negative answers in these problems fool you! Find −x, and then multiply both sides by −1 to find the value of x, as shown in the second example in your *Student Textbook*. Show your work.

a. $17 - x = 12$

   Example Meaning: Your airplane trip is expected to take 17 hours. How many hours into the trip are you if you still have 12 hours left to go, assuming you're on schedule?

b. $26.45 - x = 2.54$

   Example Meaning: You started with $26.45. How much did you spend if you ended with $2.54?

c. $56.99 - x = 35.56$

   Example Meaning: An item retails for $56.99. How much did you save if you found it on sale for $35.56?

d. Check your work in problem 1c by substituting the value you found for *x* back into the original equation. Show how you found the correct value.

You may have noticed that all of the example meanings could have been written as a straightforward subtraction problem with the two known numbers. (For example, problem 1a could be written 17 − 12.) While that may be the case for these simple problems, it's important to understand how to solve and manipulate equations in different ways so that you'll be able to apply the skills to more advanced problems.

2. **Skill Sharpening** (🖩)

   a. Simplify: $x - \frac{4}{5}x$

   Example Meaning: the net change in altitude of a plane that climbs a certain altitude and then descends $\frac{4}{5}$ of that altitude

   b. Solve: $16x - 6x = 10{,}560$ ft

   Example Meaning: Say you normally walk around a track 16 times. One day you walk around 6 fewer times. If you walked 10,560 feet (2 miles) that day, how far is it around the track?

   c. Solve: $5x - 0.5x = 550$

   Example Meaning: The cost for 5 nights at a hotel minus the discount of 50% of one hotel night's cost totals $550.

   d. Solve: $3x + 50 - x = 60$

   e. Solve: $x - \frac{7}{8}x = 18$

   f. Solve: $-9b = -225$

   g. Solve $x - y = a$ for x.

| PRINCIPLES OF MATHEMATICS 2 | When the Unknown Is on Both Sides of the Equation Pages 156–157 | Day 64 | Worksheet 8.5 | Name |

You may use a calculator on this worksheet whenever you see this symbol (🖩).

When We Have Unknowns on Both Sides — Solve.

a. $5w = 2(60 \text{ ft}) + 2w$

Example Meaning: What is the width of a rectangular garden if its length is 60 ft, and its perimeter equals 5 times its width? The formula for the perimeter of a rectangle is $P = 2\ell + 2w$.

b. $x + 150 = 31x$

Example Meaning: If the cost of one train ticket plus $150 equals the cost of 31 train tickets, how much does each ticket cost?

c. Check your work in problem 1b by substituting the value you found for x back into the original equation. Show how you found the correct value.

d. $34 - x = 16x$

e. Check your work in problem 1d by substituting the value you found for x back into the original equation. Show how you found the correct value.

2. **Skill Sharpening** (🖩)

    a. Solve: $16 - x = -46$

    b. Solve: $22x - 15x = 469$

    c. Solve: $2x - x + x = 45$

    d. Suppose you get a check for your weekly salary plus a bonus of $\frac{1}{4}$ of your weekly salary. The check for $560. How much is your weekly salary?

    e. In the situation described in 2d, how much is your bonus?

    f. Solve $a - x = c$ for a.

    g. Evaluate $8 - x$, when x is -6

You may use a calculator on this worksheet whenever you see this symbol (📱).

1. **Converting to Celsius** (📱) — Use the formula $C = \frac{5}{9}(F - 32°)$ to convert these Fahrenheit temperatures (F) to degrees Celsius (C). Use decimals rather than fractions to represent partial quantities in your answers.

   a. 80° F

   b. 20° F

   c. 32° F

2. **Nested Parentheses** — Simplify.

   a. 2[3(4 + 5)]

   Example Meaning: It costs $4 for shoe rentals plus $5 to bowl. If 3 kids in a family go bowling 2 times, how much will it cost?

   b. 6[4 + 3(5 − 2)]

   Example Meaning: It costs $5 a game, minus a $2 discount, plus a $4 fee per day. If each of 6 people plays 3 games, how much does it cost altogether?

3. **Applying Parentheses** — Show how you could write out these problems concisely using parentheses.

   Example: If you put together 40 party favors that each cost $4 plus $1.50, how much will it cost you to make all 40?
   Answer: 40($4 + $1.50)

   a. If it costs $4.50 plus $5 to crochet a baby blanket, how much will 9 blankets cost?

   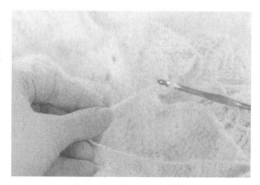

   b. If you buy items that cost $7 and $9.24, and are charged a 4% tax on your purchase, how much will you pay in tax?

4. **Solving Parentheses** — Solve each of the problems you wrote out in problem 3.

   a.   b.

5. **Skill Sharpening**

   a. If 3 of an item minus 1 of the same item equal $15, how much does the item cost?

   b. If to fix a leak, the plumber says that he'll charge you 4 man hours (i.e., 4 times his hourly rate), and that to install a faucet while he's there will be 2 more man hours (i.e., 2 times his hourly rate), making the labor $480 altogether, how much is the plumber's hourly rate?

   c. Solve: $3x - \frac{2}{8}x = 4$

   d. Solve: $75.2 - y = 108$

| PRINCIPLES OF MATHEMATICS 2 | Parentheses, the Distributive Property, and Unknowns Pages 162–167 | Day 68 | Worksheet 9.2 | Name |

You may use a calculator on this worksheet whenever you see this symbol (🖩).

Reviewing the Order of Operations — Solve each problem using the order of operations.

a. $4(5 + 10)$

   Example Meaning: If per person it costs $5 for food and $10 for admission, how much will it cost for 4 people?

b. $\frac{5}{9}(\frac{6}{5} + \frac{3}{20})$

c. $2(6 - 8)$

d. $4(6 - 4)$

Reviewing the Distributive Property — Resolve problems 1a–1d using the distributive property. Show your work.

a.

b.

c.

d.

Using the Distributive Property to Find Unknowns — Use the distributive property to find these unknowns.

a. $5(x + 2) = 30$

b. $4(3 + x + 3) = 48$ *Hint:* You'll save time if you simplify inside the parentheses before you distribute. In this case, add the $3 + 3$, simplifying the parentheses to $(6 + x)$.

c. $4(x - 2) = 28$

d. 15($12 − x) = $120

   Example Meaning: If 15 people can attend a concert for $120, and it costs $12 per person minus an unknown discount amount, how much is the discount?

e. $4(\frac{3}{4} + x) = 11$

f. (5 + 2 + x)3 = 30

   Example Meaning: A necklace has 30 beads. The beads on the necklace follow a pattern that uses 5 black beads, 2 red beads, and some silver beads. If the pattern repeats itself exactly 3 times in the necklace, how many silver beads are used in the pattern?

4. **Using Parentheses with Word Problems** — Write these problems using parentheses. Solve. *Hint*: Some problems involve an unknown; others do not.

   a. If it costs $1.50 for the stain plus $4.50 for the wood to make each wooden box, and if these are the only supplies needed, how much will 10 wooden boxes cost?

   b. If to build 10 wooden boxes it costs a total of $50, and each one costs $2 for the wood plus whatever the cost of the stain is, how much does the stain cost per wooden box?

   c. Suppose you go into business cutting trees. You pay your brother $7 an hour for his help and rent a chainsaw for $10 an hour. If you paid your brother and rented the chainsaw for 5 hours, how much did you spend?

   d. Suppose once again you paid your brother $7 an hour for his help and to rent a chainsaw by the hour. If you paid your brother and rented the chainsaw for 5 hours, how much did you spend per hour on a chainsaw if you spent $75 total? *Hint*: This time, set up your problem with x representing the hourly cost of the chainsaw.

5. **Converting to Fahrenheit** (🖩) — Use the formula $C = \frac{5}{9}(F - 32°)$ to convert these temperatures to degrees Fahrenheit.

   a. 15° Celsius

   b. 100° Celsius

Parentheses Preceded by a Positive Sign — Solve these problems by multiplying the parentheses by 1 and distributing. Notice that in each case, you'd obtain the same answer as you would if you simply removed the parentheses.

Example: $2 + (3 + 4) =$
$2 + 1(3 + 4) =$
$2 + 1(3) + 1(4) =$
$2 + 3 + 4 = 9$

a. $4 + (5 + 6)$

Example Meaning: If you collected 4 bottles for charity, and a friend collected 5 bottles plus 6 bottles, how many bottles did the two of you collect altogether?

b. $20 + (43 - 5)$

Example Meaning: If you started with $20, earned $43 babysitting but spent $5 of that, how much money do you have now?

Parentheses Preceded by a Positive Sign with Unknowns — Solve.

a. $8 + (3 + x) = 30$

Example Meaning: If you collected 8 bottles for charity and a friend collected 3 bottles, plus some additional bottles (he couldn't remember how many), how many additional bottles did your friend collect if you and your friend combined collected a total of 30 bottles?

b. $\$15 + (\$35 - x) = \$25$

Example Meaning: Say you started with $15. You then earned $35 babysitting, but spent some of that on dinner. If you ended with $25, how much did you spend on dinner?

c. In the example meaning in problem 2b, what does the x represent?

3. **Checking Your Work** — Substitute the values you found for x in 2a and 2b back into the original equation to show that you obtained the correct values.

   a.   b.

4. **Skill Sharpening**

   a. Solve: $2.5x = x + 39$

   Example Meaning: If 2.5 times an expense equals the expense plus $39, how much is the expense?

   b. Use parentheses to write this problem:

   Each of 4 sisters was given 3 books. Each sister gave 1 of the 3 books away. How many books did the sisters keep altogether?

   c. Solve 4b.

   d. Use parentheses to write this problem. Note that there is an unknown this time.

   Each of 4 brothers was given the same number of baseball cards. Each brother gave one baseball card away. Altogether, the brothers kept 60 baseball cards. How many baseball cards was each brother given?

   e. Solve 4d.

You may use a calculator on this worksheet whenever you see this symbol (🖩).

Earnings (🖩) — The steps below will help you walk through this math problem:

Suppose the total of two boys' earnings is $1,200 a month, but the first boy earns $150 a month more than the second boy. How much does the second boy earn?

a. Use words to finish expressing the relationship between the total of $1,200 and each boy's earnings.

$1,200 = *first boy's earnings* + _____

b. Now let's express each boys earnings using symbols. Below, we've used x to represent the second boy's earnings. The first boy's earnings equal x plus what amount?

first boy's earnings = x + _____

second boy's earnings = x

c. Finish rewriting the relationship between total of $1,200 and each boy's earnings using only numbers and the unknown x. Use your answers to 1a and 1b to help you.

$1,200 = (_____ + _____) + _____

d. Solve the equation you wrote in 1c to find x (the second boy's earnings).

e. Check your work by substituting the value you found for x in 1d back into the equation you found in 1c.

f. What were the *first* boy's earnings?

Skill Sharpening (🖩)

a. Solve: $6(x + 3) = 25$

b. Solve: $2(x - 2) = 20$

c. Solve: $5(x + 2) = 15x$

d. Solve: $\frac{3}{4}(5 - x) = 3$

Example Meaning: A recipe calls for 5 c of flour, but you always use less flour. If when you make $\frac{3}{4}$ of a batch you use a total of 3 c of flour, how much less flour do you use when you make a full batch?

e. Solve: $1.06(\$3.50 + \$5.50 - x) = \$5.13$

Example Meaning: Two items cost $3.50 and $5.50, minus a discount. If 6% sales tax was charged on that subtotal and if the total with the tax came to $5.13, how much was the discount?

f. Suppose you are making a quilt rack. You want to double (i.e., multiply by 2) all the dimensions to make it larger. One side in the rack is 24 inches plus 2 inches. Use parentheses to show that you want to double the sum of 24 inches and 2 inches.

g. Solve the problem in 4f

h. Simplify: $5[(1.5 + 6)5]$

i. Solve: $4x + 8 = 2x$

j. One week's paycheck includes two weeks' salary ($2x$) plus a bonus that's 10% of one week's salary ($0.1x$). The paycheck is for $800; how much is one week's salary?

| PRINCIPLES OF MATHEMATICS 2 | Parentheses, the Distributive Property, Unknowns, and Negative Numbers — Pages 172–175 | Day 72 | Worksheet 9.5 | Name |

1. **Order of Operations** — Solve each problem using the order of operations.

   a. $-3(5 + 7 + 2)$

   Example Meaning: It costs $5 for admission, $7 for dinner, and $2 for dessert at an event. Three people paid, but were unable to attend. How much will the organizers of the event owe in refunds to the 3 people who paid and couldn't come, assuming they refund the full amount?

   b. $3 - (9 - 2)$

   Example Meaning: If you have $3 in your wallet, but want to buy an item that costs $9 minus a $2 coupon, how much will you have left, assuming there's no tax on the item? (In this case, the negative answer indicates you don't have enough money to buy the item — it tells you how much money you're short.)

   c. $37 - (10 - 4)$

   Example Meaning: If you spend $37 at the store, and then return an item that cost $10 before a discount of $4, how much did you spend after the return?

2. **Distributing** — Go back and resolve problems 1a–1c, using the distributive property. Show your work.

   Example: $3 - (2 - 4) =$
   $3 + -1(2 + -4) =$
   $3 + -1(2) + -1(-4) =$
   $3 + -2 + 4 = 5$

   a.

   b.

   c.

3. **Finding Unknowns** — Solve.

   a. $-4(\$2 + x) = -\$28$

   b. $87 - 4(10 + x) = 27$

   Example Meaning: If you started with 87 cookies, and made 4 plates to give away, each of which contained 10 cookies plus the same number of additional cookies (you can't remember how many), and you ended up with 27 cookies, how many additional cookies did you add to each plate?

   c. $50 - (42 - x) = 16$

   Example Meaning: If you spend $50 at the store, and then return an item that cost $42 minus a discount, the amount of which you can't remember, spending a total of $16 after the return, what was the amount of the discount?

   d. $12 - (x - 4) = -19$

   e. In the example meaning in 3c, what does the x represent?

PAGE 126 | PRINCIPLES OF MATHEMATICS 2

Writing Inequalities — Represent the following using the appropriate symbol ($<, >, \neq, \leq,$ or $\geq$).

a. 7 is less than 8

   7 _____ 8

b. 8 is greater than 7

   8 _____ 7

c. income must be less than or equal to $6,000 for a discount

   income _____ $6,000

d. hours worked must be greater than or equal to 40

   hours worked _____ 40

e. the time does not equal 0

   time _____ 0

Question — Has $<$ always been used to show less than?

Skill Sharpening

a. Solve: $5x - 2x = 256$

b. Solve: $8 - x = -45$

c. Solve: $x + \frac{5}{6}x = 110$

   Example Meaning: If Betty can type a certain number of words per minute, and Joe can type $\frac{5}{6}$ as fast as Betty, and the two together can type 110 words per minute, how fast can Betty type?

d. In the previous problem's example meaning, what would x represent?

e. Use parentheses to write this problem:

   If each team member has to order a $10 cap and a $12 T-shirt, but gets a $2 discount, how much will the total be for a team of 20?

f. Solve problem 3e.

4. **Coins (🖩)** — The steps below will help you walk through this math problem:

   Frederick has his money in dimes, nickels, and pennies, and he has the same number of each kind of coin. The value of all the coins is $0.80. How many of each kind of coin does Frederick have?

   a. Since we were told the amount of dimes, nickels, and pennies were all the same, we can use x to stand for the total of each kind of coin. Thus, we could represent the value of Frederick's dimes as $0.10x$. (The value of the dimes will be $0.10 times the number of dimes Frederick has, since each dime is worth $0.10.) Following this same logic, represent the value of the number of nickels and pennies Frederick has.

   $$\begin{aligned} dimes &= \$0.10x \\ nickels &= \underline{\qquad} \\ pennies &= \underline{\qquad} \end{aligned}$$

   b. Now, the value of all the coins together equals $0.80. So if we add the values of the dimes, nickels, and pennies, they will total $0.80. Write out an equation showing this.

   c. Solve the equation you wrote in 3b to find the number of each coin Frederick has (i.e., the value of x).

   d. Check your work by substituting the value you found for x in 4c back into the equation you found in 4b.

PAGE 128 | PRINCIPLES OF MATHEMATICS 2

Inequalities on the Number Line — Graph each inequality on the number line.

a. $t < 0$

   Example Meaning: Water freezes and melts at 0° Celsius. So if we want ice, we could specify a temperature less than 0.

   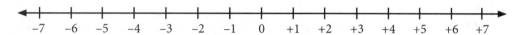

b. $a \leq 0$

   Example Meaning: We want to specify a final altitude less than or equal to 0.

   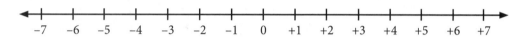

c. $x \geq 5$

   Example Meaning: We're working with an equation that only holds true if x equals 5 or more.

   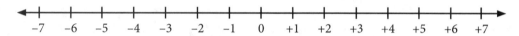

d. $x > 5$

   Example Meaning: We're working with an equation that only holds true if x is greater than 5.

   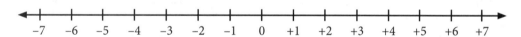

Using Inequalities and Unknowns — Using x to represent the unknown, use an inequality to show the possible values for the unknown in each scenario.

a. the amount we can spend on dinner if we have to pay cash and only have $18

b. the number of candies we need to buy if we want each guest to have at least 1 and we have 20 guests coming to our party

c. the length of a rectangle if it has to be greater than or equal to 0 in

d. our options if we have greater than 3 options

e. the temperature we can heat a substance to if we want to keep it greater than −3 degrees Fahrenheit

3. **Skill Sharpening** (🖩)

    a. Solve: $2x + 3x = 20$

    Example Meaning: If you knit 2 rows plus an additional 3 rows in 20 minutes, how long on average does it take to knit each row?

    b. Solve: $\frac{1}{8}x + x = 72$

    Example Meaning: If you received $72 for $\frac{1}{8}$ of a day's work plus a day's work, how much did you receive for a day's work?

    c. Solve: $5x + 6x = 350$

    d. Show how you could represent this problem using parentheses:

    If you spend $22 total at the store on 3 hats, each of which cost $7 plus tax, how much was the tax on each hat?

    e. Solve the problem you wrote in 3d.

    f. Solve: $14 - 2x = -8$

PRINCIPLES OF MATHEMATICS 2

Swapping Sides of an Inequality — Pages 180–182

Day 77 | Worksheet 10.3

You may use a calculator on this worksheet whenever you see this symbol (🖩).

1. **Swapping Sides** — Rewrite each inequality, putting what was on the right on the left. Remember to change the sign as needed to preserve the meaning.

   a. $5 < 9$

   b. $5 < x$

   c. $56 > 23$

   d. $14 > x$

   e. $25 < x + 5$

   f. $0 \geq x$

   g. $12 \geq x - 6$

   h. $0 \leq a + b$

2. **Inequalities on the Number Line** — Graph each inequality on the number line.

   a. $x < 10$

   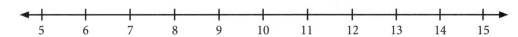

   b. $x > 0$

   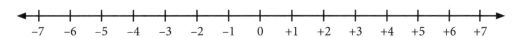

   c. $x \leq 10$

3. **Winters in St. Petersburg** (🖩) — The steps below will help you walk through this math problem:

   In midwinter in St. Petersburg, there are 13 hours more of darkness than of daylight. Each day, how many hours are there of darkness, and how many hours of daylight?

   a. Use words to finish expressing the relationship between the hours of darkness, the hours of daylight and the total hours in a day (24 hr).

   24 hr = *darkness* + _____

   b. Now let's express the hours of daylight and darkness using symbols. Below, we've used x to represent the hours of daylight. The hours of darkness equal the hours of daylight plus what amount?

   darkness = x + _____

   daylight = x

   c. Finish rewriting the relationship between the hours of darkness, the hours of daylight, and the total hours in a day using only numbers and the unknown x. Use your answers to 3a and 3b to help you.

   24 hr = (_____ + _____) + _____

   d. Solve the equation in 3c to find x (i.e., the hours of daylight).

   e. Now that you know x (i.e., the hours of daylight), find the hours of darkness.

   f. Check your work by seeing if the sum of the values you found for daylight and darkness do indeed equal the total hours in a day (24 hr), and if the value you found for the hours of darkness is indeed 13 hr more than the value you found for the hours of daylight.

Principles of Mathematics 2 — Finding the Value of an Unknown in an Inequality — Pages 182–186 — Day 78 — Worksheet 10.4 — Name

Solving Inequalities — Solve these inequalities. Be careful to change the direction of the sign when needed.

a. $x + \$100 \leq \$250$

Example Meaning: Our monthly optional expenses/savings plus our monthly $100 fixed expenses must be less than or equal to our monthly income of $250.

b. $x - \$500 \geq \$100$

Example Meaning: If our monthly income minus $500 spending must be greater than or equal to $100, what does our monthly income need to be each month?

c. $x - \$60 \geq \$10$

Example Meaning: Suppose you're heading on a camping trip and need to figure out how much money to take. How much money do you need to start with if you plan to spend $60 and need to keep at least $10 for the closing meal?

d. $30x < 60$

Example Meaning: If I drove less than 60 miles while traveling at 30 miles an hour, how long did I travel?

e. $-4x > -60$

f. $-3x \leq -30$

g. $\frac{x}{10} \leq \$20$

h. $\frac{x}{-5} > 50$

2. **Inequalities in Action**

    a. Suppose you have to get at least 60 points on a project to pass the class. If you've already completed portion of the project worth 8 points, how many additional points do you need?

    b. If it takes more than 50 points to win a game, and you expect to have 12 points deducted for mistakes, how many points do you need before the deduction to win the game?

3. **Question** — When adding, subtracting, multiplying, or dividing both sides of the inequalities <, >, ≤, and ≥ by the same amount, when do you have to change the direction of the sign in order to keep the meaning?

Reviewing Inequalities

a. Graph $x < 15$ on the number line.

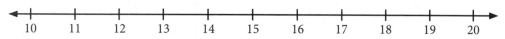

b. Graph $x \geq 10$ on the number line.

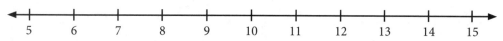

c. Swap the sides in $8 > 5 - x$, so that 8 is on the right side of an inequality symbol. Be sure to preserve the meaning.

d. Use an inequality to describe all acceptable temperatures if a substance must be kept cooler than 55 °F.

Solving Inequalities — Solve.

a. $\frac{1}{5}x > \$50$

b. $-50s < -100$

c. $x + 9 \geq 35$

d. $x - 15 \leq 80$

e. $\frac{x}{-3} > 45$

Skill Sharpening — Solve.

a. $15 - x = 25$

b. $2x = x + 6$

Collecting and Interpreting Data

a. Suppose we want to find the opinion of town residents over the age of 18 about opening up a new pool and we decide to do so by conducting a random survey of a sufficient portion of town residents over the age of 18.

Circle the population and put a star next to the sample.

town residents in favor of the pool

town residents not in favor of the pool

town residents living in the neighborhood closest to the proposed pool

town residents who returned a survey

town residents living in the town who are over 18

b. If the survey comes back that 55% support the new pool, but the MOE is ±10% and the confidence level is 95%, this means that we're 95% confident that between _____ and _____ of the population supports the new pool?

c. Suppose a store pays a company to conduct a survey to determine which of 3 color swatches teenage girls liked best. After the survey, the company makes the claim that 45% of teenage girls liked the teal color swatch the best. What additional information should the store look at in order to see how much stock to put in this result?

Organizing Data: Reading Graphs

The histogram shown is based on one from the CIA website[1] and shows the population breakdown for Sudan, Africa. The histogram is arranged as two histograms next to each other — the left side showing the male population, and the right side showing the female population. Use it to answer the questions.

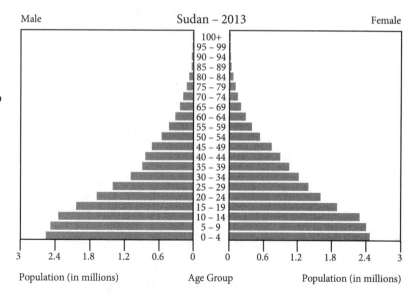

a. Approximately how many 30–34 year-old females were there in Sudan in 2013?

b. Were there more people under 50 or over 50 in Sudan in 2013?

The World Factbook 2013-14 (Washington, DC: Central Intelligence Agency, 2013), https://www.cia.gov/library/publications/the-world-factbook/geos/su.html, accessed 11/16/13.

3. **Organizing Data: Frequency Distributions and Graphs** (🖩) — For the 41 states in the USA for which data was available, below is the 2010 corn production in millions of bushels.[2]

29	5	57	35	183	20	3	36	20	1,947	898	2,153	581	153
70	46	315	1,292	91	369	5	1,469	8	12	89	76	248	533
44	8	116	30	570	75	302	4	21	26	3	502	6	

a. Finish filling out the frequency distribution table below.

States' 2010 Corn Production in Millions of Bushels	Tally	Frequency	Relative Frequency
0–499	‖‖‖ ‖‖‖ ‖‖‖ ‖‖‖ ‖‖‖ ‖‖‖ //	32	78.05%
500–999			
1,000–1,499			
1,500–1,999			
2,000–2,499			

b. Use the frequency distribution table from 3a to finish drawing the histogram below.

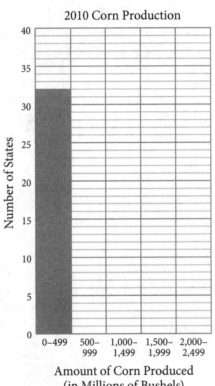

4. **Term Time** — Statistics is the "mathematics of _____, _____ and _____ of numerical data: . . ."[3]

5. **Inequalities and Electricity** — If a specific circuit breaker trips when the current sustains 15 amps for a prolonged period of time, there needs to be less than 15 amps of sustained current on the circuit. If you already have lights drawing sustained usage of 2 amps, 4 amps, and 3 amps, how many more sustained amps can you draw off the circuit?

---

[2] Data taken from "Table 859, Corn — Acreage, Production, and Value by Leading States," *The National Data Book* (United States Census Bureau), accessed 10/23/13, http://www.census.gov/compendia/statab/cats/agriculture/crops.html.
[3] *The American Heritage Dictionary of the English Language*, 1980 New College Edition, s.v. "statistics."

Principles of Mathematics 2 — Line Graphs and Trends — Pages 194–199 — Day 82 — Worksheet 11.2

You may use a calculator on this worksheet whenever you see this symbol (🖩).

Drawing Line Graphs — Finish drawing a line graph representing this data, which is of the approximate populations of New York City and Los Angeles from 1850–2000, measured every 50 years.[1] *Hint*: The New York City population and the Los Angeles population should be graphed on the same graph in the same way the two different libraries were in the *Student Textbook*.

Year	New York City Population (in millions)	Los Angeles Population (in millions)
1850	0.7	0.0
1900	3.4	0.1
1950	7.9	2.0
2000	8.0	3.7

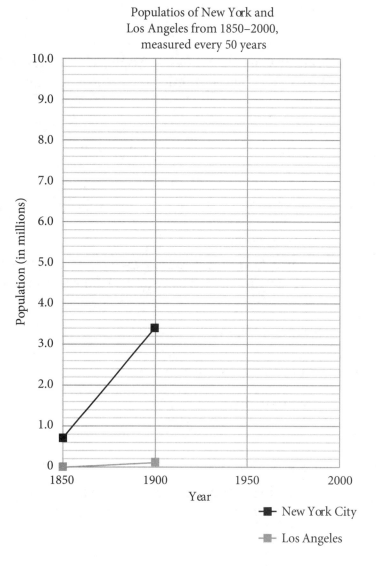

Understanding Line Graphs — Use the graph you drew in problem 1 to answer these questions.

a. Which city's population changed the most between 1850 and 2000?

b. Is the overall trend in New York City's population upward or downward?

c. Is the overall trend in Los Angeles' population upward or downward?

d. Would a city that diminishes in population each year be an example of an upward or downward trend?

Be Careful About Conclusions — In the data you graphed in problem 1 and looked at in problem 2, we were comparing two different cities for the same years. However, one city (New York City) is a much older city than Los Angeles. Before we drew conclusions comparing the two cities' growth, we might want to also look at how much each grew the first 150 years of their existence.

Source: Decennial Censuses, U.S. Census Bureau, U.S. Dept. of Commerce. Found in Sarah Janssen, sr. ed., M.L. Liu, Shmuel Ross, and Nan Badgett, eds., *The World Almanac and Book of Facts*, 2012 (New York: Infobase Learning, 2012), p. 613.

3. **Convention Check** — Circle one:
   The convention is to list the (vertical/horizontal) coordinate first.

4. **Labeling Points** — Use coordinates to label the specified points on this coordinate graph. The first one is done for you.

   a. (–4, 4) b.

   c.   d.

   e.   f.

5. **Drawing Coordinates** — Use graph paper to draw a coordinate graph. Then draw the given coordinates on the graph. Connect the points to form a triangle.

   (3, 1)

   (0, –2)

   (5, –2)

6. **Axis** — On the graph you drew in problem 3, put a star next to each axis.

7. **Skill Sharpening**

   a. If you have to read at least 25 books to qualify for a prize in a summer reading program, and you've read 5, use an inequality to show how many more books you still have to read to earn a prize.

   b. Solve: $-15x < 60$

   c. Solve: $3x < 15$

   d. Solve: $x + (x + 5) = 63$

   Example Meaning: If you want to increase the amount you read by 5 pages a week, and your goal is to read a total of 63 pages after the second week, how many pages would you have to read the first week?

   e. In the example meaning for problem 7d, what does the x stand for?

   f. In the example meaning for problem 7d, how many pages would you read the second week?

| PRINCIPLES OF MATHEMATICS 2 | Scatter Graphs and Correlation Pages 199–201 | Day 83 | Worksheet 11.3 | Name |

Driving the Selling Price — Use this hypothetical data regarding lot size, square footage, and selling price to explore scatter graphs and correlation.

Lot Size (in acres)	Square Footage	Selling Price
2.5	3,500	$349,500
0.25	3,300	$320,000
0.5	3,000	$290,000
0.8	2,500	$285,000
0.75	3,400	$280,000
4	2,400	$275,000
3.5	2,300	$255,000
0.75	2,250	$230,000
0.5	2,000	$204,000
0.75	1,500	$170,000
0.5	1,500	$150,000
3	1,000	$120,000

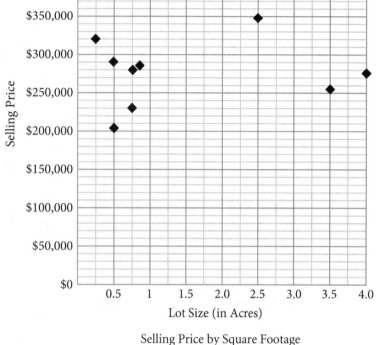

a. Graph the last three lot sizes and selling prices on the top scatter graph (ignore the square footage column). Notice that there doesn't appear to be much of a relationship, or correlation, between the lot size and the selling price for these houses.

b. Graph the last three square footages and selling prices on the bottom scatter graph (ignore the lot size column). Notice that this time, there's a definite positive correlation, or relationship, between the square footage and the selling price — in our hypothetical data anyway, larger square footages generally produced higher selling prices.

Keep in mind the data we just looked at was purely hypothetical . . . and was way too small of a sample to draw any general conclusions. The purpose of this problem wasn't to make a statement about the selling price of homes, but rather to illustrate the point that we can look for relationships, or correlations, between data in order to better understand the data . . . and that scatter graphs can be a helpful way to see those relationships visually.

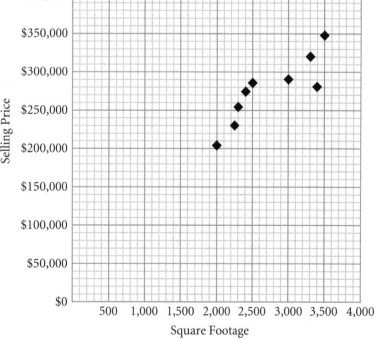

2. **Scattering Crime**

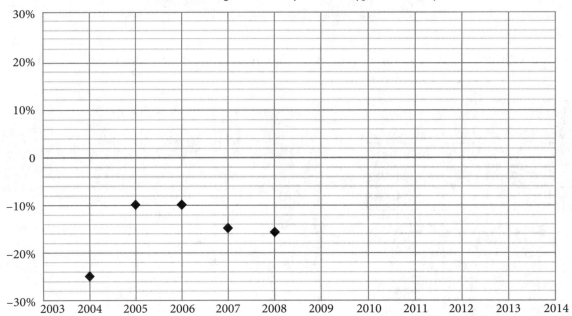

Year	Percent Change
2004	−25%
2005	−10%
2006	−10%
2007	−15%
2008	−16%
2009	1%
2010	5%
2011	6%
2012	20%
2013	21%

a. What is the general trend in crime for this city? Make your prediction before you graph the data, and then graph the rest of the data on the scatter chart.

b. By what percent did the crime change in 2012?

c. Suppose a man running for office uses this data to try to convince voters not to vote for the current mayor, as crime has increased. What are some additional facts you could look at before believing his conclusion?

3. **Skill Sharpening**

a. Graph $x > 5$ on the number line.

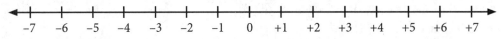

b. Solve: $x + (x + \$10) = \$180$

Example Meaning: The combined earnings of two employees is $180 a month. One employee earns $10 a month more than the other. How much does the employee that earns less earn?

c. In the example meaning for 3b, what did x represent?

d. In the example meaning for 3b, how much does the employee that earns more earn?

e. Solve: $2x > 14$ f. Solve: $-2x > 14$

Stem-and-Leaf Plots

a. Draw a stem-and-leaf plot expressing these hypothetical average monthly temperatures (in °F) for a city, based on data compiled over many years. Make the tens your stem, and the ones your leaves.

30   33   35   38   42   45   48   49   55   56   62   68

b. Are the temperatures in this city more frequently in the 30s or 60s?

c. If you were packing to visit this city, what might you want to bring with you?

Stem-and-Leaf Plots

a. Suppose the times below are the times it took for different runners in a marathon to complete a race. Round the minutes to the nearest ten.

Example: 4 hr, 15 min *rounds to* __4 hr, 20 min__

Example: 5 hr, 55 min *rounds to* ____6 hr____

5 hr, 45 min *rounds to* _____   7 hr, 8 min *rounds to* _____

4 hr, 7 min *rounds to* _____   5 hr, 40 min *rounds to* _____

6 hr, 56 min *rounds to* _____   5 hr, 10 min *rounds to* _____

7 hr, 40 min *rounds to* _____   5 hr, 23 min *rounds to* _____

b. Using the data you rounded in 2a, make a stem-and-leaf plot expressing the data. Make the hours your stems and the minutes your leaves.

c. Can we conclude from this data that more people tend to finish this course in 5 to 6 hours than in any other time span? Why or why not?

3. **Debt** — This scatter graph shows the U.S. debt by year from 1982–2014 (notice that the dollar amounts represent trillions of dollars).[1]

   a. Based on this chart, what was the general trend in national debt from 1982 to 2014? (upward or downward)

   b. If this trend continues, will the debt in 2020 be more or less than it was in 2010?

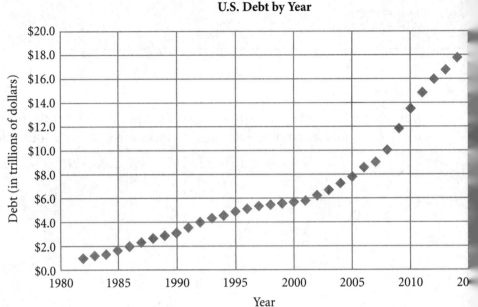

4. **Coordinate Graphs** — The point on the graph represents a ship's location. How would you describe it using coordinates?

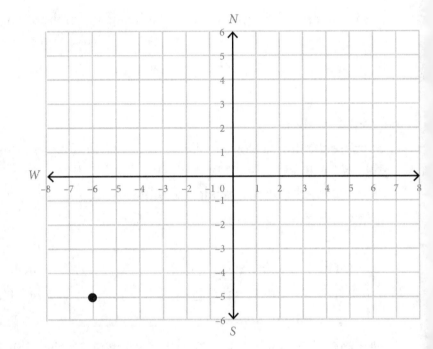

5. **Skill Sharpening** — Solve.

   a. $\dfrac{x}{-8} < 156$

   b. $\dfrac{x}{8} < 156$

   c. $179 \text{ ft} - 15 \text{ ft} = 12x$

   Example Meaning: The leaning tower of Pisa in Italy is 179 ft high, which is 15 ft more than 12 times the distance it leans over. How many feet does it lean over?

   d. $4 - (2 - x) = 20$

   e. Check your work in problem 5d by substituting the values you found for x back into the original equation.

---

[1] Data from "Historical Debt Outstanding — Annual" (TreasuryDirect), https://www.treasurydirect.gov/govt/reports/pd/histdebt/histdebt.htm, accessed 10/17/15.

PRINCIPLES OF MATHEMATICS 2
Average and Distribution — Pages 204–208
Day 85 — Worksheet 11.5

You may use a calculator on this worksheet whenever you see this symbol (🖩).

Exploring Data (🖩) — Use this data to answer the questions:

$$1, 2, 2, 3, 3, 4, 4, 4, 5, 5, 6, 6, 7$$

a. Find the average of the data.

b. Find the median of the data.

c. Find the mode of the data.

d. What do you notice about the average, median, and mode of the data?

e. Finish filling out this frequency distribution table for the data.

Data	Tally	Frequency	Relative Frequency
1	/	1	7.69%
2			
3			
4			
5			
6			
7			

f. Use the frequency distribution table from 1e to complete this column graph. Notice that the data tapers off evenly on both sides of the average.

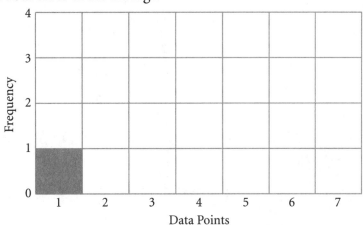

2. **More Exploring Data** (🖩) — Use this data to answer the questions:

$$1, 2, 3, 3, 4, 4, 4, 4, 5, 6, 8, 12, 15$$

a. Find the average of the data.

b. Find the median of the data.

c. Find the mode of the data.

d. What do you notice about the average, median, and mode of this data?

e. Finish filling out the frequency distribution table for the data.

Data	Tally	Frequency	Relative Frequency
1	/	1	7.69%
2			
3			
4			
5			
6			
8			
12			
15			

f. Use the frequency distribution table from 2e to complete this column graph. Notice that this time, the data does not taper off evenly from the average.

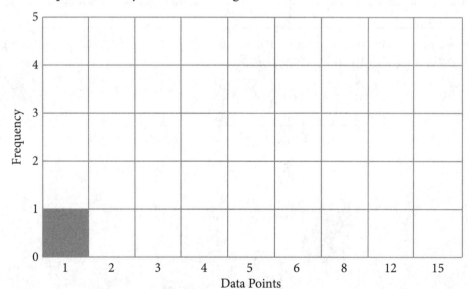

Continue to Next Page

Exploring House Prices (🖩) — Use these hypothetical sale's prices for houses in a hypothetical community to answer the questions.

$349,500, $320,000, $290,000, $285,000, $280,000, $275,000,
$255,000, $230,000, $204,000, $175,000, $150,000, $115,000

a. What is the average of the data?

b. What is the median of the data?

c. What is the mode of the data?

d. Categorize the data using the frequency distribution table below. Notice that the house prices are grouped.

Sale's Price	Tally	Number of Houses Sold in Grouping	Relative Frequency
$100,000–$149,999			
$150,000–$199,999			
$200,000–$249,999			
$250,000–$299,999			
$300,000–$349,999			

e. Use the frequency distribution table from 3d to finish the histogram showing the sales price of the houses.

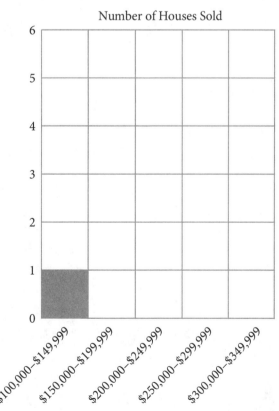

f. If trying to sell a house in this community, what are some additional things we might want to know?

4. **Coordinate Graphs** — Use graph paper to draw a coordinate graph. Then draw the given coordinates on the graph. Connect the points to form a rectangle.

   (−2, 2), (−4, 2), (−2, −3), (−4, −3)

Mixed Percents (Lesson 6.3)

a. If wages are increased 15%, what will the weekly increase be for a person whose current salary is $400 a week?

b. If you've finished 60 out of 80 rows of a crochet project, what percent have you finished?

c. In a compound made up of 5 parts zinc, 2 parts tin, and 1 part lead, what is the percentage of zinc? *Hint*: First find the total number of parts.

d. If you pay $14 in sales tax at a rate of 7.5%, how much was your purchase before tax?

Finding Unknowns — Solve.

a. $x + \frac{1}{4}x = 65$ (Lesson 7.4)

Example Meaning: If Jack's age plus $\frac{1}{4}$ of Jack's age equals 65 years, how old is Jack? *Fun Note*: An ancient Greek mathematician named Diophantus has a math puzzle about his age on his tombstone . . . only the puzzle on his tombstone is a little more involved than this one.

b. If math takes 3 times as long as spelling and if reading takes 2 times as long as spelling and if you spend 90 minutes total on math and reading, how long does it take you to do spelling? (Lesson 7.2)

c. $5\frac{1}{2} - x = 2\frac{3}{4}$ lb (Lesson 8.4)

Example Meaning: If you start with $5\frac{1}{2}$ pounds of apples on a scale, and remove enough apples so that there are only $2\frac{3}{4}$ pounds left on the scale, how many pounds of apples did you remove?

d. $x + (x - 5) - x + 3 = 10$ (Lessons 8.3 and 9.3)

e. $2(5 - x) = -2$ (Lesson 9.2)

f. $4 - (x + 3) = -6$ (Lesson 9.5)

g. $6x > 36$ (Lesson 10.4)

h. $-6x > 36$ (Lesson 10.4)

3. **Understanding Check (Lesson 8.4)** — In the example meaning in problem 2c, what does the x represent?

4. **Recipe Fun** — According to a *Fine Cooking* article,[1] in a cake, the weight (cooks will sometimes measure in weight, especially if baking in bulk) of the eggs plus the liquid should be greater than or equal to the weight of the sugar. In other words, we have this relationship: *eggs + liquid ≥ sugar*

   Let's say that you want to make a cake batter using only 12 ounces of eggs, and that the sugar weighs 28 oz. Using l to represent the weight of the liquid, you'd now have this relationship:

   $12 \text{ oz} + l \geq 28 \text{ oz}$

   a. Solve the inequality for l to see how many ounces of liquid you should put in the recipe. (Lesson 10.4)

   b. Graph the inequality you found in 4a on the number line. (Lesson 10.2)

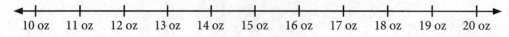

[1] Shirley Corriher, "For Great Cakes, Get the Ratios Right," *Fine Cooking*, 42, http://www.finecooking.com/articles/ratios-for-great-cakes.aspx?pg=2, accessed 10/17/15. *Note*: The website uses an equal's sign when writing the equation; as we mentioned in Lesson 10.4, we often use an equal's sign in situations that could be expressed with an inequality, knowing that we're finding the minimum or maximum amount.

Rearranging and Swapping Sides

a. Swap the sides in this equation: $A = lw$ (Lesson 6.2)

b. Rearrange this equation to solve for c; also swap the sides so c is on the left side of the equation: $a = bc$ (Lesson 6.2)

c. Swap the sides in this inequality: $-5 < x$ (Lesson 10.3)

d. Rearrange this equation to solve for c; also swap the sides so c is on the left side of the equation: $a = b + c$ (Lesson 8.2)

Omitting Multiplication Signs (Lesson 7.1) — Rewrite each of the following as multiplications, putting the coefficient directly before the unknown.

a. $s + s + s + s$

b. the opposite of 20 times an unknown amount

Understanding Check (Lesson 8.3) — Do $-x$ and $-1x$ mean the same thing? Why?

Miscellaneous Stats

a. Consider this quote: "The mean level of HDL cholesterol for American adults $\geq$ 20 years of age is 54.3 mg/dL."[2] Notice the mention of "mean." What is another word for mean? (Lesson 11.5)

b. Below are some hypothetical times in which racers completed a short run. (Lesson 11.5)

      40 min   36 min   35 min   35 min   90 min   20 min

What was the average time? Round to the nearest minute.

c. For the runners in problem 8b, what was the median time? Round to the nearest minute. (Lesson 11.5)

d. For the runners in problem 8b, what was the mode time? (Lesson 11.5)

National Health and Nutrition Examination Survey 2003–2006; National Center for Health Statistics; and National Heart, Lung, and Blood Institute; unpublished analysis. Quoted in American Heart Association, Heart Disease and Stroke Statistics—2010 Update, http://circ.ahajournals.org/content/121/7/e46.full.pdf, accessed 10/17/15, p. 104.

9. **Trends** — This scatter graph shows the temperature of a patient recovering from scarlet fever, taken every 12 hours. (Lessons 11.2 and 11.3)

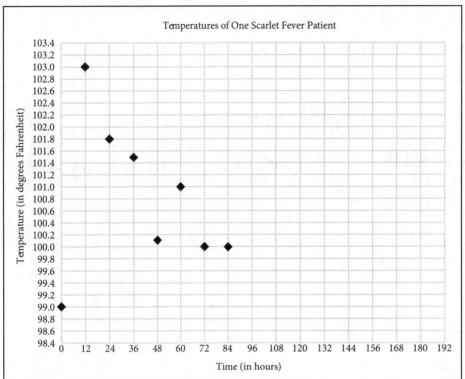

a. Finish plotting the rest of the data on the chart.

Time (in hours)	Temperature (in degrees Fahrenheit)
0	99
12	103
24	101.8
36	101.5
48	100.1
60	101
72	100
84	100

Time (in hours)	Temperature (in degrees Fahrenheit)
96	99.8
108	100.3
120	99
132	100
144	98.9
156	99.1
168	98.8
180	98.9

b. Based on this chart, what was the general trend in the fever? (upward or downward)

c. Can we conclude from this chart that all scarlet fever patients will follow this trend?

10. **Simplify** — 2[5(2+3)] (Lesson 9.1)

| PRINCIPLES OF MATHEMATICS 2 | Introduction to Probability Pages 211–213 | Day 91 | Worksheet 12.1 | Name |

You may use a calculator on this worksheet whenever you see this symbol (🖩).

probability of an event = $\frac{\text{outcomes that produce event}}{\text{total possible outcomes}}$

Unless told otherwise, specify probability as a percent rounded to two decimal places. For example, express a probability of $\frac{1}{36}$ as 2.78%.

Experiencing Probability (🖩)

a. How many possible outcomes are there when you toss a coin?

b. What is the probability of getting heads when you toss a coin?

c. Grab a coin and toss it 5 times, recording your results each time. What percent of your actual results were heads?

d. Toss the same coin 45 more times, recording your results. What percent of your actual results were heads? Notice how the more you flipped the coin, the more your actual results came closer to the mathematical probability you found in 1b.

e. The experiment you conducted in 1d illustrates what we call the law of _____.

More Experiencing Probability (🖩)

a. How many possible outcomes are there on a standard die?

b. What is the probability of rolling a ⚁ on a single roll of a die?

c. Grab a die and roll it 30 times, keeping track of how many times you rolled the ⚁. What percent of your actual results were ⚁s? The more you roll the die, the more you'll find your experimental probability and theoretical probability lining up.

Probability Expanded (🖩) — Let's suppose a game has a specialty die that has these 8 sides:

3 sides   3 sides   2 sides

a. What's the probability of rolling a 🙂 on this die?

b. What's the probability of rolling a ☹ on this die?

PRINCIPLES OF MATHEMATICS 2 | PAGE 153

4. **Graphing** — Use coordinates to describe the rectangle's corner points.

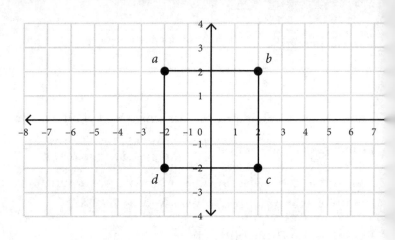

   a.

   b.

   c.

   d.

5. **Exports** ( ) — The value, in millions of dollars, of agricultural implements exported from the United States has been as follows (when rounded to the nearest million): during 1880, 2; during 1885, 3; during 1890, 4; during 1895, 5; during 1900, 16; during 1905, 21.

   a. Finish the scatter graph showing the relationship between the years and the agricultural implement exported. The first year is marked for you.

   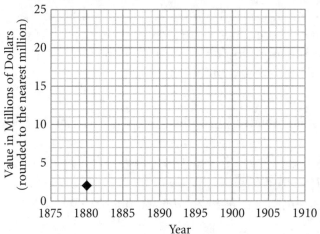

   b. What was the general trend (upward or downward) in exports between the years 1880 and 1905?

   c. What was the average value of agricultural implements for these years?

   d. What was the median?

6. **Skill Sharpening** — Solve.

   a. $-4x > -48$

   b. $4x > 48$

   c. $4 - (2 + x) = -1$

   d. $2x + x = 18$

PAGE 154 | PRINCIPLES OF MATHEMATICS 2

| PRINCIPLES OF MATHEMATICS 2 | Expressing and Applying Probability Pages 213–216 | Day 92 | Worksheet 12.2 | Name |

You may use a calculator on this worksheet whenever you see this symbol (🖩).

probability of an event = $\dfrac{\text{outcomes that produce event}}{\text{total possible outcomes}}$

Unless told otherwise, specify probability as a percent rounded to two decimal places. For example, express a probability of $\dfrac{1}{36}$ as 2.78%.

Probability Questions (🖩)

a. If a certain surgery has been performed 8,721 times and has had 5,783 successes, based on its past success, what is the probability that the surgery will be successful?

b. If on a specialty die there are 15 different numbers, including one ⑩, what's the probability of rolling a ⑩?

c. If a die has 2 letter As, 2 letter Bs, 2 letter Cs, 2 letter Ds, and 2 letter Es, what's the probability of rolling an E?

d. If a spinner has 12 options, 3 of which result in drawing a card, what's the probability of drawing a card?

e. What's the probability in the previous situation (1d) of *not* drawing a card?

100% Probable

a. If there's a 7% chance of rain, what's the probability that it won't rain?

b. If the probability of drawing the card you need to win a game is 3.13%, what's the probability of not drawing the card you need to win a game?

PRINCIPLES OF MATHEMATICS 2 | PAGE 155

3. **Probability and Baseball Stats** (🖩) — What is the probability of each player hitting the ball? In this case, the outcomes we're considering will be the hits, and the total outcomes the at-bats.

   a. Player A: 80 at-bats; 11 hits

   b. Player B: 213 at-bats; 45 hits

   c. Player C: 150 at-bats; 21 hits

   d. Player D: 197 at-bats; 50 hits

4. **More Probability and Baseball Stats**

   a. Which baseball player in problem 3 had the highest probability of hitting the ball?

   b. If a player has a 25% probability of hitting the ball, does that mean that if he's missed it the last 3 times, he's bound to hit it the next time?

   c. If a baseball player has a batting average of 0.145, what's the probability that he won't hit the ball? *Hint*: The batting average is the same as the probability of hitting the ball.

5. **Probability, the Weather, and Unknowns** — The probability of precipitation weathermen report is calculated by the formula

   Probability of Precipitation = C • A, where

   C = "the confidence that precipitation will occur somewhere in the forecast area"
   A = "the percent of the area that will receive measureable precipitation, if it occurs at all"[1]

   While we won't go into how these values are determined, if you're given C and A, you can calculate the probability of precipitation. For example, if a weatherman is 60% confident (C) that it will rain and think the rain will cover 80% of the area (A), what is the probability of precipitation that he should report?

6. **Stat Time** — Thinking back to what we discussed in the last chapter when we studied statistics, write down at least one question you might have if you were told that a surgery had a 45% probability of being successful.

---

[1] National Weather Service Weather Forecast Office, "Explaining 'Probability of Precipitation'" (Peachtree City, GA), http://www.srh.noaa.gov/ffc/?n=pop, accessed 10/19/15.

Independent Events — Worksheet 12.3

You may use a calculator on this worksheet whenever you see this symbol (🖩).

Finding the Probability (🖩)

a. What's the probability of rolling an A on an 8-sided die that has an A on 3 sides?

b. On the dice described in 1a, what's the probability of rolling an A *twice in a row*?

c. What's the probability of getting a head when you toss a coin?

d. What's the probability of getting *8 heads in a row* when you toss a coin?

e. What's the probability of getting a ⚀ when you roll a normal die?

f. What's the probability of rolling 3 ⚀s *in a row* on a normal die?

g. What's the probability of rolling a ⚂ on a normal die?

h. Suppose you and a friend are playing a game. You pick up two standard dice and roll them. What's the probability they will *both* be ⚂s?

2. **Probability in Action** — True or false: probability helps us describe atoms.

3. **Bushels of Wheat** — The steps below will walk you through finding the bushels of wheat produced inside the United States and outside the United States for 1906 given only this information regarding the wheat crop of the world:

   The wheat crop of the world in 1906 was approximately 3,423 million bushels, while the number of bushels produced outside the United States was 483 million bushels more than 3 times that produced inside of the United States.

   a. We've used x to represent the bushels produced inside of the United States. The bushels produced outside of the United States equal 3 times x plus what amount?

   bushels produced outside the United States = $3x$ + _____

   bushels produced inside the United States = x

   b. Finish rewriting this relationship between the total bushels and those produced inside the United States and those produced outside the United States using only numbers and the unknown x:

   3,423 MBU = bushels produced inside United States + bushels produced outside the United States

   3,423 MBU = _____ + (_____+_____)

   Note: MBU stands for million bushels.

   c. Solve the equation you wrote in 3b to find the bushels produced inside the United States in 1906.

   d. How many bushels were produced outside the United States in 1906?

4. **Skill Sharpening** (🖩)

   a. $x + (x - 88 \text{ ft}) = 1{,}312 \text{ ft}$

   Example Meaning: The sum of the heights of the Metropolitan Life and Singer buildings is 1,312 ft and the Singer building is 88 ft shorter than the Metropolitan Life building. What is the height of the Metropolitan Life building?

   b. In problem 4a's example meaning, what does x represent?

   c. In problem 4a's example meaning, what would the height of the Singer building be?

Dependent and Independent

a. Give an example of independent events (you can use one from the *Student Textbook* if needed).

b. Give an example of dependent events (you can use one from the *Student Textbook* if needed).

c. For both dependent and independent events, we multiply the probability of the individual events occurring to find the probability of multiple events. Only with dependent events, what else do we need to take into account?

Finding the Probability of Dependent Events

a. If the numbers 0–25 are put inside a hat, what's the probability of the first person drawing a 4? *Hint:* 0–25 is 26 numbers total, as we have to include 0.

b. If the numbers 0–25 are put inside a hat, and the number 4 has already been drawn out of the hat (leaving 25 numbers left), what's the probability of one person drawing a 2?

c. If the numbers 0–25 are put inside a hat, what's the probability of one person drawing a 4 and the next person drawing a 2, assuming each person holds on to the number he or she drew?

d. Let's say a small local store sends out scratch-off coupons to 60 customers; 20 of the coupons are worth 30% off, while the others are worth smaller percentages. If the destinations for the various coupons are randomly chosen, what is the probability that one specific customer on the list will receive a 30%-off coupon?

e. In the situation described in 2d, what is the probability that two sisters, both of whom were customers on the list, would receive a 30%-off coupon?

3. **Factorials**

   a. Rewrite 4! using multiplication.

   b. What does 4! equal?

   b. Write as a factorial: 8 • 7 • 6 • 5 • 4 • 3 • 2 • 1

4. **Skill Sharpening**

   a. Draw points at the following: (−3, −4) and (3, −4)

   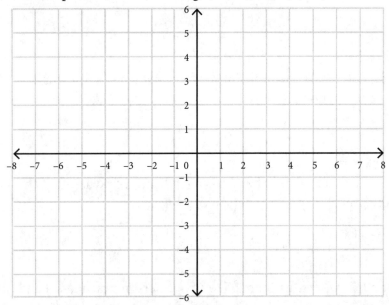

   b. What is the horizontal distance between the two points you just drew? *Hint*: Find the absolute value of the difference between the two points.

   c. $42x < 84$

   d. $-42x < -84$

   e. $45 + x + x < 105$

| PRINCIPLES OF MATHEMATICS 2 | The Fundamental Counting Principle Pages 222–225 | Day 95 | Worksheet 12.5 | Name |

Finding the Possibilities

a. The game Yahtzee® has 5 dice, each of which has 6 possible outcomes. How many possible combinations could you get on a single roll of 5 dice?

b. If you have 3 blouses and 3 skirts that all go together, how many different possible ways could you wear them?

c. If a password is 5 digits long and uses only the numbers 1–9 (so 9 possible numbers in each digit), how many possible combinations are there? *Hint*: There are 9 possibilities for the first digit, 9 possibilities for the second digit, and so forth.

d. If a password is 7 digits long and uses only the numbers 1–9, how many possible combinations are there?

e. If we allow 0-9 in our 7-digit password (so 10 possible numbers in each digit), how many possible combinations would there be?

Most websites require you to use letters (upper and lower), special symbols, and a minimum number of digits in order to make passwords harder to break. The more possibilities a hacker has to try (or have an automated computer program try for him), the harder it is for him to figure out the password.

2. **Games and Probability** (🖩) — Suppose a board game has the following cards in a stack.

     10 cards   10 cards   10 cards

 a. What's the probability of drawing a card with a ⊛ the first time a card is drawn?

 b. What's the probability of the first 3 cards that are drawn all having ⊛s?

 c. Is the scenario described in 1b is an example of a dependent or independent event?

3. **Skill Sharpening**

 a. Solve: $7 - (2 + x) = 2$

 b. If a basketball team has scored 67, 65, 40, 88, and 90 points so far in the season, what's their average score for a game so far?

 c. What is the median score for the team described in 3b?

Worksheet 12.6 — Understanding the Odds / The Dangers of Gambling

You may use a calculator on this worksheet whenever you see this symbol (🖩).

Baseball and Probability (🖩) — Express the probability of hitting the ball for each of these players. View the hits as the outcomes that produce the event, and the at-bats as the total outcomes.

Example: 80 at-bats; 15 hits *Answer*: probability of hitting the ball = $\frac{15}{80}$ = 18.75%

a. Player A: 90 at bats; 10 hits

b. Player B: 145 at bats; 18 hits

c. Player C: 220 at-bats; 35 hits

d. Player D: 124 at-bats; 30 hits

Baseball and Odds (🖩) — Express the odds of hitting the ball for each of the players in problem 1a.

Example: 80 at-bats; 15 hits *Answer*: odds for hitting the ball = 15:65

(Note on example: We used 65 rather than 80 since we want to compare the outcomes that produced the event with the outcomes that did not produce the event rather than with the total outcomes. If 15 outcomes produced the event and there are 80 outcomes, then there are 80 – 15, or 65, outcomes that did not produce the event.)

a. Player A: 90 at bats; 10 hits

b. Player B: 145 at bats; 18 hits

c. Player C: 220 at-bats; 35 hits

d. Player D: 124 at-bats; 30 hits

More Baseball and Odds — Express the odds of not hitting the ball for each of the players in problem 1.

Example: 80 at-bats; 15 hits *Answer*: odds against hitting the ball = 65:15

a. Player A: 90 at bats; 10 hits

b. Player B: 145 at bats; 18 hits

c. Player C: 220 at-bats; 35 hits

d. Player D: 124 at-bats; 30 hits

4. **Gambling**

    a. Suppose the odds of winning a contest are listed as 1:309,876. What would the odds of losing in the above contest be?

    b. Look up five verses on money, gain, or wealth from the Bible. Write the references here. *Hint*: Use a Bible concordance or the Internet to help you.

5. **Skill Sharpening**

    a. Suppose you are trying to decide who gets to go first. Seven people — one of whom is Bob — want to go first. You decide to draw to see who goes first and grab seven sticks — six long and one short — and hold them in your hand so the contestants cannot see which one is shorter. Then you have each contestant pick a stick. Whoever picks the short stick will get to go first. What's the *probability* that Bob will pick the short stick if he draws the first stick?

    b. In the situation described in 5a, what are the *odds* that Bob will pick the short stick if he draws the first stick?

    c. In the situation described in 5a, what's the *probability* that Bob will pick the short stick if he goes *third* and the short stick has not yet been chosen?

    d. If a surgery has a success rate of 69 out of 80 attempts, based on the past success rate, what is the *probability* the surgery will be successful?

    e. Consider this explanation from the United States Postal service about 5-digit zip codes: "The first digit designated a broad geographical area of the United States, ranging from zero for the Northeast to nine for the far West. This number was followed by two digits that more closely pinpointed population concentrations and those sectional centers accessible to common transportation networks. The final two digits designated small post offices or postal zones in larger zoned cities."[1]

    Delaware, New York, and Pennsylvania zip codes start with a 1. The next two digits clarify sections within those states. For example, Watertown, New York, zip codes start with a 136.

    Assuming there are no further zip code rules that interfere, how many possible 5-digit zip codes could be formed for Watertown, New York, if the last two digits could be any digit from 0-9? *Hint*: You're trying to find how many different combinations there could be given two digits (the first three are 136) that can change.

---

[1] "ZIP Code," *Publication 100 — The United States Postal Service — an American History 1775–2006* (United States Postal Service, November 2012), https://about.usps.com/publications/pub100/pub100_029.htm, accessed 10/19/15. For a list of three-digit prefixes, see "LOO2: 3-Digit ZIP Code Prefix Matrix," found in *Mailing Standards of the United States Postal service Domestic Mail Manual* (United States Postal Service), http://pe.usps.gov/Archive/HTML/DMMArchive0106/L002.htm, accessed 10/19/15.

Worksheet 12.7 — Probability and Genetics

You may use a calculator on this worksheet whenever you see this symbol (🖩).

General Note: Round pods (shown as R) in peas is a dominant trait; wrinkled pods (shown as r) is a recessive one. Thus, to end up with wrinkled pods, the pea plant must have genes of rr.

Pea Plant Fun (🖩) — The Punnett Square shows the possible offspring from two pea plants with round pods, only one of which carries the recessive trait (r). Use it to answer the following questions.

	R	R
R	RR	RR
r	rR	rR

a. What is the probability of a specific offspring from these two pea plants ending up with wrinkled pods? *Hint:* See the "General Note" in the gray box.

b. What is the probability of a specific offspring from these two pea plants ending up with one gene for a wrinkled pod (r)?

More Pea Plant Fun (🖩) — The Punnett Square shows the possible offspring from two pea plants with round pods, both of which carry the recessive trait (r).

	R	r
R	RR	Rr
r	rR	rr

a. What is the probability of a specific offspring from these two pea plants ending up with wrinkled pods?

b. What is the probability that the *fifth offspring* these pea plants produce will end up with wrinkled pods if the first four did not? *Hint:* The probability is the same for every plant. Every time, there's an equal chance that the small gene will pass along.

c. What is the probability that three offspring in a row from these two pea plants will end up with wrinkled pods?

d. What is the probability of a specific offspring from these two pea plants ending up with *one gene* for a wrinkled pod (r)?

e. What are the *odds for* a specific offspring from these two pea plants ending up with *one gene* for a wrinkled pod (r)?

f. What are the *odds against* a specific offspring from these two pea plants ending up with *one gene* for a wrinkled pod (r)?

3. **Skill Sharpening** (🖩)

   a. Draw these points on the graph: (3, 2), (0, 2), (3, 5), (0, 5); connect the points to form a square.

   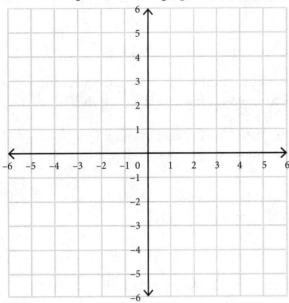

   b. What is the area of the shape you drew in 3a, if each square on the graph represents 1 mile?

   c. Solve: $56x - x < 110$

   d. Solve: $3x + 4(x - 5) > 22$

   e. Find the average of these numbers: 12, 25, 30, 45, 50, 54

   f. What was the median of the numbers in 3e?

4. **Out of the Box: More Genetics** — There's so, so much more we could have said about genetics! But don' take my word for it. Take a look at one of these additional resources, and write a paragraph summary of what you find.

   - Read "Genes and Genesis" in *Building Blocks in Life Sciences: From Genesis & Genes to Science & Scripture* by Dr. Gary Parker.[1] This section is currently available to read for free at www.MasterBooks.com (search for *Building Blocks in Life Sciences* and download the preview).
   - Visit www.AnswersinGenesis.org and read an article or watch a video on natural selection, origin of the races, fitting the animals on the ark, or mutations.

---

[1] Gary Parker, *Building Blocks in Life Science: From Genes & Genesis to Science & Scripture* (Green Forest, AR: Master Books, 2011).

Understanding Constants and Variables

a. We use the term "constant" to refer to a _____.

b. We use the term "variable" to refer to a _____.

c. The standard acceleration of gravity, often shown by the symbol g_n, is always 9.80665 meters per second squared.[1] Is the standard acceleration of gravity a constant or a variable?

d. The perimeter of a triangle (P) in the formula $P = s_1 + s_2 + s_3$ varies based on the lengths of the triangle's sides. Are we viewing the perimeter as a constant or a variable?

e. If we draw a triangle with a fixed perimeter of 20 ft, are we now viewing the perimeter as a constant or a variable?

Relationships Between Variables

a. If it costs $5 every time you park in a specific parking lot, the relationship between the total you spend in parking equals $5 times the number of times you park there, or $t = \$5n$. In this relationship, does the total you spend in parking (t) increase or decrease when you increase the number of times you park (n)?

b. In the situation described in 2a, the total you spend in parking is always ____ times the number of times you park in the parking lot.

Skill Sharpening

a. Use graph paper to draw a coordinate graph and graph these points: (–2, 2), (1, 4), (5,–6)

---

[1] Meters per second squared, typically abbreviated $\frac{m}{s^2}$, is a common unit of measure used to measure acceleration.

b. If an online spam protection screen randomly displays 3 characters, and if each character can be either a letter (uppercase or lowercase) or one of the digits 0–9, how many different combinations can it display? *Hint*: Start by finding the total possibilities for each of the 3 spaces. There are 26 letters in the alphabet (each of which can be upper or lowercase), and 0–9 is 10 digits.

c. If there are 10 slips of paper in a hat, each with a different name on it, what's the probability of randomly picking a particular name?

d. If there are 10 slips of paper in a hat, and one name is on 4 slips, what's the probability of picking that name?

e. In the problem described in 3d, what's the probability of picking the name on the 4 slips 4 times in a row if you don't put the slips of paper back into the hat once they have been selected?

| PRINCIPLES OF MATHEMATICS 2 | Independent and Dependent Variables Pages 238–241 | Day 101 | Worksheet 13.2 | Name |

You may use a calculator on this worksheet whenever you see this symbol (🖩).

Pull out the "Mathematical Relationships — Important Terms" reference sheet (p. 431). While we haven't covered all of the terms on it yet, begin using it to help you recognize the different parts of mathematical relationships.

Inputs and Outputs

a. In $y = 2x$, what is the output (y) when x (the input) is 6?

b. In $y = 8 - x$, what is the output (y) when x (the input) is 3?

c. If the value of s depends on the value chosen for t, what kind of variable do we call s?

d. If the value of s depends on the value chosen for t, what kind of variable would we call t?

e. Name one real-life example of a value that depends on another varying value. *Hint*: The *Student Textbook* gave several.

Lawn Mowing (🖩) — The total dollars you make mowing lawns depends on the number of lawns you mow. We could describe the relationship between the total dollars you make (d), the amount you charge per lawn (ℓ), and the lawns you mow (m) like this: $d = \ell m$. Say you charge $15 a lawn. You'd now have $d = \$15m$.

a. In order to better understand the relationship, let's look at a couple of inputs and find the corresponding outputs. In the table below, write the independent variable over the top of the "input" column and the dependent variable over the top the "output" column. *Hint*: Think about what value depends on the other. The variable that depends on the other value is the dependent variable, or output.

_____ (input)	$d = \$15m$	_____ (output, in dollars)
0	$d = 15(0) = 0$	
5		
10		

b. Finish filling out the table given in 2a. You can use the middle column to do the math if needed.

c. In this situation, the total dollars you make mowing is always _____ times the number of lawns you mow.

d. When you mow fewer lawns, does the total you make (d) increase or decrease?

3. **Solving for the Dependent Variable** — Rewrite each of these equations so the dependent variable (i.e., the output) is by itself on the left side of the equation. While we can arrange relationships different ways, having the output on a side by itself makes it easier to calculate the output for various inputs.

   a. $\frac{p}{c} = 15$, if the value of p depends on the value of c

   b. $\frac{P}{R} = \$200$, if the value of P depends on the value of R

4. **Distance, Time, and Speed** — As you already know, the relationship between the distance, time, and speed of an object can be expressed like this: $d = st$, or *distance = speed • time*. Let's explore this relationship a little deeper.

   Let's say you want to see how far you can drive given different amounts of time, assuming you'll average $55 \frac{mi}{hr}$. In other words, we want to see how the distance you can go varies based on the time you travel.

   a. Find the value for distance (d) for each input for time (t) given. Using the middle column is optional.

t (input, in hr)	$d = (55\frac{mi}{hr})t$	d (output, in mi)
1	$d = (55)(1) = 55$	55
5		
10		

   b. As the time you travel increases, does the distance increase or decrease?

5. **More with Distance, Time, and Speed** — Let's say that rather than seeing how the distance you can travel varies based on the time you travel, you want to see how long you'll have to travel depending on the distance you decide you want to go, given an average speed of $55 \frac{mi}{hr}$. In other words, we want to look at the same relationship we did in problem 4, only this time, we want to look at the time (t) as the dependent variable.

   The following questions will help you complete this input and output table.

d (input, in mi)		t (output, in hr)
10		
100		
300		

   a. In order to more easily find the value of time (t) for various distance (d) values, rewrite $d = (15\frac{mi}{hr})t$ so that time (t) is on the left side of the equation by itself (i.e., solve for t and swap the sides so t is on the left). Write your answer in the top row of the gray column of the table.

   b. Complete the table by finding the outputs for the given inputs.

Skill Sharpening (🖩)

a. Label the coordinates shown on the graph.

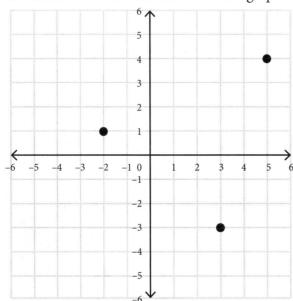

b. If an automated computer program can try 100 random passwords a second in an attempt to break into a website, how long would it take for it to guess all the possible combinations if the program knew that the website's password was only 3 digits long, each digit of which could contain one of 95 symbols (lowercase letters, uppercase letters, the digits 0–9, and special characters)? Give your answer in hours.

Note: Now you know why most online passwords have to be longer than 3 digits, why websites don't specify an exact number of digits, and why websites use additional means to protect against automated attempts to break into them (such as blocking users after a certain number of invalid login attempts).

c. If the probability of one event occurring is 1 in 4 and the probability of another independent event occurring is $\frac{2}{33}$, what's the probability of both events occurring?

			Worksheet	Name
PRINCIPLES OF MATHEMATICS 2	Using x and y for Independent and Dependent Variables Pages 241–243	Day 102	13.3	

You may use a calculator on this worksheet whenever you see this symbol (🖩).

Reminder: You may use the "Mathematical Relationships — Important Terms" reference sheet (p. 431) to help you.

Using Different Letters

a. What letter is commonly used to represent the dependent variable (i.e., the output)?

b. What letter is commonly used to represent the independent variable (i.e., the input)?

c. What letters are commonly used to represent constants?

Exploring Springs (🖩) — Let's say you are building a device with a spring. You want to see how the amount you stretch or compress the spring will affect the force the spring will exert (i.e., you want to see how the force *depends on* the displacement). The relationship between the force and the amount the spring is stretched or compressed (i.e., its displacement) is this:

$$Force = -(spring\ constant \cdot displacement)$$
or
$$F = -kd$$

The package in which you bought the spring tells you that its spring constant (k) is 7 pounds per inch (often abbreviated $\frac{lb}{in}$).

a. What are we viewing as the dependent variable (the output) and how do you know from the wording above which is the dependent variable (the output)?

b. What are we viewing as the constant in the relationship?

c. Find the force for the following displacements.

d (input, in inches)	$F = -kd$, when $k = 7$ pounds per inch	F (output, in pounds)
1	$F = -(7)(1) = -7$	–7
5		
15		

d. For these values, as the displacement increases, does the force increase in the negative or positive direction?

3. **Skill Sharpening** (🧮)

   a. A company sends out random complimentary gifts to customers along with their order. If they have 60 gifts on hand, 15 of which are a new lotion, what's the probability that a specific customer will end up with the new lotion?

   b. In the situation described in 3a, what's the probability that two sisters who order back to back will both end up with the new lotion, assuming the process is totally random and the person packaging the gifts doesn't purposefully pick different gifts for the sisters.

PRINCIPLES OF MATHEMATICS 2 | Functions Pages 241–243 | Day 103 | Worksheet 13.4 | Name

Reminder: You may use the "Mathematical Relationships — Important Terms" reference sheet (p. 431) to help you.

Functions — In a function, there's only _____ output for every input.

A Function of — As you begin exploring mathematical relationships between variables, you'll often hear the phrase *is a function of*. When you do, keep in mind that the term *is a function of* lets you know the relationship between the variables. When this term is used, it's easy to tell which variable is the input and which is the output: the output is a function of the input.

output is a function of *input*

So if *y* is the output and *x* the input of a function, we could write this:

y is a function of *x*

Since the phrase *is a function of* was used, you also know that each input has one output.

a. Suppose you want to see how the volume (*V*) depends on the height (*h*) you choose. Which variable are you viewing as the dependent variable (output) and which as the independent variable (input)?

   dependent variable (output) = ____

   independent variable (input) = ____

b. Assuming for every input there's only one output, in the situation described in 2c, we're viewing ____ as a function of ____.

c. Suppose you want to see how the height (*h*) depends on the volume (*V*) because you plan to change the height depending on what volume you decide to make the prism. Which variable are you viewing as the dependent variable (output) and which as the independent variable (input)?

   dependent variable (output) = ____

   independent variable (input) = ____

d. Assuming for every input there's only one output, in the situation described in 2c, we're viewing ____ as a function of ____.

e. If we're looking at area (*A*) as a function of the width (*w*), which variable are we viewing as the *input*?

f. If we're looking at width (*w*) as a function of the area (*A*), which variable are we viewing as the *output*?

3. **Recognizing Functions** — In upper math, there are certain techniques that are quite helpful in describing God's creation for which we need to know if we're dealing with a function or not. Thus, it's important to be able to look at a relationship or data and determine if for every input there's just one output. Practice your skills with the questions below.

   a. Given only the relationship $n > m$, can we view n as a function of m? Why or why not?

   b. The following table gives the temperature recorded by the Weather Bureau at 8 a.m. at San Francisco, California, for the six consecutive days beginning April 6, 1908. For the data shown, could we view the temperature as a function of the day? *Hint*: For every day (input), is there only one temperature (output)?

Day	Temperature (in degrees Fahrenheit)
1	46
2	54
3	54
4	50
5	52
6	54

   c. Look back at the table in 3b. Could we view the day as a function of the temperature? *Hint*: For every temperature (input) is there only one day (output)?

   d. Average scores for a hypothetical exam taken by four different classes of students are reported in the table shown. Can we view the average score as a function of the class?

Class	1	2	3	4
Average Score	80	75	80	77

   e. Look back at the table in 3d. Could we view the class as a function of the average score?

   f. Suppose a group of contestants were asked to select a number from 0 to 10. The results are recorded in the table. Can we view the number as a function of the contestant?

Contestant	A	B	C
Number	2	1	10

   g. Look back at the table in 3f. Can we view the contestant as a function of the number?

Typing Speed () — Let's say Jane can type an average of 80 words per minute. Obviously, the words Jane can type varies based on the number of minutes she spends typing. In fact, we could represent the relationship with this equation:

$$\text{total words typed} = 80(\text{minutes spent typing})$$
$$t = 80m$$

But let's say we want to see how the number of minutes she needs to spend typing varies based on the total words she needs to type. We're now viewing the minutes spent typing as a function of the total words typed.

a. Solve $t = 80m$ for m (also swapping the sides of the equation so m is on the left) so it will be easier to find the outputs.

b. Fill in the table to find the minutes spent typing (m) for the given inputs for total words typed (t). Use the equation you found in 4a to perform your calculations; you can use the middle column to do the math if needed.

t (input)		m (output)
1,000		
20,000		
30,000		

c. As the total words typed increases, does the minutes spent typing increase or decrease?

d. Convert the number of minutes you calculated for typing 20,000 words into hours.

Skill Sharpening

a. Graph the data from 3d on the graph below.

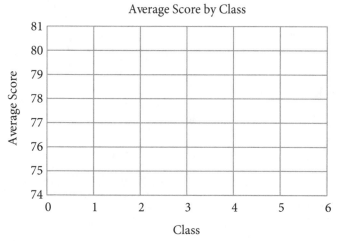

Average Score by Class

b. If there are 50 crayons in a box, and 12 of them are green, what's the probability of drawing a green crayon if you randomly pull one out?

c. In the situation described in 5b, what's the probability of randomly pulling 3 green crayons in a row, assuming you do not put the crayons back after you pull them out?

PRINCIPLES OF MATHEMATICS 2
Domains — Pages 245–247 — Day 104 — Worksheet 13.5

Reminder: You may use the "Mathematical Relationships — Important Terms" reference sheet (p. 431) to help you.

Understanding Domains — Complete the statement:

A domain is the _____.

Graphing Domains — Graph each of these domains on a number line. The first number line is drawn for you; draw your own number line for the rest.

Example: $y = 52x$, where $x < 3$

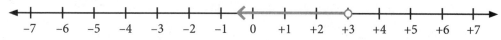

a. $x > 0$

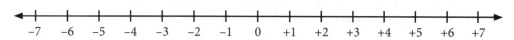

b. $x \geq 0$

c. $3 < x \leq 6$

d. $4 \geq x > 0$

e. $\{1, 4, 6\}$

Hint: Here, rather than being told a start and an end, you're being told three different values for the domain. So simply graph three closed points on the number line.

Understanding Graphs of Domains — Use symbols ($<$, $>$, $\leq$, or $\geq$) to show the domain based on the values for x shown on the number line.

Example: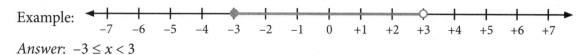

Answer: $-3 \leq x < 3$

a.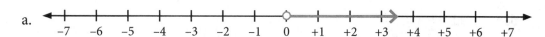

b.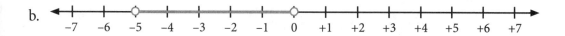

c.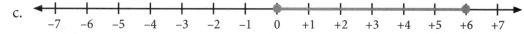

4. Specifying Domains

a. Using symbols, how would you specify that a relationship only holds true when *x* is less than 9?

b. Using symbols, how would you specify that a relationship only holds true when *s* is less than 9 but greater than −8?

c. Let's say that we're planning a wedding. We've been told it costs $12 per person to cater the reception. The $12 only holds true, though, when we have greater than 40 guests. Finish writing an inequality to specify the domain for the relationship.

   guests > _____

d. If the $12 price only holds true when the number of guests is greater than 40 but less than 100, use an inequality to finish specifying the domain for the relationship in problem 4c.

   40 _____ guests _____ 100

5. Exploring Percents with Domains
— We saw back in Chapter 6 that the rate times the base equals the percentage ($RB = P$). Let's say the sales tax in a state is 5% for purchases between 0 and $10,000 (for more expensive purchases, the rate changes). We have the equation $(0.05)B = P$, where $0 \leq B \leq \$10,000$.

a. Would −5 be a valid input for *B*?

b. Would 8 be a valid input for *B*?

c. Finish filling in the table and see how *P* (the amount paid in sales tax) changes as *B* (the purchase amount) changes. The gray column is included for you to perform the math if you like.

B (input, in dollars)	$(0.05)B = P$ where $0 \leq B \leq \$10,000$	P (output, in dollars)
100		
1,000		
10,000		

d. In $(0.05)B = P$, the value of *P* (the amount owed in sales tax) is always _____ times the value of *B* (the purchase amount).

e. Graph the domain of $(0.05)B = P$, where $0 \leq B \leq \$10,000$, on this number line.

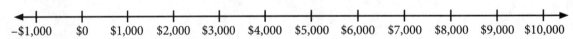

6. Mastering Functions

a. Suppose you want to see how the number of inches a plant grows (*g*) is a function of the number of days (*d*). Which variable are you viewing as the dependent variable (output) and which as the independent variable (input)?

   dependent variable (output) = _____

   independent variable (input) = _____

b. Since we were told we had a function, for each input in problem 6a, we know there will be _____ output.

Picturing Relationships

Worksheet 14.1

You may use a calculator on this worksheet whenever you see this symbol (🖩).

You may use the "Mathematical Relationships — Important Terms" reference sheet (p. 431) to help you.

Ticket Sales to a Virtual Event with No Attendee Limit Versus Number of Attendees at $15 a Ticket (🖩)

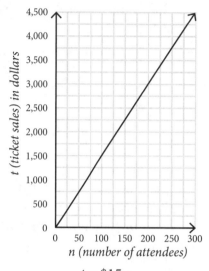

$t = \$15n$
ticket sales = 15(number of attendees)

a. Based on the graph, what will the ticket sales be when the number of attendees is 100?

b. Finish filling out the table showing different inputs and outputs for $t = \$15n$. We've omitted the column with the equation, as you can either perform the calculation on a calculator or next to the table.

n (input)	t (output, in dollars)
50	
200	
250	

c. Viewing each input as a horizontal coordinate and the corresponding output as the vertical coordinate, graph the coordinates you found in 1b on the graph shown at the beginning of problem 1. Notice that the coordinates all describe points along the line.

d. Is $t = \$15n$ a linear equation? Why or why not?

Ticket Sales Versus Ticket Price with 200 Attendees (🖩)

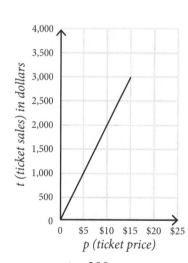

$t = 200p$
ticket sales = 200(ticket price)

a. Based on the graph, what will the total ticket sales be when the ticket price is $5?

b. Finish filling out the table showing different inputs and outputs for $t = 200p$.

p (input, in dollars)	t (output, in dollars)
10	
15	
20	

c. Viewing each input as a horizontal coordinate and the corresponding output as the vertical coordinate, graph the coordinates you found in 2b on the graph shown at the beginning of problem 2. Use a ruler to extend the line. Notice that when you do, all the coordinates describe points along the line.

d. Is $t = 200p$ a linear equation? Why or why not?

3. **Ticket Price as Number of Attendees Varies to Keep the Ticket Sales a Constant $1,000** (🖩)

    a. Based on the graph, what would the ticket price need to be when the number of attendees is 10?

    b. Rearrange $1,000 = np$ so p is on a side by itself.

    c. Use the equation you rearranged in 3b to finish filling out this table showing different inputs and outputs.

n (input)	p (output, in dollars)
5	
20	
50	

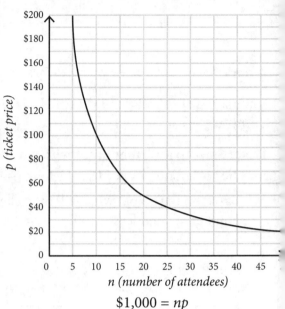

$1,000 = np$
$1,000 =$ number of tickets sold • ticket price

    d. Viewing each input as a horizontal coordinate and the corresponding output as the vertical coordinate, graph the coordinates you found in 3c on the graph shown at the beginning of problem 3. Notice that the coordinates all describe points along the curve.

    e. Is $1,000 = np$ a linear equation? Why or why not?

4. **Money Lost if a Company Loses $50 a Day** (🖩)

    a. Based on the graph, what would the change in dollars be after 5 days?

    b. Finish filling out the table showing different inputs and outputs for $d = -50t$.

t (input, in days)	d (output, in dollars)
2	
5	
10	

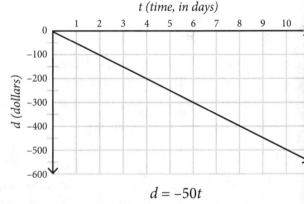

$d = -50t$
change in dollars $= (-\$50)(\text{time in days})$

    c. Viewing each input as a horizontal coordinate and the corresponding output as the vertical coordinate, graph the coordinates you found in 4b on the graph shown at the beginning of problem 4. Notice that the coordinates all describe points along the line.

    d. As the time (t) progresses in the positive direction, do the dollars lost (d) increase in the positive or the negative direction?

    e. Is $d = -40t$ a linear equation? Why or why not?

Continue to Next Page

Graphs of Functions — It's very easy to tell on a graph if the relationship between an input and output is a function or not. Remember, a function means that for every input there's one output. When you look at a graph, you can easily see if for every *x* value (i.e., every input), there's only one *y* value (i.e., one output). How? Well, using your finger, trace the *x*-axis horizontally. At any point does the line(s) or curve have two different vertical values? If it does, than it is not a function, as not every input has only one output.

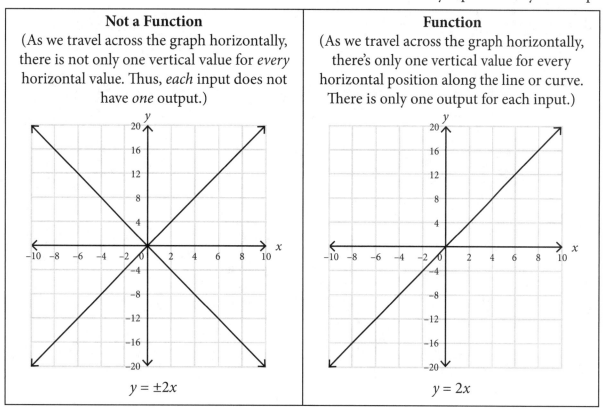

a. In the graph of $y = \pm 2x$ above, what two values can *y* be when *x* is 4?

b. In problem 2, was the graph the graph of a function?

c. In problem 3, was the graph the graph of a function?

d. Is this graph of a function? *Hint*: Don't let the curve's form fool you. If there's only one vertical value for every horizontal position along the line or curve, then it is a function.

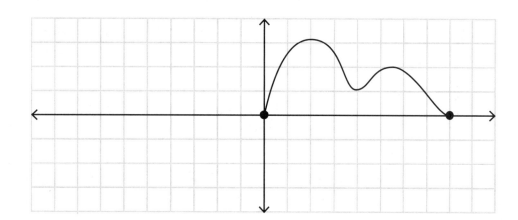

PRINCIPLES OF MATHEMATICS 2 | The Mechanics of Graphing Linear Equations Pages 254–257 | Day 108 | Worksheet 14.2 | Name

Reminder: When asked to graph an equation with *y* and *x* in this course, you can assume that *y* represents the dependent variable (and thus should be graphed on the vertical axis), while *x* represents the independent variable (and thus should be graphed on the horizontal axis).

Learning the Steps

a. Find coordinates to use to graph the linear equation $y = 2x$. Notice the example meaning — don't let the use of *y* and *x* fool you into thinking the graph is pointless.

Example Meaning: the altitude after 2 seconds when starting at sea level equals 2 seconds times the rate at which the altitude is changing

x (input)	*y* (output)
−1	
0	
1	

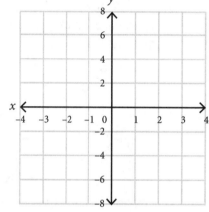

b. Graph the coordinates you found in 1a. Connect the points into a straight line using a ruler. Add arrows to both sides of the line to emphasize the fact that it can be extended. Notice how the line shows the relationship visually.

Finding Coordinates to Graph

a. $y = 7x$

x (input)	*y* (output)
−1	
0	
1	

b. $y = \frac{1}{2}x$

x (input)	*y* (output)
−1	
0	
1	

Graphing the Coordinates — Use the coordinates you found in problem 2 to graph the linear equations on the graphs below.

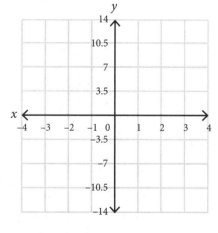
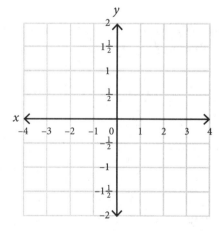

When you're graphing an equation and you don't have a reason to choose other inputs, it's often helpful to use −1, 0, and 1 as the inputs. That way, you'll see how the equation behaves with both a negative and a positive value and at 0, the outputs will be easy to calculate, and the coordinates will be easy to graph.

4. **Drawing Your Own Graph**

   a. Find coordinates to use to graph the linear equation $y = 6x$.

x (input)	y (output)
−1	
0	
1	

   b. Graph the coordinates you found in 4a. This time, draw your own graph on graph paper. Be sure to label the horizontal axis x and the vertical axis y. Connect the points you graph into a straight line using a ruler. Add arrows to both sides of the line to emphasize the fact that it can be extended. Notice how the line shows the relationship visually.

   c. Find coordinates to use to graph the linear equation $y = -2x$. This time, rather than giving you a table with inputs, pick your own three inputs and find the corresponding outputs. Pick at least one negative value and one positive value. You'll find that −1, 0, and 1 make for easy calculations and graphing.

x (input)	y (output)

   d. Graph the coordinates you found in 4c on graph paper. Label the axes x and y. Connect the points into a straight line using a ruler. Add arrows to both sides of the line to emphasize the fact that it ca be extended. Notice how the line shows the relationship visually.

5. **Graphing with Units** — Graph how the height of an elevator changes over time if the height is changing at a consistent rate of 4 meters per second and we're starting at a height of 0 m. The linear equation to graph is $h = (4 \frac{m}{sec})t + 0$ m, which simplifies to $h = (4 \frac{m}{sec})t$.

   a. What are we viewing as the dependent variable (i.e., the output)?

   b. Find 3 sets of coordinates you can use to graph this relationship. Choose at least one negative and one positive input. Remember, inputs of −1, 0, and 1 make for easy calculations and graphing.

t (input, in seconds)	h (output, in meters)

   c. Use graph paper to graph $h = (4 \frac{m}{sec})t$. Remember to put the dependent variable on the vertical axis. Label the side of the graph representing distance "h (height), in meters" and the side of the graph representing speed "t (time), in seconds".

| | PRINCIPLES OF MATHEMATICS 2 | Showing the Domain on a Graph Pages 258–260 | Day 109 | Worksheet 14.3 | Name |

You may use a calculator on this worksheet whenever you see this symbol (🖩).

Graphing with Domains (🖩) — Finish graphing the following linear equations. Notice that they are all the same equation, but have different domains.

a. $y = 3x$

x (input)	y (output)
–5	
20	
25	

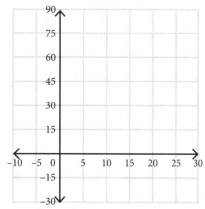

b. $y = 3x$, where $x > 10$

x (input)	y (output)
10	
20	
25	

Hint: Put an open circle at the coordinate where x is 10 to show that x must be greater than 10.

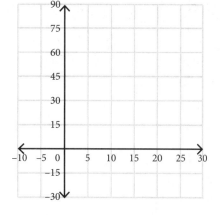

c. $y = 3x$, where $x \geq 10$

x (input)	y (output)
10	
15	
25	

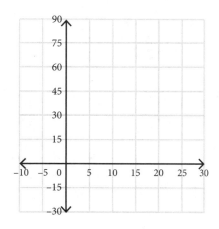

2. **Jewelry Sale** (▦) — Suppose we could purchase jewelry at $7 a piece, provided we purchased 10 or fewer pieces. This linear equation represents the total cost (t) as a function of the number of pieces purchased (n).

$$t = 7n, \text{ where } 0 < n \leq 10$$

Use this information to complete 2a and 2b.

a. In the table below, write the independent variable over the top of the "input" column and the dependent variable over the top of the "output" column. Then find 3 sets of coordinates by completing the table. Notice that we picked inputs that were within the domain.

_____n_____ (input)	_____t_____ (output)
1	7
5	35
10	70

b. Finish graphing the coordinates you found in 2a. Notice that we've already put one point on the graph — we put an open point at 0 to show that 0 is not included in the domain. Use a closed point where x equals 10 to show that 10 is included in the domain (x is less than or equal to 10). Draw a line connecting the points. Do not draw arrows, since the domain doesn't extend indefinitely. Be sure to add labels to the horizontal and vertical axes.

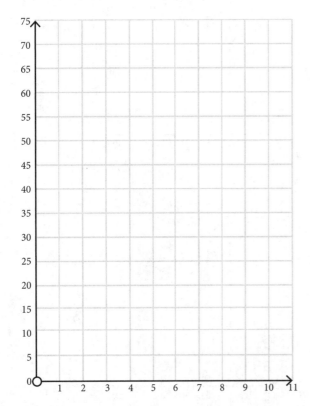

Flower Shop Time (🖩) — Suppose you own a flower shop. You buy flowers and then resell them at a profit. You've concluded that you have to charge 8 times the cost of each product you sell in order to stay in business. The sales price *is a function of* the cost of each product.

a. Finish this equation so that it will reflect the function between the sales price and the cost. The *s* represents the sales price; use *c* to represent the cost.

$s = \underline{}\,\underline{}$

b. Specify a domain for the equation you found in 3a that shows that the cost must be greater than 0, since negative numbers wouldn't make sense for this situation.

c. Find three sets of coordinates to help you graph the equation you found in 3a with the domain found in 3b. Use 1, 2, and 3 as the inputs.

d. Finish graphing the linear equation found in 3a for the domain found in 3b.

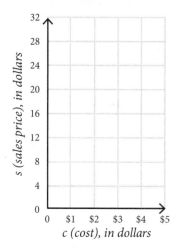

4. **Skill Sharpening**

   a. Graph this table, which shows hypothetical data of the number of patients cared for at a hospital for the given years. Do not connect the points.

Year	Patients Served (in thousands)
2010	56
2011	60
2012	62
2013	65
2014	67
2015	72

   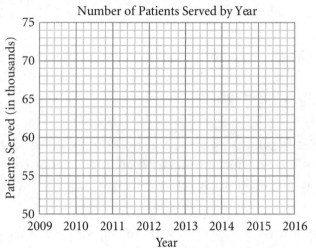

   b. For the data you graphed in 4a, can we think of the patients served as a function of the year? Why or why not?

   c. Is the trend of the number of patients at the hospital an upward or downward trend?

   d. In the graph below, what two values is y when x is 100?

   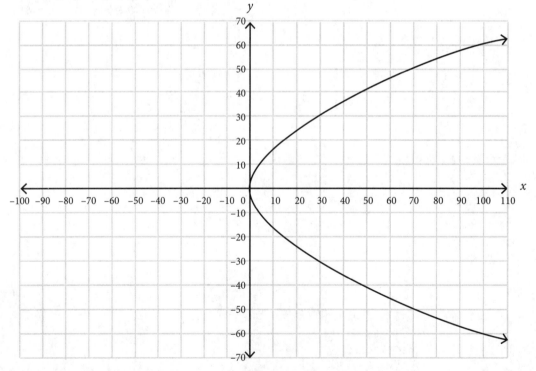

   e. Is the relationship graphed in 4d a function? Why or why not?

| PRINCIPLES OF MATHEMATICS 2 | Y-Intercept Pages 260–265 | Day 110 | Worksheet 14.4 | Name |

You may use a calculator on this worksheet whenever you see this symbol (🖩).

Y-intercept — Find the *y*-intercept for these linear equations by graphing the equation and looking at where the line intersects the *y*-axis. These problems are hypothetical explorations of a drone that is descending into a valley at a rate of $-10 \frac{ft}{min}$. Notice that we're viewing the height of the drone relative to the top of the valley (*h*) as a function of time (*t*). Times before 0 show the drone's height in the *past*. The *y*-intercept shows the drone's initial height relative to the top of the valley when the time (*t*) is 0 minutes.

a. $h = (-10)t + 0$

Example Meaning: The drone is starting at the top of a valley and descending.

b. $h = (-10)t + -5$

Example Meaning: The drone has already descended 5 ft below the top and continues descending into the valley from there.

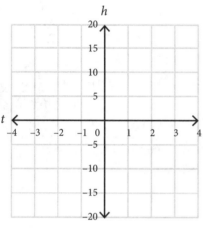
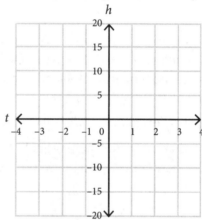

c. $h = (-10)t + 5$

Example Meaning: The drone starts its descent into a valley at 5 ft above the top of the valley.

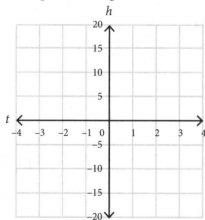

d. Look back at the graph to 1a. In the example meaning, how many minutes will it take the drone to reach the bottom of the valley if the valley's bottom is −20 ft when measured relative to the top?

. **More with the Y-Intercept** — Go back and find the *y*-intercept for problems 1a–1c by solving for when *t* equals 0. Show your work.

a.

b.

c.

3. **Notebooks and Students** — Use this hypothetical scenario to answer the questions:

   Let's say you want to see the relationship between the number of notebooks to purchase and the number of students if each student needs 4 notebooks. The number of students will be greater than or equal to 0, and we also want 4 extra notebooks on hand. *Hint*: The function between the number of students and the number of notebooks can be described by the linear equation $n = 4s + 4$, where $s \geq 0$, n represents the number of notebooks, and s represents the number of students.

   a. What is the dependent variable and what is the independent variable?

   b. Use graph paper to graph this relationship. Be sure to clearly label the graph.

4. **Skill Sharpening**

   a. Solve: $4x + x = 12$

   Example Meaning: In order to mix a specific color paint, you need 4 times as much yellow paint as green paint. If you want 12 gallons of the mixed paint, how many gallons of green paint do you need? *Note*: We have this relationship:

   gallons of yellow paint + gallons green paint = total gallons of mixed paint

   We know that the yellow paint equals 4 times the gallons of green paint. If we use x to represent the green paint, we then have this: $4x + x = 12$.

   b. In order to make a specific wooden footstool you need wood for the top of the footstool and the sides of the footstool. You need 1.5 times the length of the wood for the top of the footstool as you do for *each* of the two sides of the footstool. If you want to make the whole project out of a 35-inch long piece of wood you have, how much wood can you use for each side of the footstool?

   c. The graph below (an up-close look at an EKG) shows a graph of a heart's electrical activity (y) over time (x). In it, can we think of the electrical activity as a function of time? Why or why not?

   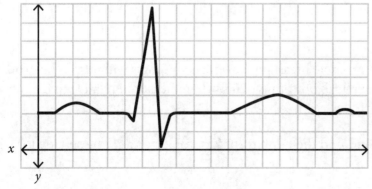

Slope — Worksheet 14.5

You may use a calculator on this worksheet whenever you see this symbol (🖩).

Understanding Slope

a. Slope is the ratio _____.

b. If a mountain trail has an average slope of $\frac{3 \text{ ft}}{11 \text{ ft}}$, there is an average of _____ feet of vertical change per _____ feet of horizontal change.

c. Slope can be thought of as the rise over the _____.

d. In $\frac{y_2 - y_1}{x_2 - x_1}$, why does it make sense to use the letter y to stand for the two vertical coordinates and the letter x to stand for the two corresponding horizontal coordinates?

Identifying the Slope (🖩) — What is the slope of the following lines?

a.

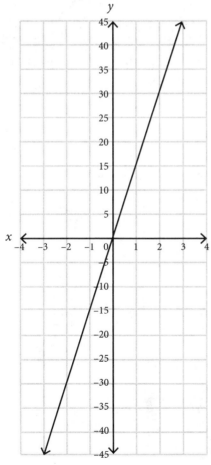

b.

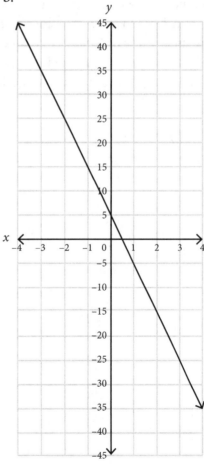

c.

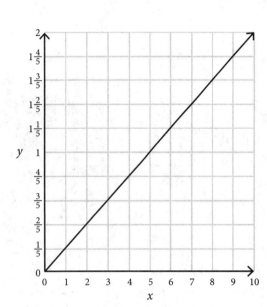

d.

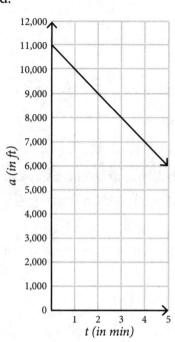

e. Look at the graph in 2d again. Let's say it represents the altitude of a skier who's skiing down a mountain where the mountain's slope is basically consistent (and thus the skier is changing altitude at a consistent rate). According to the graph, then, the skier starts at an altitude of 11,000 ft and descends to an altitude of 6,000 ft in a total of 5 minutes. The slope you found is the consistent rate at which the skier changes altitude. According to the graph, then, at what altitude is the skier at after 4 minutes?

3. **Y-intercept** — For each graph in problem 2, what was the y-intercept?

   a.

   b.

   c.

   d.

Estimated Hours (🖩) — A company is trying to estimate the cost of hiring a contractor who charges by the hour. The contractor earns $50 an hour. They expect the project to take somewhere between 40 and 50 hours.

The total cost depends on the number of hours. We could represent this function with this linear equation: $t = (\frac{\$50}{hr})h$, where 40 hr $\leq h \leq$ 50 hr. We've used t to stand for the total cost and h for the number of hours the contractor works.

a. Finish filling out the table showing different inputs and outputs for $t = (\frac{\$50}{hr})h$, where 40 hr $\leq h \leq$ 50 hr.

(input, in hours)	(output, in dollars)
40	
45	
50	

b. Graph $t = (\frac{\$50}{hr})h$, where 40 hr $\leq h \leq$ 50 hr. Be sure to clearly label each axis.

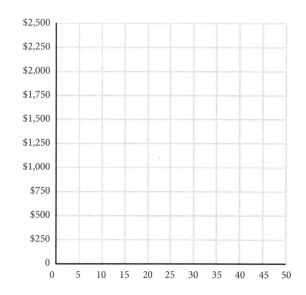

Geometry Time (🖩) — Use the reference sheets as needed to answer the questions.

a. Find the volume of a rectangular pool that is 8 ft long, 5 ft wide, and 5 ft deep.

b. What is the volume of the pool from problem 5a in cubic *inches*?

c. How many gallons could the pool hold?

d. Would it make sense to think of the number of gallons a pool is holding as a function of the depth to which we fill up the pool? Why or why not?

Finding the Equation — Worksheet 14.6

You may use a calculator on this worksheet whenever you see this symbol (🖩).

Remember, slope intercept form is an equation in this form:

$$\text{dependent variable} = \text{slope}(\text{independent variable}) + y\text{-intercept}$$
or
$$y = mx + b$$

Understanding Slope-Intercept Form

a. Is $y = 5x + 1$ written in slope-intercept form?

b. In $y = 5x + 1$, what is the slope?

c. In $y = 5x + 1$, what is the y-intercept?

d. If d is the dependent variable and s is the independent variable, is $d = 8s + 5$ written in slope-intercept form?

e. In $d = 8s + 5$, what is the slope?

f. In $d = 8s + 5$, what is the y-intercept?

g. If d is the dependent variable and s is the independent variable, is $d = 8s$ written in slope-intercept form? Remember, you do not need to show a y-intercept of 0.

h. In $d = 8s$, what is the slope?

i. In $d = 8s$, what is the y-intercept?

j. Rewrite $\frac{F}{5} = m$ in slope intercept form, if F is the dependent variable.

k. What is the slope of the equation in 1j?

l. What is the y-intercept of the equation in 1j?

2. **Finding the Equation** (🖩) — Find the equation of these lines by finding the slope and *y*-intercept, and substituting those values into the slope-intercept form. Notice that the graph in 2a is the graph with which Lesson 14.6 in your *Student Textbook* began. Since this graph is showing an experiment, in real li we'd have to use common sense regarding whether the relationship holds true for values beyond those w tested. However, in problem 2a, you do not need to specify a domain.

a.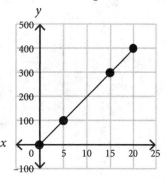

b.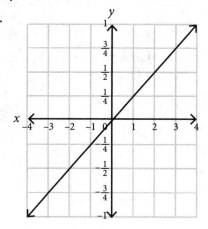

c.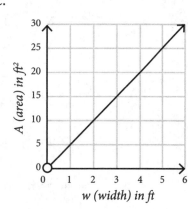

d.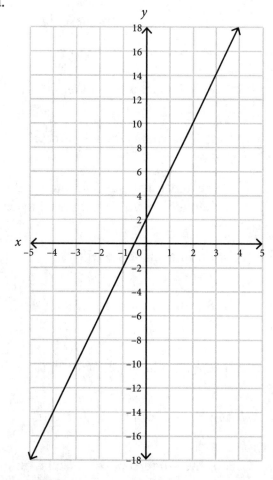

e.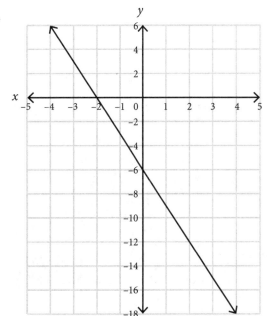

Luncheon Meat Needed (🖩) — Suppose you would like to have enough luncheon meat for each guest to have 4 oz. The total meat you need (m) depends on the number of guests (g). In fact, the meat is a *function* of the number of guests. Assuming the number of guests is greater than or equal to 0, then the total luncheon meat needed equals 4 oz times the number of guests.

$$m = (4\text{ oz})g, \text{ where } g \geq 0$$

a. Finish filling out the table of inputs and outputs below. Notice that we picked inputs that were within the domain.

(input)	(output, in oz)
0	
20	
30	

b. Graph the linear equation $m = (4\text{ oz})g$, where $g \geq 0$, to see how the meat you need changes as the number of guests changes. Be sure to clearly label each axis.

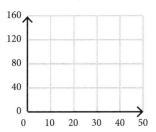

4. **Skill Sharpening** — Solve.

   a. 8 − (5 − 2)

   b. 2 − (−3 + 4)

   c. 4 + (5 + x) = 20

   d. $34 − ($3 + x) = $5

   Example Meaning: You start with $34 in your wallet and you end with $5. You know you spent $3 on ice cream and put the rest of the missing cash in the church offering. How much cash did you put in the offering?

   e. In the relationship graphed below, is y a function of x?

   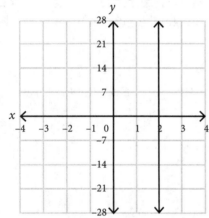

| PRINCIPLES OF MATHEMATICS 2 | The Line of Best Fit Pages 275–278 | Day 113 | Worksheet 14.7 | Name |

You may use a calculator on this worksheet whenever you see this symbol (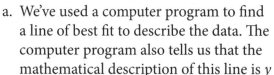).

Pressure and Temperature (🖩) — Use the graph shown to answer the questions. The graph shows the relationship between the pressure and temperature of a hypothetical ideal gas when the volume is constant. While this relationship is a constant relationship, when measuring and conducting experiments, we often have results that don't align perfectly with the relationship due to error in measurements. However, we can still use a line of best fit to see the relationship.

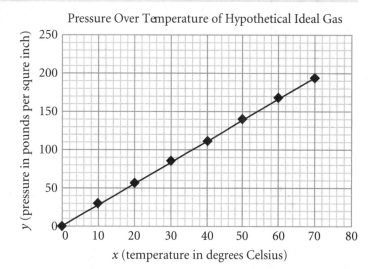

a. We've used a computer program to find a line of best fit to describe the data. The computer program also tells us that the mathematical description of this line is $y = 2.8x$. Knowing this, what is the y-intercept of this line?

b. Knowing that the equation of the line is $y = 2.8x$, what is the slope of the line?

c. Finish filling out the right-most column below, using the equation $y = 2.8x$ to find the pressure for each volume. Notice how some of the values obtained from the equation vary from the actual values ever so slightly, as the actual data doesn't fall on a perfect line (some of the points are above or below the line) due to measurement error.

Temperature Measurement (represented by x) in degrees Celsius	Pressure Measurement (represented by y) in pounds per square inch	Pressure from Formula ($y=2.8x$) in pounds per square inch
0	0	$y = 2.8(0) = 0$
10	28	$y = 2.8(10) = 28$
20	56	$y = 2.8(20) = 56$
30	85	$y = 2.8(30) = 84$
40	110	
50	141	
60	168	
70	196	

d. Based on the line of best fit formula, what should we expect the pressure to be when the temperature increases to 80 degrees Celsius?

2. **More Line of Best Fit** — The graph below is of the data we looked at on Worksheet 13.4 regarding the temperature recorded by the Weather Bureau at 8 a.m. at San Francisco, California, for the six consecutive days beginning April 6, 1908.

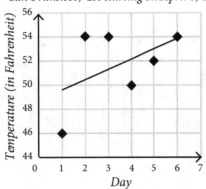
Temperature Recorded at 8 a.m. in San Fransisco, CA starting on April 6, 1908

a. We've used a computer program to find a line of best fit to describe the data. The computer program also tells us that the mathematical description of this line is $y = 0.8571x + 48.667$. Knowing this, what is the y-intercept of this line?

b. Knowing that the equation of the line is $y = 0.8571x + 48.667$, what is the slope of the line?

c. Finish filling out the right-most column, using the equation $y = 0.8571x + 48.667$ to find the temperature for each day. Notice how the value obtained from the equation varies quite significantly at times from the actual, as many of the points in this relationship did not fall near the line.

Day (represented by x)	Temperature (represented by y) in °F	Temperature from Formula ($y = 0.8571x + 48.667$) in °F
1	46	$y = 0.8571(1) + 48.667 = 49.52$
2	54	$y = 0.8571(2) + 48.667 = 50.38$
3	54	
4	50	
5	52	
6	54	

d. Based on the line of best fit, what is the general trend in temperature for these six days (upward or downward)?

e. Can we assume, based on the line of best fit, that the temperature will be warmer still on day 7? Why or why not?

Continue to Next Page

Exploring Relationships with Graphing — Let's say you want to see how far you can travel on your bike at an average speed of $10 \frac{mi}{hr}$. How far you can travel depends on how long you ride, or we could say the distance you can travel is a function of the time you spend traveling. You want to go on a trip that's between 3 and 5 hours long.

We can represent this relationship with the equation $d = (10 \frac{mi}{hr})t$, where $3 \text{ hr} \leq t \leq 5 \text{ hr}$.

a. Finish completing the table below to find coordinates to graph. Choose whole number inputs within the specified domain.

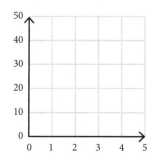

(input, in _____)	(output, in _____)

b. Finish graphing the relationship. Be sure to label the axes.

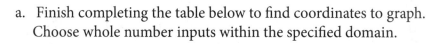

Finding the Equation — Find the equation of this line by finding the slope and y-intercept and substituting those values into the slope-intercept form.

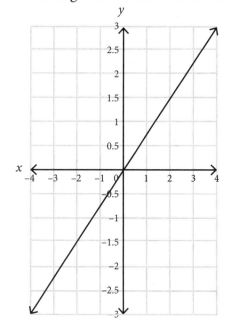

PRINCIPLES OF MATHEMATICS 2 | PAGE 203

5. **Skill Sharpening**

   a. Solve: $x + \frac{2}{7}x = 36$

   Example Meaning: One package of plates plus $\frac{2}{7}$ of a second package are enough to serve 36 people. How many plates are there in each package?

   b. To mix a specific color paint, there needs to be twice as much green paint as red paint. If you want to make a total of 6 gallons of the mixed paint, how many gallons of red paint will you need? *Hint*: Think of the red paint as x and the green paint as $2x$.

   c. In the situation described in 5b, how much green paint will you need?

   d. In the relationship graphed below, can we view y as a function of x?

   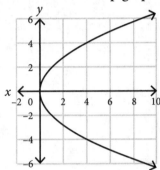

Reviewing Exponents — Worksheet 15.1

Reviewing Exponents — Use exponents to express these multiplications. Use parentheses with negative numbers or fractions, as shown in the second two examples.

Example: $2 \cdot 2 \cdot 2 = 2^3$

Example: $-7 \cdot -7 \cdot -7 = (-7)^3$

Example: $\frac{3}{5} \cdot \frac{3}{5} = (\frac{3}{5})^2$

a. $4 \cdot 4 \cdot 4$

b. $-5 \cdot -5 \cdot -5$

c. $7 \cdot 7$

d. 3 raised to the 3rd power

e. $-3 \cdot -3 \cdot -3$

f. $\frac{2}{3} \cdot \frac{2}{3} \cdot \frac{2}{3}$

More Reviewing Exponents — Convert the exponents you found in problem 1 to a single number (i.e., complete the multiplication). Be sure to watch your negative signs.

a.

b.

c.

d.

e.

f.

More Exponents — Rewrite each of these exponents as a single number.

a. 125^0

b. 15^1

c. -125^1

d. -100^0

e. 16^0

f. 60 raised to the first power

4. **Order of Operations** (🖩) — Solve.

   a. $7(4^2 + 6) + 5^2$

   b. $x \cdot 3 + 7 = 25$

   c. $2x + x \cdot 2 = 30^2$

   d. $5^2 - x = 100$

5. **Graphing Relationships** — Finish graphing this linear equation. View d as a function of t. *Hint*: Since you were told d is a function of t, view d as your dependent variable.

   $d = 6t$, where $0 \leq t \leq 10$

   Example Meaning: the distance a park train could travel at various lengths of time from 0 to 10 minutes, assuming the train travels at an average speed of $6 \ \frac{mi}{hr}$

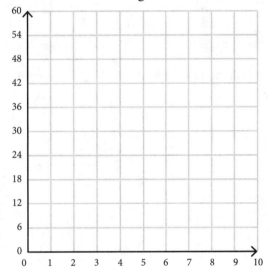

6. **Identifying Relationships**

   a. Write an equation to describe the relationship shown between the force required to move an object at a specific acceleration and the mass of an object. Notice that we're looking at force as a function of the mass of the object. *Note*: We've purposefully left off units of measure.

   b. In the equation you found in 6a, what is the slope?

   c. In the equation you found in 6a, what is the y-intercept?

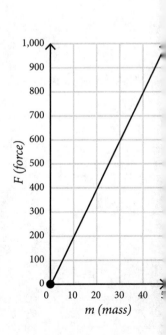

You may use a calculator on this worksheet whenever you see this symbol (🖩).

Exponents and Unknowns — Rewrite each repeated multiplication using exponents, and any repeated addition as a multiplication.

Example: $x + x = 2x$ *Example: $x \cdot x = x^2$*

a. $y \cdot y \cdot y$

b. $y + y + y$

c. $v \cdot v \cdot v \cdot v \cdot v$

d. $v + v + v + v + v$

More Exponents and Unknowns — Rewrite each exponent as repeated multiplication, and each multiplication by a coefficient as repeated addition.

Example: $2x = x + x$ *Example: $x^2 = x \cdot x$*

a. $5x$

b. x^2

c. y^5

d. $3x^2$

Evaluating Expressions — Evaluate (i.e., find the value of) these expressions for the given value of x.

a. $5x + 2$, when $x = 5$

b. $5x^2 + 2$, when $x = 5$

c. x^5, when $x = 2$

d. 5^x, when $x = 3$

e. $-r^4$, when $r = -2$

f. $(-r)^4$, when $r = -2$

Exponents of One — Just as any known quantity raised to the first power equals itself (for example, 7^1 equals 7), so any unknown raised to the first power equals itself ($x^1 = x$). Thus, we can think of any unknown without an exponent as having an exponent of 1. Rewrite each quantity below that has an exponent without an exponent, and every quantity without an exponent with an exponent of 1.

Example: $3 = 3^1$ *Example: $3^1 = 3$*
Example: $x = x^1$ *Example: $x^1 = x$*

a. $52^1 = $ _____

b. $c^1 = $ _____

c. $4 = $ ____

d. $23.5 = $ ____

e. $y = $ ____

f. $a = $ ____

5. **Geometry Time** (🖩) — Notice the exponents in the formulas for the area of a square and the volume a cube. Notice also the exponents in the units of measure in your answers.

   Area = side² or A = s²
   Volume = side³ or V = s³

   a. Find the area of a square with 8 m sides.

   b. Find the volume of a cube with 9 m sides.

   c. Find the area of a rectangle that's 6 ft long and 7 ft wide.

   d. Convert the area in 4c to square meters.

6. **Graphing Relationships** — Use graph paper to graph these linear equations. In problem 6a, view d as a function of t (thus view d as the dependent variable).

   a. $d = 40t + 60$

   Example Meaning: the relationship between distance and time, when traveling at 40 $\frac{mi}{hr}$ and starting at 60 miles

   b. $y = 7x$, where $x \geq 0$

   Example Meaning: the total cost of a trip if it costs $7 per person and x number of people come

7. **Identifying Relationships** — If 50 TVs are all purchased at the same price by a company, find the linear equation that describes the function between the total spent (t) and the cost of each TV (c), if the cost is greater than or equal to 0.

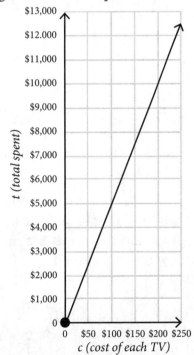

PAGE 208 | PRINCIPLES OF MATHEMATICS 2

Exponents and Graphing — The graph shows the equation $A = s^2$ (the equation for the area of a square), where $s \geq 0$. Use the graph and equation to answer the questions.

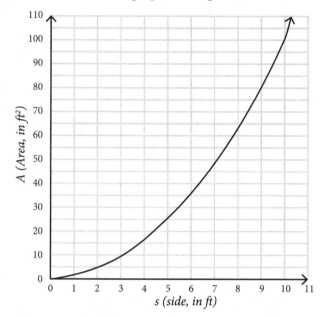

a. What is the area of a square whose sides are 5 ft?

b. What is the area of a square whose sides are 10 ft?

c. What is the y-intercept of this equation?

Skill Sharpening

a. Simplify: $25 + 3^2(12.3 + 5)$

b. Evaluate $4x^2$, when $x = 5$ m

c. Evaluate x^1, when $x = 4$

d. Simplify: $(\frac{2}{3})^2 \div (\frac{1}{4})^2$

e. Find the volume of a cube with 5 ft sides.

f. What is the volume of the cube in 2e in cubic inches?

g. In $y = 9x + 96$, what is the y-intercept?

h. In $y = 9x + 96$, what is the slope?

i. Find the equation that represents the line shown.

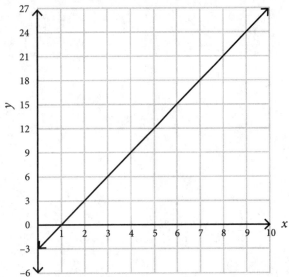

3. **More Skill Sharpening** — *Hint*: Use an exponent to simplify 3b and 3d.

   a. Simplify: $8^2 \div 2^2$

   b. Simplify: $-x \cdot -x \cdot -x$

   c. Evaluate the expression you simplified in 3b when x equals -4.

   d. Simplify: $-(x \cdot x \cdot x)$

   e. Evaluate the expression you simplified in 3d when x equals -4.

Exponents on the Calculator (🖩) — Use a calculator to simplify. Be sure to watch the order of operations where applicable.

a. 56^2

b. 101^2

c. 0.56^{20} (do not round your answer)

d. x^9, when $x = 9$

e. $5x + x^6$, when $x = 2$

f. $(-3)^6 + 56$

g. $y^2 + x^2 + 87$ in^2, when $y = 2.5$ in and $x = 1.75$ in

h. 6.25^x, when $x = 8$

i. $4(1 + 0.08)^x$, when $x = 13$

j. $5(2 + 0.68)^x$, when $x = 6$

Skill Sharpening — Simplify.

a. $x \cdot x \cdot x$

b. $-x + -x + -x$

c. x^1

Graphing Relationships — Graph these linear equations.

a. $y = 8x$

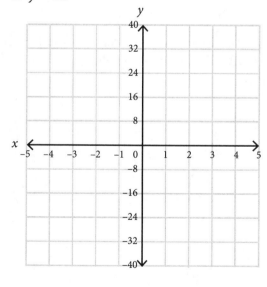

b. $y = x + 5$

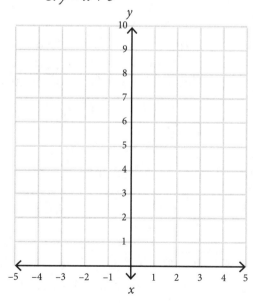

c. $y = \frac{1}{8}x$, where $x \geq 0$

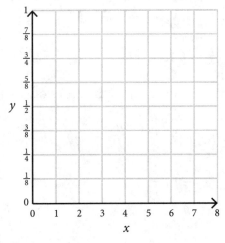

d. In the relationship in 3c, what is the y-intercept?

e. In the relationship in 3c, what is the slope?

f. In the relationship in 3b, what was the slope? *Hint*: Remember that an unknown has an assumed coefficient of 1. So you can think of x as being $1x$ in problem 3b.

4. **Identifying Relationships** — Use the graph to find an equation that expresses the relationship between purchase price (p) and amount of sales tax due (s) at a fixed sales tax rate (the rate will be the slope). We're looking at the sales tax due as a function of the purchase price.

PRINCIPLES OF MATHEMATICS 2

Exponential Growth — Pages 292–295 — Day 120 — Worksheet 15.5 — Name

You may use a calculator on this worksheet whenever you see this symbol (📱).

Exponential Growth (📱) — Use the formula $P = P_0(1 + r)^t$ to solve the following problems.

a. What will your salary be after 10 years if every year you get a 2% raise and your starting salary is $40,000 a year?

b. What will your salary be after 10 years if every year you get a 5% raise and your starting salary is $40,000 a year?

c. A store incentive program promises to increase the amount you get back in coupons by 1% every month you hold your incentive card. If you hold onto the card for 15 months, how much will you get back in coupons if when you first got the incentive card you received $60 in coupons the first month?

Graphing the Growth (📱) — This graph shows the growth of a $1,000 investment if it gains a flat $20 (which is 2% of the initial investment) a year.

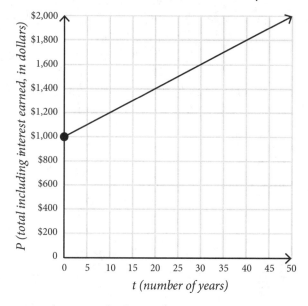

a. Is the growth shown linear? How can you tell?

b. According to the graph, what will the total including all interest earned be after 10 years?

c. What is the *y*-intercept of the line? The *y*-intercept in this case shows the starting amount invested.

d. What equation describes the line?

3. **Graphing the Growth 2** (📱) — This graph shows the growth of a $1,000 initial investment if it gains 2% a year on *both* the initial investment *and* all the previous gains.

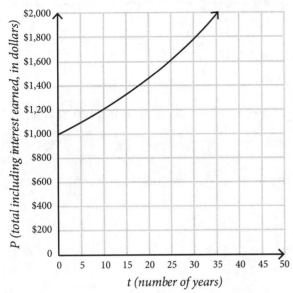

   a. Is the growth shown linear? How can you tell?

   b. This graph is showing the equation $P = \$1,000(1.02)^t$. Using the equation, calculate the total including all interest earned after 20 years.

   Most bank balances grow exponentially, although there are some ways to invest money that only grow linearly. We'll look at the difference between linear and exponential (or what we call simple and compound) interest in Chapter 19.

4. **Skill Sharpening**

   a. Simplify: $(3^2 + 5)8^2$

   b. $x^4 + y = 56$; solve for y when x is 2.

   c. Rewrite without an exponent: x^3

   d. Rewrite with an exponent: c

   e. Simplify to a decimal answer: $(\frac{2}{5})^4$

   f. Find the area of a square in square feet if the sides are 28 in long, finding the area in inches first and then converting to square feet.

PRINCIPLES OF MATHEMATICS 2 | Population Growth Pages 296–298 | Day 121 | Worksheet 15.6 | Name

You may use a calculator on this worksheet whenever you see this symbol (📱).

1. **Hypothetical Exponential Growth** (📱) — Use the formula $P = P_0(1 + r)^t$ to estimate these population growths based on purely hypothetical data.

   Round answers to the nearest whole number.

   a. If a zoo purchases 10 lizards for their rainforest exhibit, and if the lizard population grows an average of 50% a year if unchecked, about how many lizards will the zoo have after 6 years at that rate?

   b. If a mosquito population grows at the rate of 400% every month, about how many mosquitoes will a 10-mosquito population increase to over 4 months?

   c. If a pond is stocked with 100 catfish and if the population increases at a rate of 8% every year, approximately what will the population of catfish be at the end of 3 years?

2. **Identifying the Relationship** — Find the linear equation that can describe the function graphed. The graph shows how the density of a gas (ρ) in a 20 cubic meter container will vary as we put more or less of that gas (i.e., change the gases' mass, or m) into the container.

   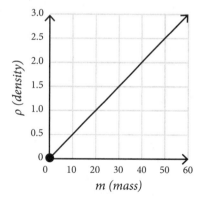

3. **Graphing the Relationship** — We've decided to build a prism that's base is a constant 10 square feet, but we want to see how changing the height affects the overall volume. Graph this linear equation showing how the volume would change as we adjust the height (that is, look at volume as a function of the height $V = Bh$, where $h > 0$ and given that $B = 10$ ft^2

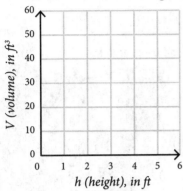

4. **Skill Sharpening** (🖩)

   a. Simplify: $5 - (2^3 + x) = 400$

   b. Evaluate $y^2 + 8^3 \cdot 1$ ft^2, when $y = 25$ ft

   c. Simplify: 152^1

Exponential Decay and Vitamins (🖩) — Use the formula $P = P_0(1 + r)^t$ to estimate these decays if you're told that vitamin C leaves your blood stream at a rate of about 2.28% per minute. *Hint*: Since the vitamin C is *leaving* the blood stream, it's *decreasing*, and thus 2.28% is a *negative rate*.

a. About how much vitamin C will you have left in the blood stream from a 1,000 mg pill after 30 minutes?

b. About how much vitamin C will you have left in the blood stream from a 1,000 mg pill after 240 minutes (4 hours)?

Drawing Conclusions – Because vitamin C leaves the blood stream so quickly, some claim you'll see better results from smaller doses administered more frequently, as that will keep the levels in your blood stream higher for a longer period of time.[1]

Eating Fresh and Nutrition Decay — Sometimes, we're not given an exponential rate or told if decay is exponential. Instead, we're only told what the decay is after a specific period of time. In these situations, we're dealing with a straightforward percent problem. Dust off your basic percent skills to answer these questions.

a. Suppose you're told that safflower oil has 4.6 mg of vitamin E per serving. You're also told that safflower oil loses about 55% of its vitamin E after three months. If that's the case, about how much vitamin E will be left per serving after 3 months?[2] *Hint*: If 55% is lost, what percent is left?

b. An article from the *Chicago Tribune* has this title: "Most produce loses 30 percent of nutrients three days after harvest."[3] If a vegetable that loses 30 percent of its nutrients after 3 days starts with 30 mg of a vitamin, how much of that vitamin will it have at the end of 3 days?

Drawing Conclusions – Nutrients decay at different rates. The claim that "most produce loses 30 percent of nutrients three days after harvest" is a broad generalization about nutrient loss. It does not mean that all nutrients in all fruits and vegetables decay at this rate. In fact, before making decisions based on this claim, you'd want to know how many produce were tested (and what kinds), what nutrients were tracked, etc.

Knowledge of Health, Inc., *Linus Pauling Vindicated; Researchers Claim RDA For Vitamin C Is Flawed* (2004), http://www.prnewswire.com/news-releases/linus-pauling-vindicated-researchers-claim-rda-for-vitamin-c-is-flawed-71172707.html, accessed 10/20/15.

Realfoodnutrients.com, "What You Can Do to Boost the Effectiveness of Vitamin C," Newsletter Issue 22 (Wellness Support Network), http://www.realfoodnutrients.com/NewsletterArticles/WhatYouCanDotoBoosttheEffectivenessofVitaminC.htm, accessed 2/1/16.

Decay after 3 months is based on Paul M Insel, R. Elaine Turner, and Don Ross, *Discovering Nutrition*, 3rd ed. (Sudbury, MA: Jones and Bartlett Publishers, 2010), p. 342. Found on Google Books.

Monica Eng, "Most Produce Loses 30 Percent Of Nutrients Three Days After Harvest," July 10, 2013, *Chicago Tribune*, 2015, http://articles.chicagotribune.com/2013-07-10/features/chi-most-produce-loses-30-percent-of-nutrients-three-days-after-harvest-20130710_1_harvest-farmers-vitamin-c, accessed 10/20/15.

3. **Radiometric Dating**

   a. List at least two assumptions that go into radiometric dating.

   b. What's one way radiometric dating differs from observations we make about the exponential decay in bacteria, vitamins, etc.?

4. **Out of the Box: Radiometric Dating** — Watch "Does Radiometric Dating Prove the Earth Is Old?" (It's only 3 minutes and 53 seconds!) or read the article by the same name. Both are currently available at www.answersingenesis.org (see footnote[4]). Write down one tidbit from the video or article. *Note*: Should these resources no longer be available, use any resource on radiometric dating from a biblical worldview. Answers in Genesis (www.answersingenesis.org) has many from which to choose.

---

[4] Article: Mike Riddle, "Does Radiometric Dating Prove the Earth Is Old?" in *The New Answers Book* (Green Forest, AR: Master Books, 2007), available online at https://answersingenesis.org/geology/radiometric-dating/does-radiometric-dating-prove-the-earth-is-old/, accessed 10/20/15. Video: Dr. Andrew A. Snelling, "Does Radiometric Dating Prove the Earth Is Old?" (KY: Answers in Genesis), available online at https://answersingenesis.org/answers-bible-curriculum/media-supplements/does-radiometric-dating-prove-earth-old/, accessed 10/20/15.

Exponents in Action — Use exponents to express these probability calculations more concisely.

Example: $\frac{1}{2} \cdot \frac{1}{2} = \frac{1}{2^2}$

a. $\frac{1}{10} \cdot \frac{1}{10} \cdot \frac{1}{10} \cdot \frac{1}{10}$

Example Meaning: Suppose there's a $\frac{1}{10}$ probability of spinning a specific number on each spin. Assuming each spin has the same probability, what's the probability of spinning that number on four spins in a row?

b. $\frac{1}{3 \cdot 3 \cdot 3}$

Example Meaning: Suppose a pea is hidden underneath a paper cup. There are 3 paper cups in the first row, 3 in the second row, and 3 in the third row. What is the probability that the pea is hidden underneath a specific paper cup?

c. $\frac{1}{4} \cdot \frac{1}{4} \cdot \frac{1}{4} \cdot \frac{1}{4} \cdot \frac{1}{4} \cdot \frac{1}{4}$

Example Meaning: In a game, if there are 4 possible results you could get when spinning, what's the probability of landing on the same result 6 spins in a row?

2. **Finding the Probabilities** (🖩) — Go back and calculate the probability for 1a–1c.

   a.   b.

   c.

3. **Find the Value** (🖩) — Convert each expression to a decimal number.

   Example: $\frac{9}{5^2} = \frac{9}{25} = 0.36$

   a. $\frac{7}{3^2}$

   b. $\frac{60}{2^4}$

   c. $\frac{6}{4^2}$

   d. $\frac{3}{5^1}$

4. **Spheres** (🖩) — The volume of a sphere is found using this formula:

   $V = \frac{4}{3}\pi r^3$ (i.e., $Volume = \frac{4}{3} \cdot \pi \cdot radius^3$)

   a. A soccer ball is basically a sphere. If a ball's radius is 4.3 in, what is its volume?

   b. A basketball is basically a sphere. If its diameter is 9.5 in, what is its volume?
   Hint: Find the radius first.

5. **Identifying the Relationship** — Write the equation that describes the function graphed.

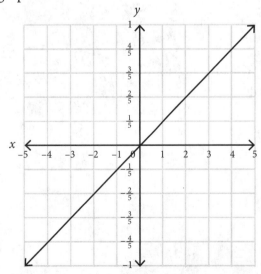

PAGE 220 | PRINCIPLES OF MATHEMATICS 2

1. **Negative Exponents** — Remember, a negative exponent is another way of writing the multiplicative inverse of the base raised to that power. Knowing this, rewrite each expression using only a positive exponent.

   Example: $8^{-2} = \frac{1}{8^2}$

   a. 2^{-3}

   b. 4^{-6}

   c. 2^{-5}

   d. s^{-2}

2. **Using Negative Exponents** — Rewrite each expression using a negative exponent. Notice that 2a, b, and c are the probabilities you simplified in problem 1 of Worksheet 16.1. Negative exponents give us another way of representing the repeated multiplication.

   Example: $\frac{1}{8^2} = 8^{-2}$

   a. $\frac{1}{10^4}$

   b. $\frac{1}{3^3}$

   c. $\frac{1}{4^6}$

   d. $\frac{1}{x^4}$

3. **Exponents on a Calculator** (🖩) — Use a calculator to find these values. Do not round (list the entire answer your calculator displays).

   a. 7^{-5}

   b. 6^6

   c. 7^{-4}

   d. $(-8)^6$

   e. $-(8^6)$

   f. 3 raised to the negative 9th power

PRINCIPLES OF MATHEMATICS 2 | PAGE 221

4. **More Exponents on a Calculator** (🖩)

    a. Evaluate x^5, when $x = -2$

    b. Evaluate x^{-1}, when $x = 2$

5. **Understanding Check** — What does the negative sign in front of an exponent mean?

Negative Exponents — Remember, a negative exponent is another way of writing *the multiplicative inverse* of the base raised to that power. Knowing this, rewrite each expression using a positive exponent.

Example: $8^{-2} = \frac{1}{8^2}$

a. 3^{-6}

b. 2^{-5}

c. 4^{-2}

d. 25.6^{-3}

More Negative Exponents — Simplify. Give your answer as a fraction.

Example: $2 \cdot 3^{-3} = 2 \cdot \frac{1}{3 \cdot 3 \cdot 3} = \frac{2}{27}$

a. $4 \cdot 10^{-2}$

b. $3 \cdot 10^{-5}$

c. $5 \cdot 6^{-2}$

d. $2 \cdot 3^{-1}$

Even More Negative Exponents — Evaluate for the given value of *x*. Give your answer as a fraction.

a. $2x^{-2}$, when $x = 4$

b. $5x^{-3}$, when $x = 2$

4. **Kepler's Third Law (🖩)**— Kepler's third law of planetary motion describes the fact that if we examine the ratio between the time it takes a planet to complete an orbit and a specific measurement regarding a planet's orbit size (the semimajor axis), we find that the ratio is always approximately the same:

$$\frac{(\text{time to complete an orbit})^2}{(\text{semimajor axis})^3} \quad \text{or} \quad \frac{T^2}{a^3}$$

Check it out by calculating this ratio yourself for some planets. Do not round.

a. Earth

   time to complete an orbit = 1

   semimajor axis = 1

b. Jupitor

   time to complete an orbit = 11.86 years

   semimajor axis = 5.2

c. Mars

   time to complete an orbit = 1.88

   semimajor axis = 1.52

Take a moment to reflect on the reality that because of the consistent way God holds this universe together, planets orbit in a consistent, predictable fashion.

The heavens declare the glory of God; and the firmament sheweth his handywork (Psalm 19:1).

Many, O LORD my God, are thy wonderful works which thou hast done, and thy thoughts which are to us-ward: they cannot be reckoned up in order unto thee: if I would declare and speak of them, they are more than can be numbered (Psalm 40:5).

Multiplying by a Power of 10 — Rewrite each exponent as multiplication and then complete the multiplication to convert to decimal notation. Do not round.

Example: $5 \times 10^{-2} = 5 \cdot \dfrac{1}{10} \cdot \dfrac{1}{10} = \dfrac{5}{100} = 0.05$

a. 7×10^4

b. 7×10^2

c. 7×10^{-4}

d. 7×10^{-2}

Converting to Scientific Notation — Represent these numbers using scientific notation.

a. 450

b. 7,240

c. 0.045

d. 0.00724

e. 5,906,400,000 km
(distance from Pluto to the sun)[1]

f. 0.0000005234
(possible size of a bacteria)

Skill Sharpening — Give all answers as in fractional form, simplified as much as possible.

a. What does 6^{-2} equal?

b. What does 7^{-2} equal?

c. What does 3^{-3} equal?

See Dr. David R. Williams, "Planetary Fact Sheet — Metric" and "Sun Fact Sheet" (NASA Goddard Space Flight Center, 07/17/15 update), http://nssdc.gsfc.nasa.gov/planetary/factsheet/.

Powers of 10

a. What does 10^{-5} equal? Give the answer as a decimal; do not round.

b. What does 10^5 equal?

Applying Scientific Notation[1] — Represent these numbers using scientific notation. *Note*: We've purposefully left off units of measure on units we haven't covered.

a. 4,870,000,000,000,000,000,000,000 kg (mass of Venus)

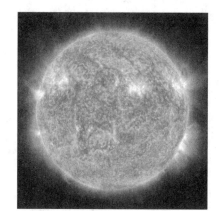

b. 1,988,500,000,000,000,000,000,000,000,000 kg (mass of the sun)

c. 108,200,000 km (distance from Venus to the sun)

d. 0.0000000000667408 (Newtonian constant of gravitation)

e. 0.000000000008854187817 (electric constant)

More Applying Scientific Notation — Convert these problems from scientific notation to standard decimal notation. Do not round. *Note*: We've purposefully left off units of measure on units we haven't covered.

a. 2.99792458×10^8 meters per second (speed of light in a vacuum)

b. $6.022140857 \times 10^{23}$ (Avogadro constant)

c. 5.670367×10^{-8} (Stefan-Boltzmann constant)

d. 1.59×10^{-8} (resistivity of silver)

e. 1.6×10^{-19} (charge of a proton)

Stop for a moment and think about the numbers you've been writing today. God holds both the vast expanses of space and the tiniest particles together. And that same mighty God came and took the penalty our sin deserved.

"O LORD, our Lord, how excellent is thy name in all the earth! who hast set thy glory above the heavens. Out of the mouth of babes and sucklings hast thou ordained strength because of thine enemies, that thou mightest still the enemy and the avenger. When I consider thy heavens, the work of thy fingers, the moon and the stars, which thou hast ordained; what is man, that thou art mindful of him? and the son of man, that thou visitest him?" (Psalm 8:1–4).

Performing Operations in Scientific Notation on a Calculator

Worksheet 16.4 — Day 129 — Pages 313–314

You may use a calculator on this worksheet whenever you see this symbol (🖩).

On a Calculator (🖩) — Perform these multiplications on a calculator. Write the answers in scientific notation, rounded to two decimal places (when written in scientific notation).

a. 251,136,000 • 562,048,200

b. 0.00000012 • 0.000369874

c. $6(2.99792458 \times 10^8)$

   Example Meaning: 6 times the speed of light in a vacuum

d. $2.5(6.67408 \times 10^{-11})$

   Example Meaning: 2.5 times the gravitational constant.

Probability Review (🖩) — Suppose 15 different letters (the letters A–O) are placed inside a hat. The probability of picking all of the letters in order is thus $\frac{1}{15!}$ (that is, 1 divided by 15 factorial, or $\frac{1}{15 \cdot 14 \cdot 13 \cdot 12 \cdot 11 \cdot 10 \cdot 9 \cdot 8 \cdot 7 \cdot 6 \cdot 5 \cdot 4 \cdot 3 \cdot 2 \cdot 1}$). Use your calculator to find the decimal equivalent of $\frac{1}{15!}$. Give the answer in scientific notation.

Scientific Notation, Graphs, and Stats (🖩) — As we've mentioned before, we can use programs like Microsoft Excel to analyze many different aspects of data. Sometimes when analyzing data we end up with really small or really large numbers, which Excel shows in — you guessed it — scientific notation. The numbers below are in a format you might encounter when analyzing data. See if you can understand them. Do not round the answers.

a. What number (in scientific notation) is 5.772E–06 representing?

b. Rewrite 5.772E–06 in decimal notation.

c. What number (in scientific notation) is 2.67616E–05 representing?

d. Rewrite 2.67616E–05 in decimal notation.

e. If a computer program shows the line of best fit for a graph as
   $y = 3.20238\text{E}{-}05(x) + -0.128571429$, what is the slope in scientific notation?

f. What is the slope in 3e in decimal notation?

4. **Exploring Energy** (🖩) — One of the most famous equations in math is Einstein's $E = mc^2$. The E represents energy, the m mass (similar to weight), and the c the speed of light (299,792,458 meters per second). While the details of the equation are beyond the scope of this course, it basically shows a relationship between energy and mass — in other words, that matter has the potential for tremendous energy.

   Solve these problems by substituting the given values into $E = mc^2$. Notice the scientific notation you encounter. Your answers will all be in a unit called joules (a joule is the result of multiplying kilograms by meters per second).

   Do not round; list all the digits your calculator displays.

   a. Find the energy of a substance with a mass of 1 kilogram.

   b. Find the energy of a substance with a mass of 45 kilogram.

Albert Einstein (1879–1955)

5. **Understanding Check**

   a. What does $3 \cdot 6^{-3}$ equal? Give the answer as a fraction, simplified as much as possible.

   b. Rewrite $\frac{1}{6^4}$ using a negative exponent.

More with Combining Like Terms

Worksheet 16.5 — Day 130 — Pages 314–316

You may use a calculator on this worksheet whenever you see this symbol (🖩).

Combining Like Terms — Simplify by combining like terms where possible. If you cannot simplify, write "cannot be simplified."

a. $4x^2 + x^2$

b. $2x^3 + 2x^2 + 3x^2$

c. $2x^2 + x$

d. $y^3 + 3y^3$

Converting to Scientific Notation — Rewrite these numbers in scientific notation. Do not round.

a. 0.000569

b. 187,256,230,000

c. 0.00000897

d. 15,425,630,000,000

Operations in Scientific Notation (🖩) — Use a calculator to solve. Give your answer in scientific notation.

a. 1.75×10^{-15} m + 1.75×10^{-15} m

Example Meaning: the approximate length of two protons, side by side. *Note:* Scientists are still studying and learning about protons — they may actually be smaller than this!

b. 1.5×10^8 km − 1.08×10^8 km

Example Meaning: the approximate distance between Earth and Venus, as found by subtracting Venus's average distance from the sun from earth's average distance from the sun, when both are rounded to the nearest hundred thousand[1]

c. 2×10^{-3} m + 8×10^{-4} m

Example Meaning: the length of a larger and smaller grain of sand added together

Think of the size of a grain of sand presented in problem 3c and how many tiny grains fill the shores. Then take a look at this Psalm and ponder again God's incredible greatness and love.

> *How precious also are thy thoughts unto me, O God! how great is the sum of them! If I should count them, they are more in number than the sand: when I awake, I am still with thee (Psalm 139:17–18).*

Based on Dr. David R. Williams, "Planetary Fact Sheet ' Metric," (NASA Goddard Space Flight Center, 07/17/15 update), http://nssdc.gsfc.nasa.gov/planetary/factsheet/.

4. **Exploring Relationships** (🖩) — Graph $a = -12t$; view a as a function of t

   Example Meaning: The relationship between altitude and time if you're changing altitude at a consistent −12 meters per second and start at sea level

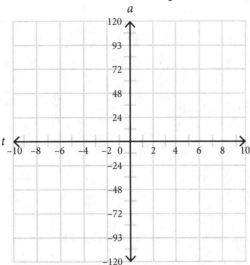

5. **Identifying the Relationship** (🖩)

   a. Use the slope-intercept formula to find the equation that describes the line shown.

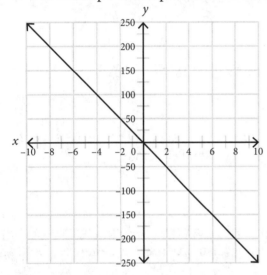

   b. What is one thing the relationship graphed in 5a could represent? *Hint*: Look at the example meaning in problem 4 for an idea.

6. **Skill Sharpening** — Give all answers as in fractional form, simplified as much as possible.

   a. What does 3^{-5} equal?
   b. What does 2^{-5} equal?

PRINCIPLES OF MATHEMATICS 2 — More with Multiplication and Division, Pages 316–319 — Day 131 — Worksheet 16.6

You may use a calculator on this worksheet whenever you see this symbol (🖩).

Understanding the Process — Rewrite each of these expressions as multiplication; do not use exponents.

Example: $5^2 \cdot 5^6 = (5 \cdot 5) \cdot (5 \cdot 5 \cdot 5 \cdot 5 \cdot 5 \cdot 5)$

a. $2^2 \cdot 2^5$

b. $\dfrac{4^3}{4^2}$

More Understanding the Process — Simplify the multiplications you wrote in problems 1a and 1b into a single number raised to a power. Notice how you could have obtained this same value by adding (in 1a) or subtracting (in 1b) the exponents in the original expression.

Example: $(5 \cdot 5) \cdot (5 \cdot 5 \cdot 5 \cdot 5 \cdot 5 \cdot 5) = 5^8$

(We could have obtained 5^8 by adding the exponents (2 and 6) in $5^2 \cdot 5^6$, like this: $5^2 \cdot 5^6 = 5^{2+6} = 5^8$.)

a.

b.

Multiplying and Dividing Unknowns with Exponents — Simplify these expressions. If the base is not the same, write "cannot be simplified."

a. $a^3 a^2$

b. $\dfrac{a^3}{a^2}$

c. $\dfrac{a^3}{v^2}$

d. $v^2 v^7$

4. **Geometry Time** — Find the requested information. Notice how you're working with exponents as you work with units of measure.

   a. Rewrite the formula for finding the volume of a rectangular prism or a cylinder ($V = Bh$) to solve for h.

   b. Use the formula you rewrote in 4a to find the height of a rectangular prism whose volume is 89 ft³ and whose base has an area of 40 ft².

   c. If the area of the base of a cylinder is 40 ft² and its height is 8 ft, what is its volume?

   d. Convert 4,000 ft³ to cubic yards.

5. **Operations with Scientific Notation** (🖩) — Part of the calculation of finding the gravitational force between the earth and the moon involves multiplying the mass of the earth by the mass of the moon. Give it a try yourself. The mass of the earth is approximately 5.97×10^{24}, and the mass of the moon is approximately 7.3×10^{22}. What is the product of their masses? Round your answer to the second decimal place (when written in scientific notation).

6. **Skill Sharpening**

   a. What does 9^{-2} equal? Give your answer as a fraction, simplified as much as possible.

   b. Rewrite 2.5×10^{-6} in decimal notation. Do not round.

   c. Simplify: $5x^2 + 2x^2$

PAGE 234 | PRINCIPLES OF MATHEMATICS 2

Probability

a. If you're rolling an 8-sided dice, one side of which has a circle, what's the probability of rolling a circle? (Lesson 12.1)

b. On the dice described in 1a, what's the probability of rolling a circle 3 times in a row? (Lesson 12.3)

c. Is the event in problem 1b an example of an independent event or a dependent event? (Lessons 12.3 and 12.4)

d. If it's 60% probable that there will be precipitation, what is the probability that there won't be any precipitation? (Lesson 12.2)

e. If John enters his name 2 times into a drawing, what is the probability that his name will be chosen on the first draw if there are 50 entries altogether? (Lesson 12.1)

f. In the situation described in 1e, suppose more than one prize is being awarded, but once an entry is chosen it is removed from the entries for the next prize. What is the probability that John's name will be chosen for the first *and* the second prize? (Lesson 12.4)

g. Is the event in problem 1f an example of an independent event or a dependent event? (Lessons 12.3 and 12.4)

h. What is the probability of randomly guessing a 4-digit bike lock code on the first try if each digit could contain only the 10 digits 0–9? (Lesson 12.5)

2. **Coordinate Graphing and Travel** (🖩) — Graph these linear equations. View d (the distance) as a function of t (the time) to see how the distance changes over time. (Lessons 14.2 and 14.3)

   a. $d = 10t$, where $t > 0$

   Example Meaning: the distance traveled over time at a speed of $10 \frac{\text{mi}}{\text{hr}}$

   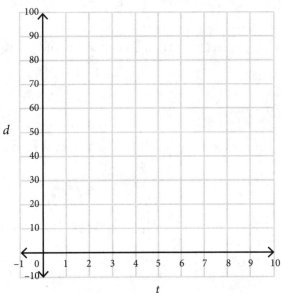

   b. $d = 30t$, where $t > 0$

   Example Meaning: the distance traveled over time at a speed of $30 \frac{\text{mi}}{\text{hr}}$

   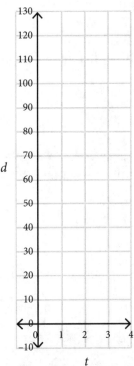

Continue to Next Page

c. $d = 30t + 10$, where $t > 0$

Example Meaning: the distance traveled over time at a speed of $30 \frac{mi}{hi}$ when starting at 10 miles

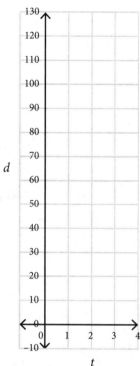

Graphing Money Loss (▦) — Graph this linear equation: $s = -\$10t$, where $t > 0$. View s (money spent) as a function of t (the time) to see how much money is spent over time if you spend $10 a day. Notice that the negative sign represents *the opposite of* gaining $10 (i.e., losing, or spending, $10).

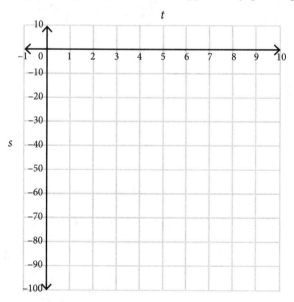

4. **Understanding Relationships**

    a. A function is a relationship, or relation, in which for each input there's only _____ output. (Lesson 13.4)

    b. In this graph of a hypothetical plant's growth over time, can we think of the growth as a function of time? Why or why not? (Lesson 13.4, Appendix B/Reference Sheets)

    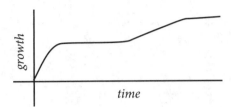

    c. In this graph, can we think of y as a function of x? Why or why not? (Lesson 13.4, Appendix B/Reference Sheets)

    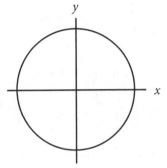

    d. In problem 2c, what did we view as the variables? (Lesson 13.1)

    e. In problem 2c, what did we view as the constants? (Lesson 13.1)

    f. What was the domain of problem 2c? (Lesson 13.5)

    g. What was the slope of problem 2c? (Lesson 14.5)

    h. What was the y-intercept of problem 2c? (Lesson 14.4)

    i. What was the y-intercept of problem 2b? (Lesson 14.4)

5. **Supports per Tree** (🖩) — Suppose we are planting trees and need 4 tree supports per tree. If we use s to represent the number of supports and t to represent the number of trees, we'd have this linear equation: $s = 4t$, where $t \geq 0$. Use graph paper to graph this function; view s as the dependent variable (i.e., the output). (Lessons 14.2 and 14.3)

Continue to Next Page

Identifying Equations (🖩) — The milligrams of a specific chemical needed for a hypothetical experiment is a function of the number of students performing the experiment. The graph to the right shows the relationship.

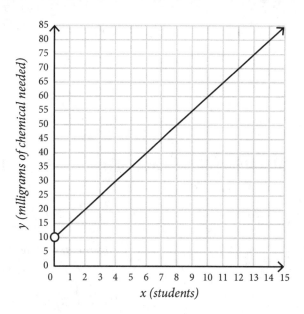

a. What is the y-intercept of the line? (Lesson 14.4)

b. What is the slope of the line? (Lesson 14.5)

c. What is the equation that describes this line? (Lesson 14.6)

Exponent Time — Simplify, or write "cannot be simplified." (Lessons 15.1, 15.2, 16.1, 16.2, 16.5, and 16.6)

a. 78^0

b. 4^{-3} (Give your answer as a fraction.)

c. $4 + 5 \cdot 20^1$

d. $\frac{1}{5^3}$ (Give your answer as a fraction.)

e. $2 \cdot 8 \cdot 6^4$

f. $v^2 v^6$

g. $\frac{v^8}{v^4}$

h. $v^2 d^3$

i. $x^2 + 3x^2$

j. $x^2 + x$

Exponents on a Calculator (🖩) — Simplify. Give all your answers in scientific notation, rounded to the second decimal. (Lessons 16.3, 16.6, and the other lessons marked)

a. $4(2 + 3)^8$ (Lesson 15.4)

b. $15(8 + 0.03)^{25}$ (Lesson 15.4)

c. 9^{-7} (Lesson 16.2)

d. $4.2 \times 10^5 \cdot 2.3 \times 10^2$ (Lesson 16.4)

PRINCIPLES OF MATHEMATICS 2 | PAGE 239

9. **Finding Unknowns with Exponents** (🖩) — Solve. (Lessons 15.1 and 16.2)

    a. $x + (-5)^3 = 50$

    b. $x + 2^{-3} = 25$

10. **Volume of the Earth** (🖩) — Use the two formulas given below to answer the questions. (Lessons 15.2 and 16.3; Worksheet 16.1)

    $$V = \frac{4}{3}\pi r^3$$

    (Volume of a sphere = $\frac{4}{3} \cdot \pi \cdot$ radius^3)

    $$C = 2\pi r$$

    (Circumference of a circle = $2 \cdot \pi \cdot r$)

    a. The earth is a sphere with a circumference at the equator of 24,873.6 mi. What is the earth's radius?[1]

    b. Use the radius you found in 10a to find the volume of the earth in cubic miles. Write your answer in scientific notation, rounded to the second decimal place when written in scientific notation.

11. **Population Growth** (🖩) — Use the formula $P = P_0(1 + r)^t$ to find the approximate ending population (P) after 60 months of a certain type of beetle that starts with a population of 4 if they grow at a rate of about 4% a month. Round to the nearest whole number. (Lesson 15.6)

---

[1] We used the equatorial circumference value listed on NASA, "Earth: By the Numbers," Solar System Exploration (beta), http://solarsystem.nasa.gov/planets/earth/facts, accessed 11/09/15.

Square Roots
Pages 321–323 — Day 136 — Worksheet 17.1

You may use a calculator on this worksheet whenever you see this symbol (🖩).

Understanding Check

a. What is a square root?

b. True or false: The square root of a positive number could be either positive or negative.

c. In this course, unless instructed otherwise, when finding a square root, you should assume _____.

Finding the Square Root (🖩) — Factor to find the requested square roots. List all of the prime factors as part of your answer. You may use a calculator to help you factor, but do not use the calculator's square root or root buttons.

a. $\sqrt{25}$

b. $\sqrt{196}$

c. $\sqrt{441}$

d. $\sqrt{900}$

e. $\sqrt{x}$, when x equals 121

Skill Sharpening (🖩)

a. Simplify, giving your answer in scientific notation (do not round): $4 \times 10^2 - 3 \times 10^{-1}$

b. Convert 2.67×10^{-5} to decimal notation. Do not round.

c. Simplify: $4x^2 + x^2$

d. Simplify: $4x^2 x^2$

e. Simplify: $\dfrac{y^3}{y^2}$

f. What does 4^{-2} equal? Give your answer as a fraction, simplified as much as possible.

g. What does 2^{-3} equal? Give your answer as a fraction, simplified as much as possible.

Worksheet 17.2

Square Roots and Unknowns (and Squaring Both Sides of an Equation) — Day 137 — Pages 323–325

You may use a calculator on this worksheet whenever you see this symbol (🖩).

Rewriting with Exponents — Rewrite each of these square roots using exponents. Solve.

Example: $\sqrt{64} = \sqrt{8^2} = 8$

a. $\sqrt{49}$

b. $\sqrt{25}$

c. $\sqrt{81}$

d. $\sqrt{100}$

Finding the Square Root of Squares

Example: $\sqrt{x^2} = x$

a. $\sqrt{12^2}$

b. $\sqrt{3.5^2}$

c. $\sqrt{y^2}$

d. $\sqrt{c^2}$

Squaring a Square Root — Simplify. *Hint*: Remember, a square root means a number that, times itself, equals the quantity under the √ sign. So when we square a square root (i.e., multiply it by itself), we end up with the number under the square root sign.

Example: $(\sqrt{8})^2 = \sqrt{8} \cdot \sqrt{8} = 8$

a. $(\sqrt{64})^2$

b. $(\sqrt{21})^2$

c. $(\sqrt{101})^2$

d. $(\sqrt{x})^2$

Squaring Both Sides of an Equation — Find these unknowns by squaring both sides of these equations.

a. $\sqrt{x} = 9$

b. $\sqrt{x} = 4$

c. $\sqrt{x} = 2$

d. $\sqrt{x} = 5$

5. **Checking Your Work** — Go back and check your work in problems 4a–4d by substituting the value you obtained for x into the original equation. Show your work.

   a.

   b.

   c.

   d.

6. **Factoring** (🖩) — Factor to find the square root of 484. List all the prime factors as part of your answer. You may use a calculator, but do not use the calculator's square root or root buttons.

7. **Skill Sharpening** (🖩)
   a. Simplify, giving your answer in scientific notation (do not round): $4.7 \times 10^{-5} + 5.2 \times 10^{-4}$

   Example Meaning: the mass of two tiny particles added together

   b. Rewrite 4.2×10^{-7} in decimal notation. Do not round.

   c. Simplify: $(7a)(3a)(2a^2)$ *Hint*: Even though you've not seen a problem just like this one before, you have all the skills you need. Remember, multiplication is commutative and associative, so you can multiply in any order. Remember also that $a = a^1$.

   d. Simplify: $\frac{7a^2}{a^2}$ *Hint*: Again, you've not seen a problem exactly like this before, but you have the skills you need.

Worksheet 17.3 — Taking the Square Root of Both Sides

You may use a calculator on this worksheet whenever you see this symbol (🖩).

Taking the Square Root of Both Sides — Find the unknown by taking the square root of both sides of these equations.

a. $y^2 = 16$

b. $v^2 = 169$

c. If a square has an area of 256 in², what length is its sides?

Checking Your Work — Go back and check your work in problems 1a–1c by substituting the value you obtained for *x* into the original equation. Show your work.

a.

b.

c.

Origami Paper Size — If you need a square piece of paper with an area of 144 in² to make a specific origami pattern, what length should you make each side of the paper? *Hint*: The area of a square equals the length of one of the sides squared ($A = s^2$).

Skill Sharpening (🖩) — Do not round your answers.

a. Find the square root of 576 by factoring. List the prime factors as part of your answer. Do not use a calculator's square root or root buttons.

b. Solve: $\sqrt{v} = 60$

c. Solve: $2x^2 = 32$ *Hint*: This is another type of problem you've not seen before, but you have all the skills you need. Divide *both* sides by 2 and then take the square root of *both* sides to find *x*.

d. Simplify, giving your answer in scientific notation: $\dfrac{4 \times 10^{-3}}{2 \times 10^{5}}$

PRINCIPLES OF MATHEMATICS 2 | Approximating Square Roots and Finding Square Roots on a Calculator | Pages 327–328 | Day 139 | Worksheet 17.4 | Name

You may use a calculator on this worksheet whenever you see this symbol (🖩).

Approximating the Square Root — Between what two integers are each of these square roots?

Example: $\sqrt{18}$ = between 4 and 5

(4 • 4 is 16, and 5 • 5 is 25, so $\sqrt{18}$ is between 4 and 5.)

a. $\sqrt{83}$

b. $\sqrt{75}$

More Approximating the Square Root (🖩) — Between what two integers are each of these square roots? You may use a calculator to help, but do not use the square root or root buttons.

Example: $\sqrt{250}$ = between 15 and 16

(15 • 15 is 225, and 16 • 16 is 256, so $\sqrt{250}$ is between 15 and 16.)

a. $\sqrt{475}$

b. $\sqrt{580}$

Finding the Square Root with a Calculator (🖩) — Use the square root button to find an exact square root.

a. $\sqrt{420}$

b. $\sqrt{800}$

c. $\sqrt{1,265}$

Square Roots Applied (🖩)

a. If $c^2 = 780$, what does c equal?

b. If a square has an area of 108 in², what is the length of each side?

c. If a square has an area of 674 m², what is the length of each side?

5. **Skill Sharpening**
    a. Convert to scientific notation (do not round): 0.000005678

    b. Solve: $x \cdot x = 64$

    c. Simplify: $2x^2 + 4x^2$

    d. Simplify: $x^4 x^6$

    e. Factor to find the $\sqrt{1{,}225}$. List all of the prime factors as part of your answer.

5. **Out of the Box: History of the Calculator** — Research the history of calculators online or in an encyclopedia and write down one fact you discovered.

You may use a calculator on this worksheet whenever you see this symbol (🖩).

Right Triangles — Circle all the right triangles shown (i.e., the triangles with a 90° angle). Put a star next to the legs and a dot next to the hypotenuse of each right triangle.

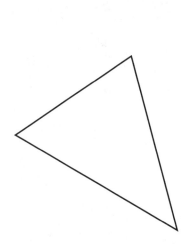 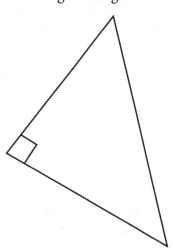 

Pythagorean Theorem (🖩) — Find the hypotenuse of these right triangles using the Pythagorean theorem.

a.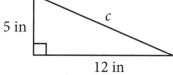

b.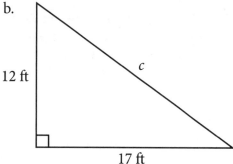

c.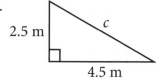

d. A right triangle with 7 in and 9 in legs

e. A right triangle with 6 m and 10 m legs

f. A right triangle with sides 8 m and 15 m long

3. **Navigation**[1] (🖩)

   a. Suppose a sailor needs to travel to a location 5 miles to the south and 3 miles to the west of his current location. If he takes a diagonal line to that location, how far will he need to travel? *Hint*: Notice from the picture that we can think of the diagonal as the hypotenuse of a right triangle of which the sides are the distances south and west.

   Use the Pythagorean theorem to find the hypotenuse, which in this case would find the distance the sailor needs to travel.

   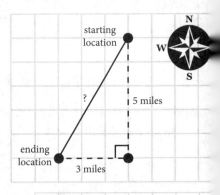

   b. Suppose a sailor traveled 9 miles north and then 2 miles east. How far would it be to take a diagonal line back to his starting location?

   c. How much shorter is it for the sailor in 3b to take a diagonal line than it would be to go back 9 miles south and 2 miles west (i.e., to travel along legs of the triangle instead of traveling along the hypotenuse)?

4. **Baseball** (🖩) — If the distance between bases on a baseball diamond is 90 feet, how far is the throw from first base to third? *Hint*: You're trying to find the distance marked c in the picture.

   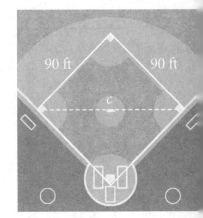

5. **Skill Sharpening** (🖩)

   a. Simplify: $5.79 \times 10^{29} + 6.5 \times 10^{25}$

      Example Meaning: the sum of two distances in outer space

   b. Find the two integers between which this square root lies; do not use the calculator's root or square root buttons: $\sqrt{640}$

   c. Simplify, leaving your answer as a base raised to a power: $5^6(5^8)$

   d. Simplify: $x^6 x^8$

   e. Factor to find the $\sqrt{1{,}296}$. List all of the prime factors as part of your answer. You may use a calculator to help you factor, but do not use the calculator's square root or root buttons.

---

[1] Problem adapted from Katherine Loop, *Revealing Arithmetic: Math Concepts from a Biblical Worldview* (Fairfax, VA: Christian Perspective, 2010). Used with permission.

| PRINCIPLES OF MATHEMATICS 2 | More with the Pythagorean Theorem Pages 333–334 | Day 142 | Worksheet 17.6 | Name |

You may use a calculator on this worksheet whenever you see this symbol (🧮).

Learning the Skill: Finding Unknowns with Exponents (🧮) — Solve.

a. $x^2 + 25 = 155$

b. $-18 + x^2 = 300$

c. $58 + y^2 = 879$

d. $5x^2 = 400$

Triangle Time (🧮) — Use the Pythagorean theorem to find the missing sides of these right triangles.

a.
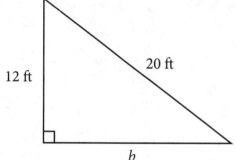

b.
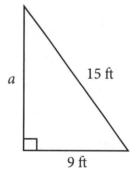

More Triangle Time (🧮)

a. Using the information given, can you use the Pythagorean theorem to find the length of the side of this triangle marked with a question mark? Why or why not?

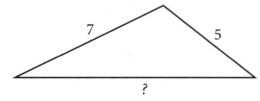

b. You want to form a regulation size soccer field.[1] The length of the touchline has to be a minimum of 100 yards, while the width of the goal line has to be a minimum of 50 yards. If you make the field with these minimum dimensions and truly make the field with right angles, what will the length of the diagonal from one corner to the other corner be?

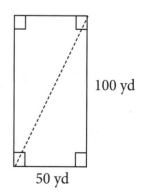

Dimmensions based on Fédération Internationale de Football Association, Laws of the Game, 2015–2016 (Zurich, Switzerland), p. 7, http://www.fifa.com/mm/Document/FootballDevelopment/Refereeing/02/36/01/11/LawsofthegamewebEN_Neutral.pdf.

c. Use the Pythagorean theorem to find the missing side of the triangle shown.

4. Skill Sharpening

a. Simplify: $17.58(1 + 0.09)^{15}$

b. Solve: $2x^2 + 3x^2 = 100$

c. The square root of 245 is between what two integers? You may use a calculator to help approximate, but do not use the calculator's square root or root buttons.

d. Simplify: $\dfrac{4^5}{4^3}$

e. Simplify, giving your answer in scientific notation (do not round): $4.2 \times 10^{-5} + 2.33 \times 10^2$

f. Factor to find $\sqrt{1{,}024}$. List all of the prime factors as part of your answer. You may use a calculator to help you factor, but do not use the calculator's square root or root buttons.

Applying the Converse

a. Suppose you're trying to mark off a rectangular garden in your yard. You want the length of the garden to be 10 ft, and the width 5 ft. How long should the diagonal from one corner to the opposite corner be if you really have laid out a rectangle?

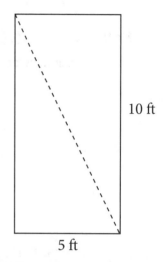

b. Suppose you're framing a house, and you want to see if the doorway you're framing forms right angles. If the length measures at 6.5 ft and the width at 3 ft, what would the length marked c in the picture have to measure in order for the doorway to be built with right angles?

c. You measure the diagonal of the doorway in problem 1b, and it's 9 ft. Is the doorway laid out with right angles?

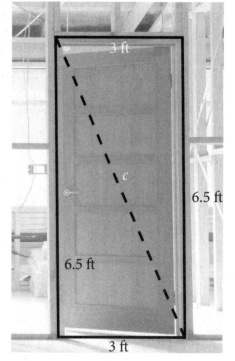

More with Triangles

a. What is the hypotenuse of a right triangle with a 4 ft and 6 ft leg?

b. What is the missing side of a right triangle with one 10.5 in leg and a 20.5 in hypotenuse?

c. Can you find the missing leg of the triangle shown using the Pythagorean theorem? Why or why not?

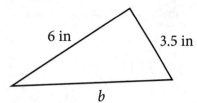

3. **Skill Sharpening** (🖩)

   a. Rewrite in scientific notation (do not round): 0.000000026147

   b. Solve: $5x^2 + 3x^2 = 1{,}024$

   c. Factor to find the $\sqrt{10{,}000}$. List all of the prime factors as part of your answer. You may use a calculator to help you factor, but do not use the calculator's square root or root buttons.

   d. The square root of 750 is between what two integers? You may use a calculator to help approximate, but do not use the calculator's square root or root buttons.

   e. Simplify: $v^4 v^2$

| PRINCIPLES OF MATHEMATICS 2 | Other Roots — Pages 336–339 | Day 144 | Worksheet 17.8 | Name |

You may use a calculator on this worksheet whenever you see this symbol (🖩).

Language Check

a. $\sqrt[6]{50}$ means the number that, times itself _____ times equals _____.

b. In $\sqrt[6]{50}$, what is the radicand?

c. In $\sqrt[6]{50}$, what is the index?

d. Draw a radical sign.

Finding Cubed Roots (🖩) — Factor to find the requested roots. List all of the prime factors as part of your answer. You may use a calculator to help you factor, but do not use the calculator's root button.

a. $\sqrt[3]{8}$

b. $\sqrt[3]{512}$

c. $\sqrt[3]{216}$

Geometry Time (🖩)

a. If the area of a square is 850 meters squared, what is the length of each of its sides?

b. What will the length of a diagonal dividing the square in problem 3a into two right triangles be? Use the Pythagorean theorem to help you. Round to the nearest whole number.

c. If the volume of a cube is 343 ft³, what is the length of each of its sides? *Hint*: Just as we have been with square roots, we can take the cubed root of both sides of an equation without changing the meaning.

4. **Missing Sides** (🖩) — Find the length of the missing side of this right triangle.

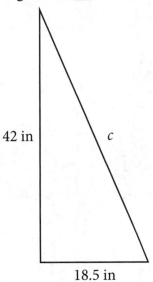

5. **Skill Sharpening** (🖩)

   a. Simplify, giving your answer in scientific notation: $7.8 \times 10^{-6} - 5.2 \times 10^{-5}$

   b. What do you need to know before you can find the missing leg of this triangle using the Pythagorean theorem?

   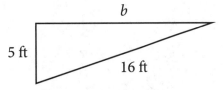

   c. Simplify: $4x^2 x^3$

   d. Simplify: $\dfrac{4x^2}{x^3}$

6. **Challenge Problem** (🖩) — Here's another problem that's different than any you've seen yet. But you have all the skills you need to solve it.

   $3x^3 + 6x^3 + 6 = 1{,}131$

| PRINCIPLES OF MATHEMATICS 2 | Introduction and Review Pages 343–347 | Day 148 | Worksheet 18.1 | Name |

You may use a calculator on this worksheet whenever you see this symbol (🖩).

1. **Congruency** — Circle all the angles congruent to ∠ABC.

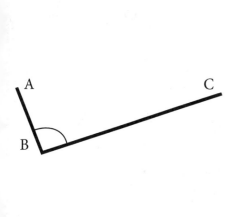

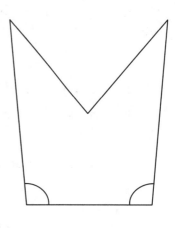

2. **Similar Shapes** (🖩) — These two rectangles are similar (the rectangle on the right is a scale drawing of the tabletop on the left). Set up a proportion to find the length of x.

width = 2.5 ft

length = 8 ft

3 in

x

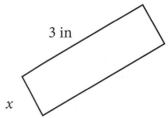

3. **Angles in a Triangle** — Shapes are often used in graphic design. Use your knowledge of triangles to find the marked angle in these graphic design pieces.

a.

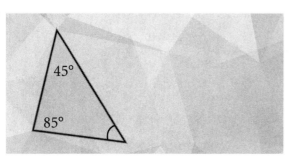

b.

c.

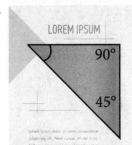

4. **More Angles in a Triangle** — In spherical geometry, do the sum of the angles of a triangle always equal 180°? If not, why not?

5. **AA Similarity Theorem** (🖩)

   a. Two triangles have to be similar if _____ sets of their corresponding angles are congruent.

   b. Circle all of the triangles that we know are similar from the information given.

   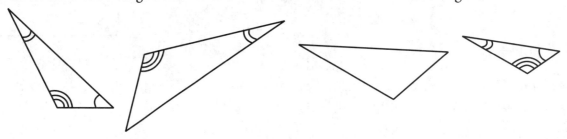

   c. We know these triangles are right triangles; how many other sets of corresponding angles do we have to know are congruent in order to know the triangles are similar using the AA similarity theorem?

   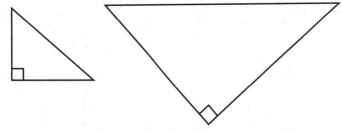

d. With the information given, how do we know that these two triangles are similar?

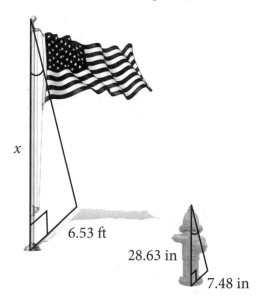

e. Set up a proportion to find the height of the flagpole in problem 5d. Round your answer to the nearest whole number.

Right Triangle Review

a. Which triangle in problem 3 is a right triangle?

b. Put a star next to the legs and a dot next to the hypotenuse of the right triangle in problem 3.

Pythagorean Theorem (🖩) — Suppose you're trying to draw a rectangle that's 3 inches by 2 inches. If you divide the rectangle in half to form two right triangles, how long should the distance from corner to corner be?

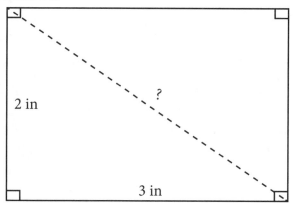

8. **Square Root Reminder** (🖩) — Factor to find the $\sqrt{2{,}025}$. List all of the prime factors as part of your answer. You may use a calculator to help you factor, but do not use the calculator's square root or root buttons.

| PRINCIPLES OF MATHEMATICS 2 | Tangent: A Ratio in Right Triangles Pages 347–352 | Day 149 | Worksheet 18.2 | Name |

You may use a calculator on this worksheet whenever you see this symbol (🖩).

Remember, a tangent is the ratio between the opposite and adjacent leg of either of the non-right angles in a right triangle.

$$\text{tangent of an angle} = \frac{\text{opposite leg}}{\text{adjacent leg}}$$

Understanding Tangents (🖩) — Round your answers to the nearest hundredth.

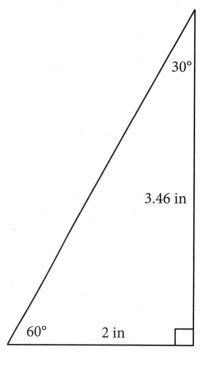

a. Find the tangent of the 60° angle in the right triangle shown by dividing the side opposite the angle by the side adjacent to it.

b. If we were to have another right triangle with a 60° angle and sides that have totally different measurements, what would the tangent of that 60° angle be?

c. Find the tangent of the 30° angle in the right triangle shown by dividing the side opposite the angle by the side adjacent to it.

Tangents on the Calculator (🖩) — Find the requested tangents using your calculator.

a. 80°

b. 73°

c. 35°

d. 15°

3. **Understanding Tangents** (🖩)

   a. The tangent of 45° is 1. This means that the ratio between the leg opposite a 45° angle of a right triangle and the leg adjacent to the 45° angle equals 1.

   $$1 = \frac{opposite\ leg}{adjacent\ leg}$$

   So if the leg adjacent to a 45° angle in a right triangle is 4 ft, what must the leg opposite the angle be?

   b. Knowing that the tangent of 20° is 0.36, what must the opposite leg be in a right triangle with a 20° angle if the adjacent leg is 4 in?

4. **Applying Tangents** (🖩) — Use the information given in the picture and what you know about tangents to answer the questions. Look at the example in your *Student Textbook* to help you.

   a. What is the length of the side marked *x*? Round to the nearest whole number.

   b. What is the height of the house?

5. **Question** — Based on the AA similarity theorem, can we conclude that all right triangles with a 30° angle are similar? Why or why not?

6. **Skill Sharpening** (🖩)

   a. Between what two integers is the square root of 650? Do not use a calculator's square root or root buttons.

   b. If a right triangle has a hypotenuse that's 78 ft and a leg that's 50 ft, what dimension must the other leg be?

   c. Factor to find $\sqrt{2{,}916}$. List all of the prime factors as part of your answer. You may use a calculator to help you factor, but do not use the calculator's square root or root buttons.

| PRINCIPLES OF MATHEMATICS 2 | Sines and Cosines: More Ratios in Right Triangles Pages 352–354 | Day 151 | Worksheet 18.3 | Name |

You may use a calculator on this worksheet whenever you see this symbol (🖩).

Remember, a sine is the ratio between the opposite leg of either of the non-right angles in a right triangle and the hypotenuse.

sine of an angle = $\dfrac{\text{opposite leg}}{\text{hypotenuse}}$

A cosine is the ratio between the adjacent leg of either of the non-right angles in a right triangle and the hypotenuse.

cosine of an angle = $\dfrac{\text{adjacent leg}}{\text{hypotenuse}}$

1. **Understanding Sines** (🖩) — Find the sine of each of the marked non-right angles in these right triangles.

   a.
   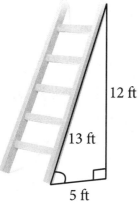

   b.
   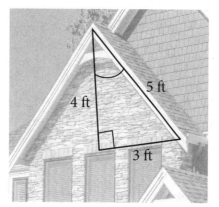

2. **Understanding Cosines** (🖩) — Find the cosine of each of the non-right marked angles in problem 1.
   a.   b.

3. **Reviewing Tangents** (🖩) — Find the tangent of each of the non-right marked angles in problem 1.
   a.   b.

4. **More Understanding Sines and Cosines** (🖩)

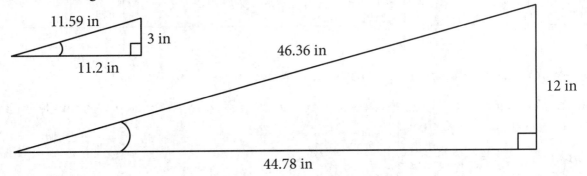

   a. Are these triangles similar? If so, how do you know by looking at only their angles?

   b. Are these triangles right triangles? If so, how do you know by looking at only their angles?

   c. Find the sine of the marked non-right angle in the larger triangle.

   d. Find the sine of the marked non-right angle in the smaller triangle. *Hint*: If the triangles are similar, the sine will be the same as the sine of the same angle in the larger triangle.

   e. Find the cosine of the marked non-right angle in the larger triangle.

   f. Find the cosine of the marked non-right angle in the smaller triangle.

5. **Sines and Cosines on a Calculator** (🖩) — Find the requested sines and cosines using your calculator.

   a. sine of 65°

   b. cosine of 22°

   c. sine of 90°

   d. cosine of 35°

   e. sine of 35°

Question — Finish the statement: If two or more shapes are similar, their corresponding sides are _____ and their corresponding angles are _____.

Basketball Time (🖩) — If a basketball player fires a ball at a 65° angle to the hoop from a distance of 5 ft off the ground, how far is he from the hoop? *Hint*: A basketball hoop is 10 ft from the ground, so if the player fires it at 5 ft, the distance from where he fires it to the rim is also going to be 5 ft. Thus, we could use this formula to find the distance to the hoop: tangent of $65° = \dfrac{5 \text{ ft}}{x}$

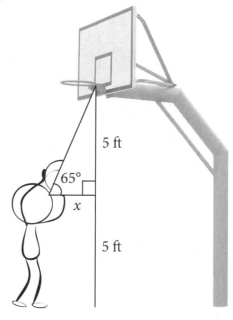

Skill Sharpening (🖩) — Solve. Problems 8a–8d, which appear similar but result in very different answers, will help you practice different skills you have acquired.

a. $15x = 45$

b. $15x + x = 45$

c. $-15x + x = 45$

d. $15x^2 + x^2 = 45$

e. Factor to find $\sqrt{3{,}025}$. List all of the prime factors as part of your answer. You may use a calculator to help you factor, but do not use the calculator's square root or root buttons.

More Skill Sharpening (🖩)

a. If the diagonal of a bookshelf is 8 ft and one side is 6.5 ft, what must the other side be if the bookshelf is truly rectangular (and thus has right angles)?

b. Between what two integers is the square root of 11,300? Do not use the calculator's square root or root buttons.

Representing Trigonometric Functions (Function Notation) — Worksheet 18.4

You may use a calculator on this worksheet whenever you see this symbol (📱).

1. **Sines, Cosines, Tangents, and Functions** (📱) — Use a calculator to find the requested values.

    a. sin(50°)

    b. cos(50°)

    c. tan(50°)

    d. cos(75°)

    e. sin(75°)

    f. tan(75°)

2. **Ratio Review** (📱)

    a. If a right triangle has a 28° angle, what is the ratio between the leg adjacent to that 28° angle and the hypotenuse?

    b. If a right triangle has a 28° angle, what is the ratio between the leg opposite and adjacent to that 28° angle?

    c. If a right triangle has a 28° angle, what is the ratio between the leg opposite to that 28° angle and the hypotenuse?

3. **Questions**

    a. In sin(45°), what is the input to the sine function?

    b. True or false: In function notation, parentheses mean to multiply.

    c. Similar shapes have _____ sides. This means that the ratio between their corresponding sides will be _____.

4. **Coordinate Graphing and Tangents** (🖩)

   a. Find the slope of the line shown.

   b. Use a calculator to find the tangent of the angle marked on the graph. How does it compare with the slope?

   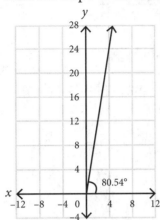

5. **Height of a Light** (🖩)

   a. What is the length of the side marked x?

   b. What is the height of the light?

   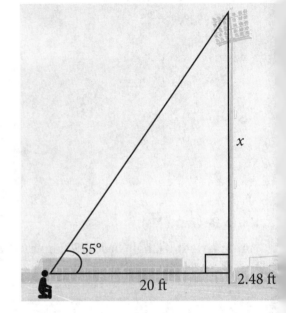

6. **Distance Through a Hill** (🖩) — Suppose a surveyor needs to find the distance between two points (we'll call them A and B) that are on opposite sides of a hill. The surveyor starts at point A and walks in a straight line 4,000 ft, then turns 90° and walks in a straight line for 3,000 ft until he arrives at point B. He has thus formed a right triangle. Use the Pythagorean theorem to find the distance between A and B (i.e., the distance through the hill).

   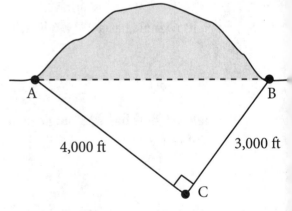

7. **Skill Sharpening** (🖩)

   a. Between what two integers does the square root of 879 fall? Do not use the calculator's square root or root buttons.

   b. Solve: $\sqrt{x} = 15$

   c. Find the cubed root of 343. List all of the prime factors as part of your answer. You may use a calculator to help you factor, but do not use the calculator's root button.

Worksheet 18.5 — Chapter Synopsis and Sound Waves

You may use a calculator on this worksheet whenever you see this symbol (🖩).

1. **Finding Sines, Cosines, and Tangents** (🖩) — Find the requested sines, cosines, and tangents. Notice that some results are negative.

   a. tan(180°)
   b. tan(200°)
   c. tan(325°)

   d. sin(180°)
   e. sin(200°)
   f. sin(325°)

   g. cos(180°)
   h. cos(200°)
   i. cos(325°)

2. **Questions**

   a. What is one way that describing sounds mathematically helps us?

   b. In question 1h, what was the input to the cosine function (i.e., what was the angle of which you found the cosine)?

3. **Exploring Cosines** — Just as we graph sines (see the *Student Textbook*), we can also graph the values for cosines by picturing a triangle as moving around a circle. When we do, we end up with a very similar, although shifted, graph. Cosine waves, like sine waves, are also useful in describing sounds. Use the graph to answer the questions.

   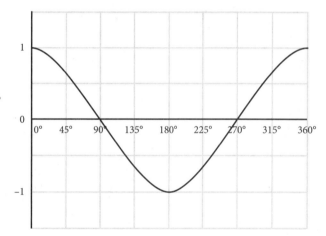

   a. What is the cosine of 0°?

   b. What is the cosine of 90°?

   c. Knowing what you know about recognizing functions on a graph (see Appendix B in the *Student Textbook*), is the cosine a function of the angle size?

4. **Study** — Look back over the chapter and review the different concepts in preparation for the quiz. Make sure you know the definitions of a tangent, sine, and cosine.

PRINCIPLES OF MATHEMATICS 2 | Sets and Symbols Pages 365–367 | Day 155 | Worksheet 19.1 | Name

You may use a calculator on this worksheet whenever you see this symbol (🖩).

Understanding Sets — Suppose you're trying to organize pictures for the year on a computer using a program in which the same picture can be put into multiple folders. List each picture letter under all appropriate folders. Assume any girl in the photos is Brittany, and any boy is William. A girl and a boy are sledding in picture *a*. *Note*: You are really organizing the photos into sets, or collections.

Folders:

Seasons

Winter {any photo taken in the winter}

Spring/Summer/Fall {any photo taken in the spring, summer, or fall}

People

Brittany

William

Symbol Time

a. What does the symbol ∈ mean?

b. $4 \in A$ means that 4 is an element of what set?

3. **Venn Diagrams and Letters for Sets**

   a. According to the diagram, which set is a subset of Airplanes?

   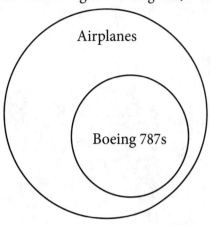

   b. Redraw the diagram, using A to name the set of all airplanes, and B to name the set of all Boeing 787s.

4. **Term Time** — Can sets be random?

5. **Skill Sharpening** (🖩)

   a. Find the height of the tree shown, using the information given. Don't forget to add the height from the ground to eye level in your final answer.

   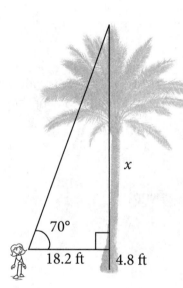

   b. $\cos(59°)$

   c. In 5b, what was the input to the function?

   d. In 5b, what was the output of the function?

   e. The cosine of 59° tells us the ratio between the leg _____ to a 59° angle and the _____ in a _____ triangle.

   f. The $\sqrt{313}$ is between what two integers? Do not use the calculator's square root or root buttons.

Specifying a Set

a. Let's say you are digitally cropping a picture to fit inside a frame. The picture's width has to be either 5 in, 8 in, or 11 in to fit inside the standard frames you own.

Finish specifying what the width must be by writing the values inside the brackets.

   width ∈ {   }

b. Specify that this equation only holds true when x is either 5 or 7:

   $y = 9x$, where _____

c. Let's say that participants in a contest have to pick either a 20 min, 25 min, or 30 min test. Specify that the time (t) has to be either 20 min, 25 min, or 30 min.

Symbols for Number Sets

a. Redraw the Venn diagram shown on the left using the symbols you learned about in Lesson 19.2 to stand for the different number sets.

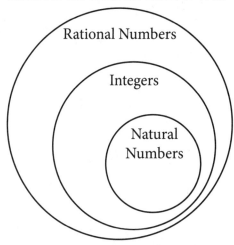 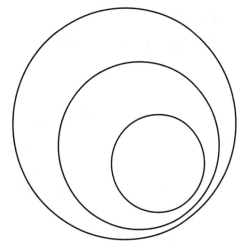

b. Looking back at Lesson 2.4 in your *Student Textbook*, write the definition for each of these sets.

   Rational Numbers:

   Integers:

   Natural Numbers:

Element of — Write true or false next to each statement. Remember that ∈ means "element of."

a. $4 \in \mathbb{N}$ b. $-4 \in \mathbb{N}$

c. $3 \in \mathbb{Q}$ d. $\frac{1}{2} \in \mathbb{Z}$

4. **Specifying a Type of Number**

    a. If $x \in \mathbb{Q}$, is π a valid value for x? *Hint*: Remember, while we typically use 3.14 as the value for π, π's actual value goes on and on. It cannot be expressed as a ratio of one integer to another.

    b. If $x \in \mathbb{Z}$, is –1 a valid value for x?

    c. If $x \in \mathbb{N}$, is –1 a valid value for x?

5. **Finding the Height of a Cliff** (🖩) — Suppose you're in a small boat slightly offshore. You need to know the height of a cliff on the shore. You measure the angle from where you're sitting and get a measurement of 45°. You then proceed to shore, measuring your distance as you go. You discover you were 50 ft from the bottom of the cliff when you measured the angle to the top. Assuming you are trying to get a rough estimate of the cliff's height (and thus don't need to worry about your height when you measured the angle), about how tall is the cliff?

6. **Skill Sharpening** (🖩)

    a. What is the sine of the marked angle?

    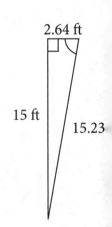

    b. What is the cosine of the marked angle?

    c. What is the tangent of the marked angle?

You may use a calculator on this worksheet whenever you see this symbol (🖩).

1. **Reviewing Sequences** — A sequence is _____.

2. **Sequences and Unknowns** (🖩)

    a. Find the first four numbers in the sequence $\{s, 7s, 14s, 28s, \ldots\}$ when s is 2.

    b. Find the first four numbers in the sequence $\{s, 7s, 14s, 28s, \ldots\}$ when s is 3.

    c. Find the first four numbers in the sequence $\{x, 3x, 6x, 9x, \ldots\}$ when x is 5.

    d. Find the first four numbers in the sequence $\{x, 2x, 3x, 4x, \ldots\}$ when x is 5.

    e. True or false: the sequence in 2d is the one we'd be counting if we counted a stack of nickels one at a time.

3. **Sequences in Music** (🖩) — The main sound of the lowest G on the piano has a frequency of approximately 49 Hz. Find the approximate frequencies of its first 5 overtones by substituting 49 Hz for f in this sequence: $\{f, 2f, 3f, 4f, 5f, \ldots\}$.

4. **Random Sequences**

    a. Can sequences be random?

    b. Write a random sequence of integers inside these braces: {   }

    Hint: You've been asked to write a random sequence, so pick *any* integers!

5. **Skill Sharpening** (🖩)

    a. Is 4.5 a valid input for x if $x \in \mathbb{Q}$?

    b. Is 4.5 a valid input for x if $x \in \mathbb{N}$?

    c. How would you specify that x must be an integer?

d. What is the sin(42°)?

e. If the hypotenuse of a right triangle with a 53° angle is 9 ft, what must the side opposite the 53° angle be?

f. True or false: all right triangles with a 50° angle are *congruent*.

g. What will the ratio between the side opposite of and adjacent to a 30° angle in a right triangle be?

h. Factor to find $\sqrt[3]{3{,}375}$. List all of the prime factors as part of your answer. You may use a calculator to help you factor, but do not use the calculator's root button.

6. **Out of the Box (optional)** — The frequencies you found in problem 3 are very close to those of the main sounds of the notes shown in the picture.

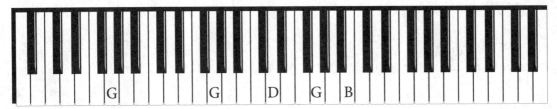

If you can, play these notes on a piano. (The left-most G in the picture is the lowest G on the piano — find it by looking for the lowest set of 3 black keys. The note to the right of the left-most black key in that set is the G. You can find the other notes by looking for where they are in relation to the sets of 2 and 3 black keys.) The sounds should be pleasing when played together. There's a mathematical reason why! In fact, if you study music, you'll learn that the notes G, B, and D are commonly played together.

Principles of Mathematics 2
Arithmetic and Geometric Sequences — Pages 371–374
Day 158 — Worksheet 19.4

You may use a calculator on this worksheet whenever you see this symbol (🖩).

Identifying Types of Sequences and Recognizing Patterns (🖩)
   a. Arithmetic sequences have a common _____.
   b. Geometric sequences have a common _____.
   c. Is there a common difference or ratio in {2, 5, 8, 11, . . .}? If so, what is it?

   d. Is the sequence in 1c an arithmetic sequence, a geometric sequence, or neither?

   e. Is there a common difference or ratio in {5, 15, 45, . . .}? If so, what is it?

   f. Is the sequence in 1e an arithmetic sequence, geometric sequence, or neither?

   g. Is there a common difference or ratio in {4, 2, 8, 6, 12, . . .}? If so, what is it?

   h. Is the sequence in 1g an arithmetic sequence, a geometric sequence, or neither?

   i. What are the next two elements in {4, 2, 8, 6, 12, 10, 16, . . .}, assuming the pattern continues? *Hint:* Subtract each element from the one before it to identify the pattern.

Geometric Sequences and Unknowns
   a. Find the first three elements of the sequence {7s, 14s, 28s, . . .} if s is 4.

   b. Look for a common ratio by finding the ratio between each element in the sequence. Remember, a ratio is a comparison via division.

   $\frac{28s}{14s} =$ _____ $\frac{14s}{7s} =$ _____

   c. Now that you know the common ratio, what would the next element in the sequence be, assuming the pattern continues?
   {7s, 14s, 28s, _____ . . .}

Arithmetic Sequences and Unknowns
   a. Find the first three elements of the sequence {6x, 9x, 12x , . . .} if x is 3.
   b. Look for a common difference by subtracting each number from the one before it.
   $12x - 9x =$ _____ $9x - 6x =$ _____

   c. Now that you know the common difference, what would the next element in the sequence be, assuming the pattern continues?
   {6x, 9x, 12x, _____ . . .}

4. **Musical Explorations** — Knowing that the main sound of the lowest G on the piano has a frequency of approximately 49 Hz, find the approximate frequency of the next 4 Gs on the piano by substituting 49 Hz for f in this sequence: $\{f, 2f, 4f, 8f, 16f, \ldots\}$

5. **True or False** — Sequences cannot be random.

6. **Exploring Ratios in Triangles** (🖩)
    a. Find the cosine of the marked angle.

    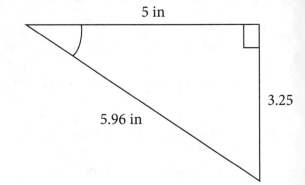

    b. Find the sine of the marked angle.

    c. Find the tangent of the marked angle.

7. **Skill Sharpening**
    a. Is 20.3 a valid input for x if $x \in \mathbb{N}$?

    b. Is -5 a valid input for x if $x \in \mathbb{N}$?

    c. How would you specify that the value of s must be an integer?

    d. In a right triangle, what will the ratio between the side opposite a 55° angle and the hypotenuse be?

Out of the Box — Pick two words or phrases and search for them on the Internet using a capitalized OR between them; now search for them without the OR. Write a short paragraph describing how including OR affected your results.

Study on Your Own — Be sure to review the chapter in preparation for the quiz.

PRINCIPLES OF MATHEMATICS 2 | Compound Interest, Pages 377–380 | Day 161 | Worksheet 20.1 | Name

You may use a calculator on this worksheet whenever you see this symbol (📱).

Percent Review — In order to calculate the value of an investment plus all the interest earned, you'll need to convert the interest rate (a percent) to a decimal. Remember, a % means *per hundred*. So you can convert a % to a decimal by dividing by 100 — that is, by moving the decimal place 2 more digits to the left.

Convert these percents to decimals.

    Example: 0.05% = 0.0005

a. 4%

b. 0.6%

c. 0.02%

d. 500%

Finding the Ending Balance (📱) — Use the formula $P = P_0(1 + r)^t$ to answer the questions. Assume that no additional money is deposited or withdrawn from the investments.

a. Find the balance of an initial investment of $400 after 3 years if it is invested at a 6% yearly interest rate and the interest is compounded yearly?

b. Find the balance of an initial investment of $600 after 60 months if it is invested at a 0.25% monthly interest rate and the interest is compounded monthly.

Finding the Interest (📱) — In problem 2a, how much was earned in interest?

Skill Sharpening: Other Consumer Math Problems (📱)

a. If you've finished 40 out of 150 pages in a book, what percent have you completed?

b. If you're told you need to purchase 10% extra fabric than what the pattern calls for, how much fabric do you need to purchase if the pattern calls for 4.5 yards? Round your answer up to the nearest quarter of a yard.

c. If you pay a bill in several payments, where each payment of $350 is 25% of the total bill, what is the total bill?

5. **More Skill Sharpening** (🖩)

    a. Find the first three elements of the sequence $\{p, 6p, 36p, \ldots\}$ if p is 5.

    b. Look for a common ratio by finding the ratio between each element in the sequence. Remember, a ratio is a comparison via division.

    $$\frac{36p}{6p} = \underline{\hspace{2cm}} \qquad \frac{6p}{p} = \underline{\hspace{2cm}}$$

    c. We would call the sequence $\{p, 6p, 36p, \ldots\}$ a _____ sequence.

    d. Now that you know the common ratio, what would the next element in the sequence be, assuming the pattern continues?

    $\{p, 6p, 36p, \underline{\hspace{1cm}}, \ldots\}$

Principles of Mathematics 2

Using the Correct Time and Rate — Pages 380–383 — Day 162 — Worksheet 20.2

You may use a calculator on this worksheet whenever you see this symbol (🖩).

Think of a year as having 365 days unless otherwise specified.

Finding the Number of Compound Periods (🖩)

Example: How many compound periods are there in 6 years if the interest is compounded quarterly? *Answer:* 6 • 4 = 24

a. How many compound periods are there in 6 years if the interest is compounded monthly?

b. How many compound periods are there in 6 years if the interest is compounded daily?

Finding the Rate per Compound Period (🖩) — Give your answer as a decimal; do not round.

Example: What is the rate per compound period if interest is compounded quarterly and a 3% annual rate is given? *Answer:* $\frac{0.03}{4} = 0.0075$

a. What is the rate per compound period if interest is compounded monthly and a 3% annual rate is given?

b. What is the rate per compound period if interest is compounded daily and a 3% annual rate is given?

Comparing Options (🖩) — Use your answers to problems 1 and 2 and the formula $P = P_0(1 + r)^t$ to find how much $10,000 will grow to after 6 years at 3% annual rate for the various compound periods listed.

Example: compounded quarterly *Answer:* $P = \$10,000(1 + 0.0075)^{24}$; $P = \$11,964.14$

a. compounded monthly

b. compounded daily

Understanding Interest Rates – Look carefully at your answers to problem 3. Notice that while the annual interest rate was the same for both 3a and 3b, you earned more interest on 3b when the interest was compounded daily rather than monthly. This is because every time the interest is compounded, that interest is added to the amount off which the interest is calculated the next time. The more often the interest gets added to the balance, then, the more exponential growth occurs. So at the same annual interest rate, money will grow faster the more frequently it is compounded. While the difference wasn't much in the problems you solved, the difference becomes much greater with larger investments or longer periods of time.

4. **Comparing Options on Your Own** (🧮) — What will $500 grow to after 3 years at 2.5% interest compounded daily? *Hint*: Break this problem down yourself by first finding the number of compound periods and the interest rate per compound period.

5. **Skill Sharpening: Other Consumer Math Problems** (🧮) — Watch your units and convert where necessary.

    a. How far can you travel in 4 hours if you travel at the speed of 1 mile per 20 minutes? *Hint*: Remember, distance equals the speed times the time (i.e., $d = st$).

    b. How many inches of fabric do you need if you need 50% of 4 yards?

6. **More Skill Sharpening**

    a. Find the first three elements of the sequence $\{p, 4p, 7p, \ldots\}$ if p is 2.

    b. Look for a common difference by subtracting each number from the one before it.
    $7p - 4p =$ _____ $4p - p =$ _____

    c. Would we call the sequence $\{p, 4p, 7p, \ldots\}$ an arithmetic sequence, geometric sequence, or neither?

    d. Now that you know the common difference, what would the next element in the sequence be, assuming the pattern continues?
    $\{p, 4p, 7p,$ _____ $\ldots\}$

| PRINCIPLES OF MATHEMATICS 2 | Simple Interest Pages 383–385 | Day 163 | Worksheet 20.3 | Name |

You may use a calculator on this worksheet whenever you see this symbol (🖩).

Calculating Simple Interest

Example: How much interest will you earn each time interest is paid at a simple interest rate of 6% on a $550 investment? *Answer:* 0.06 • $550 = $33

a. How much interest will you earn each period on a $10,000 investment at a 4% simple interest rate?

b. How much interest will you earn each period on a $3,000 investment at a 2.6% simple interest rate?

Describing Growth at Simple Interest

a. Find the equation that describes this line, which shows the relationship between the total of a $10,000 investment and the number of years, if $400 simple interest is earned each year. *Hint:* Use the marked coordinates to help you find the slope.

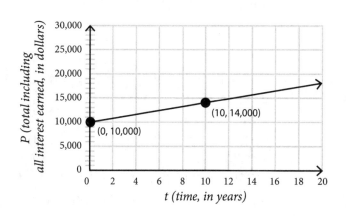

b. In the equation in 2a, is the slope the *interest earned each year* or the *initial investment*?

c. In the equation in 2a, is the *y*-intercept the *interest earned each year* or the *initial investment*?

Simple Versus Compound Interest — The graph on the left shows $10,000 invested at 4% simple interest, while the graph on the right shows the same amount invested at 4% compound interest, compounded yearly. At the same interest rate over the same number of years, does simple or compound interest result in more interest?

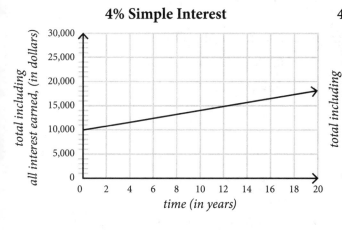
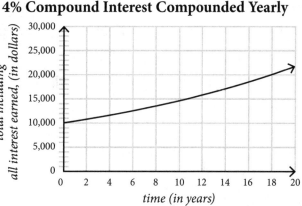

4. **Comparing Options with APYs** (🖩) — If you invest $5,000, how much more will you earn in interest the first year at an APY of 2.2% than at an APY of 1.5%?

5. **Skill Sharpening: Other Consumer Math Problems** (🖩)
    a. If you accidentally think of a yard as 35 inches instead of as the correct 36 inches, you were off by 1 inch. What percent of a yard (36 inches) does the 1 inch you were off represent?

    b. If you pay your car insurance bill in a series of $145 payments, each of which is 25% of the total, how much is the total?

    c. Which is the better price per pound: an item that's $4.50 for 4 lbs, with a 12%-off coupon, or an item that's $3.75 for 3.5 lbs?

    d. Suppose you have a copy of the blueprint to an office building you're considering renting. You know the building has $\frac{1}{18}$ of an acre thumbprint (in other words, its area is $\frac{1}{18}$ of an acre). You've also been told it's a rectangle. What is the building's length in feet if its width is 40 ft? (1 acre equals 43,560 square feet)

    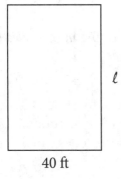
    40 ft

6. **More Skill Sharpening**
    a. Is {−5, −10, −20, ...} an arithmetic sequence, geometric sequence, or neither?
    b. Is {20, 18, 16, 14, ...} an arithmetic sequence, geometric sequence, or neither?
    c. Simplify this sequence by using multiplication instead of addition:
        $\{x, x + x, x + x + x, x + x + x + x, ...\}$

    d. If $x \in \mathbb{N}$, is −5 a valid value for x?

Understanding Income and Expenses

a. What's one benefit of a budget?

b. If your income is $1,200 a month, and your mandatory expenses are $800, how much extra does that leave you with each month?

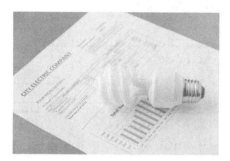

c. If it costs $450 a year in electricity, how much do you need to budget each month for electricity?

d. If you make $5,000 a year at a hobby business, how much should you budget as income from the hobby business each month?

e. If you make $25 per time babysitting and on average you babysit one time a week, how much on average do you make a month in babysitting if there are 4.33 weeks per month?

f. Over the last 4 weeks, Sue's grocery bills were $130, $150, $99, and $111. Based on this, how much on average does Sue spend in groceries per week? *Note:* It would be helpful if we could look at bills over more than 4 weeks to get a better estimate.

2. **Vacation Time** (🖩) — Suppose you're planning a 3-day vacation. Figure out how much you need to budget for the vacation if you choose Plan A and if you choose Plan B. Fill in the blanks in the first column with your answers.

Hypothetical Vacation Budget	Plan A (airplane trip to city)	Plan B (drive to campground)
Transportation Total for Plan A = _____ Total for Plan B = _____	$450 for airline ticket; $25 each way for luggage; $55 for transportation to the airport (you have a friend giving you a ride home)	$0.50 a mile for 700 miles; $15 in tolls.
Lodging Total for Plan A = _____ Total for Plan B = _____	3 nights at a hotel at $70 a night	3 nights at a campground at $15 a night
Meals Total for Plan A = _____ Total for Plan B = _____	Eating Out — 5 days of eating out, with an average of $6 for breakfast, $8 for lunch, and $10 for dinner	Cooking — $4 for eggs, $4 for bread, $10 for canned meat, $10 for meat to grill, plus $30 for miscellaneous food
Activities Total for Plan A = _____ Total for Plan B = _____	$25 for a show, $50 for boating, and $10 for a museum	$5 for bait with which to fish
GRAND TOTAL Grand Total for Plan A = _____ Grand Total for Plan B = _____		

3. **Skill Sharpening: Salesman Problems** (🖩)

    a. What is the monthly income from commission of a salesman who sells $60,000 worth of goods at a 7.5% commission each month?

    b. A salesman who earns a 5% commission on everything he sells earned $3,500 one month. How much did he sell?

    c. If a salesman earned $6,500 in commission by selling $65,000, what rate does he earn in commission?

    d. If the monthly expenses of the salesman in problem 3a are $150, how much monthly income does he have from commission after deducting his expenses?

    e. Suppose a salesman had the choice to be paid by commission or by salary. He chose to be paid a 4% commission. If he ended up only selling an average of $1,000 a week, how much more could he have made per year if he had opted instead for a $400 weekly salary? Use 52 weeks to a year.

4. **More Skill Sharpening** (🖩)

    a. Is the sequence {7, 5, 6, 4, . . .} an arithmetic sequence, geometric sequence, or neither?

    b. Assuming the pattern continues, what are the next two elements of the sequence in 4e?

Review of Chapters 17–20
Worksheet 20.5 — Day 168

You may use a calculator on this worksheet whenever you see this symbol (🖩).

Reviewing Roots

a. The $\sqrt{234}$ is between what 2 integers? (Lesson 17.4)

b. Find $\sqrt[3]{1,000}$. List all of the prime factors as part of your answer. (Lesson 17.8)

c. Find the $\sqrt{1,764}$. List all of the prime factors as part of your answer. (Lesson 17.1)

More with Roots (🖩)

a. Solve: $\sqrt{x} = 11$ (Lesson 17.2)

b. Find the measurement of each side of a square if its area is 156.25 ft². (Lesson 17.3)

c. Solve: $a^2 + 79 = 500$ (Lesson 17.6)

Reviewing Trigonometry (🖩)

a. Are all right triangles with a 40° angle similar? If so, how do we know? (Lesson 18.2)

b. Is the sine of a right triangle with a 40° angle equal to the sine of another right triangle with a 40° angle? (Lesson 18.3)

c. Find: sin(40°) (Lesson 18.4)

4. **Right Triangle Time** (📱) — Think through how to find the requested information based on what you know. You may need to use either the Pythagorean theorem or what you know about tangents, sines, and cosines. (Lessons 17.5, 17.6, 18.2, and 18.3)

   a. Circle the right triangles shown. *Hint*: Use the Pythagorean theorem to figure out if the second two triangles are truly right triangles.

   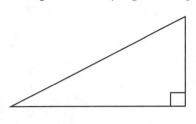 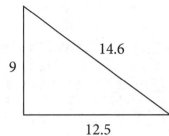 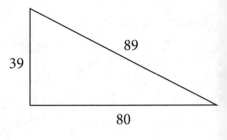

   b. Find the sine of the marked angle in the triangular wooden block.

   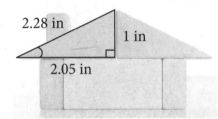

   c. Find the tangent of the marked angle in the triangular wooden block in 4b.

   d. Find the cosine of the marked angle in the triangular wooden block in 4b.

   e. Suppose you want to build a pyramid with a square base and an outside angle of 78°. You also want the distance from each corner to the center to be 7 ft. Use a tangent to help you find the distance marked a (i.e., the height of the pyramid).

   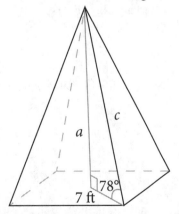

   f. How long should the distance marked c in the pyramid be? While you could use a sine or cosine, use the Pythagorean theorem and the value you found for a in 4e.

Continue to Next Page

Sets and Sequences (🖩)

a. If $x \in \mathbb{N}$, is −9 a valid value for x? (Lesson 19.2)

b. If $x \in \{4, 9, 11\}$, is 9 a valid value for x? (Lesson 19.2)

c. Find the first 3 values in this sequence $\{x, x + 3, x + 6, \ldots\}$ if x is 4. (Lesson 19.3)

d. Look for a common difference by subtracting each element from the one before it. (Lesson 19.4)
   Hint: Use the distributive property where necessary.

   $(x + 6) - (x + 3) =$ _____ $(x + 3) - (x) =$ _____

e. Now that you know the common difference, what would the next element in the sequence $\{x, x + 3, x + 6, \ldots\}$ be, assuming the pattern continues? (Lesson 19.4)

   $\{x, x + 3, x + 6,$ _____ $\ldots\}$

f. Would we call the sequence $\{x, x + 3, x + 6, \ldots\}$ an arithmetic sequence, geometric sequence, or neither? (Lesson 19.4)

g. Find the first 4 values in this sequence $\{x, x^2, x^3, x^4, \ldots\}$ if x is 3. (Lesson 19.3)

h. Look for a common ratio by looking at the ratio between each element in the sequence. Remember, a ratio is a comparison via division. (Lesson 19.4)

   $\dfrac{x^4}{x^3} =$ _____ $\dfrac{x^2}{x} =$ _____

i. Now that you know the common ratio, what would the next element be in the sequence $\{x, x^2, x^3, x^4, \ldots\}$, assuming the pattern continues? (Lesson 19.4)

   $\{x, x^2, x^3, x^4,$ _____ $\ldots\}$

j. Would we call the sequence $\{x, x^2, x^3, x^4, \ldots\}$ an arithmetic sequence, geometric sequence, or neither? (Lesson 19.4)

6. **Consumer Math** (🖩)

   a. Use the formula $P = P_0(1 + r)^t$ to find what $29,000 will grow to after 5 years at 3.25% interest compounded monthly. *Hint*: First find the number of monthly compound periods in 5 years and the rate per monthly compound period. Use those values in the formula. (Lessons 20.1 and 20.2)

   b. Which will earn more interest after 15 years: $500 invested at 5% simple interest or at 5% compound interest? (Lesson 20.3)

   c. If you spent a total of $400 eating out last year, how much should you budget per month for the next year, if you want to budget enough for the previous year plus a 10% increase? (Lesson 20.4)

   d. If you have two coupons you could use — one for 15% off your entire purchase, or one for $5 your purchase of $40 or more — which will save you more money on a $45 purchase and how much more will it save you? (Miscellaneous)

   e. If you only have 20 minutes to walk, how fast do you have to go in miles per hour in order to walk 1.5 miles? (Miscellaneous)

Algebra Synopsis — Pages 389–390 — Day 171 — Worksheet 21.1

You may use a calculator on this worksheet whenever you see this symbol (🖩).

End-of-Year Project — As you review the course, complete one of the end-of-the-year projects found on page 303 and 305. Your project is due on Test 5 (the final test).

Finding Unknowns (🖩) — Solve.

a. $\$3x = \$15$

   Example Meaning: If you were given $15 for your birthday and want to spend it on books, how many books can you buy if each one costs $3?

b. $x + -\$90 = \$120$

   Example Meaning: We know we have $120 left after spending $90. How much did we have before we spent the $90?

c. $\dfrac{x}{-5} = 100$

d. $x - \dfrac{4}{5}x = 120$

e. $\dfrac{1}{10}x = \$250$

f. If an employer gives their employees $\dfrac{1}{60}$ of the hours they work back in vacation time, how many hours must an employee work to earn 40 hours of vacation?

g. How many days at 8 hours a day must the employee in problem 2f work to earn the 40 hours of vacation?

h. $x - \dfrac{2}{3}x = 67$

i. $2x + 3x = 45$

j. $8 - (2 + x) = 20$

k. $6 + 2(x + 5) = 86$

3. **Find Those Missing Sides** (🖩)

    a. A manufacturer wants to make crates that can hold 12,000 in³ and that have a base with an area of 400 in². What height do they need to make the crates? *Hint:* The volume of a rectangular prism equals the area of the base times the height ($V = Bh$).

    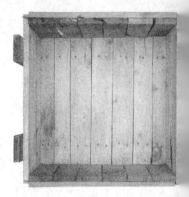

    b. Find the height of this triangle if the area is 18 in².

    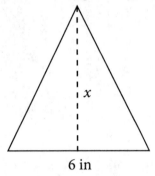

4. **Time and Distance** (🖩)

    a. If you're training for a race and decide you need to run 10 miles on your treadmill but only have 2 hours in which to run, at what speed do you need to set your treadmill?

    b. If you can run at 6.5 miles an hour, how long will it take you to run 12 miles? Give fractional portions of an hour in minutes, rounded to the nearest minute.

    c. If you're traveling 50 miles per hour, how far can you go in 25 minutes?

Statistics, Probability, Trigonometry, and Consumer Math Synopsis

PRINCIPLES OF MATHEMATICS 2 — Pages 390–391 — Day 172 — Worksheet 21.2 — Name _____

You may use a calculator on this worksheet whenever you see this symbol (📱).

Statistics (📱)

a. Finish filling out the frequency table illustrating the following data.

The breakdown by age of lawful permanent residents[1] who were naturalized between 1973–1975 is as follows:

- 18–24:   130,675
- 25–34:   197,111
- 35–44:   78,160
- 45+:   59,214

Ages of Lawful Permanent Residents Who Were Naturalized Between 1973 and 1975	Frequency	Relative Frequency
18–24	130,675	28.09%

b. List at least one reason you should question or ask for additional information if an article concluded, based on the data in problem 1a alone, that more people naturalize when age 34 or under than when over age 34.

c. Find the average speed at which contestants crossed the finish line if the finishing speeds (in miles per hour) were 0.5, 1.9, 2.4, 2.9, 3.3, 3.5, 3.5, 5.5, 7.5, 8.

d. Find the mode of the speeds in problem 1c.

e. Find the median of the speeds in problem 1c.

Probability (📱)

a. What is the probability of getting 3 heads in a row when you toss a coin?

b. What are the *odds* of getting 3 heads in a row when you toss a coin?

James Yankay, "Interstate Migration of Lawful Permanent Residents Who Migrate," *Fact Sheet: November 2013* (Department of Homeland Security, Office of Immigration Statistics), http://www.dhs.gov/sites/default/files/publications/ois_geo_mob_fs.pdf, accessed 01/8/14.

c. If a completely random number generator randomly selects a number between 1 and 20 (20 number total), what is the probability that a number between 8 and 10 (3 numbers total) will be chosen?

d. In the situation described in 2c, if the random number generator is programmed not to repeat the same number twice, what is the probability that a number between 8 and 10 will be chosen 3 times in a row?

e. In the situation described in 2c, if the random number generator can repeat the same number multiple times, what is the probability that a number between 8 and 10 will be chosen 3 times in a row?

3. **Trigonometry** (🖩)

   a. Find the sin(45°)

   b. Find the missing side of the right triangle shown.

   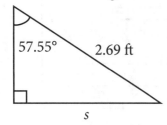

   c. Find the cosine of the marked angle.

   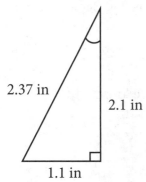

4. **Consumer Math** (🖩)

   a. If an account earns 5.4% interest compounded daily, what is the interest rate per compound period? Give your answer as a decimal; do not round. *Hint*: Remember, when not otherwise specified, assume the interest rate given is the annual rate.

   b. What percent tip are you leaving if you leave $8.33 on a $55.53 total?

   c. How much do you spend a month in car insurance if your bi-annual bill (i.e., your bill for 6 months) is for $532?

5. **Project** (🖩) — Continue to work on the project assigned in Worksheet 21.1.

You may use a calculator on this worksheet whenever you see this symbol (🖩).

Reviewing Without a Calculator
a. The $\sqrt{540}$ is between what two integers? Do not use the calculator's square root button.

b. Factor to find $\sqrt[3]{343}$. List all of the prime factors as part of your answer.

c. Simplify: $f + f + f$

d. Simplify: $-x + -x$

e. Simplify: $s \cdot s \cdot s \cdot s \cdot s$

Miscellaneous Review (🖩)
a. Solve: $x^2 + 89 = 315$

b. Simplify: $60(7 + 0.015)^7$

c. Rewrite your answer to 2b using scientific notation. Do not round.

d. If you want the area of a painting to be 289 in², and you want the canvas to be square, what should you make the length of each side?

e. Find the cos(12°)

f. $x + 5 < 86$

g. $6x < 180$

h. $-6x < 180$

More Miscellaneous Review (🖩)
a. If a company spends $450 a month on electricity, and that represents 5% of their total budget, what is their total budget?

b. Find the dimension of the leg marked *s*:

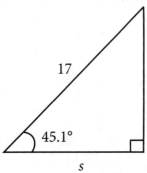

c. What are the first 4 values of the sequence $\{x, x - \frac{1}{2}, x - 1, x - 1\frac{1}{2} \ldots\}$ when *x* equals 4?

d. Let's say that we need to sell a product for 7 times our cost in order to make a profit, and that we know the cost is greater than $5. Our selling price is a function of the cost. Using *s* to represent the selling price and *c* to represent the cost, we have this equation: $s = 7c$, where $c > \$5$. Finish graphing the equation.

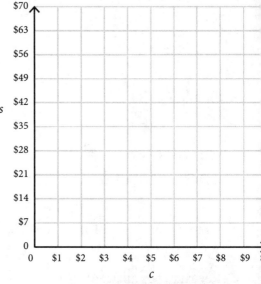

4. **Cross Multiplication** ( ) — Use a proportion and cross multiplication to solve.

    a. Suppose you want to draw a scale drawing of a hockey rink. If the rink is a standard 200 ft long by 85 ft wide and you want your drawing to be 10 in long, how many inches wide should it be?

    b. The room of a house is 14 feet wide by 20 feet long. If, in the plan, the width is represented by a line 3 inches, how many inches should the line be that represents the length?

    c. If 1 degree equals 60 arcminutes, how many degrees are 8,090 arcminutes? *Hint*: While you might not be familiar with arcminutes, you can use the principles you have learned on units to solve this problem.

5. **End-of-Year Project** — Continue to work on the project assigned in Worksheet 21.1.

Miscellaneous

a. Use graph paper to graph $y = 3x$, where $x > 0$.

b. Rearrange this relationship to solve for y: $y - x = 56 \frac{mi}{hr}$

c. Solve: $x - 7\frac{7}{8} = 20$

d. Solve: $100 - 4(2 + x) = 20$

e. If Jill lost 87 pounds total during a weight loss competition, and lost 25 pounds the last week, what percent of her total poundage lost occurred during the last week?

f. Rewrite in decimal notation (do not round): 2.64×10^{-6}

g. Express in scientific notation: 0.000025
   Example Meaning: possible size of a yeast cell

h. Solve: $-2x < 100$

i. Find $\sqrt{1{,}089}$. List all of the prime factors as part of your answer. You may use a calculator to help you factor, but do not use the calculator's square root or root buttons.

j. In the graph shown, can we think of y as a function of x?

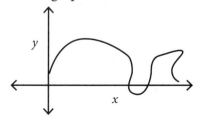

2. **Pythagorean Theorem** — Find the missing side of the right triangle. The dimensions are in feet.

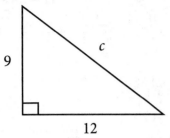

3. **Math in Action: Pressure, Force, and Area** (📱) — Because of the consistent way God holds all things together, the pressure on an object consistently equals the force on that object divided by the area of that object. We could represent that in this way:

$$pressure = \frac{force}{area} \quad \text{or} \quad P = \frac{F}{A}$$

While we won't actually be exploring this formula in depth (you'll get to do that in physics), notice from the example meanings that the skills you've learned would help you explore real-life consistencies such as pressure, force, and area.

a. $0.7 = \frac{700}{A}$

Example Meaning: finding the area when the pressure and force are known

b. $0.09 = \frac{F}{60}$

Example Meaning: finding the force when the pressure and area are known

4. **End-of-Year Project** — Continue to work on the project assigned in Worksheet 21.1.

Miscellaneous (📱)

a. Simplify: $4y^2 + 2y^2 + y + y$

b. Rewrite using a negative exponent: $\dfrac{1}{8^3}$

c. If based on previous statistics it's 30% probable that a baseball player will hit a ball, how probable is it that he'll miss?

d. Between what two integers is $\sqrt{879}$? Do not use the calculator's square root or root buttons.

Problem Solving (📱)

a. In seasoning, oak shrinks about 3.1% across the grain. If an oak board is 2.5 feet when measured across the grain, what will its finished distance across the grain be after it shrinks? Do not round until you arrive at your final answer.

b. If 1.75 barrels of lime (from limestone) are required for plastering 50 square yards, how many barrels would be required for a job of plastering 600 square yards?

3. **Math in Action: Gears** — Math applies in all sorts of places. This problem will let you explore the math behind gears (such as the gears on your bike or the gears in a car). While you may never have to calculate a gear ratio yourself, know that you constantly use items that took math to design. Since math is a way of describing the consistencies God created and sustains, it proves quite useful outside of a textbook, both directly (as we use it personally) and indirectly (as we benefit from the math other people have used).

The revolutions per minute of the larger gear (R) times the number of teeth in the larger gear (T) equals the revolutions per minute in the smaller gear (r) times the number of teeth in the smaller gear (t). This easier to see as a formula:

$RT = rt$

Use this knowledge and the skills you've learned to answer these questions.

   a. If a 28-tooth gear is driving a 14-tooth gear, and the 28-tooth gear makes 200 revolutions per minute, how many revolutions per minute does the 14-tooth gear make?

   b. In the bicycle shown, how many times will the back gear revolve (and with it the wheels of the bike) if the front gear (the one turned by pedaling) revolves 100 times each minute?

4. **End-of-Year Project** — Continue to work on the project assigned in Worksheet 21.1.

| PRINCIPLES OF MATHEMATICS 2 | End-of-the-Year Project #1: Budgeting | Day 171 | Project 1 | Name |

Plan a budget for an actual hypothetical three-day vacation. Have backup for what you've based your expenses on (i.e., actually look up reasonable values online, by visiting a grocery store and pricing out the cost of food, etc.).

Hypothetical Vacation Budget	Notes	Amount Set Aside for Expense
A. Transportation		
B. Lodging		
C. Meals		
D. Activities		
E. Other		
F. GRAND TOTAL		

Specific Instructions

A. Plan how you'll get to your destination. Will you drive or fly? How much will it cost you? If you drive, assume a cost of $0.50 a mile (to cover gas and wear-and-tear on the car), plus the cost of any toll roads. You can figure out the total miles by putting your starting and ending points into an online map. If you fly, find the cost of a flight (don't forget to add in the cost per bag each way you fly), plus the cost of getting to and from the airport (such as taking a taxi or parking).

B. Pick a hotel or campground at which to stay. How much will that cost?

C. Plan your meals. Where will you eat? Keep in mind that you could buy food at the grocery store for some meals. Approximate how much food will cost. Document what you're basing your estimate on.

D. Pick three different activities to do (one per day). How much will they cost you? Look online at the actual costs.

E. How much extra do you need to budget for the whole trip? Be sure to include a little extra money for souvenirs or extra (unexpected) expenses.

PRINCIPLES OF MATHEMATICS 2 | End-of-the-Year Project #2: Bank Account Comparison | Day 171 | Project 2 | Name

Go online or visit several banks and compare 5 different savings accounts Complete the chart and write a summarizing paragraph about the different accounts, including any other advantages or disadvantages about the different accounts that you noticed.

A. Account Name					
B. APY					
C. Interest earned on $1,000 after 1 year					
D. Annual Rate You will usually need to look at the fine print or account details.					
E. Compound Period					
F. Rate per compound period Give your answer as a decimal; do not round.					
G. Number of compound periods in 10 years					
H. Growth of $1,000 after 10 years Use the formula $P = P_0(1 + r)^t$ Use your answer to F. as the value for r, and your answer to G. as the value for t.					
I. Fees					
J. Total fees after 10 years					
K. Column H minus Column J					

Summarizing Paragraph:

Principles of Mathematics 2
Quizzes and Tests

| PRINCIPLES OF MATHEMATICS 2 | Chapters 1–2 | Day 13 | Quiz 1 | Name |

You may use a calculator (▦) on *all* problems on this quiz.

You may consult the reference sheets (p. 423–428) as needed.

Skill Check — Simplify, except where otherwise instructed.

a. $7 + 8.2(1.5 - 1.25) - 8$

b. $-8 \cdot -1 \cdot -1$

c. $|-9|$

d. $\frac{1}{9} \div \frac{2}{3}$

e. $2\frac{1}{2} \cdot \frac{3}{10}$

f. $2\frac{1}{3} + 5\frac{6}{9}$

g. Solve using the distributive property, showing your work: $5(7 + 8)$

h. $8 + -7 + -3$

More with Fractions and Factoring

a. Simplify: $\frac{85 \text{ ft}}{1{,}045 \text{ ft}}$

b. What are the prime factors of 8 and of 88?

c. What is the greatest common factor of 8 and 88?

d. Rewrite as an improper fraction (do not simplify): 55 ÷ 10

e. Rewrite $\frac{17}{50}$ as a decimal.

3. Geometry Time

a. What is the cost of putting a 4-foot wide sidewalk along the front and one side of a lot 60 ft by 160 at $2.50 a square foot?

b. What is the volume of a bin that is 24 in deep, 42 in long, and 8 in tall?

4. Questions

a. What does a negative sign mean?

b. True or false: Math helped in discovering the speed of light.

5. Miscellaneous

a. If you make $62.54 at a job 15 days in a row, how much will you make altogether?

b. If you cool a solution to 5 °C, and then decrease its heat by 63 °C, what will the ending temperature be?

c. A farmer spent the following amounts on a 12-acre field: $30 on plowing, $22 on harrowing and rolling, $16 on seed, $2.75 on drilling, and $27 on cutting and threshing. His income from the field was 240 bushels of wheat that he sold for $2 a bushel, plus $5 he earned renting out part of the field for pasturage. How much did the farmer make after deducting his expenses (i.e., what was his profit)? *Note*: As you might have guessed from the prices, this problem came from an early 1900s textbook.

| PRINCIPLES OF MATHEMATICS 2 | Chapter 3 | Day 24 | Quiz 2 | Name |

1. **Finding Unknowns** — Solve each equation for x (that is, isolate x on a side by itself so as to find its value). Show how you added, subtracted (i.e., added a negative number), multiplied, or divided the same amount to both sides.

   Problems will not be counted as correct unless you show how you obtained the answer by adding, subtracting, multiplying, or dividing both sides by the same quantity.

   a. $x \cdot 12 = 480$

   Example Meaning: How many books can a company buy if each book costs $12 and the company has set aside $480 to spend?

   b. $\frac{x}{7} = 7$

   Example Meaning: How much will a company spend in appreciation gifts if they spend $7 per employee and have 7 employees?

   c. $x - 87 = 14$

   d. $42 \cdot x = 126$

   e. $x + 99 = 214$

2. **Unknowns in Action** — Solve.

   a. If it takes 20 hours to go 800 miles, how fast are you traveling on average?

   b. If a whale takes 6 minutes to go from sea level to an altitude of –1,000 ft, at what rate did the whale change altitude?

3. **Find the Missing Side** — Find the missing sides.

   a. The perimeter is 392 ft.

   b. The perimeter is 265 m.

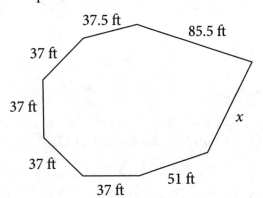
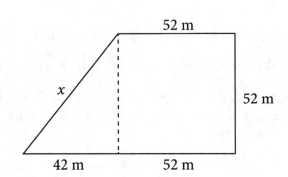

4. **Applying the Skill** — Suppose you were helping your father prepare the garden for planting. Together, you had calculated the area of the rectangular garden as 55.5 square feet. While at the store purchasing soil conditioner, your dad comes up with the idea of edging the garden to help keep the weeds out. There's just one problem: you remember the width was 5 feet, but neither of you can remember the dimensions of the length. Use what you know about finding unknowns to find the missing side.

5. **Equality** — If two expressions are equal and you add the same amount to both of them, will the expressions still be equal?

| PRINCIPLES OF MATHEMATICS 2 | Chapter 4 | Day 33 | Quiz 3 | Name |

You may use a calculator (🖩) on *all* problems on this quiz.

You may consult the reference sheets (p. 423–428) as needed.

Miscellaneous Fraction Problems — For each problem, show how you found the value of the unknown by adding, subtracting, multiplying, or dividing both sides by the same quantity.

Problems will not be counted as correct unless you show how you obtained the answer by adding, subtracting, multiplying, or dividing both sides by the same quantity.

a. $\frac{1}{3} + x = 2\frac{2}{3}$

Example Meaning: If we start at a force of $\frac{1}{3}$ lb, by how much are we increasing the force if we increase it to $2\frac{2}{3}$ lb?

b. $x - \frac{5}{6} = 6\frac{1}{2}$

Example Meaning: If we start with a certain yardage, subtract $\frac{5}{6}$ of a yard, and end up with $6\frac{1}{2}$ yards, how many yards did we have to start?

c. $\frac{2}{3} \cdot x = \$2$

Example Meaning: If $\frac{2}{3}$ of a pound of apples cost $2, how much do the apples cost per pound?

d. $\frac{1}{3} \cdot x = 88$

Example Meaning: If $\frac{1}{3}$ of the total customers surveyed voted for carrying a new brand, how many total customers were surveyed?

e. $\dfrac{80}{x} = 20$

f. $x - \dfrac{-1}{2} = 15$

2. **Pyramid** — The Louvre Pyramid in France[1] has a square base with sides approximately 35.4 m and a height of approximately 21.6 m. What is its volume?

---

[1] Dimensions rounded but based on those given on Structurae, "Louvre Pyramid," (International Database for Civil and Structural Engineering), http://structurae.net/structures/louvre-pyramid, accessed 11/6/15.

| PRINCIPLES OF MATHEMATICS 2 | Chapter 5 | Day 42 | Quiz 4 | Name |

You may use a calculator (🖩) on *all* problems on this quiz.

You may use the reference sheets (p. 423–428) to help answer the questions if needed.

1. **Proportion Time** — Use cross multiplication to solve; show your work.

   a. If there are 3 quarter notes or their equivalent per measure, how many quarter notes or their equivalent are there in a piece of music that has 32 measures?

   b. If a certain milk sample yields 2.5 pounds of butter fat per gallon, how many pounds of butter fat will 100 gallons of such milk yield?

   c. If two rectangles (which we'll call Rectangle A and Rectangle B) are similar, and Rectangle A has a width of 6 ft and a length of 10 ft and Rectangle B has a length of 15 ft, what is Rectangle B's width?

2. **Unit Conversions**

   a. If a compost bin has a volume of 207,360 cubic inches, what is its volume in cubic feet?

   b. How many gallons can a water drum hold if it has a volume of 4,620 in^3.

3. **Time for Time** — Give your final answer to 3a and 3b in hours and minutes, rounding to the nearest minute.

   a. If you travel at a speed of 400 $\frac{mi}{hr}$ (perhaps in a plane!), how long will it take you to go 5,659 miles?

b. If you travel at 500 $\frac{mi}{hr}$, how long will it take you to go 6,862 miles?

c. If it takes 8 min for an object being lowered into a pit at a rate of –0.75 feet per second to go from the top of the pit (view the top of the pit as your reference level of 0 ft) to reach the bottom of the pit how deep is the pit (i.e., what would the height be at the bottom of the pit relative to the top)?
Hint: Be sure to watch your units.

4. **Lever** — Use the relationship $\frac{F_1}{F_2} = \frac{d_2}{d_1}$ and the picture shown to answer the questions.

   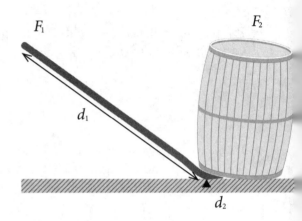

   a. A man is trying to lift a barrel using a cross bar. The distance between the pivot point and the force of the barrel is 0.25 feet (d_2). The barrel weighs 100 pounds (F_2). If the man applies his force 3 feet (d_1) from the pivot point, how much force must he apply?

   b. The same man is trying to lift the same 100 pound (F_2) barrel located 0.25 feet (d_2) from the pivot point, only this time he has a shorter cross bar and applies his force 2 feet (d_1) from the pivot point. How much force must he now apply?

Bonus Question — What's one lesson we can learn from the life of Archimedes?

| PRINCIPLES OF MATHEMATICS 2 | Chapter 6 | Day 53 | Quiz 5 | Name |

You may use a calculator (🖩) on *all* problems on this quiz.

You may consult the reference sheets (p. 423–428) as needed.

Percent Time

a. Let's say you buy a book at a garage sale for $2 and want to sell it for 40% more than you spent for it (which means you want to sell it for 140% of your cost). What would your selling price have to be?

b. A small business has $7,000 of expenses a year and $15,000 in sales. What percent of their sales do their expenses represent?

c. If 25 students are enrolled in a college class and 8 students were absent for class, what percent of the students were absent?

d. In problem 1c, what percent of the students were present?

e. If 58% of a business's earnings go toward covering its expenses, and if its expenses are $10,530 for the year, what are the businesses' total earnings?

f. If the daily value (DV) for sodium[1] is 2,400 mg, and a food source says it contains 22% of the daily value for sodium, how much sodium does it contain?

2. **Rearranging Formulas** — Solve $A = \ell \cdot w$ for w. Also swap the entire sides so that w is on the left side of the equation.

3. **Comprehension Check**

    a. True or false: We can perform the same operation to both sides of an equation, whether we do so with known quantities or unknowns.

    b. Name one fact from Sir Isaac Newton's life.

| PRINCIPLES OF MATHEMATICS 2 | Chapter 7 | Day 59 | Quiz 6 | Name |

You may use a calculator (🖩) on *all* problems on this quiz.

You may consult the reference sheets (p. 423–428) as needed.

Understanding the Language

a. What is the coefficient of x in $5x$?

b. Rewrite $5 \cdot y$ by putting the coefficient directly before the unknown.

c. Why do x and $1x$ mean the same thing?

Finding Unknowns — Solve.

a. $x + \frac{2}{5}x = 5$

b. $2x + x = 18$

c. $2x + 8x = 190$

d. $3x + 4x = 80$

Percent Reminder — From a farm of 160 acres, 30 acres were sold. What percent was sold?

Bonus Question — Archimedes found a mathematical way to test whether or not a crown was _____.

| PRINCIPLES OF MATHEMATICS 2 | Chapter 8 | Day 66 | Quiz 7 | Name |

You may use a calculator (🖩) on *all* problems on this quiz.

You may consult the reference sheets (p. 423–428) as needed.

1. Solve:

   $106 - x = 86$

2. Solve:

   $x - y = 108$, when $y = -6$

3. Evaluate:

   $-3x$, when $x = -6$

4. Solve:

   $3x - x = 89$

5. Solve:

   $7x - 4x = 135$

6. Solve:

   $85.42 - x = 62.78$

7. Solve:

   $3x = 40 + x$

8. A negative sign means *the* _____ *of*.

9. Pick a problem on this quiz and write a word problem for it.

| PRINCIPLES OF MATHEMATICS 2 | Chapter 9 | Day 74 | Quiz 8 | Name |

You may use a calculator (🖩) on *all* problems on this quiz.

You may consult the reference sheets (p. 423–428) as needed.

Parentheses — Use parentheses to show this situation, and then solve: You bought an item that costs $7 minus a $2.50 coupon, and were charged 8% tax on the difference. How much did you pay in tax?

Solving with Parentheses — Solve.

a. $3(\frac{2}{3} + x) = 8$

   Example Meaning: You are tripling a batch of cookies that calls for $\frac{2}{3}$ c. of flour. You know your mother used to add some extra flour, but you can't remember how much. You do remember, though, that she would use 8 cups altogether when tripling the batch. How much flour did your mother add when making a single batch?

b. $1.08(\$70 + \$8 - x) = \$75$

   Example Meaning: If you have a $75 gift certificate you can spend, how much less do you need to spend to get your total to $75 if you've selected a $70 and a $8 item, both of which are subject to a 8% tax?

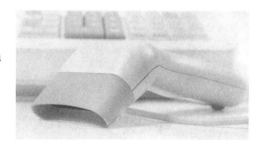

c. $-5(8 - x) = -20$

   Example Meaning: You are returning 5 items, each of which cost $8 minus a per-item discount you'd used. You get back $20. How much was the per-item discount?

d. $800 - (\$4 + x) = \$795.75$

Example Meaning: You're given $800 to spend, and you buy an item that costs $4 plus an unknown amount in tax. If you still have $795.75, what was the tax amount?

3. **Nested Parentheses** — Simplify: $2[3(5 + 15)]$

    Example Meaning: If on average it takes you 5 minutes to read a math lesson and 15 minutes to solve the problems and you complete 3 lessons a day, 2 times a week, how long do you spend on math each week on average?

4. **Understanding the Meaning** — In the example meaning in problem 3, what does the 3 stand for?

Using Inequalities and Unknowns

a. According to the American Heart Association and American Stroke Association website, an HDL of 60 $\frac{mg}{dL}$ "and above is considered protective against heart disease."[1] Use an inequality and the letter x to represent the HDL level that's considered protective against heart disease.

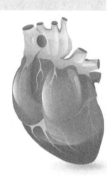

b. Represent a shopping cart total that's greater than $50 with an inequality, using x to represent the cart total.

Inequalities on the Number Line

a. Graph the inequality you wrote in 1a on this number line.

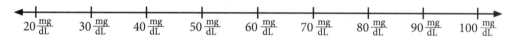

b. Graph the inequality you wrote in 1b on this number line.

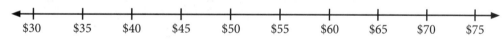

Swapping Sides — Swap the sides in these inequalities, so that the expression on the left is on the right. Be sure to preserve the meaning.

a. $20 < x + 5$

b. $-16 \geq -4x$

c. $25 > x - 6$

d. $1{,}600 \leq 80x$

American Heart Association and American Stroke Association, "Controllable Risk Factors," http://powertoendstroke.org/stroke-reduce-risk-controllable.html, accessed 10/16/15.

4. **Solving Inequalities** — Solve each of the inequalities you wrote as your answers to problem 3.
   a.   b.

   c.   d.

PRINCIPLES OF MATHEMATICS 2 | Chapter 11 | Day 87 | Quiz 10 | Name

This quiz is going to be a little different than normal. Rather than give you questions, it's time to apply what you learned on your own! You may use a computer, library, calculator, etc., to help in completing the assignment. Your analysis must be your own, however.

Find at least one real-life use of statistics. — To find one, pull out a newspaper or business magazine or look online (www.USA.gov/statistics offers links to many of the different statistics our government tracks).

Write a one to three paragraph analysis of the use you found. — Here are some possible questions to address in your analysis:

- Was a conclusion drawn from the statistics presented? If so, was the conclusion drawn accurate? Why or why not?
- Is further research needed before you could know if the statistic was accurate? If so, what research?
- If there was no conclusion or slant presented on the statistical use you found, what kind of conclusions (if any) could be drawn . . . or what information is missing in order to draw a conclusion?
- If there's a graph, does the graph accurately express the data?

Chocolate Probability

a. Let's suppose you do a survey regarding the average age that people first tasted chocolate, and it showed that 15,000 out of the 30,000 participants surveyed first tasted chocolate by age 1. Based on that data alone, how probable is it that a random 1-year-old you meet will have tasted chocolate?

b. Based on the data in 1a, how probable is it that two random 1-year-olds you meet will both have tasted chocolate?

c. If it's 95% probable that the results of the hypothetical survey in 1a are accurate within a specific margin of error, how probable is it that the results are off by more than that margin of error?

Miscellaneous Probability

a. If you have a 12-sided die, 3 sides of which have a dot on them, how probable is it that you'll roll a dot?

b. If you have 30 prizes to give away, 4 of which are candy, and if the prizes are randomly chosen and then given away (causing there to be one less prize after each giveaway), how probable is it that a candy will be chosen first?

c. In the situation described in 2b, what are the odds of a candy being chosen first?

d. In the situation described in 2b, how probable is it that the first two prizes chosen will be candy?

3. **Fundamental Counting Principle** — How many possible combinations are there on a four-digit ATM pin if you can use the digits 0–9?

Bonus Question — List three applications of probability that are not already mentioned on this quiz.

Term Time

a. Is π a variable or a constant?

b. In a function, there's only _____ output for every input.

c. In $y > 8x$, for every value we could input for x, is there only one value for y (i.e., only 1 output), or could y have multiple values?

d. Based on your answer to 3c, given $y > 8x$, can we think of y as a function of x?

Exploring Relationships — If you plan on working two jobs (we'll call them Job A and Job B), then your total earnings equal your earnings from Job A plus your earnings from Job B ($T = A + B$). If one of your jobs (Job A) has a steady monthly salary of $800 and the other (Job B) varies, we would have this equation: $T = \$800 + B$.

a. If you want to see how your total earnings (T) depend on the amount you earn on Job B, what are you viewing as your dependent variable (i.e., output)?

b. Complete this sentence: In problem 2a, we're viewing _____ as a function of _____.

c. Let's say you are considering getting a second job (Job B), but currently only have one job (Job A). The amount you need to earn at Job B depends on how much total earnings (T) you determine you need. In this case, what are you viewing as your dependent variable (i.e., output)?

d. Complete this sentence: In problem 2c, we're viewing ____ as a function of _____.

3. **Exploring Relationships** — The distance we can travel in 5 hr depends on the speed at which we travel. We can describe it with this equation, which shows the function between distance (d) and speed (s): $d = s(5 \text{ hr})$, where $s \geq 0$.

   a. Fill out the rest of the table showing three different inputs and outputs.

s (input, in $\frac{mi}{hr}$)	$d = s(5 \text{ hr})$ where $s \geq 0$	d (output, in mi)
15		
45		
60		

   b. Graph the domain for this function on this number line.

   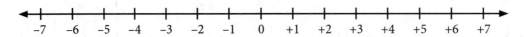

PAGE 332 | PRINCIPLES OF MATHEMATICS 2

PRINCIPLES OF MATHEMATICS 2 — Chapter 14 — Day 114 — Quiz 13 — Name

You may use a calculator (🖩) on *all* problems on this quiz.

1. **Graphing Equations** — Graph the equations shown.

    a. $y = 2x + 4$

    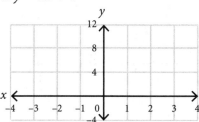

    b. $y = 100x$, where $-2 \leq x < 2$

    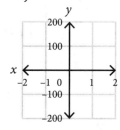

2. **Term Time**

    a. What is the slope of problem 1a?

    b. What is the slope of problem 1b?

    c. What is the *y*-intercept of problem 1a?

    d. What is the *y*-intercept of problem 1b?

    e. Draw a box around any domains that were specified in problems 1a or 1b.

3. **Describing Lines** — Find the linear equations that describe these lines.

    a.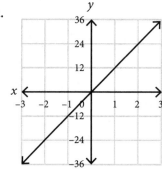

    b.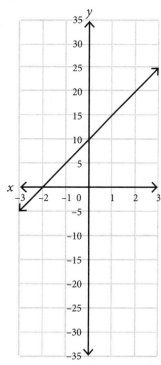

4. **Understanding Check** — Specify whether the following statements are true or false.

   a. The y-intercept is the value at which the line intercepts horizontal axis.

   b. The slope is the ratio of the change in the vertical coordinates and the change in the horizontal coordinates.

   c. In the graph below (which is of a sound wave), we can think of y as a function of x.

   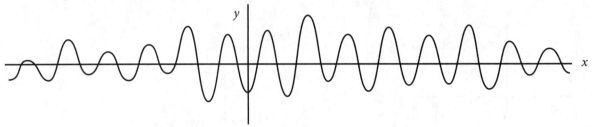

5. **Volume and Base** — Finish graphing how the volume of a rectangular prism would change depending on what was chosen for the area of the base, assuming a constant height of 8 ft and that the area of the base is greater than or equal to 4 ft². Here is the relationship: $V = (8 \text{ ft})B$, where $B \geq 4 \text{ ft}^2$.

   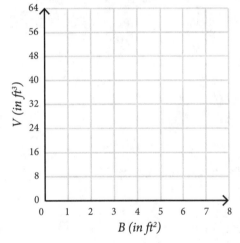

Bonus Question — Write a couple of sentences about Descartes' statement that "I think, hence I am" and his general philosophy.

PRINCIPLES OF MATHEMATICS 2

Chapter 15 | **Day 123** | **Quiz 14** | Name _____

You may use a calculator (🖩) on *all* problems on this quiz.

You may consult the reference sheets (p. 425–434) as needed.

Testing the Language

a. Simplify: $4^2 + 4(3^3 - 2)$

b. Evaluate $x^4 + 5$, when $x = 9$

c. Simplify: $x \cdot x \cdot x \cdot x \cdot x$

d. Simplify: $x + x + x$

Exponents in Action

a. Find the area of a square if the sides are 7.6 ft long.

b. Find the volume of a rectangular prism with sides 30 in, 20 in, and 4 in.

c. Find the volume of a cube with sides 4 m long.

3. **Exponential Growth and Decay** — Use the formula $P = P_0(1 + r)^t$ to find these approximate population growths or decays.

   a. If a bacteria population grows 5% an hour, about how much bacteria will there be after 20 hours if there were 10 bacteria to start? Round to the nearest whole number.

   b. If a vitamin decays at a rate of 1% an hour, about how much will a vitamin that has 15 mg decay to after 1 day (i.e., 24 hours)?

Bonus Question — Why do we find suffering and death in the world?

Negative Exponents

a. Simplify (give the answer as a fraction): 5^{-2}

b. Rewrite using only a positive exponent: 3^{-4}

Scientific Notation — Do not round.

a. Rewrite 0.0000056247 in scientific notation.

b. Rewrite 526,415,800 in scientific notation.

c. Rewrite 5.62×10^{15} in decimal notation.

d. Rewrite 3.12×10^{-8} in decimal notation.

Simplifying — Simplify as much as possible. Give the answers for 3d and 3e in scientific notation.

a. $x^3 x^6$

b. $\frac{x^6}{x^3}$

c. $x^5 + 2x^5$

d. $4 \times 10^2 + 6 \times 10^2$

e. $2 \times 10^8 \cdot 4 \times 10^{-2}$

Bonus Question — Modern algebra is known as symbolic algebra, where we use symbols to describe quantities and relationships between those quantities. What was used in rhetorical and syncopated algebra?

| PRINCIPLES OF MATHEMATICS 2 | Chapter 17 | Day 147 | Quiz 16 | Name |

You may use a calculator (🖩) on *all* problems on this quiz.

Root Time

a. Factor to find the $\sqrt{324}$. List all of the prime factors of 324 as part of your answer.

b. Factor to find $\sqrt[3]{64}$. List all of the prime factors of 64 as part of your answer.

c. Solve: $\sqrt{x} = 241$

d. If the area of a square equals 456 in², what is the length of each side?

Pythagorean Theorem — Use the Pythagorean theorem to find the unknown sides when you can. Remember that the Pythagorean theorem only works when the triangle is a right triangle. If you cannot find a missing side, write "not enough information."

a.
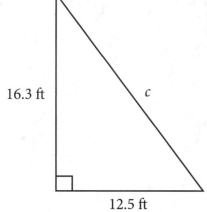
16.3 ft, 12.5 ft, c

b.
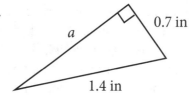
a, 0.7 in, 1.4 in

c.

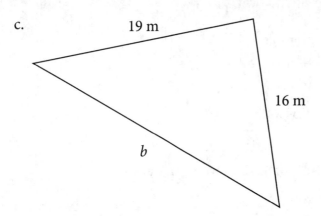

3. **Building a Stool**

   a. You're building a stool, and you want to make sure that the top you've finished really has 90° corners. Your length equals 12 inches and your width equals 5 inches. What should the diagonal across the top equal if the top really has 90° corners?

   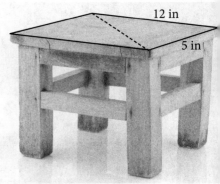

   b. The diagonal of the stool in problem 3a from corner to corner equals 13 inches. Is the top of the stool a rectangle (i.e., does the diagonal cut it into two right triangles — that is, triangles with a 90° angle)?

4. **Surveying** — A surveyor, wishing to determine the distance between two points, A and B, that are separated by a lake, measures a straight line that is 250 yards long that is perpendicular to another line that is 325 yards, thus forming two legs of a right triangle. What is the distance from A to B?

   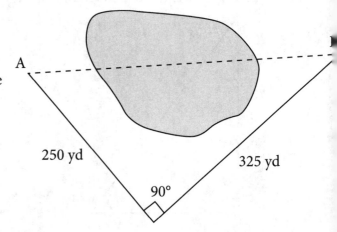

Bonus Question — How does the Pythagorean theorem itself discredit the Pythagorean worldview?

| PRINCIPLES OF MATHEMATICS 2 | Chapter 18 | Day 154 | Quiz 17 | Name |

You may use a calculator (🖩) on *all* problems on this quiz.

Exploring the Ratios in a Right Triangle

a. Find the tangent of the non-right marked angle.

b. Find the sine of the non-right marked angle.

c. Find the cosine of the non-right marked angle.

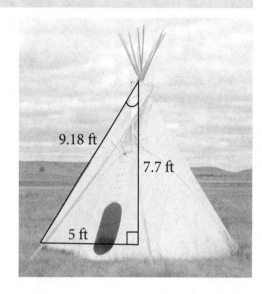

Understanding Calculating Ratios on Calculators

a. We know that all right triangles with a 40° angle are similar, as they have two corresponding angles that are congruent: the 40° angle and the _____ angle.

b. The corresponding sides in similar shapes are proportional/congruent (circle one).

c. What is the ratio between the side opposite a 40° angle in a right triangle and the hypotenuse?

Calculating in Function Notation — Find the requested values.

a. tan(15°)

b. cos(52°)

Find the Missing Side — What is the length of the missing side in the triangle shown?

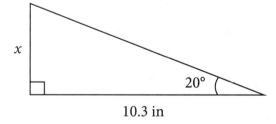

Exploring Sets

a. Suppose set C contains these values: {57, 62, 75, 74, 73, 80, 82, 99}. Use the symbol ∈ to show that 57 is an element of set C.

b. If set C contains the values listed in 1a and is a subset of set E as shown in the diagram, is 57 also an element of the set E?

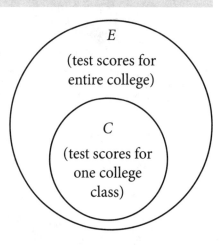

More Sets

a. Is 45 a valid input for x if $x \in \mathbb{Q}$?

b. Is –50 a valid input for x if $x \in \mathbb{Z}$?

c. How would you specify that x must be a natural number?

Sequences

a. Find the first 5 values in $\{r, 4r, 8r, 12r, 16r, \ldots\}$ when r is 3.

b. Does the sequence {7, 21, 63, ...} have a common difference, a common ratio, or neither? If it has one, what is it?

c. Is the sequence in 3b an arithmetic sequence, geometric sequence, or neither?

d. If the pattern continues, what would the next two values of the sequence in 3b be?

In the Interest of Interest

a. How many compound periods are there in 10 years if the interest is compounded monthly?

b. If an account earns 3.3% interest, and that interest is compounded monthly, what is the interest rate per compound period? Give your answer as a decimal; do not round.

c. Use your answers to 1a and 1b and the formula $P = P_0(1 + r)^t$ to find what $700 would grow to after 10 years at 3.3% interest compounded monthly.

d. How much will $6,000 earn in interest after one year at 5% APY?

Budgeting

a. If your health insurance premium is $700 a quarter (every 3 months), how much should you budget per month for it?

b. If you earn $450 a week, how much should you budget as your income per month? Use 4.33 weeks per month.

Other Consumer Math Problems

a. If the instructions call for 10 gallons, and you want to make 40% of the amount in the instructions, how many cups will you need? There are 16 cups in a gallon.

b. If at a dealer's special you pay $500 for a used car that the original asking price was $1,200, what percent of the asking price did you pay?

Bonus Question — Name one truth from Scripture to keep in mind while working with money.

| PRINCIPLES OF MATHEMATICS 2 | Chapters 1–5 | Day 45 | Test 1 | Name |

You may use a calculator (🖩) on *all* problems on this test.

You may consult the reference sheets (p. 423–428) as needed.

Math in Action

a. If a stenographer writes at the rate of 250 words per minute, how long at the same rate would it take him to write 2,000 words? Show how you obtained your answer using cross multiplication.

b. If a mechanically operated hacksaw makes 90 strokes per minute, how many strokes will it make in 60 minutes? Show how you obtained your answer using cross multiplication.

c. How many meters long is a 5-mile race?

d. If a field has an area of 85 square feet, what is its area in square yards?

e. $\frac{4}{5} \cdot x = 52$

Example Meaning: If $\frac{4}{5}$ of the people on the trip wanted Italian dressing, and 52 people wanted Italian dressing, how many people are on the trip?

f. If we travel 400 miles in 8 hours, what is our speed?

g. About how many bushels of grain could the cylinder portion of these 4 silos hold combined if the cylinder portion of each one has a radius of 6 ft and a height of 32 ft?

h. If the area of a rectangle is 80 in² and the length is 5.5 in, what is the width?

2. **Skill Test** — Simplify.

   a. $\dfrac{6}{\frac{1}{4}}$

   b. $\dfrac{35}{5}$

   c. $\dfrac{8}{-2}$

   d. $20 + -3$

3. **Unknowns** — Solve.

   a. $x + 6 = 24.6$

   b. $4.5 \bullet x = 35$

   c. $\dfrac{25}{x} = 5$

   d. $x - 8 = 32$

Math in Action

a. The first week of choir practice there were 45 people at practice, the next 31, the next 35, the next 41, the next 28, and the next 40. What was the average number of people at choir practice over these weeks? Round to the nearest whole number.

b. What was the median attendance at choir practice for the weeks described in 1a? Round to the nearest whole number.

c. The total supplies needed for the children's ministry equals the supplies needed for the children registered plus any extra supplies needed for children who show up that day. In other words, we have this relationship: *total supplies = supplies for registered + extra supplies*, or $t = r + e$. Rearrange $t = r + e$ to solve for r. Also, swap the sides so that r is on the left of the equation.

d. If a church must receive an offering of $6,000 each week to meet its expenses, complete the inequality showing what the offering amount must be to meet expenses.

x _____ $6,000

e. If 6 people register for a retreat and then another 3 register for the same retreat (all at the same price), and if altogether they pay $495, how much does the retreat cost per person?

f. If 55 people had registered for a class but only 44 showed up, what percent of those registered showed?

g. If the 55 people who registered for the class represent 2.5% of the people invited to the class, how many people were invited to the class?

2. **Unknowns** — Solve.

   a. $3x + x = 48$

   b. $22 - 2(5 + x) = 22$

   c. $\$5 + x < \$65$

   d. $x + \frac{1}{4}x = 8$

   e. $-4x < 104$

   f. $50 - (1 + x) = 2$

   g. $5x > 10$

3. **Miscellaneous**

   a. Rewrite so the unknown is on the left side of the inequality: $-105 < x$

   b. Show $x \leq 2$ on the number line.

   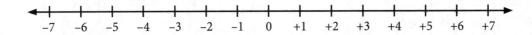

   c. Find 5.5% of $78.50.

   d. 5.04 is 6% of what number?

Test 3

PRINCIPLES OF MATHEMATICS 2 — Chapters 12–18 — Day 135

You may use a calculator (🖩) on *all* problems on this test.

1. How Probable Is That?

a. If there are 4 boxes contestants can choose from, and a $1,000 prize is hidden underneath 1 of the 4 boxes, what is the probability of picking the prize?

b. In the situation described in 1a, what is the probability of picking the prize two times in a row if you got to choose a second time with four new boxes?

c. How many different possible combinations are there for a garage door opener combination if the combination must be 4 digits long, and each digit can contain the numbers 0–4?

2. Graphing — Graph each of the following linear equations. The equations are written in slope-intercept form.

a. $h = (20)t - 100$

Example Meaning: the height (relative to ground level) over time if you lift a bucket out of a well from a depth of 100 m at a rate of $20 \frac{m}{min}$.

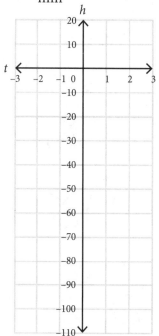

b. $d = \frac{1}{3}b$, where $b \geq 0$

   Example Meaning: the relationship between the number of days the chips you purchased will last and the number of chips you buy if your family eats $\frac{1}{3}$ a bag a day

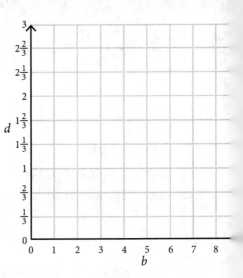

3. **Understanding Relationships**

   a. In a function, for every input there's only _____ output.

   b. In the graph shown, is y a function of x?

   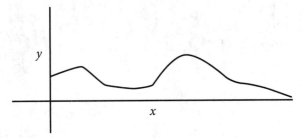

4. **Representing Lines** — The graph shows the amount paid in tax (P) at a specific tax rate (the slope) as the purchase price (B) varies.

   a. What is the slope of the line (i.e., the tax rate)?

   b. What is the y-intercept of the line?

   c. What is the equation that describes the line?

   d. In this graph, we can look at _____ as a function of _____.

Checking Exponents — Simplify.
   a. $(3 + 5)^2$
   b. 5^{-2} (Give your answer as a fraction.)
   c. $16(1 - 0.56)^6$
   d. $4x^2 + 2x^2$

Scientific Notation — Convert these numbers to scientific notation. Do not round.
   a. 0.00435

   b. 142,325,000,000

Spheres — The volume of a sphere is found using this formula: $V = \frac{4}{3}\pi r^3$ (i.e., Volume = $\frac{4}{3} \cdot \pi \cdot$ radius^3). If a volleyball's radius is 4.1 in, what is its volume?

Solve

a. The $\sqrt{500}$ is between what 2 integers?

a. What is the $\sqrt{1{,}936}$? List all of the prime factors as part of your answer.

c. What is the $\sqrt[3]{729}$? List all of the prime factors as part of your answer.

Miscellaneous

a. Solve: $\sqrt{x} = 86$

b. Find the measurements of the side of a square with an area of 78 in².

c. Find: $\tan(15°)$

Right Triangle Time

a. What is the hypotenuse of a right triangle whose legs are 15 feet and 8 feet?

b. Suppose we're building a shed. What height (h) would we have to make the roof if we make the width from the center to the edge 3.5 ft, and want the slanted part of the roof to be 5 ft?

c. Find the cosine of the marked angle in the drawing in problem 3b.

d. Suppose again that we're designing a shed. This time, we know we want the angle of the roof of a shed to be 45°. We also know that we want the slanted part of the roof to be 8 ft. What does the height (h) of the roof of the shed need to be?

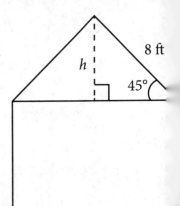

e. In a right triangle, what will the ratio be between the side adjacent to a 35° angle and the hypotenuse?

4. Sets and Sequences

a. If the domain is $x \in \{5, 7, 20\}$, is 25.6 a valid value for x?

b. Look for a common difference in $\{x, 2x, 3x, \ldots\}$ by subtracting each element from the one before it.

$3x - 2x =$ _____ $2x - x =$ _____

c. Would we call $\{x, 2x, 3x, \ldots\}$ an arithmetic sequence, a geometric sequence, or neither?

d. If the pattern continues, what would the next element be in $\{x, 2x, 3x, \ldots\}$ be?

$\{x, 2x, 3x,$ _____ $, \ldots\}$

e. Find the first 4 elements in this sequence $\{x, \frac{1}{2}x, \frac{1}{4}x, \frac{1}{8}x, \ldots\}$, when x is 3.

f. Find the next two elements in $\{2, 5, 3, 5, \ldots\}$, assuming the pattern continues.

$\{2, 5, 3, 5,$ _____ $,$ _____ $\ldots\}$

5. Consumer Math

a. How many compound periods are there in 5 years if the interest is compounded monthly?

b. If an account earns 2.5% interest, and that interest is compounded monthly, what is the interest rate per compound period? Give your answer as a decimal; do not round.

c. Use your answers to 5a and 5b and the formula $P = P_0(1 + r)^t$ to find what $15,000 will grow to after 5 years at 2.5% interest compounded monthly.

d. If you earn $60,000 a year, how much do you earn on average per month?

e. If you want to set aside 10% of your income for savings, how much should you set aside each month if you earn $30,000 a year?

| PRINCIPLES OF MATHEMATICS 2 | Final Test | Day 180 | Test 5 | Name |

You may use a calculator (🖩) on *all* problems on this test.

You may use your reference sheets (423–428) to help answer the questions

Math in Everyday Life

a. If you've finished 23 out of 144 pages of a book, what percent have you finished?

b. Solve: $\frac{1}{50}x = \$15,000$

Example Meaning: A city wants to increase spending by $\frac{1}{50}$ of the current spending. They say that will only increase the spending $15,000 a month. What is the current monthly spending?

c. If you left a $6 tip and the total of your meal was $50, what percent tip did you leave?

d. Solve: $5(\$6 - x) = \$20$

Example Meaning: If you bought 5 shirts at $6 each minus a discount, and ended up spending $20, what was the discount?

e. Solve: $\frac{1}{4}x = \$35$

Example Meaning: If $\frac{1}{4}$ of the total cost is $35, what is the total cost?

f. Suppose you have 495 miles to travel in 9 hours. How fast do you have to travel per hour to arrive on schedule?

g. Suppose you're running late to work. You're on the highway going 65 miles per hour, and your work is still 5 miles away. How many minutes will it take you to get to work if you maintain your current speed? Round your answer to the nearest minute.

h. If you're billed each quarter for $\frac{1}{4}$ of your yearly website hosting bill, and your yearly bill is $80, how much do you pay each quarter?

2. **Shapes, Missing Sides, and More**

   a. Say you want to plant a rectangular garden with an area of 80 ft². You know you want the width to be 8 ft, as that's all that will fit in the side yard. What should the length be to get your desired area?

   b. Find the hypotenuse of a right triangle whose legs are 20 ft and 15 ft.

   c. Find tan(45°)

   d. Find the sine of the marked angle.

   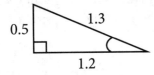

   e. If the area of a square is 89 ft², what is the length of each side?

   f. If you're drawing a blueprint of a home that's 40 ft wide and 50 ft long, and you make the width 0.2 ft on the drawing, how long should you make your drawing?

3. **Graphing Relationships**

   a. Suppose you go into business with someone in a 50–50 partnership. That means that you get $\frac{1}{2}$ of all the profits . . . and $\frac{1}{2}$ of all the losses. Your profits or losses are a function of the business's profits or losses. The function could be expressed with this linear equation: $p = \frac{1}{2}b$, where b represents the business's profits or losses, and p represents your personal profits or losses. Finish completing the table showing three inputs and outputs and graphing $p = \frac{1}{2}b$.

b (input)	p (output)
−600	
0	
600	

   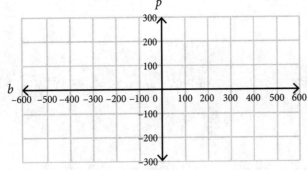

PAGE 358 | PRINCIPLES OF MATHEMATICS 2   Continue to Next Page

b. what equation describes this line?

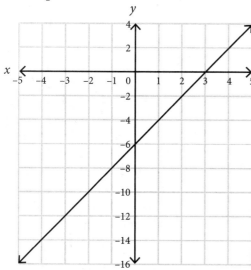

Probability and Stats

a. If you roll a standard die 4 times in a row, what's the probability of rolling a ⚁ all four times?

b. What is the average snow accumulation for the week in a hypothetical city if the snow accumulation per day was 3 in, 4 in, 2.5 in, 0 in, 8.8 in, 0 in, and 0.5 in?

c. Could we conclude off the data in problem 4b that the average you found for the hypothetical city is reflective of the city's typical snowfall? Why or why not?

d. What is the mode for the snow accumulation given in problem 4b?

e. What is the median for the snow accumulation given in problem 5d?

5. **Miscellaneous**

   a. Rewrite in decimal notation (do not round): 2.56×10^{-11}

   b. Simplify: $5(1 + 2.03)^{15}$

   c. What are the first 4 values in $\{x, 4x, 8x, 24x, \ldots\}$ when x is 2?

   d. Solve: $y + 2y = 9$

   e. Evaluate $4x^2$, when x equals 3

   f. Solve: $4x < 64$

   g. Find the $\sqrt{784}$. List all of the prime factors as part of your answer.

6. **Math In Action: Cones** — Given that the formula for finding the volume of a cone is the same as for a pyramid ($\frac{1}{3}$ • area of the base • height, or $\frac{1}{3}Bh$), what is the volume of a construction cone whose base has a radius of 6 in and whose height is 28 in?

7. **End-of-the-Year Project** — Submit your end-of-the-year project that was assigned on Worksheet 21.1.

Principles of Mathematics 2
Answer Key

General Grading Notes

Please use your own judgment when grading. Below are some general principles to keep in mind.

- **Different Strategies** — There is often more than one legitimate approach to a problem. You want to evaluate whether the students are learning the concepts and solving the problems carefully, correctly, and logically.

- **Different Arrangement** — When grading, keep in mind that you can swap the entire sides of an equation without changing the meaning. For example, $8 = x$ and $x = 8$ both mean the same thing and would be equally correct, unless the students were told specifically to arrange the equation a certain way.

- **Open-Ended Questions** — On open-ended questions, answers may vary significantly from what is listed.

- **Partial Credit** — Feel free to give partial credit if a student set up the problem correctly but made a calculation error.

- **Units of Measurement** — If a unit of measure is given in the problem (dollars, feet, etc.), students need to include the unit of measure in their answer. For example, if a student lists "6" instead of "6 in" on a problem where the answer key lists "6 in," the student's answer is only partially correct. Watching units carefully will serve students well, both in real life and in upper-level courses.

- **Showing Steps** — While mental arithmetic should be encouraged, students will sometimes be instructed to show their work (there will be a note in the answer key letting you know this). Showing their work is especially important when students are first learning a skill, as they need to practice the process on simple problems so they'll be able to solve more advanced ones.

- **Word Problems** — Students should always write down the equation(s) they used to solve word problems so you can see what process they followed. Writing down enough steps that someone can see the process followed is a helpful habit to develop, as it makes it easier to find any errors.

- **Rounding** — Unless otherwise instructed, answers should be rounded to two decimal places. When using a calculator, students should not round until the final answer. When answers are written as a percent, the percent should be rounded to two decimal places.

    Example: 4.567 rounds to 4.57

    Example: 26.3574% rounds to 26.36%

    Be aware that an answer may still vary slightly from the one in the answer key due to differences in rounding. This is not typically a problem. The important thing is that students followed instructions (including any instructions given in the problem regarding rounding) and solved the problem accurately.

- **Fractions** — Fractional answers should be denoted in lowest terms, unless otherwise specified. This includes writing improper fractions as mixed numbers. Not only will this make it easier to grade and avoid confusion, it will also provide the student with practice forming equivalent fractions.

    If a problem is given with a fraction in it, students should list any partial quantities in their answer as a fraction so as to become proficient in working with fractions. There is an exception to this: if the problem includes both fractions and decimals, students may give their answer in either notation.

- **Pi (π)** — To keep grading simpler and to help students memorize the approximate value of π, students have been instructed to use 3.14 as the value for π when solving problems in this course.

Assigning a Grade

The grade column in the Suggested Schedule (p. 6–18) is available for you to keep track of a student's grade should you choose to do so. Feel free to use whatever method for grading you've chosen to adopt, or to leave those columns blank if you prefer not to assign grades.

Bonus Questions

Some quizzes include bonus questions, and the final test includes a project. It is up to you to decide how the bonus questions and project should affect the student's grade.

Additional Resources and Course Notes

Please see http://www.christianperspective.net/math/pom2 for links to helpful online resources, along with additional notes and information related to this course. There is also a way to ask questions there.

Chapter 1:

Worksheet 1.1

Math notebook should be prepped.

Student should have added terms to notebook and (optionally) made flashcards for them.

Answer should be 10 ways math applies outside of a textbook. See the "Where Did Math Originate?" section of Lesson 1.1 in the *Student Textbook* for ideas.

a. A worldview is a set of truths (or falsehoods we believe to be true) through which we interpret life.
b. Math is a way of describing God's creation that works because of God's faithfulness.
c. We find evidence of God's wisdom and care because a wise and caring God created all things very good, and we find evidence of suffering and death because this world is marred by sin and no longer the perfect world God created.

a. an expression
b. 14

Note on questions 6b and 6c: Rounding was taught back in Book 1, Lesson 3.2. Please review if needed.
a. I can use a calculator whenever I see the symbol 🖩 or when instructed to on a quiz or test.
b. 0.54
c. 0.9
d. no
e. whenever one is given
f. Answer should be one of the study day suggestions given on p. 421 of this *Teacher Guide*.

Worksheet 1.2

Note: On this worksheet and the next, students will be reviewing a lot of the basics of arithmetic, including adding, subtracting, multiplying, and dividing both whole and decimal numbers. The book assumes students already know how to perform these mechanics; if they do not, do not start this book until they do.

a. name, identify, and order
b. $-, +, =, \neq$
c. Three of these methods should be listed: 20 x 6, 20 • 6, 20(6), (20)6
d. Conventions are agreed-upon protocols or rules that aid us in communication.

a. 8 tens *or* eighty
b. 8 hundredths *or* $\frac{8}{100}$

Students were told to both rewrite the multiplication with parentheses and solve.
a. 5(6) = 30
b. 2(105) = 210

Students were told to both rewrite the multiplication with a • and solve.
a. 8 • 9 = 72
b. 7 • 218 = 1,526

a. 8 − 3 + 2 =

    5 + 2 = 7
b. (8 − 2)10 ÷ 2 =
    (6)10 ÷ 2 =
    60 ÷ 2 =
    30
c. 7.5(0.23 + 0.96) − 1.8 =
    7.5(1.19) − 1.8 =
    8.925 − 1.8 =
    7.13
d. $4\overline{)4 + 9 + 7} = 4\overline{)20} = 5$
e. 2.5 + 4.1(5.6 − 3) ÷ 2 =
    2.5 + 4.1(2.6) ÷ 2 =
    2.5 + 10.66 ÷ 2 =
    2.5 + 5.33 = 7.83

6. a. an expression
   b. 4.25

Worksheet 1.3

1. a. ≠
   b. =
   c. associative property of addition
   d. ≠
   e. =
   f. identity property of multiplication
   g. =
   h. identity property of addition
   i. =
   j. =

2. Check to make sure problems were solved using the distributive property.
   a. 9(15 + 22) =
      9(15) + 9(22) =
      135 + 198 = 333
   b. 5($8.45 + $3.99) =
      5($8.45) + 5($3.99) =
      $42.25 + $19.95 = $62.20

3. a. 256
   b. 256 ÷ 3 = 85.33
   c. $11.36
   d. $2,918.58

Worksheet 1.4

1. total cost of Option B = 50($5.50 + $25.30) + $50 = $1,590
   cost per employee of Option B = $1,590 ÷ 50 = $31.80
   difference in cost per employee = $32.50 − $31.80 = $0.70
   Option B is less expensive by $0.70 per employee.

2. Plan A = $76.45 + $19.99 + $19.99 = $116.43
   Plan B = 4($23.45 + $35.40) = $235.40
   difference in monthly cost = $235.40 − $116.43 = $118.97

3. amount made = income − expenses
   income = $6 + 3(280)($0.05) + $12 = $60
   expenses =
      $6 + 3.5($6.50) + (1,200 ÷ 100)$0.75 =
      $6 + $22.75 + (12)$0.75 =
      $28.75 + $9 = $37.75
   amount made = $60 − $37.75 = $22.25

4. a. 8 + (164)5 + 5 =

8 + 820 + 5 = 833
  b. 88
  c. 13 − 3 + 2 =
  10 + 2 = 12

Worksheet 1.5

1. a. square
   b. circle
   c. octagon
   d. equilateral, acute triangle
   e. rectangle

2. a. $P = 6 \cdot 0.5$ cm = 3 cm
   b. $A = 8$ ft $\cdot$ 8 ft = 64 ft^2
   c. $V = (36$ in $\cdot$ 13 in$)(24$ in$) = 11{,}232$ in^3
   d. $A = (9.5$ in$)(3.3$in$) = 31.35$ in^2

3. a. a shorthand way of representing repeated multiplication
   b. $8 \cdot 8$ or $8(8)$
   c. ft $\cdot$ ft or ft(ft)

4. a. "a mathematical relationship or rule expressed in symbols."[1]
   b. $P = 120$ volts $\cdot$ 25 amps = 3,000 volts $\cdot$ amps = 3,000 watts
   c. length
   d. $62.54 + $587.89 = $650.43
   e. $56.15 − $19.29 = $36.86

5. Geometry means "earth measure."

Worksheet 2.1

1. Students were told they did not need to include units of measure.
   a. $\frac{58}{3}$
   b. $19\frac{1}{3}$
   c. $\frac{4}{3}$
   d. $\frac{45}{5}$
   e. 3
   f. 11
   g. Students should give an example meaning for $\frac{50}{6}$. *Suggestions*: 50 dollars divided by 6 people, 50 miles divided by 6 hours, 50 days divided by 6, etc.
   h. 0.6
   i. 1.33
   j. $\frac{16}{2} = 8$

2. $A = (6$ ft$)(8$ ft$) = 48$ ft^2
   $48 \cdot $23.50 = $1,128

Worksheet 2.2

1. Factor trees may vary slightly, but the circled numbers should be the same.
   a. 26
      ╱ ╲
     ⑬ ⋅ ②

b. 54
   ╱ ╲
  9 ⋅ 6
  ╱╲ ╱╲
 ③⋅③ ②⋅③

2. a. Yes; they both represent the same quantity. They both simplify to $\frac{1}{2}$ or 0.5.
   b. No; they do not represent the same quantity.

3. a. $56 = 2 \cdot 2 \cdot 2 \cdot 7$
      $36 = 2 \cdot 2 \cdot 3 \cdot 3$
      GCF $= 2 \cdot 2 = 4$
   b. $\frac{36}{56} \div \frac{4}{4} = \frac{9}{14}$
   c. $60 = 2 \cdot 2 \cdot 3 \cdot 5$
      $40 = 2 \cdot 2 \cdot 2 \cdot 5$
      GCF $= 2 \cdot 2 \cdot 5 = 20$
   d. $\frac{40}{60} \div \frac{20}{20} = \frac{2}{3}$

4. a. $\frac{1}{32}$
      Note: Notice that the units of measure canceled out.
   b. 22 ft
      Note: Canceling the units of measure left us with an answer in ft.

5. a. $\frac{2 \cdot 2 \cdot 3 \cdot 47}{2 \cdot 2 \cdot 2 \cdot 5 \cdot 5 \cdot 5}$
   b. Two 2s in the fraction in problem 3a should be circled in both the numerator and the denominator.
   c. 4
   (The greatest common factor is the result of multiplying all the common prime factors—in this case, $2 \cdot 2$—together.)
   d. $\frac{564}{1{,}000} \div \frac{4}{4} = \frac{141}{250}$

6. a. $\frac{60 \text{ ft}^2}{7 \text{ ft}}$
   b. $8\frac{4}{7}$ ft
   c. 8.57 ft

Worksheet 2.3

1. a. $\frac{7}{10} + \frac{2}{5} =$
      $\frac{7}{10} + \frac{4}{10} = \frac{11}{10} =$
      $1\frac{1}{10}$
   b. $5\frac{1}{2} + 6\frac{2}{3} =$
      $5\frac{3}{6} + 6\frac{4}{6} =$
      $11\frac{7}{6} =$
      $12\frac{1}{6}$
   c. $\frac{8}{9} - \frac{3}{6} =$
      $\frac{16}{18} - \frac{9}{18} = \frac{7}{18}$
   d. $1\frac{1}{3} - \frac{2}{7} =$
      $\frac{4}{3} - \frac{2}{7} =$
      $\frac{28}{21} - \frac{6}{21} =$
      $\frac{22}{21} = 1\frac{1}{21}$

2. Check to make sure student simplified while completing the multiplication when possible.
   a. $4 \cdot \frac{2}{3} =$
      $\frac{8}{3} = 2\frac{2}{3}$
   b. $\frac{8}{7} \cdot \frac{14^2}{24_3} = \frac{2}{3}$

---

[1] *New Oxford American Dictionary*, 3rd ed. (Oxford University Press, 2012), Version 2.2.1 (156) (Apple, 2011), s.v., "formula."

c. $5\frac{1}{7} \cdot \frac{8}{9} =$

$\overset{4}{\frac{36}{7}} \cdot \frac{8}{9} = \frac{8}{9}$

$\frac{32}{7} = 4\frac{4}{7}$

d. $2 \div \frac{2}{3} = \overset{1}{2} \cdot \frac{3}{\underset{1}{2}} = 3$

e. $\frac{\frac{9}{12}}{\frac{6}{18}} = \frac{9}{12} \div \frac{6}{18} =$

$\overset{3}{\underset{2}{\frac{9}{12}}} \cdot \frac{18}{6}\overset{3}{\underset{2}{}} =$

$\frac{9}{4} = 2\frac{1}{4}$

f. $\frac{\frac{7}{8}}{1\frac{1}{2}} = \frac{7}{8} \div 1\frac{1}{2} =$

$\frac{7}{8} \div \frac{3}{2} =$

$\overset{}{\underset{4}{\frac{7}{8}}} \cdot \frac{2}{3} = \frac{7}{12}$

a. tripling the recipe:

$3 \cdot \frac{3}{4} c = \frac{9}{4} c$

halving the sugar:

$\frac{1}{2} \cdot \frac{9}{4} c = \frac{9}{8} c = 1\frac{1}{8} c$

Note: Students could have halved the sugar and then tripled the recipe as well.

halving the sugar:

$\frac{1}{2} \cdot \frac{3}{4} c = \frac{3}{8} c$

tripling the recipe:

$3 \cdot \frac{3}{8} c = \frac{9}{8} c = 1\frac{1}{8} c$

b. $5 \cdot 56\frac{1}{2}$ in $=$

$5 \cdot \frac{113}{2}$ in $=$

$\frac{565}{2}$ in $= 282\frac{1}{2}$ in

c. $24\frac{1}{2} + 18\frac{2}{5} + 15\frac{2}{5} + 28 + 17\frac{4}{5} + 32\frac{3}{5} + 27\frac{2}{3} =$

$24\frac{15}{30} + 18\frac{12}{30} + 15\frac{12}{30} + 28 + 17\frac{24}{30} + 32\frac{18}{30} + 27\frac{20}{30} =$

$161\frac{101}{30} =$

$164\frac{11}{30}$ tons

a. $\frac{700}{3}$

b. 233.33

c. 4.17

Worksheet 2.4

a. -50
b. $-9\,°C$
c. -80 mi

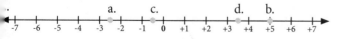

a. Negative Numbers, Rational Numbers
b. Integers, Prime Numbers
c. Rational Numbers, Whole Numbers
d. Irrational Numbers

a. -5 mi
b. 6 mi
c. $-\frac{2}{5}$ ft
d. $\frac{5}{9}$ ft

5. On problems 5b and 5d, check to see that students simplified from right to left, viewing the subtraction as an addition of negative numbers.

a. $5 - 3 - 1 =$
$2 - 1 = 1$

b. $5 - 3 - 1 =$
$5 + -3 + -1 =$
$5 + -4 = 1$

c. $23 - 6 - 2 =$
$17 - 2 = 15$

d. $23 - 6 - 2 =$
$23 + -6 + -2 =$
$23 + -8 = 15$

6. $30\,°F - 50\,°F = -20\,°F$

7. a. -63
b. $-5 - -9 = -5 + 9 = 4$
c. $-5 - - - -9 = -5 + 9 = 4$
d. -4
(The mi canceled out.)
e. 6
f. -10
g. -210 mi
h. 60
i. -5
j. 749 pounds

Worksheet 2.5

1. a. 9
b. 6.89
c. $\frac{2}{3}$
d. $\frac{2}{3}$

2. a. $-118.24° - -71.06° =$
$-118.24° + 71.06° =$
-47.18
$|-47.18| = 47.18$
Note: We could have also found the answer by subtracting $-118.24°$ from $-71.06°$.
$-71.06° - -118.24° = 47.18°$
$|47.18°| = 47.18°$
b. negative

3. a. $-12.09°$
b. $32.80°\,N = 32.80°$
$12.09°\,S = -12.09°$
$32.80° - -12.09° =$
$32.80° + 12.09° = 44.89°$
$|44.89°| = 44.89°$
Note: We could have also found the answer by subtracting $32.80°$ from $-12.09°$.
$-12.09° - 32.80° = -44.89°$
$|-44.89°| = 44.89°$
c. $-79.38° - -71.24° =$
$-79.38° + 71.24° = -8.14°$
$|-8.14°| = 8.14°$
Note: We could have also found the answer by subtracting $-79.38°$ from $-71.24°$.
$-71.24° - -79.38° = 8.14°$
$|8.14°| = 8.14°$

4. a. −2
   b. 2
   c. $7 - 5(2\frac{1}{2}) =$
   $7 - 5(\frac{5}{2}) =$
   $7 - \frac{25}{2} =$
   $\frac{14}{2} - \frac{25}{2} =$
   $-\frac{11}{2} = -5\frac{1}{2}$
   d. $\frac{1}{{}_3 6} \cdot \frac{4^2}{3} = \frac{2}{9}$
   e. $\frac{2}{16} = \frac{1}{8}$

5. Each plant needs 1.5 ft in each direction, so each plant needs 1.5 ft + 1.5 ft, or 3 ft of length. The total length is 6 ft, so we can fit 2 plants across the length. The total width is 6 ft, so we can fit 2 plants across the width. Thus we can fit 2 • 2, or 4 plants total.

Worksheet 2.6

1. a. $-6 - +1 = -7$
   $|-7| = 7$
   There's a 7 hour difference in time.
   b. 8 a.m. minus 7 hours is 1 a.m.
   It is 1 a.m. in Kansas City.
   c. 5 p.m.
   d. 10 a.m. on August 6
   e. finding the difference in time:
   $-7 - +1 = -8$
   $|-8| = 8$
   finding the time in Berlin: 5 p.m. + 8 hrs = 1 a.m. the next day, October 30
   It is 1 a.m. on October 30.

2. 20 °F

3. $42.89° - -34.61° = 42.89° + 34.61° = 77.5°$
   $|77.5°| = 77.5°$
   Note: We could have also found the answer by subtracting 42.89° from −34.61°.
   $-34.61° - 42.89° = -77.5°$
   $|-77.5°| = 77.5°$

4. a. $\frac{7}{8} \cdot \frac{3}{2} = \frac{21}{16} = 1\frac{5}{16}$
   b. $\frac{1}{5} \div 8 = \frac{1}{5} \cdot \frac{1}{8} = \frac{1}{40}$
   c. −4
   d. 24
   e. 42

Worksheet 3.1

1. a. 2
   b. 6
   c. 0
   d. 6
   e. 45

2. a. 9
   b. 6
   c. 9
   d. 4
   e. 5
   f. 27

3. a. The x represents the additional flower bouquets needed
   b. The x represents the amount we can spend.
   c. The x represents the amount we can spend on each package.
   d. The x represents the number of pizzas we can buy.

4. false

5. a. x, y, and z, along with a, b, and c
   b. name, identity, and order

Worksheet 3.2

1. a. =
   b. =
   c. ≠
   d. =
   e. ≠
   f. =
   g. =
   h. =
   i. ≠

2. a. $3 + 20 = 23$
   b. $2.5 = 5 \div 2$
   c. $54 = 6 \cdot 9$
   d. $15 = x - 6$

3. a. 23
   b. 9

4. a. radius
   b. 3.14
   c. $C = 2(3.14)(8 \text{ ft}) = 50.24 \text{ ft}$
   d. $A = \pi \cdot r^2$
   Note: See reference sheet (p. 427–428) for additional ways this formula can be written.
   e. $A = 3.14(8 \text{ ft})(8 \text{ ft}) = 200.96 \text{ ft}^2$
   f. $t = p + f$, where t is the total cost, p is the ticket price, and f is the food.
   Note: Letters used to show the relationship may vary.

5. a. $5 \cdot \$29.99 = \$149.95$
   b. $43° - -17° =$
   $43° + 17° = 60°$
   $|60°| = 60°$
   Note: We could have also found the answer by subtracting 43° from −17°.
   $-17° - 43° = -60°$
   $|-60°| = 60°$
   c. $-5 - +2 = -7$
   $|-7| = 7$
   They are 7 hours apart.
   d. It is 4 a.m. on December 2.
   e. Check to make sure problem was solved using the distributive property.
   $2(10) + 2(3) + 2(\frac{1}{4}) =$
   $20 + 6 + \frac{1}{2} = 26\frac{1}{2}$

Worksheet 3.3

1. Check to make sure students showed how they obtained the answer by adding or subtracting (i.e., adding a negative number) the same amount to both sides, as shown in 1a.

a. $x - 7 + 7 = 20 + 7$
$x = 27$
b. $x = 31$ (added –7 to both sides)
c. $x = 18$ (added –8 to both sides)
d. $x = 211$ (added 98 to both sides)
e. $x = 162$ (added –78 to both sides)
f. $x = 106$ (added –15 to both sides)

Students were instructed to show their work.
a. $27 - 7 = 20$
$20 = 20$
b. $31 + 7 = 38$
$38 = 38$
c. $18 + 8 = 26$
$26 = 26$
d. $211 - 98 = 113$
$113 = 113$
e. $78 + 162 = 240$
$240 = 240$
f. $15 + 106 = 121$
$121 = 121$

a. The x would represent how many brownies there were before dinner.
b. The x would represent how much more you have to save.
c. Answer should be a word problem for $x + 8 = 26$. See the example meaning of problem 1b and the example meanings of problem 2a and 2e of Worksheet 3.1 for ideas.

$x = 18$ (added 8 to both sides)

a. $-1{,}035$
b. -9
c. -9
d. -495
e. $-\frac{4}{7}$
f. $\frac{5}{3} \cdot \frac{3}{2} = \frac{5}{2} = 2\frac{1}{2}$
g. $\overset{3}{6} \cdot \frac{3}{2} = 9$
h. 6 m
a. $\frac{\$55{,}670}{12} = \$4{,}639.17$
b. $\$32.56 \cdot 12 = \$390.72$

To find an unknown in an equation, <u>get the unknown on a side by itself</u>. Do this by performing the <u>same</u> operation using the <u>same quantity</u> to <u>both sides</u> of the equation.

Worksheet 3.4

Check to make sure students showed how they obtained the answer by adding, subtracting (i.e., adding a negative number), multiplying, or dividing the same amount to both sides, as shown in 1a.
a. $\frac{7 \cdot x}{7} \cdot \frac{21}{7}^3$
$x = 3$
b. $x = 6$ (divided both sides by 4)
c. $x = 8$ (divided both sides by 8)
d. $x = 56$ (multiplied both sides by 8)
e. $x = 81$ (multiplied both sides by 9)
f. $x = 171$ (added 91 to both sides)
g. $x = 133$ (added 108 to both sides)
h. $x = 147$ (added –87 to both sides)

i. $x = 68$ (added –36 to both sides)

2. a. $7 \cdot 3 = 21$
$21 = 21$
b. $4 \cdot 6 = 24$
$24 = 24$
c. $8 \cdot 8 = 64$
$64 = 64$
d. $\frac{56}{8} = 7$
$7 = 7$

3. a. The x would represent the amount you can spend per gift.
b. The x would represent the total cost of the event.
c. Answer should be a word problem for $4 \cdot x = 24$. See the example meaning of problem 1a and of other similar problems in previous lessons for ideas.

4. a. -8
b. -80
c. $\frac{3}{2} = 1\frac{1}{2}$
d. 75 m²
e. 10
f. $\frac{50}{10} = 5$

Worksheet 3.5

1. Check to make sure students showed how they obtained the answer by adding, subtracting (i.e., adding a negative number), multiplying, or dividing the same amount to both sides, as shown in 1a.
a. $\frac{8 \cdot x}{8} \cdot \frac{72}{8}^9$
$x = 9$
b. $x = 911$ (added 408 to both sides)
c. $x = 128$ (added –12 to both sides)
d. $x = 7$ (divided both sides by 9)
e. $x = 384$ (multiplied both sides by 8)
f. $x = 2.67$ (divided both sides by 30)

2. a. The x would represent the amount spent on each gift.
b. Answer should be an example meaning for $4 \cdot x = \$2.50$. One possibility is this: Suppose you go to the store and buy 4 cans of beans. How much did each can cost if the cost of all of them combined was $2.50?

3. On 3c–3e, look for any one of the answers listed.
a. yes
b. yes
c. $30\frac{mi}{hr}$ or $\frac{30 \text{ mi}}{hr}$ or $\frac{30 \text{ mi}}{1 \text{ hr}}$
d. $15\frac{m}{s}$ or $\frac{15 \text{ m}}{s}$ or $\frac{15 \text{ m}}{1 \text{ s}}$
e. $2\frac{lb}{in^2}$ or $\frac{2 \text{ lb}}{in^2}$ or $\frac{2 \text{ lb}}{1 \text{ in}^2}$

4. Students were instructed to show their work.
a. $16 \text{ mi} = s \cdot 2 \text{ hr}$
$\frac{\overset{8}{16} \text{ mi}}{2 \text{ hr}} = \frac{s \cdot 2 \text{ hr}}{2 \text{ hr}}$
$8\frac{mi}{hr} = s$
b. $200 \text{ mi} = s \cdot 5 \text{ hr}$
$\frac{\overset{40}{200} \text{ mi}}{5 \text{ hr}} = \frac{s \cdot 5 \text{ hr}}{5 \text{ hr}}$
$40\frac{mi}{hr} = s$

c. 40 mi = $s \cdot$ 3 hr
$$\frac{40 \text{ mi}}{3 \text{ hr}} = \frac{s \cdot 3 \text{ hr}}{3 \text{ hr}}$$
$13.33 \frac{\text{mi}}{\text{hr}} = s$

5. $V = B \cdot h$
    $V = (3.14 \cdot 4 \text{ ft} \cdot 4 \text{ ft})28 \text{ ft}$
    $V = 1{,}406.72 \text{ ft}^3$

Worksheet 3.6

1. a. 27 m + 58 m + 27 m + x = 149 m
    112 m + x = 149 m
    x = 37 m   (added –112 m to both sides)
    b. 45 in + x + 52 in = 187 in
    97 in + x = 187 in
    x = 90 in   (added –97 in to both sides)
    c. 30 ft + 60 ft + 19 ft + 28 ft + x = 183 ft
    137 ft + x = 183 ft
    x = 46 ft   (added –137 ft to both sides)

2. a. 200 cm³ = 4 cm $\cdot$ 5 cm $\cdot$ h
    200 cm³ = 20 cm² $\cdot$ h
    $$\frac{200 \text{ cm}^3}{20 \text{ cm}^2} = \frac{20 \text{ cm}^2 \cdot h}{20 \text{ cm}^2}$$
    $$\frac{\overset{10}{\cancel{200}} \text{ cm}^{3\text{ cm}}}{\cancel{20} \text{ cm}^2} = \frac{20 \text{ cm}^2 \cdot h}{20 \text{ cm}^2}$$
    10 cm = h
    b. 1,600 ft³ = $\ell \cdot$ 10 ft $\cdot$ 8 ft
    1,600 ft³ = $\ell \cdot$ 80 ft²
    $$\frac{1{,}600 \text{ ft}^3}{80 \text{ ft}^2} = \frac{\ell \cdot 80 \text{ ft}^2}{80 \text{ ft}^2}$$
    $$\frac{\overset{20}{\cancel{1{,}600}} \text{ ft}^{3\text{ ft}}}{\cancel{80} \text{ ft}^2} = \frac{\ell \cdot 80 \text{ ft}^2}{80 \text{ ft}^2}$$
    20 ft = ℓ

3. Answer should be an example meaning for 18 + x = 20. For ideas, see the example meanings of similar problems under problem 2 of Worksheet 3.1.

4. 5 = 10 ÷ 2

5. a. yes
    b. Look for any one of the answers listed.
    $100 \frac{\text{lb}}{\text{ft}}$ or $\frac{100 \text{ lb}}{\text{ft}}$ or $\frac{100 \text{ lb}}{1 \text{ ft}}$

Worksheet 3.7

1. Check to make sure students showed how they obtained the answer by adding, subtracting (i.e., adding a negative number), multiplying, or dividing the same amount to both sides, as shown in 1a.
    a. $\frac{5 \cdot r}{5} \cdot \frac{-25}{5}^5$
    $r = -5$
    b. $x = -395$ (added –605 to both sides)
    c. $x = -44$ (added –15 to both sides)
    d. $x = -216$ (multiplied both sides by 6)

2. a. 12,000 ft = $r \cdot$ 15 min + 0 ft
    12,000 ft = $r \cdot$ 15 min
    $$\frac{\overset{800}{\cancel{12{,}000}} \text{ ft}}{\cancel{15} \text{ min}} = \frac{r \cdot 15 \text{ min}}{15 \text{ min}}$$
    $800 \frac{\text{ft}}{\text{min}} = r$
    b. 1,050 ft = $r \cdot$ 5 min + 0 ft
    1,050 ft = $r \cdot$ 5 min
    $$\frac{\overset{210}{\cancel{1{,}050}} \text{ ft}}{\cancel{5} \text{ min}} = \frac{r \cdot 5 \text{ min}}{5 \text{ min}}$$
    $210 \frac{\text{ft}}{\text{min}} = r$
    c. –100 ft = $r \cdot$ 30 min + 0 ft
    –100 ft = $r \cdot$ 30 min
    $$\frac{\overset{10}{\cancel{-100}} \text{ ft}}{\underset{3}{\cancel{30}} \text{ min}} = \frac{r \cdot 30 \text{ min}}{30 \text{ min}}$$
    $-3.33 \frac{\text{ft}}{\text{min}} = r$
    d. –45 m = $r \cdot$ 15 sec + 0 m
    –45 m = $r \cdot$ 15 sec
    $$\frac{\overset{3}{\cancel{-45}} \text{ m}}{\cancel{15} \text{ sec}} = \frac{r \cdot 15 \text{ sec}}{15 \text{ sec}}$$
    $-3 \frac{\text{m}}{\text{sec}} = r$
    e. –70 ft = $r \cdot$ 1.5 min + 0 ft
    –70 ft = $r \cdot$ 1.5 min
    $$\frac{-70 \text{ ft}}{1.5 \text{ min}} = \frac{r \cdot 1.5 \text{ min}}{1.5 \text{ min}}$$
    $-46.67 \frac{\text{ft}}{\text{min}} = r$

3. the height

4. a. –3
    b. 13
    c. –3
    d. –10
    e. –10
    f. –5
    g. $-\frac{1}{2}$
    h. 5 – 2 = 7

5. a. *dimensions of each side of square* = 2 $\cdot$ 44 in = 88 in
    area for each hill = (88 in)(88 in) = 7,744 in²
    hills per acre = $\frac{6{,}272{,}640 \text{ in}^2}{7{,}744 \text{ in}^2}$ = 810 hills
    b. *total number of ears produced* = 810 $\cdot$ 3 = 2,430 ears
    bushels produced = $\frac{2{,}430}{120}$ = 20.25 bushels

Worksheet 4.1

1. a. $\frac{2}{3} + x = \frac{12}{3}$
    $x = \frac{10}{3}$ (added $-\frac{2}{3}$ to both sides)
    $x = 3\frac{1}{3}$
    b. $x = 304\frac{2}{3}$ lb   (added $4\frac{2}{3}$ lb to both sides)
    c. $-\frac{3}{4}$ lb = x
    d. $x = 6\frac{1}{12}$ (added $\frac{3}{4}$ to both sides)

2. a. $x + 70\frac{4}{13}$ lb = $650\frac{1}{3}$ lb
    $x = 580\frac{1}{39}$ (added $-70\frac{4}{13}$ lb to both sides)
    b. $x - 10\frac{1}{10}$ lb = $400\frac{4}{5}$ lb
    $x = 410\frac{9}{10}$ (added $10\frac{1}{10}$ lb to both sides)

3. a. –40 ft = $r \cdot$ 1.5 hr + 0 ft
    –40 ft = $r \cdot$ 1.5 hr
    $-26.67 \frac{\text{ft}}{\text{hr}} = r$ (divided both sides by 1.5 hr)
    b. $200 \frac{\text{km}}{\text{hr}}$ or $\frac{200 \text{ km}}{\text{hr}}$ or $\frac{200 \text{ km}}{1 \text{ hr}}$

Worksheet 4.2

1. a. $\frac{\frac{2}{3} \cdot x}{\frac{2}{3}} = \frac{30}{\frac{2}{3}}$
    $\frac{\cancel{2}}{\cancel{3}} \cdot x \cdot \frac{\cancel{3}}{\cancel{2}} = \overset{15}{\cancel{30}} \cdot \frac{3}{\cancel{2}}$

$x = 45$

b. $\dfrac{\frac{4}{5} \cdot x}{\frac{4}{5}} = \dfrac{60}{\frac{4}{5}}$

$\dfrac{\cancel{4}}{\cancel{5}} \cdot x \cdot \dfrac{\cancel{5}}{\cancel{4}} = \overset{15}{\cancel{60}} \cdot \dfrac{5}{\cancel{4}}$

$x = 75$

c. $\dfrac{x}{\frac{5}{2}} = 49$

$\dfrac{x}{\frac{\cancel{5}}{\cancel{2}}} \cdot \dfrac{\cancel{5}}{\cancel{2}} = 49 \cdot \dfrac{5}{2}$

$x = 122\frac{1}{2}$

a. $\frac{8}{27}$

b. $5\frac{1}{2} \div \frac{1}{3} =$

$\dfrac{11}{2} \div \dfrac{1}{3} = \dfrac{11}{2} \cdot \dfrac{3}{1} =$

$\dfrac{33}{2} = 16\frac{1}{2}$ hats

a. $V = \frac{1}{3} \cdot B \cdot h$

$V = \frac{1}{3}(53{,}074.94 \text{ m}^2)(146.5 \text{ m})$

$V = 2{,}591{,}826.24 \text{ m}^3$

$V = 2{,}591{,}826 \text{ m}^3$ (rounded per instructions)

b. $V = \frac{1}{3} \cdot B \cdot h$

$V = \frac{1}{3}(240.5 \text{ ft} \cdot 240.5 \text{ ft})163 \text{ ft}$

$V = 3{,}142{,}653.58 \text{ ft}^3$

$V = 3{,}142{,}654 \text{ ft}^3$ (rounded per instructions)

a. $C = \pi \cdot d$

$45 \text{ ft} = 3.14 \cdot d$

$\dfrac{45 \text{ ft}}{3.14} = \dfrac{\cancel{3.14} \cdot d}{\cancel{3.14}}$

$14.33 \text{ ft} = d$

b. $x - \frac{3}{4} = 4\frac{2}{3}$

c. $x = 5\frac{5}{12}$ (added $\frac{3}{4}$ to both sides)

d. $-36 \text{ ft} = r \cdot 4 \text{ sec} + 0 \text{ ft}$

$-36 \text{ ft} = r \cdot 4 \text{ sec}$

$-9 \dfrac{\text{ft}}{\text{sec}} = r$ (divided both sides by 4 sec)

Worksheet 4.3

Check to make sure students showed how they obtained the answer via multiplication, as shown in 1a.

a. $\cancel{4} \cdot x \cdot \dfrac{1}{\cancel{4}} = \overset{5}{\cancel{20}} \cdot \dfrac{1}{\cancel{4}}$

$x = 5$

b. $x = 6$ (divided both sides by 6 by multiplying them by $\frac{1}{6}$)

c. $x = 40$ (divided both sides by 5 by multiplying them by $\frac{1}{5}$)

d. $x = 63$ (divided both sides by $\frac{1}{3}$ by multiplying them by $\frac{3}{1}$)

e. $x = 90$ (divided both sides by $\frac{3}{9}$ by multiplying them by $\frac{9}{3}$)

f. $x = 1\frac{1}{3}$ (divided both sides by $\frac{3}{4}$ by multiplying them by $\frac{4}{3}$)

g. $x = \$75$ (divided both sides by $\frac{2}{3}$ by multiplying them by $\frac{3}{2}$)

h. $x = 15$ (divided both sides by 4 by multiplying them by $\frac{1}{4}$)

2. $\frac{1}{3} \cdot 63 = 21$

$21 = 21$

Yes; 21 is the correct value for x.

3. $A = \frac{1}{2} \cdot b \cdot h$

$A = \frac{1}{2} \cdot 53 \text{ m} \cdot 46 \text{ m} = 1{,}219 \text{ m}^2$

4. a. 2

b. $-1\frac{1}{5}$

c. $\frac{7}{4} - \frac{21}{4} = -\frac{14}{4} = -3\frac{2}{4} = -3\frac{1}{2}$

5. $V = \frac{1}{3} \cdot B \cdot h$

$V = \frac{1}{3}(78 \text{ m} \cdot 78 \text{ m})(52 \text{ m})$

$V = 105{,}456 \text{ m}^3$

6. $24 \text{ mi} = s \cdot 4 \text{ hr}$

$6\dfrac{\text{mi}}{\text{hr}} = s$ (divided both sides by 4 hr)

Worksheet 4.4

1. a. $\dfrac{8}{x}$

b. $\dfrac{x}{70}$

c. $\dfrac{100}{x}$

2. a. $\dfrac{70 \text{ mi}}{1 \text{ hr}}$ or $70 \dfrac{\text{mi}}{\text{hr}}$

b. $\dfrac{250 \text{ mi}}{x}$

c. $\dfrac{1 \text{ day}}{31 \text{ days}}$

d. $\dfrac{x}{4.33 \text{ weeks}}$

3. Students should show that they found the unknown by multiplying both sides by the same quantity, as shown in 3a and 3b.

a. $\cancel{8} \cdot \dfrac{x}{\cancel{8}} = 9 \cdot 8$

$x = 72$

b. $\cancel{x} \cdot \dfrac{\$54}{\cancel{x}} = \$9 \cdot x$

$\$54 = \$9 \cdot x$

$\dfrac{\overset{6}{\cancel{\$54}}}{\cancel{\$9}} = \dfrac{\cancel{\$9} \cdot x}{\cancel{\$9}}$

$6 = x$ (divided both sides by $9)

c. $\$80 = \$20 \cdot x$ (multiplied both sides by x)

$4 = x$ (divided both sides by $20)

d. $-40 = -20 \cdot x$ (multiplied both sides by x)

$2 = x$ (divided both sides by -20)

e. $\dfrac{-40}{2} = -20$

$-20 = -20$

Yes, -20 is the correct value.

4. Students were asked to write and solve example meanings for $\dfrac{24}{x} = 8$ and $\dfrac{30}{x} = 15$. The solution and an example meaning for each equation is listed below.

a. $\dfrac{24}{x} = 8$

$24 = 8 \cdot x$ (multiplied both sides by x)

$x = 3$ (divided both sides by 8)

Example Meaning: 24 items divided evenly among how many people will give each person 8 items?

b. $\dfrac{30}{x} = 15$

$30 = 15 \cdot x$ (multiplied both sides by x)

$2 = x$ (divided both sides by 15)

Example Meaning: If we have $30 in the scholarship fund to use to help pay people's admission to an event, for how many people can we pay if the event costs $15 per person?

5. a. −11
   b. −4
   c. 8
   d. $2 \div \frac{1}{3} = 2 \cdot \frac{3}{1} = 6$

6. $A = \ell \cdot w$
   $84 \text{ ft}^2 = \ell \cdot 6 \text{ ft}$
   $14 \text{ ft} = \ell$ (divided both sides by 6 ft)

Worksheet 4.5

1. a. −2
   b. $40 − 2 = 38$
   c. $70 + \frac{39}{40} = x$
      $70\frac{39}{40} = x$
   d. $60 + \frac{25}{10} = x$
      $62\frac{1}{2} = x$
   e. $x = 10\frac{2}{21}$ (added $\frac{2}{21}$ to both sides)
   f. $x + \frac{40}{2} = 50$
      $x + 20 = 50$
      $x = 30$ (added −20 to both sides)
   g. $x + \frac{39}{2} = 80$
      $x = 60\frac{1}{2}$ (added $-\frac{39}{2}$ to both sides)

2. $60\frac{1}{2} - \frac{39}{-2} = 80$
   $60\frac{1}{2} + 19\frac{1}{2} = 80$
   $80 = 80$
   Yes, $60\frac{1}{2}$ is the correct value for x.

3. $V = \frac{1}{3} \cdot B \cdot h$
   $V = \frac{1}{3}(6 \cdot \frac{1}{2} \cdot 20 \text{ ft} \cdot 17.32 \text{ ft})(54 \text{ ft}) = 18,705.6 \text{ ft}^3$

4. a. $64 = 8 \cdot x$ (multiplied both sides by x)
      $8 = x$ (divided both sides by 8)
   b. $200 = 10 \cdot x$ (multiplied both sides by x)
      $20 = x$ (divided both sides by 10)
   c. $52 \div \frac{2}{4} = 52 \cdot \frac{4}{2} = $
      112

Worksheet 5.1A

1. a fancy name for using division to compare quantities
2. a. $\frac{\$20}{3 \text{ bushels}}$
   b. $\frac{30 \text{ oz}}{10 \text{ oz}}$
   c. $\frac{45 \text{ mi}}{5 \text{ hr}}$
   d. $\frac{60 \text{ min}}{1 \text{ hr}}$ or $\frac{60 \text{ min}}{\text{hr}}$
   e. $\frac{1 \text{ hr}}{60 \text{ min}}$
   f. $\frac{\$60}{x}$
   g. $\frac{x}{6 \text{ hr}}$
3. $6.67 per bushel
4. a. $x = 20$ qt

Note: Since the numerator was multiplied by 20, we multiplied the denominator (1 qt) by 20 also in order to form an equivalent ratio.
   b. $x = 192$ pt
   Note: Since the denominator was multiplied by 24, we multiplied the numerator (8 pt) by 24 also in order to form an equivalent ratio.

5. $\frac{3 \text{ c}}{1 \text{ gal}} = \frac{x}{7 \text{ gal}}$; $x = 21$ c
   Note: Since the denominator was multiplied by 7, we multiplied the numerator (3 c) by 7 also in order to for an equivalent ratio.

6. a. 2 and 5
   b. 1 and 10

7. Students were instructed to use the ratio shortcut method
   a. $67.8 \text{ mi} \cdot \frac{1.609344 \text{ km}}{1 \text{ mi}} = 109.11$ km
   b. $58.3 \text{ mi}^2 \cdot \frac{1.609344 \text{ km}}{1 \text{ mi}} \cdot \frac{1.609344 \text{ km}}{1 \text{ mi}} = 151$ km²
   c. $60 \text{ ft}^3 \cdot \frac{12 \text{ in}}{1 \text{ ft}} \cdot \frac{12 \text{ in}}{1 \text{ ft}} \cdot \frac{12 \text{ in}}{1 \text{ ft}} = 103,680$ in³
   d. $103,680 \text{ in}^3 \cdot \frac{1 \text{ gal}}{231 \text{ in}^3} = 448.83$ gal

Worksheet 5.1B

1. a. $345 \text{ min} \cdot \frac{1 \text{ hr}}{60 \text{ min}} = 5.75$ hr
   b. $5 \text{ ton} \cdot \frac{2,000 \text{ lb}}{1 \text{ ton}} = 10,000$ lb
2. a. $52 \text{ picas} \cdot \frac{1 \text{ in}}{6 \text{ picas}} = 8.67$ in
   b. $28 \text{ in} \cdot \frac{6 \text{ picas}}{1 \text{ in}} = 168$ picas
3. $\frac{132 \text{ m}}{78 \text{ m}} = \frac{33 \text{ m}}{x}$
   $x = 19.5$ m
   Note: Students may have set up proportion differently; check for final answer being correct.
4. $\frac{3 \text{ in}}{6 \text{ in}} = \frac{1 \text{ in}}{x}$
   $x = 2$ in
   Note: Students may have set up proportion differently; check for final answer being correct.
5. a. $x = 800$ (divided both sides by $\frac{1}{2}$ by multiplying them by $\frac{2}{1}$)
   b. $\frac{1}{3} \cdot x = \$500$
      $x = \$1,500$ (divided both sides by $\frac{1}{3}$ by multiplying both sides by $\frac{3}{1}$)
   c. $8 \cdot \frac{3}{2} = 12$

Worksheet 5.2

On some problems, students may have set up the proportions differently; check that students found the correct final answer and, in problems 1–2, used cross multiplication.

1. a. $5 \text{ c} \cdot 15 \text{ gal} = 3 \text{ gal} \cdot x$ (cross multiplied)
      $75 \text{ c} \cdot \text{gal} = 3 \text{ gal} \cdot x$
      $\frac{25 \overline{75 \text{ c} \cdot \text{gal}}}{3 \text{ gal}} = \frac{3 \text{ gal} \cdot x}{3 \text{ gal}}$
      $25 \text{ c} = x$
   b. $5 \text{ mi} \cdot x = 20 \text{ hr} \cdot 25 \text{ mi}$ (cross multiplied)
      $5 \text{ mi} \cdot x = 500 \text{ hr} \cdot \text{mi}$
      $\frac{5 \text{ mi} \cdot x}{5 \text{ mi}} = \frac{100 \overline{500 \text{ hr} \cdot \text{mi}}}{5 \text{ mi}}$
      $x = 100$ hr

c. $\frac{2\,c}{4\,\text{gal}} = \frac{x}{18\,\text{gal}}$
2 c • 18 gal = 4 gal • x   (cross multiplied)
36 c • gal = 4 gal • x
$\frac{\cancel{36}^9 c \cdot \cancel{\text{gal}}}{\cancel{4\,\text{gal}}} = \frac{\cancel{4\,\text{gal}} \cdot x}{\cancel{4\,\text{gal}}}$
9 c = x

d. $\frac{15\,\text{mi}}{1\,\text{hr}} = \frac{x}{14\,\text{hr}}$
15 mi • 14 hr = 1 hr • x   (cross multiplied)
210 mi • hr = 1 hr • x
$\frac{210\,\text{mi} \cdot \cancel{\text{hr}}}{\cancel{1\,\text{hr}}} = \frac{\cancel{1\,\text{hr}} \cdot x}{\cancel{1\,\text{hr}}}$
210 mi = x

$\frac{52\,\text{in}}{83\,\text{in}} = \frac{17.33\,\text{in}}{s}$
52 in • s = 83 in • 17.33 in   (cross multiplied)
52 in • s = 1,438.39 in²
$\frac{\cancel{52\,\text{in}} \cdot s}{\cancel{52\,\text{in}}} = \frac{1,438.39\,\text{in}^{2\,\text{in}}}{52\,\text{in}}$
s = 27.66 in

a. $\frac{16\,\text{ft}}{18\,\text{ft}} = \frac{0.8\,\text{ft}}{x}$; x = 0.9 ft
b. $\frac{250\,\text{mi}}{2.5\,\text{in}} = \frac{372\,\text{mi}}{x}$; x = 3.72 in

a. 780 points • $\frac{1\,\text{in}}{72\,\text{points}}$ = 10.83 in
b. 50 points • $\frac{1\,\text{in}}{72\,\text{points}}$ • $\frac{2.54\,\text{cm}}{1\,\text{in}}$ = 1.76 cm

65 ft² • $\frac{1\,\text{yd}}{3\,\text{ft}}$ • $\frac{1\,\text{yd}}{3\,\text{ft}}$ = 7.22 yd²; round up to 8 yd², as we were told we could not buy a portion of a yard.
8 • $4.50 = $36

a. 150   (multiplied both sides by 5)
b. $\frac{x}{5} = \$50$
   x = $250   (multiplied both sides by 5)
c. 6 • $\frac{3}{4} = 4\frac{1}{2}$
d. 33 = 11 • x   (multiplied both sides by x)
   3 = x   (divided both sides by 11)

Worksheet 5.3A

a. $8\,\frac{\text{mi}}{\text{hr}} \cdot \frac{\text{hr}}{8\,\text{mi}} = 1$
b. $\frac{60\,\text{m}}{s} \cdot \frac{s}{60\,\text{m}} = 1$
c. $\frac{1\,\text{gal}}{213\,\text{in}^3} = \frac{231\,\text{in}^3}{1\,\text{gal}}$

Students were told to give the answers to 2b–2d in minutes.

a. $d = \frac{40\,\text{mi}}{1\,\text{hr}} \cdot 20\,\text{min}$
$d = \frac{40\,\text{mi}}{60\,\text{min}} \cdot 20\,\text{min}$
$d = \frac{40\,\text{mi}}{{}_3 60\,\text{min}} \cdot 20\,\text{min}$
d = 13.33 mi
Note: Students needed to convert hours to minutes (or minutes to hours) in order to solve the problem.

b. 20 mi = $\frac{60\,\text{mi}}{1\,\text{hr}} \cdot t$
$20\,\text{mi} \cdot \frac{1\,\text{hr}}{{}_3 60\,\text{mi}} = \frac{60\,\text{mi}}{1\,\text{hr}} \cdot t \cdot \frac{1\,\text{hr}}{60\,\text{mi}}$
$\frac{1}{3}\,\text{hr} = t$
converting to minutes: $\frac{1}{3}\,\text{hr} \cdot \frac{{}^{20}60\,\text{min}}{1\,\text{hr}} = 20\,\text{min}$
20 min = t

c. 20 mi = $\frac{40\,\text{mi}}{1\,\text{hr}} \cdot t$
$20\,\text{mi} \cdot \frac{1\,\text{hr}}{{}_2 40\,\text{mi}} = \frac{40\,\text{mi}}{1\,\text{hr}} \cdot \frac{1\,\text{hr}}{40\,\text{mi}} \cdot t$
$\frac{1}{2}\,\text{hr} = t$
converting to minutes: $\frac{1}{2}\,\text{hr} \cdot \frac{{}^{30}60\,\text{min}}{1\,\text{hr}} = 30\,\text{min}$

30 min = t

d. 10 mi = $\frac{40\,\text{mi}}{1\,\text{hr}} \cdot t$
$10\,\text{mi} \cdot \frac{1\,\text{hr}}{{}_4 40\,\text{mi}} = \frac{40\,\text{mi}}{1\,\text{hr}} \cdot t \cdot \frac{1\,\text{hr}}{40\,\text{mi}}$
$\frac{1}{4}\,\text{hr} = t$
converting to minutes: $\frac{1}{4}\,\text{hr} \cdot \frac{{}^{15}60\,\text{min}}{1\,\text{hr}} = 15\,\text{min}$
15 min = t

3. a. 400 barrels • $\frac{\$1.75}{\text{barrel}} = \$700$

b. total sales of apples:
$\frac{3}{4} \cdot \overset{100}{400}\,\text{barrels} \cdot \frac{\$2.50}{\text{barrel}} = \$750$
amount made:
$750 – $700 = $50

c. $\frac{3\,\text{quarts}}{\text{day}} \cdot \frac{280\,\text{days}}{\text{year}} = \frac{840\,\text{quarts}}{\text{year}}$ or 840 quarts per year
d. $\frac{840\,\text{quarts}}{\text{year}} \cdot \frac{\$2}{\text{quart}} = \frac{\$1,680}{\text{year}}$ or $1,680 per year

4. a. 900 ft = $\frac{400\,\text{ft}}{1\,\text{min}} \cdot t + 0\,\text{ft}$
900 ft = $\frac{400\,\text{ft}}{1\,\text{min}} \cdot t$
2.25 min = t   (divided both sides by $\frac{400\,\text{ft}}{1\,\text{min}}$ by multiplying them by $\frac{1\,\text{min}}{400\,\text{ft}}$)

b. 900 ft = $\frac{70\,\text{ft}}{1\,\text{min}} \cdot t + 0\,\text{ft}$
900 ft = $\frac{70\,\text{ft}}{1\,\text{min}} \cdot t$
12.86 min = t   (divided both sides by $\frac{70\,\text{ft}}{1\,\text{min}}$ by multiplying them by $\frac{1\,\text{min}}{70\,\text{ft}}$)

Worksheet 5.3B

1. a. $\frac{7,000\,\text{lb}}{x} = \frac{2,000\,\text{lb}}{1\,\text{ton}}$; x = 3.5 tons
b. $\frac{2.5\,\text{tons}}{x} = \frac{1\,\text{ton}}{2,000\,\text{lb}}$; x = 5,000 lb
c. $\frac{130\,\text{lb}}{x} = \frac{1\,\text{lb}}{16\,\text{oz}}$; x = 2,080 oz
d. Answer should be student's weight in ounces. The problem can be solved the same way as problem 1c.

2. Students were told to use cross multiplication to solve.
a. 8 • x = 12 • 54   (cross multiplied)
   8 • x = 648
   x = 81   (divided both sides by 8)
b. 25 • 500 = x • 450   (cross multiplied)
   12,500 = x • 450
   27.78 = x   (divided both sides by 450)
c. $\frac{94\,\text{ft}}{50\,\text{ft}} = \frac{9.4\,\text{in}}{x}$
94 ft • x = 50 ft • 9.4 in   (cross multiplied)
94 ft • x = 470 in • ft
$\frac{\cancel{94\,\text{ft}} \cdot x}{\cancel{94\,\text{ft}}} = \frac{\overset{5}{470}\,\text{in} \cdot \cancel{\text{ft}}}{\cancel{94\,\text{ft}}}$
x = 5 in

Note: Students may have set up proportion differently; check for final answer being correct and for cross multiplication being used.

3. a. 15 mi = $\frac{35\,\text{mi}}{1\,\text{hr}} \cdot t$
$\overset{3}{15}\,\text{mi} \cdot \frac{1\,\text{hr}}{{}_7 35\,\text{mi}} = \frac{35\,\text{mi}}{1\,\text{hr}} \cdot t \cdot \frac{1\,\text{hr}}{35\,\text{mi}}$
$\frac{3}{7}\,\text{hr} = t$
converting to minutes:
$\frac{3}{7}\,\text{hr} \cdot \frac{60\,\text{min}}{1\,\text{hr}} = \frac{180\,\text{min}}{7} = 25.71\,\text{min}$

b. 15 mi = $\frac{20\,\text{mi}}{1\,\text{hr}} \cdot t$

$^3 15 \text{ mi} \cdot \frac{1 \text{ hr}}{_4 20 \text{ mi}} = \frac{20 \text{ mi}}{1 \text{ hr}} \cdot t \cdot \frac{1 \text{ hr}}{20 \text{ mi}}$

$\frac{3}{4} \text{ hr} = t$

converting to minutes: $\frac{3}{4} \text{ hr} \cdot \frac{^{15}60 \text{ min}}{1 \text{ hr}} = 45 \text{ min}$

4. a. $x = 75$ (divided both sides by $\frac{2}{3}$ by multiplying them by $\frac{3}{2}$)

  b. If $\frac{15}{16}$ are above freezing, then $\frac{1}{16}$ are below freezing.
  $\frac{1}{16} \cdot 365 \text{ days} = 22.81 \text{ days}$
  23 days   (rounded per instructions)

  c. $\frac{1}{3} \cdot x = 66$ pages
  $x = 198$ pages   (divided both sides by $\frac{1}{3}$ by multiplying them by $\frac{3}{1}$)

  d. $x = 11\frac{1}{3} + \frac{4}{5}$
  $x = 12\frac{2}{15}$ (added $\frac{4}{5}$ to both sides)

  e. $x - \frac{-8}{-9} = 25$
  $x - \frac{8}{9} = 25$
  $x = 25\frac{8}{9}$ (added $\frac{8}{9}$ to both sides)

  f. $3 \cdot \frac{5}{2} = \frac{15}{2} = 7\frac{1}{2}$

Worksheet 5.4

1. Check to see that cross multiplication was used. Only the original proportion and final answer are shown here.

  a. $\frac{40 \text{ lb}}{100 \text{ lb}} = \frac{V_2}{24 \text{ in}^3}$; $V_2 = 9.6 \text{ in}^3$
  b. $\frac{35 \text{ lb}}{10 \text{ lb}} = \frac{V_2}{15 \text{ yd}^3}$; $V_2 = 52.5 \text{ yd}^3$

2. Students may have set up proportions differently; check for final answer being correct.

  a. $\frac{0.1 \text{ in}}{100 \text{ ft}} = \frac{x}{2{,}600 \text{ ft}}$; $x = 2.6 \text{ in}$
  b. alfalfa per time cut:
  $\frac{1.5 \text{ tons}}{1 \text{ acre}} = \frac{x}{12 \text{ acres}}$; $x = 18$ tons
  alfalfa per growing season:
  $7 \cdot 18 \text{ tons} = 126$ tons

  c. $x = 8$ sec
  d. $\frac{1 \text{ in}}{11 \text{ ft}} = \frac{x}{75 \text{ ft}}$; $x = 6.82$ in

3. $\frac{4 \text{ in}}{8 \text{ in}} = \frac{3 \text{ in}}{x}$; $x = 6$ in

4. a. $400 \text{ mi} = s \cdot 5 \text{ hr}$
  $\frac{^{80}400 \text{ mi}}{5 \text{ hr}} = \frac{s \cdot 5 \text{ hr}}{5 \text{ hr}}$
  $80 \frac{\text{mi}}{\text{hr}} = s$

  b. Traveling at $65 \frac{\text{mi}}{\text{hr}}$:
  $400 \text{ mi} = \frac{65 \text{ mi}}{1 \text{ hr}} \cdot t$
  $400 \text{ mi} \cdot \frac{1 \text{ hr}}{65 \text{ mi}} = \frac{65 \text{ mi}}{1 \text{ hr}} \cdot \frac{1 \text{ hr}}{65 \text{ mi}} \cdot t$
  $6.15 \text{ hr} = t$

  Traveling at $55 \frac{\text{mi}}{\text{hr}}$:
  $400 \text{ mi} = \frac{55 \text{ mi}}{1 \text{ hr}} \cdot t$
  $400 \text{ mi} \cdot \frac{1 \text{ hr}}{55 \text{ mi}} = \frac{55 \text{ mi}}{1 \text{ hr}} \cdot \frac{1 \text{ hr}}{55 \text{ mi}} \cdot t$
  $7.27 \text{ hr} = t$
  $7.27 \text{ hr} - 6.15 \text{ hr} = 1.12 \text{ hr}$
  Converting fractional portion to minutes:
  $0.12 \text{ hr} \cdot \frac{60 \text{ min}}{1 \text{ hr}} = 7.2$ min

It would take you 1 hr and 7 min less.
Note: We rounded the minutes per instructions.

5. a. $x + \frac{3}{7} = 5\frac{1}{3}$
  $x = 5\frac{1}{3} - \frac{3}{7}$ (added $-\frac{3}{7}$ to both sides)
  $x = 4\frac{19}{21}$

  b. $x + \frac{2}{7} = 2\frac{1}{4}$
  $x = 2\frac{1}{4} + -\frac{2}{7}$ (added $-\frac{2}{7}$ to both sides)
  $x = 1\frac{27}{28}$

  c. $\frac{7}{9} \cdot x = 6$ acres
  $x = \frac{54}{7}$ acres   (divided both sides by $\frac{7}{9}$ by multiplying them by $\frac{9}{7}$)
  $x = 7\frac{5}{7}$ acres

  d. $x = \frac{84}{8}$ (divided both sides by $\frac{8}{7}$ by multiplying them by $\frac{7}{8}$)
  $x = 10\frac{1}{2}$

  e. $5 \cdot \frac{6}{5} = 6$

  f. $26 \text{ m} \cdot \frac{1 \text{ yd}}{0.9144 \text{ m}} \cdot \frac{3 \text{ ft}}{1 \text{ yd}} = 85.3$ ft
  Note: Students could have also converted from m to cm and then to ft.

Worksheet 5.5

1. Check to see that students used cross multiplication to solve, as shown in 1a.

  a. $\frac{F_1}{800 \text{ lb}} = \frac{0.5 \text{ ft}}{4 \text{ ft}}$
  $F_1 \cdot 4 \text{ ft} = 800 \text{ lb} \cdot 0.5 \text{ ft}$ (cross multiplied)
  $F_1 \cdot 4 \text{ ft} = 400 \text{ ft} \cdot \text{lb}$
  $\frac{F_1 \cdot 4 \text{ ft}}{4 \text{ ft}} = \frac{^{100}400 \text{ ft} \cdot \text{lb}}{4 \text{ ft}}$
  $F_1 = 100$ lb

  b. $\frac{50 \text{ lb}}{F_2} = \frac{2 \text{ ft}}{5 \text{ ft}}$
  $F_2 = 125$ lb

  c. $\frac{100 \text{ lb}}{5{,}000 \text{ lb}} = \frac{1 \text{ ft}}{d_1}$
  $d_1 = 50$ ft

2. a. $300 \text{ mi} = \frac{65 \text{ mi}}{1 \text{ hr}} \cdot t$
  $300 \text{ mi} \cdot \frac{1 \text{ hr}}{65 \text{ mi}} = \frac{65 \text{ mi}}{1 \text{ hr}} \cdot t \cdot \frac{1 \text{ hr}}{65 \text{ mi}}$
  $4.62 \text{ hr} = t$
  Converting the fractional portion to minutes:
  $0.62 \text{ hr} \cdot \frac{60 \text{ min}}{1 \text{ hr}} = 37.2$ min
  4 hr, 37 min $= t$ (rounded per instructions)

  b. $300 \text{ mi} = \frac{45 \text{ mi}}{1 \text{ hr}} \cdot t$
  $6.67 \text{ hr} = t$ (divided both sides by $\frac{45 \text{ mi}}{1 \text{ hr}}$ by multiplying them by $\frac{1 \text{ hr}}{45 \text{ min}}$)
  Converting the fractional portion to minutes:
  $0.67 \text{ hr} \cdot \frac{60 \text{ min}}{1 \text{ hr}} = 40.2$ min
  6 hr, 40 min $= t$ (rounded per instructions)

3. a. $4 \cdot \frac{5}{1} = 20$
  b. $64\frac{1}{5}$ (added $-\frac{4}{5}$ to both sides)
  c. $65\frac{4}{5}$ (added $\frac{4}{5}$ to both sides)
  d. $\frac{2}{3} \cdot 2 c = 1\frac{1}{3} c$
  e. $10 \text{ m} \cdot \frac{1 \text{ yd}}{0.9144 \text{ m}} \cdot \frac{3 \text{ ft}}{1 \text{ yd}} = 32.81$ ft

Note: Students could have also converted from m to cm and then to ft.

Worksheet 5.6

a. Students should have solved using the order of operations.
$7.8(1.2 + 0.8)$
$7.8(2) =$
15.6

b. Check to make sure problem was solved using the distributive property.
$7.8(1.2 + 0.8) =$
$7.8(1.2) + 7.8(0.8) =$
$9.36 + 6.24 = 15.6$

a. -8
b. $7 \cdot \frac{3}{2} = \frac{21}{2} = 10\frac{1}{2}$
c. 2
d. -2
e. 6

a. $x = 16$ (added -9 to both sides)
b. $x = 12$ (divided both sides by 5)
c. $x = 84$ (divided both sides by $\frac{2}{3}$ by multiplying them by $\frac{3}{2}$)
d. $x = 89\frac{7}{8}$ (added $\frac{7}{8}$ to both sides)
e. $x - \frac{1}{2} = 6$
$x = 6\frac{1}{2}$ (added $\frac{1}{2}$ to both sides)
f. $55.6 = 5 \cdot x$ (multiplied both sides by x)
$11.12 = x$ (divided both sides by 5)

prime factors $= 2 \cdot 2 \cdot 19$

a. the opposite of
b. placeholders
c. yes

a. $30\frac{1}{3}$ ft $- 15\frac{1}{2}$ ft $+ 45\frac{1}{6}$ ft $+ 18$ ft $- 33$ ft $=$
$30\frac{2}{6}$ ft $- 15\frac{3}{6}$ ft $+ 45\frac{1}{6}$ ft $+ 18$ ft $+ -33$ ft $= 45$ ft

b. $5\frac{2}{3} + 3\frac{7}{8} =$
$5\frac{16}{24} + 3\frac{21}{24} = 9\frac{13}{24}$ miles per hour

c. $6 + -3\frac{7}{8} = 2\frac{1}{8}$ miles per hour
d. $x = 115$ (divided both sides by $\frac{4}{5}$ by multiplying them by $\frac{5}{4}$)
e. the total number of people surveyed

a. 30 ft² $= \frac{1}{2} \cdot 12$ ft $\cdot h$
30 ft² $= 6$ ft $\cdot h$
$\frac{^5 30\text{ ft}^2}{6\text{ ft}} = \frac{6\text{ ft} \cdot h}{6\text{ ft}}$
5 ft $= h$

b. $V = \frac{1}{3}(43$ ft $\cdot 43$ ft$)(60$ ft$) = 36,980$ ft³

c. 75 m² $\cdot \frac{1\text{ yd}}{0.9144\text{ m}} \cdot \frac{1\text{ yd}}{0.9144\text{ m}} \cdot \frac{3\text{ ft}}{1\text{ yd}} \cdot \frac{3\text{ ft}}{1\text{ yd}} = 807.29$ ft²
Note: Students could have also converted from m² to cm² and then to ft².

d. Finding the volume of 1 crate:
$V = (232.5$ in $\cdot 92.5$ in$)(93.9$ in$) = 2,019,436.875$ in³
Finding the volume of 6 crates:
$6 \cdot 2,019,436.875$ in³ $= 12,116,621.25$ in³

Converting to feet:
$12,116,621.25$ in³ $\cdot \frac{1\text{ ft}}{12\text{ in}} \cdot \frac{1\text{ ft}}{12\text{ in}} \cdot \frac{1\text{ ft}}{12\text{ in}} = 7,011.93$ ft³

8. a. 40 mi $= s \cdot 2.25$ hr
$17.78 \frac{\text{mi}}{\text{hr}} = s$ (divided both sides by 2.25 hr)

b. -500 ft $= \frac{-25\text{ ft}}{1\text{ sec}} \cdot t + 0$
-500 ft $= \frac{-25\text{ ft}}{1\text{ sec}} \cdot t$
20 sec $= t$ (divided both sides by $\frac{-25\text{ ft}}{1\text{ sec}}$ by multiplying them by $\frac{1\text{ sec}}{-25\text{ ft}}$)

9. Students should have used cross multiplication to solve.
a. $\frac{F_1}{500\text{ lb}} \cdot \frac{1\text{ ft}}{8\text{ ft}}$
$F_1 \cdot 8$ ft $= 500$ lb $\cdot 1$ ft (cross multiplied)
$\frac{F_1 \cdot 8\text{ ft}}{8\text{ ft}} = \frac{500\text{ lb} \cdot 1\text{ ft}}{8\text{ ft}}$
$F_1 = 62.5$ lb

b. $\frac{F_1}{500\text{ lb}} \cdot \frac{1\text{ ft}}{20\text{ ft}}$
$F_1 \cdot 20$ ft $= 500$ lb $\cdot 1$ ft (cross multiplied)
$\frac{F_1 \cdot 20\text{ ft}}{20\text{ ft}} = \frac{^{25}500\text{ lb} \cdot 1\text{ ft}}{20\text{ ft}}$
$F_1 = 25$ lb

10. Students should have used cross multiplication to solve. Proportion could have been set up differently.
$\frac{2.5\text{ ft}}{4\text{ ft}} = \frac{3\text{ ft}}{x}$
2.5 ft $\cdot x = 4$ ft $\cdot 3$ ft (cross multiplied)
2.5 ft $\cdot x = 12$ ft²
$\frac{2.5\text{ ft} \cdot x}{2.5\text{ ft}} = \frac{12\text{ ft}^2}{2.5\text{ ft}}$
$x = 4.8$ ft

Worksheet 6.1

1. a. 80%
   b. 85%
   c. $\frac{56}{100} = \frac{14}{25}$
   d. 0.56
   e. 0.5785
      Note: Students were told not to round.
   f. 88.89%
   g. $1.3333 = 133.33\%$
   h. 42.35%
   i. 87.2%
   j. $12.53 \div 0.2 = 62.65$
   k. $0.05 \cdot \$800 = \$40$

2. Students should have solved using the method shown.
   a. $\frac{20}{100} = \frac{x}{156.24}$; $x = 31.25$
   b. $\frac{12}{100} = \frac{x}{46}$; $x = 5.52$
   c. $\frac{62}{100} = \frac{x}{40\text{ tons}}$; $x = 24.8$ tons
   d. total percent expected to not survive:
      $10\% + 15\% = 25\%$
      number of seeds expected to not survive:
      $\frac{25}{100} = \frac{x}{1,000\text{ seeds}} = 250$ seeds
   e. $1,000 - 250 = 750$ seeds
      or
      $100\% - 25\% = 75\%$
      $\frac{75}{100} = \frac{x}{1,000\text{ seeds}}$; $x = 750$ seeds

PRINCIPLES OF MATHEMATICS 2 | PAGE 373

3. a. $400 \text{ mi} = \frac{60 \text{ mi}}{1 \text{ hr}} \cdot t$

    $400 \text{ mi} \cdot \frac{1 \text{ hr}}{60 \text{ mi}} = \frac{60 \text{ mi}}{1 \text{ hr}} \cdot t \cdot \frac{1 \text{ hr}}{60 \text{ mi}}$

    $6.67 \text{ hr} = t$

    Converting fractional portion to minutes:

    $0.67 \text{ hr} \cdot \frac{60 \text{ mi}}{1 \text{ hr}} = 40.2 \text{ min}$

    $6 \text{ hr } 40 \text{ min} = t$ (rounded per instructions)

    b. $\frac{5 \text{ yd}}{s} = \frac{12.5 \text{ yd}}{0.25 \text{ yd}}$; $s = 1 \text{ yd}$

    c. $x = \$328.75$ (added –$96.50 to both sides)

    d. $x + \frac{3}{5} = 7$

    $x = 6\frac{2}{5}$ (added $-\frac{3}{5}$ to both sides)

    e. $\frac{8}{5} = 1\frac{3}{5}$

Worksheet 6.2A

1. a. $x + 10 = 45$
    b. $3 = 6 - x$
    c. $d = s \cdot t$

2. a. $V = B \cdot h$

    $\frac{V}{h} = \frac{B \cdot h}{h}$

    $\frac{V}{h} = \frac{B \cdot \cancel{h}}{\cancel{h}}$

    $\frac{V}{h} = B$

    b. $B = \frac{V}{h}$

    c. $B = \frac{70 \text{ m}^3}{7 \text{ m}}$

    $B = \frac{10 \cancel{70} \text{ m}^{3 \text{ m}^2}}{\cancel{7} \cancel{\text{m}}} = 10 \text{ m}^2$

    d. $V = B \cdot h$

    $\frac{V}{B} = \frac{B \cdot h}{B}$

    $\frac{V}{B} = \frac{\cancel{B} \cdot h}{\cancel{B}}$

    $\frac{V}{B} = h$

    e. $h = \frac{V}{B}$

    f. $h = \frac{60 \text{ ft}^3}{9 \text{ ft}^2}$

    $h = \frac{60 \text{ ft}^{3 \text{ ft}}}{9 \text{ ft}^2} = 6.67 \text{ ft}$

    g. $C = 2 \cdot \pi \cdot r$

    $\frac{C}{2 \cdot \pi} = \frac{2 \cdot \pi \cdot r}{2 \cdot \pi}$

    $\frac{C}{2 \cdot \pi} = \frac{\cancel{2} \cdot \cancel{\pi} \cdot r}{\cancel{2} \cdot \cancel{\pi}}$

    $\frac{C}{2 \cdot \pi} = r$

    h. $r = \frac{C}{2 \cdot \pi}$

    i. $r = \frac{6 \text{ cm}}{2 \cdot 3.14} =$

    $\frac{6 \text{ cm}}{6.28} = 0.96 \text{ cm}$

3. Check that students found answers using the method shown.
    a. $0.06 \cdot \$450 = \$27$
    b. $0.2 \cdot \$75.67 = \$15.13$

4. a. $x - \frac{1}{5} \text{ lb} = 300 \text{ lb}$

    $x = 300\frac{1}{5} \text{ lb}$ (added $\frac{1}{5}$ lb to both sides)

    b. Students were told to use cross multiplication to solve.

    $\frac{30 \text{ gal}}{3 \text{ wk}} = \frac{x}{72 \text{ wk}}$

    $30 \text{ gal} \cdot 72 \text{ wk} = 3 \text{ wk} \cdot x$ (cross multiplied)

    $\frac{^{10}\cancel{30} \text{ gal} \cdot 72 \text{ wk}}{\cancel{3} \text{ wk}} = \frac{3 \text{ wk} \cdot x}{3 \text{ wk}}$

    $720 \text{ gal} = x$

Worksheet 6.2B

1. Check that students found answers using the method shown.
    a. $0.05 \cdot 85 = 4.25$
    b. $0.3 \cdot 180 = 54$

2. Students should have found percentages using the method shown.
    a. $0.07 \cdot 5{,}000 \text{ IUs} = 350 \text{ IUs}$
    b. $\frac{1}{4} \cdot 350 \text{ IUs} = 87.5 \text{ IUs}$
    c. $0.15 \cdot 60 \text{ mg} = 9 \text{ mg}$
    d. calcium in 2 cups:
    $20\% + 20\% = 40\%$
    $0.4 \cdot 1{,}000 \text{ mg} = 400 \text{ mg}$
    Note: Students may have found the answer by multiplying 20% of 1,000 mg and then multiplying that by 2.
    e. iron in cereal = $0.32 \cdot 18 \text{ mg} = 5.76 \text{ mg}$
    additional iron needed = $65 \text{ mg} - 5.76 \text{ mg} = 59.24 \text{ mg}$

3. a. $x = 2\frac{4}{5}$ (added $-\frac{1}{5}$ to both sides)

    b. $-\frac{8}{5} = -1\frac{3}{5}$

    c. -5

    d. $\frac{7}{3} - \frac{21}{4} =$

    $\frac{28}{12} - \frac{63}{12} =$

    $-\frac{35}{12} = -2\frac{11}{12}$

    e. $x = 9\frac{9}{14}$ (added $3\frac{1}{2}$ to both sides)

Worksheet 6.3A

1. a. $R \cdot 60 = 30$
    $R = 0.5$ (divided both sides by 60)
    $R = 50\%$ (converted to a percent)

    b. $R \cdot 160 \text{ ac} = 30 \text{ ac}$
    $R = 0.1875$ (divided both sides by 160 ac)
    $R = 18.75\%$ (converted to a percent)

    c. $R \cdot 120 = 14$
    $R = 0.1167$ (divided both sides by 120)
    $R = 11.67\%$ (converted to a percent)

    d. $100\% - 11.67\% = 88.33\%$
    Note: We could also have found the number of trees that survived (120 – 14 = 106) and then figured out what percent survived (i.e., found R using this equation: $R \cdot 120 = 106$).

2. a. $0.15 \cdot B = 12$
    $B = 80$ (divided both sides by 0.15)

    b. $0.4 \cdot B = 4{,}000 \text{ bushels}$
    $B = 10{,}000 \text{ bushels}$ (divided both sides by 0.4)

    c. $0.4 \cdot B = \$2{,}500$
    $B = \$6{,}250$ (divided both sides by 0.4)

3. a. -72

    b. $2 + x = 20$
    $x = 18$ (added –2 to both sides)

    c. $x = 75$ (divided both sides by $\frac{1}{5}$ by multiplying them by 5)

    d. $\frac{5}{8} \cdot x = 11{,}565$
    $x = 18{,}504$ (divided both sides by $\frac{5}{8}$ by

e. 0.52 • 5,000 IUs = 2,600 IUs
f. 5 • x = 75   (multiplied both sides by x)
    x = 15   (divided both sides by 5)

Worksheet 6.3B

a. R • 250 = 217
    R = 0.868   (divided both sides by 250)
    R = 86.8%   (converted to a percent)
b. 0.02 • B = $400
    B = $20,000   (divided both sides by 0.02)
c. 0.6 • $75,000 = P
    $45,000 = P
d. R • 200 = 45
    R = 0.225   (divided both sides by 200)
    R = 22.5%   (converted to a percent)
e. 0.16 • B = 800 people
    B = 5,000 people   (divided both sides by 0.16)
f. 8 • $1.56 = P
    $12.48 = P
g. R • 60,000 mi = 10,000 mi
    R = 0.1667   (divided both sides by 60,000 mi)
    R = 16.67%   (converted to a percent)

a. $\frac{d}{s} = t$ (divided both sides by s)
    $t = \frac{d}{s}$ (swapped the entire sides of the equation)

b. $t = \frac{300 \text{ mi}}{50 \frac{\text{mi}}{\text{hr}}} =$

$\overset{6}{300} \text{ mi} \cdot \frac{1 \text{ hr}}{50 \text{ mi}} = 6 \text{ hr}$

a. $50 = $5 • x   (multiplied both sides by x)
    10 = x   (divided both sides by $5)
b. Check that problem was written in addition to the answer.
    $\frac{x}{5} = 7$
    x = 35   (multiplied both sides by 5)
c. $V = \frac{1}{3} \cdot B \cdot h$
    $V = \frac{1}{3}(60 \text{ m} \cdot 60 \text{ m})(20 \text{ m}) = 24{,}000 \text{ m}^3$
d. x = 21 min

Worksheet 6.4

Students were instructed not to round their answers.

a. F = −40
b. $\frac{F}{m} = a$ (divided both sides by m)
    $a = \frac{F}{m}$ (swapped the entire sides of the equation)
c. $a = \frac{5}{40} = 0.125$
d. m = 0.175   (divided both sides by 40)

a. R • $300 = $135
    R = 0.45   (divided both sides by $300)
    R = 45%   (converted to a percent)
b. 0.15 • B = $560
    B = $3,733.33   (divided both sides by 0.15)
c. 4.25 • $0.50 = P
    $2.13 = P
d. R • 125 = 70

    R = 0.56   (divided both sides by 125)
    R = 56%   (converted to a percent)
e. 100% − 56% = 44%

3. a. $V = \frac{1}{3} \cdot B \cdot h$
    Convert height from meters to feet:
    $8 \text{ m} \cdot \frac{1 \text{ yd}}{0.9144 \text{ m}} \cdot \frac{3 \text{ ft}}{1 \text{ yd}} = 26.24671916 \text{ ft}$
    $V = \frac{1}{3}(7 \text{ ft} \cdot 7 \text{ ft})(26.24671916 \text{ ft})$
    $V = 428.7 \text{ ft}^3$
    $V = 429 \text{ ft}^3$ (rounded per instructions)
    Note: Students could have also converted from meters to centimeters and then to feet.
b. $A = \ell \cdot w$
    A = 8 in • 9 in
    A = 72 in²
c. $P = 2(\ell) + 2(w)$
    P = 2(8 in) + 2(9 in)
    P = 34 in

4. a. $M = \frac{F_2}{F_1}$ (divided both sides by F_1)
b. $M = \frac{300 \text{ lb}}{20 \text{ lb}} = 15$
c. $M = \frac{300 \text{ lb}}{40 \text{ lb}} = 7.5$
d. $4 = \frac{F_2}{50 \text{ lb}}$
    200 lb = F_2 (multiplied both sides by 50 lb)

Worksheet 7.1

1. a. 8x
    b. 6x
    c. 24x
    d. 7y

2. a. 3 • $6
    Note: It is fine if the student shows the multiplication a different way, such as this: 3($6).
    b. 5s
    c. 7d
    d. 3x

3. a. 4($5) = $20
    b. 3(−2) = −6
    c. 2(−8) = −16
    d. $4(10 \frac{\text{mi}}{\text{hr}}) = 40 \frac{\text{mi}}{\text{hr}}$
    e. 3($6) = $18

4. a. $\frac{A}{w} = \ell$ (divided both sides by w)
    $\ell = \frac{A}{w}$ (swapped the entire sides of the equation)
b. 0.05 • B = $14.32
    B = $286.40   (divided both sides by 0.05)
c. 1.15 • $620 = P
    $713 = P
    Note: We could also have found 15% of $620, and then added that to $620 to get the new wage.
d. Room A:
    R • 33 = 31
    R = 0.9394   (divided both sides by 33)
    R = 93.94%   (converted to a percent)
    Room B:
    R • 42 = 39
    R = 0.9286   (divided both sides by 42)

$R = 92.86\%$ (converted to a percent)
Room C:
$R \cdot 26 = 24$
$R = 0.9231$ (divided both sides by 26)
$R = 92.31\%$ (converted to a percent)
Room A has the highest percentage of attendance.

Worksheet 7.2
1. a. We are referring to the multiplier of one or more unknowns.
   b. 8
   c. 45
   d. no

2. a. $13x$
   b. $11x$
   c. already simplified

3. a. $13x = \$65$ (combined like terms)
      $x = \$5$ (divided both sides by 13)
   b. $6x = 18$ (combined like terms)
      $x = 3$ (divided both sides by 6)
   c. Students were instructed to show their work.
      $4(3) + 2(3) = 18$
      $12 + 6 = 18$
      $18 = 18$

4. a. $7x + 2x = \$81$
      $9x = \$81$ (combined like terms)
      $x = \$9$ (divided both sides by 9)
   b. $3x + 6x = 72$ pages
      $9x = 72$ pages (combined like terms)
      $x = 8$ pages (divided both sides by 9)

5. a. weight of milk per day:
      $3 \cdot 8.5$ lb $= 25.5$ lb
      weight of milk per year:
      $365.25 \cdot 25.5$ lb $= 9{,}313.88$ lb
   b. weight of butterfat per year:
      $0.04 \cdot 9{,}313.88$ lb $= 372.56$ lb
   c. pounds of butter per year:
      $\frac{372.56 \text{ lb}}{x} = \frac{1 \text{ lb}}{1.17 \text{ lb}}$
      $x = 435.9$ lb

Worksheet 7.3
1. a. $1s$
   b. $1t$
   c. $1x$
   d. $1d$

2. a. $4x = 28$ (combined like terms)
      $x = 7$ (divided both sides by 4)
   b. $8x = 32$ (combined like terms)
      $x = 4$ (divided both sides by 8)
   c. $x + 0.15x = \$250$
      $1.15x = \$250$ (combined like terms)
      $x = \$217.39$ (divided both sides by 1.15)

3. a. Apple Trees:
      $R \cdot 120 = 14$
      $R = 0.1167$ (divided both sides by 120)
      $R = 11.67\%$ (converted to a percent)
      Raspberry Bushes:
      $R \cdot 70 = 0$
      $R = 0$ (divided both sides by 70)
      $R = 0\%$ (converted to a percent)
      Grapevines:
      $R \cdot 1{,}000 = 35$
      $R = 0.035$ (divided both sides by 1,000)
      $R = 3.5\%$ (converted to a percent)
   b. total planted $= 120 + 70 + 1{,}000 = 1{,}190$
      total that did not survive $= 14 + 0 + 35 = 49$
      $R \cdot 1{,}190 = 49$
      $R = 0.0412$ (divided both sides by 1,190)
      $R = 4.12\%$ (converted to a percent)
   c. $0.01 \cdot \$4{,}000 = \$40$
   d. $0.01 \cdot \$2{,}500 = \$25$
      $\$40 - \$25 = \$15$
      His premium would reduce by $15.

Worksheet 7.4
1. a. $\frac{1}{4}(\$200) = \$50$
   b. $\frac{1}{4}(-\$500) = -\$125$
   c. $\frac{5}{3}(5) = \frac{25}{3} = 8\frac{1}{3}$
   d. $\frac{2}{3}(-10 \text{ lb}) = \frac{-20 \text{ lb}}{3} = -6\frac{2}{3}$ lb

2. Students were told to leave any improper fractions as improper fractions.
   a. $\frac{2}{6}x + \frac{3}{6}x = \frac{5}{6}x$
   b. $\frac{5}{5}x + \frac{3}{5}x = \frac{8}{5}x$

3. a. $\frac{2}{6}x + \frac{3}{6}x = 40$
      $\frac{5}{6}x = 40$ (combined like terms)
      $x = 48$ (divided both sides by $\frac{5}{6}$ by multiplying them by $\frac{6}{5}$)
   b. $\frac{5}{5}x + \frac{3}{5}x = 350$
      $\frac{8}{5}x = 350$ (combined like terms)
      $x = \frac{1{,}750}{8} = 218\frac{3}{4}$ (divided both sides by $\frac{8}{5}$ by multiplying them by $\frac{5}{8}$)

4. $\frac{1}{3} \cdot 48 + \frac{1}{2} \cdot 48 = 40$
   $16 + 24 = 40$
   $40 = 40$

5. $\frac{7}{7}x + \frac{1}{7}x = 19$
   $\frac{8}{7}x = 19$ (combined like terms)
   $x = \frac{133}{8} = 16\frac{5}{8}$ (divided both sides by $\frac{8}{7}$ by multiplying them by $\frac{7}{8}$)

6. $\frac{2}{3}$

Worksheet 7.5
1. a. $2x = \$45$ (added $-\$5$ to both sides)
      $x = \$22.50$ (divided both sides by 2)
   b. $4x = 1{,}600$ m (added $-5{,}000$ m to both sides)
      $x = 400$ m (divided both sides by 4)
   c. $9x + \$28 = \$75$
      $9x = \$47$ (added $-\$28$ to both sides)
      $x = \$5.22$ (divided both sides by 9)
   d. $12x + \$5 + \$20 = \$90$

$12x + \$25 = \$90$
$12x = \$65$ (added –$25 to both sides)
$x = \$5.42$ (divided both sides by 12)
e. $2x - 11 = 50$ (combined like terms)
$2x = 61$ (added 11 to both sides)
$x = 30.5$ (divided both sides by 2)
f. $10x - 12 = 24$ (combined like terms)
$10x = 36$ (added 12 to both sides)
$x = 3.6$ (divided both sides by 10)
g. $\frac{3}{3}x + \frac{1}{3}x = 28$
$\frac{4}{3}x = 28$ (combined like terms)
$x = 21$ (divided both sides by $\frac{4}{3}$ by multiplying both sides by $\frac{3}{4}$)
h. $\frac{5}{5}x + \frac{4}{5}x = 25$
$\frac{9}{5}x = 25$ (combined like terms)
$x = \frac{125}{9} = 13\frac{8}{9}$ (divided both sides by $\frac{9}{5}$ by multiplying them by $\frac{5}{9}$)

a. $4x$
b. $40x$
$V = \frac{1}{3}Bh$

Worksheet 8.1

a. $2 + 5 = 7$
b. $3 - 8 = -5$
c. 45
d. -45
e. 3
f. -3

a. $7 - 5 = 2$
b. $7 - -5 = 7 + 5 = 12$
c. $15 - -2 = 15 + 2 = 17$
d. $15 - - -2 = 15 - 2 = 13$

opposite

a. $x = 5$ (divided both sides by 2)
b. $8a = 18$ (combined like terms)
$a = 2.25$ (divided both sides by 8)
c. $\frac{1}{8}x + \frac{32}{8}x = 6$
$\frac{33}{8}x = 6$ (combined like terms)
$x = \frac{48}{33}$ (divided both sides by $\frac{33}{8}$ by multiplying them by $\frac{8}{33}$)
$x = 1\frac{15}{33} = 1\frac{5}{11}$
d. $\frac{1}{2}x + 3x = 35$ hr
$\frac{1}{2}x + \frac{6}{2}x = 35$ hr
$\frac{7}{2}x = 35$ hr (combined like terms)
$x = 10$ hr (divided both sides by $\frac{7}{2}$ by multiplying them by $\frac{2}{7}$)

Worksheet 8.2

a. -8
b. 6
c. $-y$
d. s
e. $-t$
f. v

2. Check to make sure starting equations are correct as well as final answers.
   a. $\$15,000 = g - \$5,000$
      $\$20,000 = g$ (added $5,000 to both sides)
   b. $g = \$15,000 + \$5,000$
      $g = \$20,000$

3. a. $a = c - b$ or $a = c + -b$ (added $-b$ to both sides)
   b. $v = 56 - v_o$ or
      $v = 56 + -v_o$ (added $-v_o$ to both sides)
   c. $\ell = 10$ ft $+ w$ (added w to both sides)
   d. $t + -a = s$ or $t - a = s$ (added $-a$ to both sides)
      $s = t + -a$ or $s = t - a$ (swapped the entire sides of the equation)

4. a. $\frac{2}{3}x + \frac{3}{3}x = 1{,}820$
      $\frac{5}{3}x = 1{,}820$ (combined like terms)
      $x = 1{,}092$ (divided both sides by $\frac{5}{3}$ by multiplying them by $\frac{3}{5}$)
   b. $\frac{5}{30}x + \frac{12}{30}x = 85$
      $\frac{17}{30}x = 85$ (combined like terms)
      $x = 150$ (divided both sides by $\frac{17}{30}$ by multiplying them by $\frac{30}{17}$)
   c. -132.6

Worksheet 8.3

1. a. $-2s$
   b. $-1x$, which simplifies to $-x$
   c. $-\frac{2}{5}y$
   d. $\frac{1}{3}x$
   e. $-8x$
   f. $-7x$

2. a. $-2p$
   b. $-4a$
   c. $-3s$

3. a. $-5(\$6) = -\$30$
   b. $-4(4) = -16$
   c. $-2(5$ lb$) = -10$ lb
   d. $- -9 = 9$

4. Students were told to leave any improper fractions as improper fractions.
   a. $5x$
   b. $4x$
   c. $-5x$
   d. $-3x$
   e. $\frac{3}{3}x - \frac{1}{3}x = \frac{2}{3}x$ (combined like terms)
   f. $\frac{15}{5}x - \frac{2}{5}x = \frac{13}{5}x$ (combined like terms)

5. a. $3x = 21$ (combined like terms)
      $x = 7$ (divided both sides by 3)
   b. $\frac{3}{3}x - \frac{1}{3}x = 24$
      $\frac{2}{3}x = 24$ (combined like terms)
      $x = 36$ (divided both sides by $\frac{2}{3}$ by

c. $2a = 6$
   $a = 3$ (divided both sides by 2)
d. Students were instructed to show their work.
   $7(3) - 5(3) = 6$
   $21 - 15 = 6$
   $6 = 6$

6. a. $9x - 3x = \$96$
      $6x = \$96$ (combined like terms)
      $x = \$16$ (divided both sides by 6)
   b. $x - \frac{1}{4}x = 15$
      $\frac{4}{4}x - \frac{1}{4}x = 15$
      $\frac{3}{4}x = 15$ (combined like terms)
      $x = 20$ (divided both sides by $\frac{3}{4}$ by multiplying them by $\frac{4}{3}$)

7. true
   (We know from the identity property of multiplication that multiplying by 1 doesn't change the value of a quantity.)

Worksheet 8.4

1. Students were instructed to show their work.
   a. $-x = -5$ (added -17 to both sides)
      $(-1)(-x) = (-5)(-1)$
      $x = 5$
   b. $-x = -23.91$ (added -26.45 to both sides)
      $(-1)(-x) = (-23.91)(-1)$
      $x = 23.91$
   c. $-x = -21.43$ (added -56.99 to both sides)
      $(-1)(-x) = (-21.43)(-1)$
      $x = 21.43$
   d. $56.99 - 21.43 = 35.56$
      $35.56 = 35.56$

2. a. $\frac{5}{5}x - \frac{4}{5}x = \frac{1}{5}x$ (combined like terms)
   b. $10x = 10,560$ ft (combined like terms)
      $x = 1,056$ ft (divided both sides by 10)
   c. $4.5x = 550$ (combined like terms)
      $x = 122.22$ (divided both sides by 4.5)
   d. $2x + 50 = 60$ (combined like terms)
      $2x = 10$ (added -50 to both sides)
      $x = 5$ (divided both sides by 2)
   e. $\frac{8}{8}x - \frac{7}{8}x = 18$
      $\frac{1}{8}x = 18$ (combined like terms)
      $x = 144$ (divided both sides by $\frac{1}{8}$ by multiplying them by $\frac{8}{1}$)
   f. $b = 25$ (divided both sides by -9)
   g. $x = a + y$ (added y to both sides)

Worksheet 8.5

1. On problems 1c and 1e, students were instructed to show their work.
   a. $5w = 120$ ft $+ 2w$
      $3w = 120$ ft (added $-2w$ to both sides)
      $w = 40$ ft (divided both sides by 3)
   b. $150 = 30x$ (added $-x$ to both sides)
      $5 = x$ (divided both sides by 30)
   c. $5 + 150 = 31(5)$
      $155 = 155$
   d. $34 = 17x$ (added x to both sides)
      $2 = x$ (divided both sides by 17)
   e. $34 - 2 = 16(2)$
      $32 = 32$

2. a. $-x = -62$ (added -16 to both sides)
      $x = 62$ (multiplied both sides by -1)
   b. $7x = 469$ (combined like terms)
      $x = 67$ (divided both sides by 7)
   c. $2x = 45$ (combined like terms)
      $x = 22.5$ (divided both sides by 2)
   d. $x + \frac{1}{4}x = \$560$
      $\frac{4}{4}x + \frac{1}{4}x = \$560$
      $\frac{5}{4}x = \$560$ (combined like terms)
      $x = \$448$ (divided both sides by $\frac{5}{4}$ by multiplying them by $\frac{4}{5}$)
   e. $\frac{1}{4}(\$448) = \$112$
      (We knew that the bonus was $\frac{1}{4}$ of the weekly salary, so we multiplied the weekly salary we found in 2d by $\frac{1}{4}$.)
   f. $a = c + x$ (added x to both sides)
   g. $8 - -6 =$
      $8 + 6 = 14$

Worksheet 9.1

1. Students were told to use decimals rather than fractions to represent partial quantities in the answers.
   a. $C = \frac{5}{9}(80° - 32°)$
      $C = 26.67°$
   b. $C = \frac{5}{9}(20° - 32°)$
      $C = -6.67°$
   c. $C = \frac{5}{9}(32° - 32°)$
      $C = 0°$

2. a. $2[3(9)] =$
      $2[27] =$
      54
   b. $6[4 + 3(3)] =$
      $6[4 + 9] =$
      $6[13] =$
      78

3. Check to make sure parentheses were used in writing each problem.
   a. $9(\$4.50 + \$5)$
   b. $0.04(\$7 + \$9.24)$

4. a. $9(\$9.50) = \$85.50$
   b. $0.04(\$16.24) = \$0.65$

5. a. $3x - x = \$15$
      $2x = \$15$ (combined like terms)
      $x = \$7.50$ (divided both sides by 2)
   b. $4x + 2x = \$480$
      $6x = \$480$ (combined like terms)
      $x = \$80$ (divided both sides by 6)
   c. $\frac{24}{8}x - \frac{2}{8}x = 40$
      $\frac{22}{8}x = 4$ (combined like terms)

$x = \frac{32}{22} = 1\frac{10}{22} = 1\frac{5}{11}$ (divided both sides by $\frac{22}{8}$ by multiplying them by $\frac{8}{22}$)

d. $-y = 32.8$ (added –75.2 to both sides)
$y = -32.8$ (multiplied both sides by –1)

Worksheet 9.2

Check to make sure problems were solved using the order of operations.
a. $4(15) = 60$
b. $\frac{5}{9}(\frac{24}{20} + \frac{3}{20}) =$
$\frac{5}{9}(\frac{27}{20}) =$
$\frac{5}{9}(\frac{27}{20}\substack{3\\4}) = \frac{3}{4}$
c. $2(-2) = -4$
d. $4(2) = 8$

Check to make sure problems were solved using the distributive property.
a. $4(5) + 4(10) = 20 + 40 = 60$
b. $\frac{5}{9}(\frac{6}{5}) + \frac{5}{9}(\frac{3}{20}) =$
$\frac{2}{3} + \frac{1}{12} =$
$\frac{8}{12} + \frac{1}{12} =$
$\frac{9}{12} = \frac{3}{4}$
c. $2(6 + -8)$
$2(6) + 2(-8) =$
$12 + -16 = -4$
d. $4(6 + -4)$
$4(6) + 4(-4) =$
$24 + -16 = 8$

a. $5x + 5(2) = 30$
$5x + 10 = 30$
$5x = 20$ (added –10 to both sides)
$x = 4$ (divided both sides by 5)
b. $4(6 + x) = 48$
$4(6) + 4x = 48$
$24 + 4x = 48$
$4x = 24$ (added –24 to both sides)
$x = 6$ (divided both sides by 4)
c. $4(x + -2) = 28$
$4x + 4(-2) = 28$
$4x + -8 = 28$
$4x = 36$ (added 8 to both sides)
$x = 9$ (divided both sides by 4)
d. $15(\$12 + -x) = \$120$
$15(\$12) + 15(-x) = \$120$
$\$180 + -15x = \$120$
$-15x = -\$60$ (added –$180 to both sides)
$x = \$4$ (divided both sides by –15)
e. $4(\frac{3}{4}) + 4x = 11$
$3 + 4x = 11$
$4x = 8$ (added –3 to both sides)
$x = 2$ (divided both sides by 4)
f. $(7 + x)3 = 30$
$(7)3 + 3x = 30$
$21 + 3x = 30$
$3x = 9$ (added –21 to both sides)
$x = 3$ (divided both sides by 3)

4. Students were instructed to write each problem using parentheses.
a. $10(\$1.50 + \$4.50) =$
$10(\$6) = \$60$
b. $10(\$2 + x) = \$50$
$\$20 + 10x = \$50$
$10x = \$30$ (added –$20 to both sides)
$x = \$3$ (divided both sides by 10)
c. $5(\$7 + \$10) =$
$5(\$17) = \$85$
d. $5(\$7 + x) = \$75$
$\$35 + 5x = \$75$
$5x = \$40$ (added –$35 to both sides)
$x = \$8$ (divided both sides by 5)

5. a. $15° = \frac{5}{9}(F + -32°)$
$15° = \frac{5}{9}(F) + \frac{5}{9}(-32°)$
$15° = \frac{5}{9}F + -\frac{160}{9}°$
$\frac{295}{9}° = \frac{5}{9}F$ (added $\frac{160}{9}°$ to both sides)
$59° = F$ (divided both sides by $\frac{5}{9}$ by multiplying them by $\frac{9}{5}$)

b. $100° = \frac{5}{9}(F + -32°)$
$100° = \frac{5}{9}(F) + \frac{5}{9}(-32°)$
$100° = \frac{5}{9}F + -\frac{160}{9}°$
$\frac{1,060}{9}° = \frac{5}{9}F$ (added $\frac{160}{9}°$ to both sides)
$212° = F$ (divided both sides by $\frac{5}{9}$ by multiplying them by $\frac{9}{5}$)

Worksheet 9.3

1. Check to make sure problems were solved using the distributive property.
a. $4 + 1(5 + 6) =$
$4 + 1(5) + 1(6) =$
$4 + 5 + 6 = 15$
b. $20 + 1(43 + -5) =$
$20 + 1(43) + 1(-5) =$
$20 + 43 + -5 = 58$

2. a. $8 + 3 + x = 30$
$11 + x = 30$
$x = 19$ (added –11 to both sides)
b. $\$15 + \$35 - x = \$25$
$\$50 - x = \$25$
$-x = -\$25$ (added –$50 to both sides)
$x = \$25$ (multiplied both sides by –1)
c. the amount spent on dinner

3. a. $8 + (3 + 19) = 30$
$30 = 30$
b. $\$15 + (\$35 - \$25) = \$25$
$\$25 = \$25$

4. a. $1.5x = 39$ (added –x to both sides)
$x = 26$ (divided both sides by 1.5)
b. $4(3 - 1)$
c. $4(2) = 8$
d. $4(x - 1) = 60$
e. $4(x + -1) = 60$

PRINCIPLES OF MATHEMATICS 2 | PAGE 379

$4x + -4 = 60$
$4x = 64$ (added 4 to both sides)
$x = 16$ (divided both sides by 4)

Worksheet 9.4

1. a. *second boy's earnings*
   b. $150
   c. $1,200 = (x + \$150) + x$
   d. $1,200 = 2x + \$150$ (removed parentheses and combined like terms)
   $1,050 = 2x$ (added −$150 to both sides)
   $525 = x$ (divided both sides by 2)
   e. $1,200 = (\$525 + \$150) + \$525$
   $1,200 = \$1,200$
   f. *first boy's earnings* $= x + \$150$
   first boy's earnings $= \$525 + \$150 = \$675$

2. a. $6x + 18 = 25$
   $6x = 7$ (added −18 to both sides)
   $x = 1.17$ (divided both sides by 6)
   b. $2(x + -2) = 20$
   $2x + -4 = 20$
   $2x = 24$ (added 4 to both sides)
   $x = 12$ (divided both sides by 2)
   c. $5x + 10 = 15x$
   $10 = 10x$ (added −5x to both sides)
   $1 = x$ (divided both sides by 10)
   d. $\frac{3}{4}(5 + -x) = 3$
   $\frac{15}{4} + -\frac{3}{4}x = 3$
   $-\frac{3}{4}x = -\frac{3}{4}$ (added $-\frac{15}{4}$ to both sides)
   $x = 1$ (divided both sides by $-\frac{3}{4}$ by multiplying them both by $-\frac{4}{3}$)
   e. $1.06(\$9 + -x) = \$5.13$
   $1.06(\$9) + 1.06(-x) = \$5.13$
   $\$9.54 + -1.06x = \$5.13$
   $-1.06x = -\$4.41$ (added −9.54 to both sides)
   $x = \$4.16$ (divided both sides by −1.06)
   f. $2(24 \text{ in} + 2 \text{ in})$
   g. $2(26 \text{ in}) = 52 \text{ in}$
   h. $5[(7.5)5] =$
   $5[37.5] = 187.5$
   i. $2x + 8 = 0$ (added −2x to both sides)
   $2x = -8$ (added −8 to both sides)
   $x = -4$ (divided both sides by 2)
   j. $2x + 0.1x = \$800$
   $2.1x = \$800$ (combined like terms)
   $x = \$380.95$ (divided both sides by 2.1)

Worksheet 9.5

1. Check to make sure problems were solved using the order of operations.
   a. $-3(14) = -42$
   b. $3 - (7) = -4$
   c. $37 - (6) = 31$

2. Check to make sure problems were solved using the distributive property.
   a. $-3(5) + -3(7) + -3(2) =$
   $-15 + -21 + -6 = -42$
   b. $3 + -1(9 + -2) =$
   $3 + -1(9) + -1(-2) =$
   $3 + -9 + 2 = -4$
   c. $37 + -1(10 + -4) =$
   $37 + -1(10) + -1(-4) =$
   $37 + -10 + 4 = 31$

3. a. $-4(\$2) + -4x = -\$28$
   $-\$8 + -4x = -\$28$
   $-4x = -\$20$ (added $8 to both sides)
   $x = \$5$ (divided both sides by −4)
   b. $87 + -4(10 + x) = 27$
   $87 + -4(10) + -4x = 27$
   $87 - 40 + -4x = 27$
   $47 + -4x = 27$
   $-4x = -20$ (added −47 to both sides)
   $x = 5$ (divided both sides by −4)
   c. $50 + -1(42 + -x) = 16$
   $50 + -1(42) + -1(-x) = 16$
   $50 + -42 + x = 16$
   $8 + x = 16$
   $x = 8$ (added −8 to both sides)
   d. $12 + -1(x + -4) = -19$
   $12 + -1(x) + -1(-4) = -19$
   $12 + -x + 4 = -19$
   $16 + -x = -19$
   $-x = -35$ (added −16 to both sides)
   $x = 35$ (multiplied both sides by −1)
   e. *the discount*

Worksheet 10.1

1. a. $7 < 8$
   b. $8 > 7$
   c. *income* $\leq \$6,000$
   d. *hours worked* ≥ 40
   e. *time* $\neq 0$

2. no
   (Lesson 10.1 in the *Student Textbook* showed other less than symbols that have also been used.)

3. a. $3x = 256$ (combined like terms)
   $x = 85.33$ (divided both sides by 3)
   b. $-x = -53$ (added −8 to both sides)
   $x = 53$ (multiplied both sides by −1)
   c. $\frac{6}{6}x + \frac{5}{6}x = 110$
   $\frac{11}{6}x = 110$ (combined like terms)
   $x = 60$ (divided both sides by $\frac{11}{6}$ by multiplying them by $\frac{6}{11}$)
   d. *the speed Betty can type*
   e. $20(\$10 + \$12 - \$2)$
   f. $20(\$20) = \$400$

4. a. *nickels* $= \$0.05x$
   pennies $= \$0.01x$
   b. $\$0.10x + \$0.05x + \$0.01x = \$0.80$
   c. $\$0.16x = \$0.80$ (combined like terms)
   $x = 5$ (divided both sides by $0.16)
   d. $\$0.10(5) + \$0.05(5) + \$0.01(5) = \$0.80$
   $\$0.50 + \$0.25 + \$0.05 = \$0.80$
   $\$0.80 = \$0.80$

Worksheet 10.2

a.

b.

c.

d.

a. $x \leq \$18$
b. $x \geq 20$
c. $x \geq 0$ in
d. $x > 3$
e. $x > -3°$ F

a. $5x = 20$	(combined like terms)
$x = 4$	(divided both sides by 5)
b. $\frac{1}{8}x + \frac{8}{8}x = 72$	
$\frac{9}{8}x = 72$	(combined like terms)
$x = 64$	(divided both sides by $\frac{9}{8}$ by multiplying them by $\frac{8}{9}$)
c. $11x = 350$	(combined like terms)
$x = 31.82$	(divided both sides by 11)
d. $3(\$7 + x) = \$22$	
e. $\$21 + 3x = \$22$	
$3x = \$1$	(added –$21 to both sides)
$x = \$0.33$	(divided both sides by 3)
f. $-2x = -22$	(added –14 to both sides)
$x = 11$	(divided both sides by –2)

Worksheet 10.3

a. $9 > 5$
b. $x > 5$
c. $23 < 56$
d. $x < 14$
e. $x + 5 > 25$
f. $x \leq 0$
g. $x - 6 \leq 12$
h. $a + b \geq 0$

a.

b.

c.

3. a. *daylight* or *hours of daylight*
b. 13 hr
c. 24 hr = $(x + 13$ hr$) + x$
d. 24 hr = $2x + 13$ hr (removed parentheses and combined like terms)

  11 hr = $2x$ (added –13 hr to both sides)

5.5 hr = x or
5 hr, 30 min = x (divided both sides by 2)
e. *darkness* = $x + 13$ hr
  darkness = 5.5 hr + 13 hr
  darkness = 18.5 hr or 18 hr, 30 min
f. 24 hr = 18.5 hr + 5.5 hr
  24 hr = 24 hr
  darkness = 5.5 hr + 13 hr = 18.5 hr

Worksheet 10.4

1. Note that the direction of the sign changed whenever both sides were multiplied or divided by a negative number.
   a. $x \leq \$150$ (added –$100 to both sides)
   b. $x \geq \$600$ (added $500 to both sides)
   c. $x \geq \$70$ (added $60 to both sides)
   d. $x < 2$ (divided both sides by 30)
   e. $x < 15$ (divided both sides by –4 and changed the direction of the sign)
   f. $x \geq 10$ (divided both sides by –3 and changed the direction of the sign)
   g. $x \leq \$200$ (multiplied both sides by 10)
   h. $x < -250$ (multiplied both sides by –5 and changed the direction of the sign)

2. a. $8 + x \geq 60$
     $x \geq 52$ (added –8 to both sides)
   b. $x - 12 > 50$
     $x > 62$ (added 12 to both sides)

3. when multiplying or dividing by a negative number

Worksheet 10.5

1. a.

   b.

   c. $5 - x < 8$
   d. $x \leq 55$ °F

2. a. $x > \$250$ (divided both sides by $\frac{1}{5}$ by multiplying them by $\frac{5}{1}$)
   b. $s > 2$ (divided both sides by –50 and changed the direction of the sign)
   c. $x \geq 26$ (added –9 to both sides)
   d. $x < 95$ (added 15 to both sides)
   e. $x < -135$ (multiplied both sides by –3 and changed the direction of the sign)

3. a. $-x = 10$
     $x = -10$ (multiplied both sides by –1)
   b. $x = 6$ (added $-x$ to both sides)

Worksheet 11.1

1. a. "town residents who are over 18" should be circled;
      "town residents who returned a survey" should be starred.

b. 45% to 65%

c. Answers should include the MOE and the confidence level. Give a bonus if a student also thinks of additional things to question, such as the time of year (which could affect people's color choices), the randomness of the sample, the region sampled (the claim was that teenage girls liked the teal color swatch best—were girls from around the world sampled? Just America? Only a region within America?), etc.

2. a. 1.2 million or 1,200,000
    b. under 50

3. a.

States' 2010 Corn Production in Millions of Bushels	Tally	Frequency	Relative Frequency
0–499	𝍷𝍷𝍷 𝍷𝍷𝍷 𝍷𝍷𝍷 𝍷𝍷𝍷 𝍷𝍷𝍷 𝍷𝍷𝍷 //	32	78.05%
500–999	𝍷𝍷𝍷	5	12.20%
1,000–1,499	//	2	4.88%
1,500–1,999	/	1	2.44%
2,000–2,499	/	1	2.44%

Note: Due to rounding, the relative frequencies total 100.01%. The unrounded values would total 100%. The relative frequencies were obtained by dividing the value in the frequency column by the total number of data points (in this case, 41).

b.

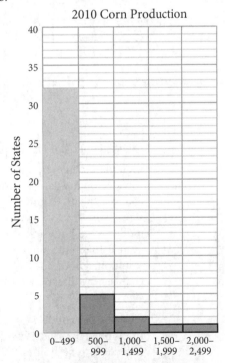

4. collection, organization and interpretation

5. $2 \text{ amp} + 4 \text{ amp} + 3 \text{ amp} + x < 15 \text{ amp}$
    $9 \text{ amp} + x < 15 \text{ amp}$
    $x < 6 \text{ amp}$ (added –9 amp to both sides)

Worksheet 11.2

1.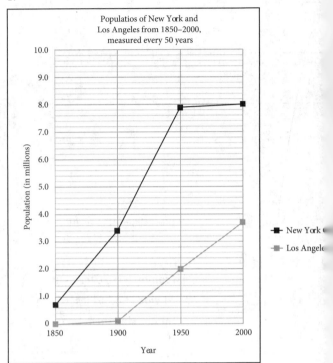

2. a. New York City's
    b. upward
    c. upward
    d. downward

3. horizontal

4. a. (–4, 4)
    b. (3, 4)
    c. (–4, –3)
    d. (–2, –2)
    e. (2, –2)
    f. (6, –3)

5–6.

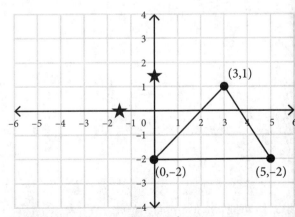

Note: Stars can be anywhere on the axes.

7. a. $5 + x \geq 25$ or
    $x \geq 20$ (added –5 to both sides)
    b. $x > -4$ (divided both sides by –15 and

c. $x < 5$ (divided both sides by 3)
d. $2x + 5 = 63$ (removed parentheses and combined like terms)
   $2x = 58$ (added –5 to both sides)
   $x = 29$ (divided both sides by 2)
e. the number of pages to read the first week
f. $x + 5 = 29$ pages + 5 pages = 34 pages

Worksheet 11.3

a.

b.

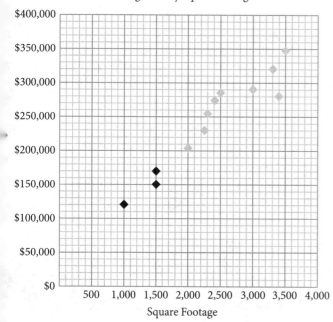

2. a. upward trend

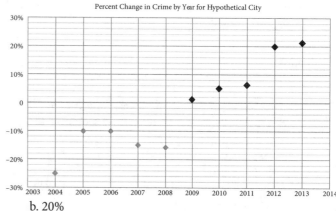

b. 20%
c. Answers should convey some additional facts to look at regarding whether the mayor is responsible for the increased crime. Possibilities include how long the mayor's been in office, national or state legislation that led to higher unemployment or worse schools, a hurricane, an earthquake, or other factors outside of the mayor's control. There may also be other issues besides crime to consider.

3. a.

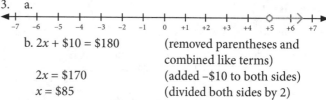

b. $2x + \$10 = \$180$ (removed parentheses and combined like terms)
   $2x = \$170$ (added –$10 to both sides)
   $x = \$85$ (divided both sides by 2)
c. the earnings of the employee who earns less
d. *earnings of employee that earns more* $= x + \$10$
   earnings of employee that earns more $= \$85 + \$10 = \$95$
e. $x > 7$ (divided both sides by 2)
f. $x < -7$ (divided both sides by –2 and changed the direction of the sign)

Worksheet 11.4

1. a.
Stems	Leaves
6	2 8
5	5 6
4	2 5 8 9
3	0 3 5 8

b. 30s
b. a coat

2. a.
5 hr 45 min	*rounds to*	5 hr, 50 min
7 hr 8 min	*rounds to*	7 hr, 10 min
4 hr 7 min	*rounds to*	4 hr, 10 min
5 hr 40 min	*rounds to*	5 hr, 40 min
6 hr 56 min	*rounds to*	7 hr
5 hr 10 min	*rounds to*	5 hr, 10 min
7 hr 40 min	*rounds to*	7 hr, 40 min
5 hr 23 min	*rounds to*	5 hr, 20 min

b.
Stems	Leaves
7	1 0 4
6	
5	5 4 1 2
4	1

c. Not entirely. We need more information. Were all these runners in a specific age group? Health condition? Were they an abnormally fast or slow group?

3. a. upward
   b. more

4. (–6, –5)

5. a. $x > -1{,}248$ (multiplied both sides by –8 and changed the direction of the sign)
   b. $x < 1{,}248$ (multiplied both sides by 8)
   c. 164 ft = 12x
   13.67 ft = x (divided both sides by 12)
   d. $4 + -1(2 + -x) = 20$
   $4 + -1(2) + -1(-x) = 20$
   $4 + -2 + x = 20$
   $2 + x = 20$
   $x = 18$ (added –2 to both sides)
   e. $4 - (2 - 18) = 20$
   $4 - (-16) = 20$
   $4 + 16 = 20$
   $20 = 20$

Worksheet 11.5

1. a. average = $\frac{52}{13} = 4$
   b. 6 data points   6 data points
   1, 2, 2, 3, 3, 4, ④, 4, 5, 5, 6, 6, 7

   median = 4
   c. mode = 4
   d. They are all the same.

   e.

Data	Tally	Frequency	Relative Frequency
1	/	1	7.69%
2	//	2	15.38%
3	//	2	15.38%
4	///	3	23.08%
5	//	2	15.38%
6	//	2	15.38%
7	/	1	7.69%

   Note: Due to rounding, the relative frequencies only total 99.98%. The unrounded values would total 100%. The relative frequencies were obtained by dividing the value in the frequency column by the total number of data points (in this case, 13).

f.

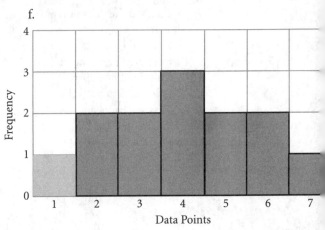

2. a. average = $\frac{71}{13} = 5.46$
   b. 6 data points   6 data points
   1, 2, 3, 3, 4, 4, ④, 4, 5, 6, 8, 12, 15

   median = 4
   c. mode = 4
   d. The average is different than the median and the mode.

   e.

Data	Tally	Frequency	Relative Frequency
1	/	1	7.69%
2	/	1	7.69%
3	//	2	15.38%
4	////	4	30.77%
5	/	1	7.69%
6	/	1	7.69%
8	/	1	7.69%
12	/	1	7.69%
15	/	1	7.69%

   Note: Due to rounding, the relative frequencies only total 99.98%. The unrounded values would total 100%. The relative frequencies were obtained by dividing the value in the frequency column by the total number of data points (in this case, 13).

f.

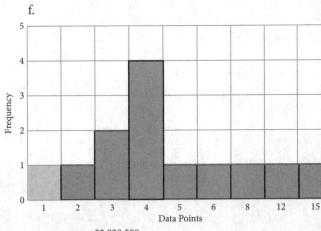

3. a. average = $\frac{\$2{,}928{,}500}{12} = \$244{,}041.67$
   b. median = $\frac{\$255{,}000 + \$275{,}000}{2} = \$265{,}000$

c. There is no mode, as no number appears more frequently than any other.

d.

Sale's Price	Tally	Number of Houses Sold in Grouping	Relative Frequency
$100,000–$149,999	/	1	8.33%
$150,000–$199,999	//	2	16.67%
$200,000–$249,999	//	2	16.67%
$250,000–$299,999	ＴＨＬ	5	41.67%
$300,000–$349,999	//	2	16.67%

Note: Due to rounding, the relative frequencies total 100.01%. The unrounded values would total 100%. The relative frequencies were obtained by dividing the value in the frequency column by the total number of data points (in this case, 12).

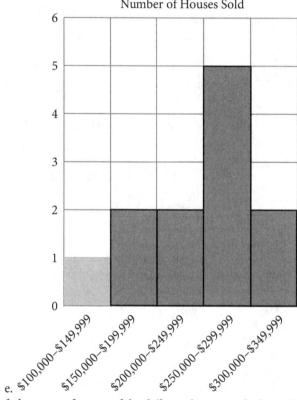

e.

f. the square footage of the different homes and what other features drove their selling prices so we can price the house competitively

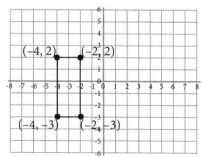

Worksheet 11.6

1. a. $0.15 \cdot \$400 = \$60$
   b. $R \cdot 80 = 60$
   $R = 0.75$ (divided both sides by 80)
   $R = 75\%$ (converted to a percent)
   c. *total number of parts* $= 5 + 2 + 1 = 8$
   $R \cdot 8 = 5$
   $R = 0.625$ (divided both sides by 8)
   $R = 62.5\%$ (converted to a percent)
   d. $0.075 \cdot B = \$14$
   $B = \$186.67$ (divided both sides by 0.075)

2. a. $\frac{4}{4}x + \frac{1}{4}x = 65$
   $\frac{5}{4}x = 65$ (combined like terms)
   $x = 52$ (divided both sides by $\frac{5}{4}$ by multiplying them by $\frac{4}{5}$)
   b. $3x + 2x = 90$ min
   $5x = 90$ min (combined like terms)
   $x = 18$ min (divided both sides by 5)
   c. $-x = 2\frac{3}{4} + -\frac{11}{2}$ (added $-5\frac{1}{2}$, or $-\frac{11}{2}$, to both sides)
   $-x = \frac{11}{4} + -\frac{22}{4}$
   $-x = -\frac{11}{4}$ lb
   $x = \frac{11}{4}$ lb (multiplied both sides by –1)
   $x = 2\frac{3}{4}$ lb (expressed as a mixed number)
   d. $x + x + -5 + -x + 3 = 10$ (removed parentheses and added plus signs for clarity)
   $x + x + -2 + -x = 10$
   $x - 2 = 10$ (combined like terms)
   $x = 12$ (added 2 to both sides)
   e. $2(5 + -x) = -2$
   $2(5) + -2x = -2$
   $10 + -2x = -2$
   $-2x = -12$ (added –10 to both sides)
   $x = 6$ (divided both sides by –2)
   f. $4 + -1(x + 3) = -6$
   $4 + -x + -3 = -6$
   $1 + -x = -6$
   $-x = -7$ (added –1 to both sides)
   $x = 7$ (multiplied both sides by –1)
   g. $x > 6$ (divided both sides by 6)
   h. $x < -6$ (divided both sides by –6 and changed the direction of the sign)

3. the pounds of apples removed from the scale

4. a. $\ell \geq 16$ oz (added –12 oz to both sides)
   b.
   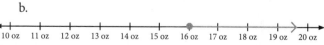

5. a. $\ell w = A$
   b. $\frac{a}{b} = c$ (divided both sides by b)
   $c = \frac{a}{b}$ (swapped the entire sides of the equation)
   c. $x > -5$
   d. $a - b = c$ or $a + -b = c$ (added –b to both sides)
   $c = a - b$ or $c = a + -b$ (swapped the entire sides of the equation)

6. a. $4s$
   b. $-20x$
7. yes; the identity property of multiplication (multiplying by 1 doesn't change the value)
8. a. average
   b. $average = \frac{40\ min + 36\ min + 35\ min + 35\ min + 90\ min + 20\ min}{6}$
   $average = \frac{256\ min}{6}$
   $average = 42.67$ min, which rounds to 43 min
   c. 2 data points   2 data points
   20 min + 35 min + 35 min + 36 min + 40 min + 90 min
   $median = \frac{35\ min + 36\ min}{2} = 35.5$ min, which rounds to 36 min
   d. $mode = 35$ min
9. a.

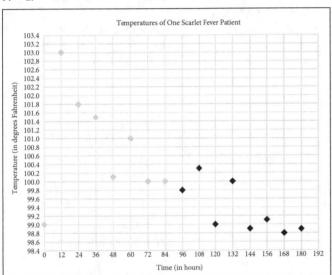

   b. downward
   c. no
   (This graph only tells us what happened to the fever of one patient.)
10. $2[5(5)] =$
    $2[25] =$
    50

Worksheet 12.1

1. a. 2
   (The coin could land on either heads or tails.)
   b. $probability\ of\ getting\ heads = \frac{1}{2} = 0.5 = 50\%$
   c. Answer should be a percent found by dividing the number of heads obtained in the experiment (the outcomes that produced the event) by 5 (the total outcomes).
   Note: Another way to think of calculating the percent is by using $RB = P$. In this case, 5 is the base (B), and the number of heads obtained is the percentage (P). Both methods will obtain the same answer.
   d. Answer should be a percent found by dividing the number of heads obtained in the experiment by 45. The percent should be close to 50%.
   e. large numbers
2. a. 6
(You could roll any of these 6 sides: ⚀ ⚁ ⚂ ⚃ ⚄ ⚅)
   b. $probability\ of\ rolling\ a\ \text{⚂} = \frac{1}{6} = 16.67\%$
   c. Answer should be a percent found by dividing the number of ⚂s rolled in experiment by 30.
3. a. $probability\ of\ rolling\ a\ ☺ = \frac{3}{8} = 37.5\%$
   b. $probability\ of\ rolling\ a\ ☹ = \frac{2}{8} = 25\%$
4. a. $(-2, 2)$
   b. $(2, 2)$
   c. $(2, -2)$
   d. $(-2, -2)$
5. a.
Value of Agricultural Implements Exported from the U.S

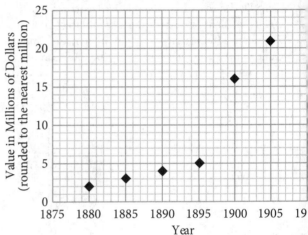

   b. upward
   c. $average = \frac{2 + 3 + 4 + 5 + 16 + 21}{6} = 8.5$ million dollars
   d. $2 + 3 + 4 + 5 + 16 + 21$
   $median = \frac{4 + 5}{2} = 4.5$ million dollars
6. a. $x < 12$ (divided both sides by -4 and changed direction of sign)
   b. $x > 12$ (divided both sides by 4)
   c. $4 + -1(2 + x) = -1$
   $4 + -2 + -x = -1$
   $2 + -x = -1$
   $-x = -3$ (added -2 to both sides)
   $x = 3$ (multiplied both sides by -1)
   d. $3x = 18$ (combined like terms)
   $x = 6$ (divided both sides by 3)

Worksheet 12.2

1. a. $\frac{5{,}783}{8{,}721} = 0.6631 = 66.31\%$
   b. $\frac{1}{15} = 0.0667 = 6.67\%$
   c. $\frac{2}{10} = 0.2 = 20\%$
   d. $\frac{3}{12} = 0.25 = 25\%$
   e. $100\% - 25\% = 75\%$ or $\frac{9}{12} = 0.75 = 75\%$
2. a. $100\% - 7\% = 93\%$
   b. $100\% - 3.13\% = 96.87\%$
3. a. $\frac{11}{80} = 0.1375 = 13.75\%$
   b. $\frac{45}{213} = 0.2113 = 21.13\%$
   c. $\frac{21}{150} = 0.14 = 14\%$
   d. $\frac{50}{197} = 0.2538 = 25.38\%$

a. Player D
b. no
(A 25% probability of hitting the ball means that over the games he's played in the past, the player has hit an average of 1 out of 4 tries, 25%. He may have missed 8 in a row ... and then hit 2 in a row. Besides, a 25% probability of hitting the ball means that's what the player has done historically; players can (and do!) change in their performance.)
c. The batting average tells us that the probability of hitting the ball is 14.5%. Thus, the probability of missing is 100% − 14.5% = 85.5%.

Probability of Precipitation = 0.6 • 0.8 = 0.48 = 48%

Answer should be questions along the lines of the following: What ages was the surgery performed on? How far advanced in the illness were the patients? How did they define "successful" (complete healing or partial)? (The success of a surgery could vary greatly based on age, health, etc.)

Worksheet 12.3

a. $\frac{3}{8} = 0.375 = 37.5\%$
b. $\frac{3}{8} \cdot \frac{3}{8} = \frac{9}{64} = 0.1406 = 14.06\%$
c. $\frac{1}{2} = 0.5 = 50\%$
d. $\frac{1}{2} \cdot \frac{1}{2} \cdot \frac{1}{2} \cdot \frac{1}{2} \cdot \frac{1}{2} \cdot \frac{1}{2} \cdot \frac{1}{2} \cdot \frac{1}{2} = \frac{1}{256} = 0.0039 = 0.39\%$
e. $\frac{1}{6} = 0.1667 = 16.67\%$
f. $\frac{1}{6} \cdot \frac{1}{6} \cdot \frac{1}{6} = \frac{1}{216} = 0.0046 = 0.46\%$
g. $\frac{1}{6} = 0.1667 = 16.67\%$
h. $\frac{1}{6} \cdot \frac{1}{6} = \frac{1}{36} = 0.0278 = 2.78\%$

true

Note: MBU stands for million bushels.
a. 483 MBU
b. 3,423 MBU = x + (3x + 483 MBU)
c. 3,423 MBU = 4x + 483 MBU
  2,940 MBU = 4x (added −483 MBU to both sides)
  735 MBU = x (divided both sides by 4)
  There were approximately 735 million bushels of wheat produced inside of the United States in 1906.
d. 3(735 MBU) + 483 MBU = 2,688 MBU
  There were approximately 2,688 million bushels of wheat produced outside of the United States in 1906.

a. 2x − 88 ft = 1,312 ft   (removed parentheses and combined like terms)
  2x = 1,400 ft   (added 88 ft to both sides)
  x = 700 ft   (divided both sides by 2)
b. the height of the Metropolitan Life building
c. 700 ft − 88 ft = 612 ft

Worksheet 12.4

a. Answer should be an example of an independent event, where the result of one event does *not* affect the result of the next event. One possibility is rolling a die multiple times in a row.
b. Answer should be an example of a dependent event, where the result of one event *does* affect the result of the next event. One possibility is drawing numbers out of a hat.
c. We have to take into account any change the previous event made to the outcomes that produce the event and the total possible outcomes.

2. a. $\frac{1}{26} = 0.0385 = 3.85\%$
   b. $\frac{1}{25} = 0.04 = 4\%$
   c. $\frac{1}{26} \cdot \frac{1}{25} = \frac{1}{650} = 0.0015 = 0.15\%$
   d. $\frac{20}{60} = 0.3333 = 33.33\%$
   e. $\frac{20}{60} \cdot \frac{19}{59} = \frac{380}{3,540} = 0.1073 = 10.73\%$

3. a. 4 • 3 • 2 • 1
   b. 24
   c. 8!

4. a.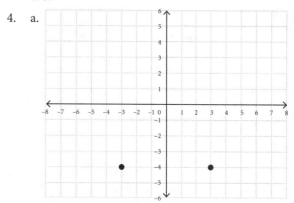

b. 3 − −3 = 3 + 3 = 6
   |6| = 6
   Note: We could have also found the answer by subtracting 3 from −3.
   −3 − 3 = −6
   |−6| = 6
c. $x < 2$ (divided both sides by 42)
d. $x > 2$ (divided both sides by −42 and changed direction of the sign)
e. 45 + 2x < 105   (combined like terms)
   2x < 60   (added −45 to both sides)
   x < 30   (divided both sides by 2)

Worksheet 12.5

1. a. 6 • 6 • 6 • 6 • 6 = 7,776
   b. 3 • 3 = 9
   c. 9 • 9 • 9 • 9 • 9 = 59,049
   d. 9 • 9 • 9 • 9 • 9 • 9 • 9 = 4,782,969
   e. 10 • 10 • 10 • 10 • 10 • 10 • 10 = 10,000,000

2. a. $\frac{10}{30} = 0.3333 = 33.33\%$
   b. $\frac{10}{30} \cdot \frac{9}{29} \cdot \frac{8}{28} = \frac{720}{24,360} = 0.0296 = 2.96\%$
   c. dependent

3. a. 7 + −1(2 + x) = 2
   7 + −2 + −x = 2
   5 + −x = 2
   −x = −3   (added −5 to both sides)
   x = 3   (multiplied both sides by −1)
   b. $\frac{350 \text{ points}}{5} = 70$ points
   c. 40, 65, ⓖ67, 88, 90
   median = 67

Worksheet 12.6

1. a. $\frac{10}{90} = 0.1111 = 11.11\%$
   b. $\frac{18}{145} = 0.1241 = 12.41\%$
   c. $\frac{35}{220} = 0.1591 = 15.91\%$
   d. $\frac{30}{124} = 0.2419 = 24.19\%$

2. a. 10:80
   (The 80 was found by subtracting 10 from 90.)
   b. 18:127
   (The 127 was found by subtracting 18 from 145.)
   c. 35:185
   (The 185 was found by subtracting 35 from 220.)
   d. 30:94
   (The 94 was found by subtracting 30 from 124.)

3. a. 80:10
   b. 127:18
   c. 185:35
   d. 94:30

4. a. 309,876:1
   b. Answer should be five references to Bible verses about money, gain, or wealth.

5. a. $\frac{1}{7} = 0.1429 = 14.29\%$
   b. 1:6
   (The 6 was found by subtracting 1 from 7.)
   c. By the third draw, there will be 2 fewer choices, as the first 2 people to draw would each have taken a short stick. So there'd be 5 sticks left, 1 of which is short. Thus, the probability of drawing the short stick is now $\frac{1}{5} = 0.2 = 20\%$.
   d. $\frac{69}{80} = 0.8625 = 86.25\%$
   e. 10 • 10 = 100

Worksheet 12.7

1. a. $\frac{0}{4} = 0 = 0\%$
   b. $\frac{2}{4} = 0.5 = 50\%$

2. a. $\frac{1}{4} = 0.25 = 25\%$
   b. $\frac{1}{4} = 0.25 = 25\%$
   c. $\frac{1}{4} \cdot \frac{1}{4} \cdot \frac{1}{4} = \frac{1}{64} = 0.0156 = 1.56\%$
   d. $\frac{3}{4} = 0.75 = 75\%$
   e. 3:1
   f. 1:3

3. a.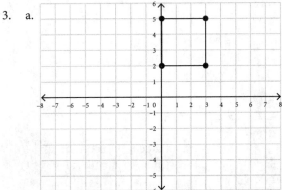
   b. 3 mi • 3 mi = 9 mi²
   c. $55x < 110$ (combined like terms)

$x < 2$ (divided both sides by 55)

   d. $3x + 4(x + -5) > 22$
   $3x + 4x + -20 > 22$
   $7x + -20 > 22$ (combined like terms)
   $7x > 42$ (added 20 to both sides)
   $x > 6$ (divided both sides by 7)
   e. $\frac{216}{6} = 36$
   f. 12, 25, ㉚, 45, 50, 54
   median = $\frac{30 + 45}{2} = 37.5$

4. Students were instructed to read or watch one of the resources mentioned on the worksheet and write a paragraph summary.

Worksheet 13.1

1. a. quantity whose value we know is constant (i.e., fixed or unchanging)
   b. quantity whose value can vary
   c. constant
   (Its value is fixed even though we often use a letter to stand for it.)
   d. variable
   (Its value can vary based on the length of its sides.)
   e. constant
   (We know its value.)

2. a. The total increases.
   (We're multiplying the number of times we park by $5.)
   b. $5

3. a.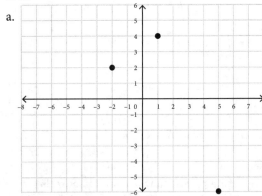
   b. 62 • 62 • 62 = 238,328
   (Each character has 62 options: 26 lowercase letters, 26 uppercase letters, and 10 digits.)
   c. $\frac{1}{10} = 0.1 = 10\%$
   d. $\frac{4}{10} = 0.4 = 40\%$
   e. $\frac{4}{10} \cdot \frac{3}{9} \cdot \frac{2}{8} \cdot \frac{1}{7} = \frac{24}{5,040} = 0.0048 = 0.48\%$

Worksheet 13.2

1. a. $y = 2(6) = 12$
   b. $y = 8 - 3 = 5$
   c. dependent variable
   d. independent variable
   e. Answer should show a dependent relationship, such as how the total slices of pizza that need to be ordered for an event depends on the number of guests, or how, if the

length is constant, we can think of the area of a sign as depending on the width chosen.

a.–b. *Note*: The gray column is optional.

m (input)	$d = \$15m$	d (output, in dollars)
0	$d = 15(0) = 0$	0
5	$d = 15(5) = 75$	75
10	$d = 15(10) = 150$	150

c. $15
d. decrease

a. $p = 15c$ (multiplied both sides by c)
b. $P = \$200R$ (multiplied both sides by R)

a. *Note*: The gray column is optional.

t (input, in hr)	$d = (55 \frac{\text{mi}}{\text{hr}})t$	d (output, in mi)
1	$d = (55)(1) = 55$	55
5	$d = (55)(5) = 275$	275
10	$d = (55)(10) = 550$	550

Note: While we didn't write out the units of measure when performing each calculation, it's worth pointing out that if we had, the units would have worked out appropriately. For example, when t is 1, we have this:
$d = (55 \frac{\text{mi}}{\text{hr}})(1 \text{ hr}) = 55 \text{ mi}$

b. increase

a.–b.

d (input, in mi)	$t = \frac{d}{55 \frac{\text{mi}}{\text{hr}}}$	t (output, in hr)
10	$t = \frac{10}{55} = 0.18$	0.18
100	$t = \frac{100}{55} = 1.82$	1.82
300	$t = \frac{300}{55} = 5.45$	5.45

a.

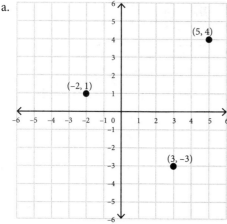

b. number of possibilities to try = $95 \cdot 95 \cdot 95 = 857,375$
time to guess all:
$\frac{857,375 \text{ passwords}}{x} = \frac{100 \text{ passwords}}{1 \text{ sec}}$
$x = 8,573.75$ sec
Converting to hours:
$8,573.75 \text{ sec} \cdot \frac{1 \text{ min}}{60 \text{ sec}} \cdot \frac{1 \text{ hr}}{60 \text{ min}} = 2.38$ hr

c. $\frac{1}{4} \cdot \frac{2}{33} = \frac{1}{66} = 0.0152 = 1.52\%$

Worksheet 13.3

1. a. y
   b. x
   c. a, b, and c

2. a. F; we were told we want to see how the force *depends on* the displacement.
   b. 7 pounds per inch *or* $7 \frac{\text{lb}}{\text{in}}$
   c. *Note*: The gray column is optional.

d (input, in inches)	$F = -kd$, when $k = 7$ pounds per inch	F (output, in pounds)
1	$F = -(7)(1) = -7$	-7
5	$F = -(7)(5) = -35$	-35
15	$F = -(7)(15) = -105$	-105

Note: While we write out the units of measure when performing each calculation, it's worth pointing out that if we had, the units would have worked out appropriately. For example, when d is 1 in, we have this:
$F = -(7 \frac{\text{lb}}{\text{in}})(1 \text{ in}) = -7$ lb

d. The force increases in the *negative* direction.

3. a. $\frac{15}{60} = 0.25 = 25\%$
   b. $\frac{15}{60} \cdot \frac{14}{59} = \frac{210}{3,540} = 0.0593 = 5.93\%$

Worksheet 13.4

1. one

2. a. dependent variable (output) = $\underline{V}$
      independent variable (input) = $\underline{h}$
   b. $\underline{V}$ as a function of $\underline{h}$
   c. dependent variable (output) = $\underline{h}$
      independent variable (input) = $\underline{V}$
   d. $\underline{h}$ as a function of $\underline{V}$
   e. w
   f. w

3. a. No; for every input for m, there's more than one output for n.
   b. yes
      (It doesn't matter that some days had the same temperature. We still only recorded one temperature per day — one output per input.)
   c. no
      (For the input of 54, there are multiple outputs. So for every input, there's not only one output.)
   d. yes
      (It doesn't matter that two classes had the same average score. We still only had one average score per class — one output (average score) per input (class).)
   e. no
      (Two classes had an average score of 80. So if we view the average scores as the inputs, for an input of 80, we'd have two different outputs.)
   f. yes
      (For each contestant, there's only one number.)
   g. yes
      (For each number, there's only one contestant.)

4. a. $\frac{t}{80} = m$ (divided both sides by 80)

$m = \frac{t}{80}$ (swapped the entire sides of the equation)

b. *Note*: The gray column is optional.

t (input)	$m = \frac{t}{80}$	m (output)
1,000	$m = \frac{1,000}{80} = 12.5$	12.5
20,000	$m = \frac{20,000}{80} = 250$	250
30,000	$m = \frac{30,000}{80} = 375$	375

c. increase

d. 250 min • $\frac{1 \text{ hr}}{60 \text{ min}}$ = 4.17 hr

5. a.

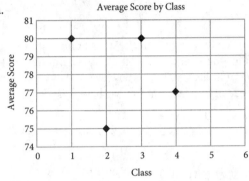

b. $\frac{12}{50} = 0.24 = 24\%$

c. $\frac{12}{50} \cdot \frac{11}{49} \cdot \frac{10}{48} = \frac{1,320}{117,600} = 0.0112 = 1.12\%$

Worksheet 13.5

1. set of values the independent variable can possibly be

2. a.
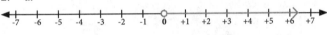
   b.

   c.
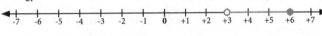
   d.
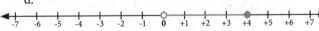
   e.
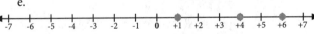

3. a. $x > 0$
   b. $-5 < x < 0$ or $0 > x > -5$
   c. $0 \le x \le 6$ or $6 \ge x \ge 0$

4. a. $x < 9$
   b. $-8 < s < 9$ or $9 > s > -8$
   c. 40
   d. $40 <$ guests < 100

5. a. no
   (B must be *greater than or equal to* 0.)
   b. yes

c. *Note*: The gray column is optional.

B (input, in dollars)	$(0.05)B = P$ where $0 \le B \le \$10,000$	P (output, in dollars)
100	$(0.05)(100) = 5$	5
1,000	$(0.05)(1,000) = 50$	50
10,000	$(0.05)(10,000) = 500$	500

d. 0.05

e.
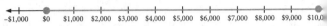

6. a. dependent variable (output) = g
   independent variable (input) = d
   b. one

Worksheet 14.1

1. a. $1,500

   b.

n (input)	t (output, in dollars)
50	750
200	3,000
250	3,750

   c.
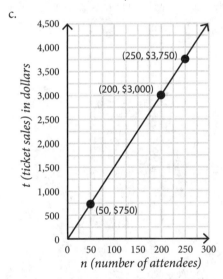

   d. Yes; it results in a straight line when graphed.

2. a. $1,000

   b.

p (input, in dollars)	t (output, in dollars)
10	2,000
15	3,000
20	4,000

c.

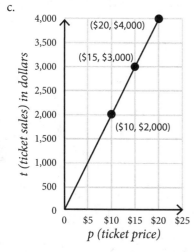

d. Yes; it results in a straight line when graphed.

a. $100

b. $\frac{\$1,000}{n} = p$ (divided both sides by n)
Note: We could also write $p = \frac{\$1,000}{n}$, as we can swap the entire expressions on both sides of the equal sign without changing the meaning.

c.

n (input)	p (output, in dollars)
5	200
20	50
50	20

d.

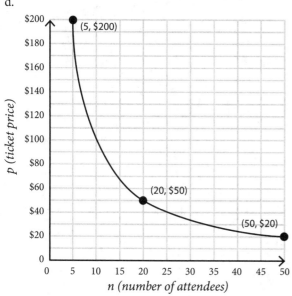

e. No; it does not result in a straight line when graphed.

a. −$250

b.

t (input, in days)	d (output, in dollars)
2	−100
5	−250
10	−500

c.

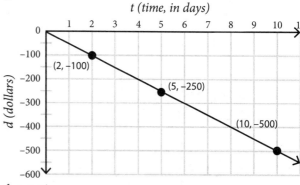

d. negative

e. Yes; it results in a straight line when graphed.

5. a. 8 and −8
   b. yes
   c. yes
   d. yes

Worksheet 14.2

1. a.

x (input)	y (output)
−1	−2
0	0
1	2

b.

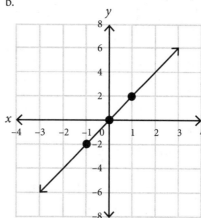

2. a.

x (input)	y (output)
−1	−7
0	0
1	7

b.

x (input)	y (output)
−1	$-\frac{1}{2}$
0	0
1	$\frac{1}{2}$

3. a.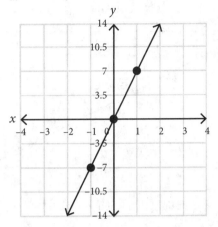

b.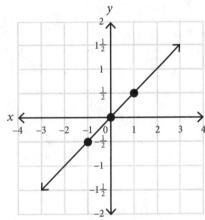

4. a.

x (input)	y (output)
−1	−6
0	0
1	6

b. Graph may vary in scale, but should show the relationship $y = 6x$. Check that the vertical and horizontal axes are labeled.

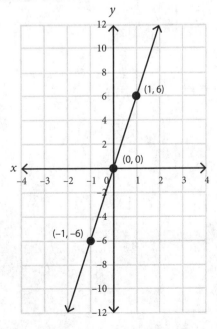

c. Answer should be three inputs and corresponding outputs to $y = -2x$.

d. Graph may vary in scale, but should show the relationship $y = -2x$.

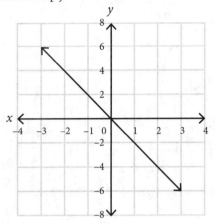

5. a. h or height

b. Answer should be three inputs and corresponding outputs to $h = (4 \frac{m}{sec})t$.

c. Check to make sure graph clearly shows units of measure. Graph may vary in scale.

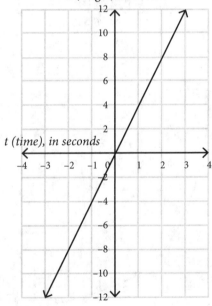

Worksheet 14.3

1. a.

x (input)	y (output)
−5	−15
20	60
25	75

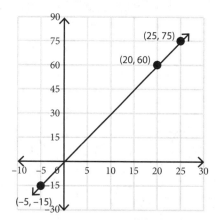

b.

x (input)	y (output)
10	30
20	60
25	75

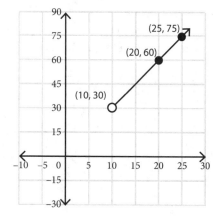

c.

x (input)	y (output)
10	30
15	45
25	75

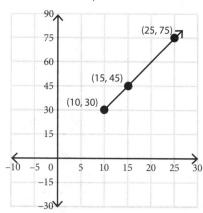

2. a.

n (input)	t (output)
1	7
5	35
10	70

b.

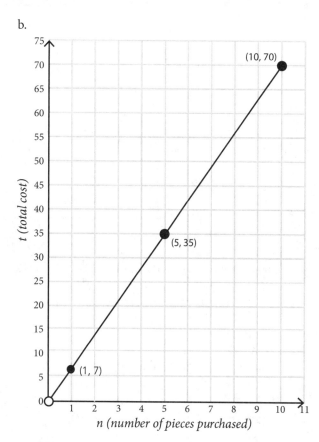

3. a. $s = 8c$
b. $c > 0$
c.

c (input)	s (output)
1	8
2	16
3	24

d.

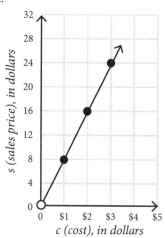

4. a.

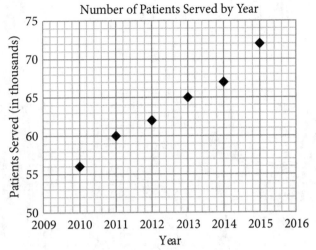

b. Yes; for every year, there's only one value for patients served.
c. upward
d. 60 and –60
e. No; there's *not* only one value for y for *every* value of x.

Worksheet 14.4

1. Check that students found the answer by graphing the equations.

   a. y-intercept = 0

   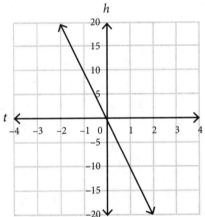

   b. y-intercept = –5

   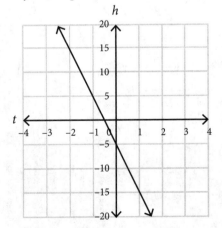

   c. y-intercept = 5

   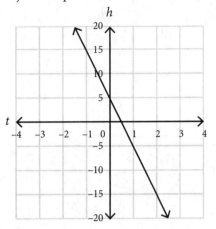

   d. 2 minutes

2. Check to see that students found the answer by solving fo when t equals 0.
   a. $h = (-10)(0) = 0$; y-intercept = 0
   b. $h = (-10)(0) + -5 = -5$; y-intercept = –5
   c. $h = (-10)(0) + 5 = 5$; y-intercept = 5

3. a. n is the dependent variable and s is the independent variable.
   b. Graph may vary in scale.

   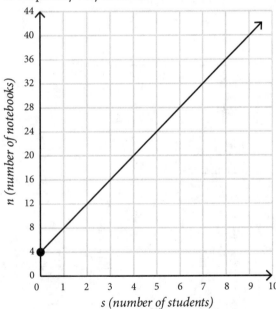

4. a. $5x = 12$ (combined like terms)
   $x = \frac{12}{5}$ (divided both sides by 5)
   $x = 2.4$

   b. $1.5x + x + x = 35$ in
   $3.5x = 35$ in   (combined like terms)
   $x = 10$ in   (divided both sides by 2.5)
   Note: The x here represents each side of the footstool. We know the top will be 1.5 times the length of each side, and that combined the top and both sides total 35 in. Thus, we have $1.5x + x + x = 35$ in as our starting equation.

   c. Yes; for every value for time (x), there's only one value fo the electrical activity (y).

Worksheet 14.5

a. between the vertical change and the horizontal change
b. <u>3</u> feet of vertical change per <u>11</u> feet of horizontal change
c. run
d. It made sense to use y for the vertical coordinates and x for the horizontal coordinates because the convention is to use y for the dependent variable (which we graph on the vertical axis) and x for the independent variable (which we graph on the horizontal axis).

Students may have chosen different coordinates off which to find the slope. Look for a correct final answer.

a. $\frac{15-0}{1-0} = 15$
b. $\frac{-5-5}{1-0} = -10$
c. $\frac{\frac{1}{5}-0}{1-0} = \frac{1}{5}$
d. $\frac{10{,}000\text{ ft} - 11{,}000\text{ ft}}{1\text{ min} - 0\text{ min}} = \frac{-1{,}000\text{ ft}}{1\text{ min}} = -1{,}000\,\frac{\text{ft}}{\text{min}}$
e. 7,000 ft

a. 0
b. 5
c. 0
d. 11,000 ft

a.

h (input, in hours)	t (output, in dollars)
40	2,000
45	2,250
50	2,500

b.

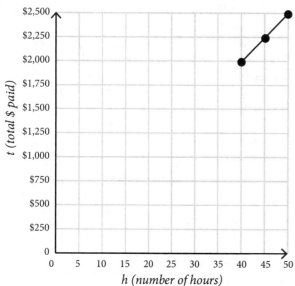

a. $V = 8\text{ ft} \cdot 5\text{ ft} \cdot 5\text{ ft} = 200\text{ ft}^3$
b. $200\text{ ft}^3 \cdot \frac{12\text{ in}}{1\text{ ft}} \cdot \frac{12\text{ in}}{1\text{ ft}} \cdot \frac{12\text{ in}}{1\text{ ft}} = 345{,}600\text{ in}^3$
c. $345{,}600\text{ in}^3 \cdot \frac{1\text{ gal}}{231\text{ in}^3} = 1{,}496.1\text{ gal}$
d. Yes; because the area of the base is constant (the size of a pool doesn't change), so the volume (or gallons) it is holding depends on to what depth we fill it. For any depth we pick, they'll be one value for the volume.

Worksheet 14.6

1. a. yes
   b. 5
   c. 1
   d. yes
   e. 8
   f. 5
   g. yes
   h. 8
   i. 0
   j. $F = 5m$ (multiplied both sides by 5)
   k. 5
   l. 0

2. a. $y = 20x$
   b. $y = \frac{1}{4}x$
   c. $A = (5\text{ ft})w$, where $w > 0$
   d. $y = 4x + 2$
   e. $y = -3x - 6$

3. a.

g (input)	m (output)
0	0
20	80
30	120

   b.

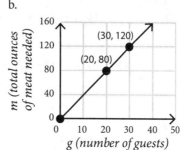

4. a. $8 - 3 = 5$
   b. $2 - 1 = 1$
   c. $4 + 5 + x = 20$
      $9 + x = 20$
      $x = 11$ (added –9 to both sides)
   d. $\$34 + -\$3 + -x = \$5$
      $\$31 + -x = \$5$
      $-x = -\$26$ (added –$31 to both sides)
      $x = \$26$ (multiplied both sides by –1)
   e. no
      (y could be any value along the vertical line; there's *not* only one value for y for *every* value for x.)

Worksheet 14.7

1. a. 0
   b. 2.8

c.

Temperature Measurement (represented by x) in degrees Celsius	Pressure Measurement (represented by y) in pounds per square inch	Pressure from Formula ($y = 2.8x$) in pounds per square inch
0	0	$y = 2.8(0) = 0$
10	28	$y = 2.8(10) = 28$
20	56	$y = 2.8(20) = 56$
30	85	$y = 2.8(30) = 84$
40	110	$y = 2.8(40) = 112$
50	141	$y = 2.8(50) = 140$
60	168	$y = 2.8(60) = 168$
70	196	$y = 2.8(70) = 196$

  d. $y = 2.8(80) = 224$
  224 pounds per square inch

2. a. 48.667
   b. 0.8571
   c.

Day (represented by x)	Temperature (represented by y) in °F	c. Temperature from Formula ($y = 0.8571x + 48.667$) in °F
1	46	$y = 0.8571(1) + 48.667 = 49.52$
2	54	$y = 0.8571(2) + 48.667 = 50.38$
3	54	$y = 0.8571(3) + 48.667 = 51.24$
4	50	$y = 0.8571(4) + 48.667 = 52.10$
5	52	$y = 0.8571(5) + 48.667 = 52.95$
6	54	$y = 0.8571(6) + 48.667 = 53.81$

   d. upward
   e. No; we have too limited of a sample size to draw a conclusion. The temperature could be radically different the next day. In order to make general weather assumptions, we'd need to look at years' worth of data to see in general what the weather is like for that location for a specific time of year.

3. a.

t (input, in hr)	d (output, in mi)
3	30
4	40
5	50

   b.

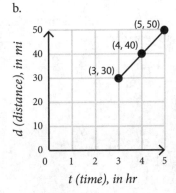

4. $y = 0.75x$
5. a. $\frac{9}{7}x = 36$ (combined like terms)

$x = 28$ (divided both sides by $\frac{9}{7}$ by multiplying them by $\frac{7}{9}$)

   b. $2x + x = 4$ gal
   $3x = 6$ gal (combined like terms)
   $x = 2$ gal (divided both sides by 3)
   c. $2 \cdot 2$ gal $= 4$ gal
   d. no
   (There's *not* only one y value for *every* value for x.)

Worksheet 15.1

1. a. 4^3
   b. $(-5)^3$
   c. 7^2
   d. 3^3
   e. $(-3)^3$
   f. $(\frac{2}{3})^3$

2. a. 64
   b. –125
   c. 49
   d. 27
   e. –27
   f. $\frac{8}{27}$

3. a. 1
   b. 15
   c. –125
   d. –1
   e. 1
   f. 60

4. a. $7(16 + 6) + 25 = 7(22) + 25 = 179$
   b. $3x + 7 = 25$
   $3x = 18$ (added –7 to both sides)
   $x = 6$ (divided both sides by 3)
   c. $2x + 2x = 900$
   $4x = 900$ (combined like terms)
   $x = 225$ (divided both sides by 4)
   d. $25 - x = 100$
   $-x = 75$ (added –25 to both sides)
   $x = -75$ (multiplied both sides by –1)

5.

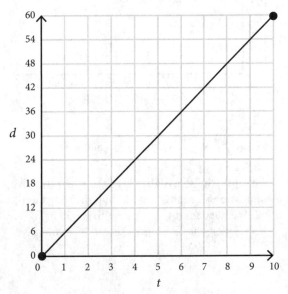

a. $F = 20m$
b. 20
c. 0

Worksheet 15.2

a. y^3
b. $3y$
c. v^5
d. $5v$

a. $x + x + x + x + x$
b. $x \cdot x$
c. $y \cdot y \cdot y \cdot y \cdot y$
d. $3 \cdot x \cdot x$

a. $5(5) + 2 = 27$
b. $5(5^2) + 2 = 5(25) + 2 = 127$
c. $2^5 = 32$
d. $5^3 = 125$
e. $-(-2)^4 = -(-2 \cdot -2 \cdot -2 \cdot -2) = -16$
f. $(--2)^4 = (2)^4 = 2 \cdot 2 \cdot 2 \cdot 2 = 16$

a. 52
b. c
c. 4^1
d. 23.5^1
e. y^1
f. a^1

a. $A = (8 \text{ m})^2 = 64 \text{ m}^2$
b. $V = (9 \text{ m})^3 = 729 \text{ m}^3$
c. $A = 6 \text{ ft} \cdot 7 \text{ ft} = 42 \text{ ft}^2$
d. $42 \text{ ft}^2 \cdot \frac{30.48 \text{ cm}}{1 \text{ ft}} \cdot \frac{30.48 \text{ cm}}{1 \text{ ft}} \cdot \frac{1 \text{ m}}{100 \text{ cm}} \cdot \frac{1 \text{ m}}{100 \text{ cm}} = 3.9 \text{ m}^2$
Note: Students could have also converted from feet to yards and then to meters.

Graphs may vary in scale.

a.

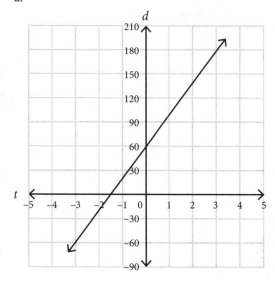

b.

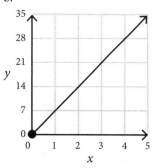

7. $t = 50c$, when $c \geq 0$

Worksheet 15.3

1. a. 25 ft²
   b. 100 ft²
   c. 0

2. a. $25 + 9(17.3) =$
      $25 + 155.7 = 180.7$
   b. $4(5 \text{ m})^2 =$
      $4(25 \text{ m}^2) = 100 \text{ m}^2$
   c. $4^1 = 4$
   d. $\frac{2}{3} \cdot \frac{2}{3} \div \frac{1}{4} \cdot \frac{1}{4} = \frac{4}{9} \div \frac{1}{16} =$
      $\frac{4}{9} \cdot \frac{16}{1} =$
      $\frac{64}{9} = 7\frac{1}{9}$
   e. $V = (5 \text{ ft})^3$
      $V = 125 \text{ ft}^3$
   f. $125 \text{ ft}^3 \cdot \frac{12 \text{ in}}{1 \text{ ft}} \cdot \frac{12 \text{ in}}{1 \text{ ft}} \cdot \frac{12 \text{ in}}{1 \text{ ft}} = 216,000 \text{ in}^3$
   g. 96
   h. 9
   i. $y = 3x - 3$

3. a. $64 \div 4 = 16$
   b. $(-x)^3$
   c. $(--4)^3 = 4^3 = 4 \cdot 4 \cdot 4 = 64$
   d. $-(x)^3$
   e. $-(-4 \cdot -4 \cdot -4) =$
      $-(-64) = 64$

Worksheet 15.4

1. a. 3,136
   b. 10,201
   c. 0.000009199
   d. 387,420,489
   e. $5(2) + 2^6 =$
      $10 + 64 = 74$
   f. $729 + 56 = 785$
      Note: 729 is positive because multiplying -3 by itself 6 times is an even number of negative signs, which results in a positive product.
   g. $(2.5 \text{ in})^2 + (1.75 \text{ in})^2 + 87 \text{ in}^2 =$
      $6.25 \text{ in}^2 + 3.06 \text{ in}^2 + 87 \text{ in}^2 = 96.31 \text{ in}^2$
   h. $6.25^8 = 2,328,306.44$
   i. $4(1.08)^{13} = 10.88$
      (We found 1.08^{13} first, and then multiplied that by 4.)
   j. $5(2.68)^6 = 1,852.59$
      (We found 2.68^6 first, and then multiplied that by 5.)

2. a. x^3

b. –3x
c. x

3. a.

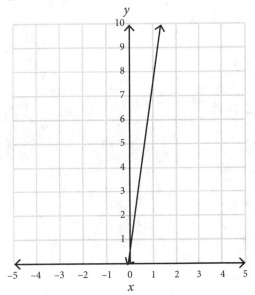

b.

c.

d. 0
e. $\frac{1}{8}$

f. 1

4. $s = 0.12p$, where p is ≥ 0

Worksheet 15.5

1. a. $P = \$40{,}000(1 + 0.02)^{10}$
   $P = \$48{,}759.78$
   b. $P = \$40{,}000(1 + 0.05)^{10}$
   $P = \$65{,}155.79$
   c. $P = \$60(1 + 0.01)^{15}$
   $P = \$69.66$

2. a. Yes; it forms a straight line.
   b. $1,200
   c. $1,000
   d. $y = \$20x + \$1{,}000$, where $x \geq 0$

3. a. No; it does not form a straight line.
   b. $P = \$1{,}000(1.02)^{20}$
   $P = \$1{,}485.95$

4. a. $(9 + 5)64 =$
   $(14)64 = 896$
   b. $2^4 + y = 56$
   $16 + y = 56$
   $y = 40$ (added –16 to both sides)
   c. $x \cdot x \cdot x$
   d. c^1
   e. $\frac{2}{5} \cdot \frac{2}{5} \cdot \frac{2}{5} \cdot \frac{2}{5} = \frac{16}{625} = 0.03$
   f. $A = (28 \text{ in})^2 = 784 \text{ in}^2$
   $784 \text{ in}^2 \cdot \frac{1 \text{ ft}}{12 \text{ in}} \cdot \frac{1 \text{ ft}}{12 \text{ in}} = 5.44 \text{ ft}^2$

Worksheet 15.6

1. a. $P = 10(1 + 0.5)^6$
   $P = 113.91$ lizards
   $P = 114$ lizards   (rounded per instructions)
   b. $P = 10(1 + 4)^4$
   $P = 6{,}250$ mosquitoes
   c. $P = 100(1 + 0.08)^3$
   $P = 125.97$
   $P = 126$ catfish   (rounded per instructions)

2. $\rho = 0.05m$ or $\rho = \frac{1}{20}m$, where $m \geq 0$

3. $V = (10 \text{ ft}^2)h$, where $x \geq 0$

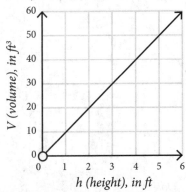

4. a. $5 + -1(8 + x) = 400$
   $5 + -8 + -x = 400$
   $-3 + -x = 400$
   $-x = 403$ (added 3 to both sides)
   $x = -403$ (multiplied both sides by –1)

b. $(25 \text{ ft})^2 + 512 \cdot 1 \text{ ft}^2 = 1{,}137 \text{ ft}^2$
625 ft² + 512 ft² = 1,137 ft²
c. 152

Worksheet 15.7

a. $P = (1{,}000 \text{ mg})(1 - 0.0228)^{30}$
$P = 500.61$ mg
b. $P = (1{,}000 \text{ mg})(1 - 0.0228)^{240}$
$P = 3.94$ mg

a. 0.45 • 4.6 mg = 2.07 mg
(If 55% is lost, then 45% remains.)
b. 0.7 • 30 mg = 21 mg
(If 30% is lost, then 70% remains.)

a. Look for at least two of these assumptions: original number of elements, rate of decay always being the same as in the present, and no "daughter" elements escaping or getting added to the rock[2]
b. Radiometric dating is dealing with the past, while the decay of bacteria, vitamins, etc., can all be observed in the present.

Students should watch the suggested video or read the suggested article and write down one tidbit from it.

Worksheet 16.1

a. $\frac{1}{10^4}$
b. $\frac{1}{3^3}$
c. $\frac{1}{4^6}$

a. $\frac{1}{10{,}000} = 0.0001 = 0.01\%$
b. $\frac{1}{27} = 0.037 = 3.7\%$
c. $\frac{1}{4{,}096} = 0.0002 = 0.02\%$

a. $\frac{7}{9} = 0.78$
b. $\frac{60}{16} = 3.75$
c. $\frac{6}{16} = 0.38$
d. $\frac{3}{5} = 0.6$

a. $V = \frac{4}{3}(3.14)(4.3 \text{ in})^3$
$V = 332.87$ in³
b. $r = \frac{1}{2}(9.5 \text{ in})$
$r = 4.75$ in
$V = \frac{4}{3}(3.14)(4.75 \text{ in})^3$
$V = 448.69$ in³

$y = \frac{1}{5}x$

Worksheet 16.2A

1. a. $\frac{1}{2^3}$
   b. $\frac{1}{4^6}$
   c. $\frac{1}{2^5}$
   d. $\frac{1}{s^2}$

2. a. 10^{-4}
   b. 3^{-3}
   c. 4^{-6}
   d. x^{-4}

3. a. 0.000059499
   b. 46,656
   c. 0.000416493
   d. 262,144
   e. –262,144
   f. $3^{-9} = 0.000050805$

4. a. $(-2)^5 = -32$
   b. $2^{-1} = \frac{1}{2^1} = \frac{1}{2}$ or 0.5

5. the multiplicative inverse of the base raised to that power

Worksheet 16.2B

1. a. $\frac{1}{3^6}$
   b. $\frac{1}{2^5}$
   c. $\frac{1}{4^2}$
   d. $\frac{1}{25.6^3}$

2. a. $4 \cdot \frac{1}{10 \cdot 10} = \frac{4}{100} = \frac{1}{25}$
   b. $3 \cdot \frac{1}{10 \cdot 10 \cdot 10 \cdot 10 \cdot 10} = \frac{3}{100{,}000}$
   c. $5 \cdot \frac{1}{6 \cdot 6} = \frac{5}{36}$
   d. $2 \cdot \frac{1}{3} = \frac{2}{3}$

3. a. $2 \cdot 4^{-2} = 2 \cdot \frac{1}{4 \cdot 4} = \frac{2}{16} = \frac{1}{8}$
   b. $5 \cdot 2^{-3} = 5 \cdot \frac{1}{2 \cdot 2 \cdot 2} = \frac{5}{8}$

4. Students were told not to round, but point out that all the answers clearly round to 1.
   a. $\frac{1^2}{1^3} = 1$
   b. $\frac{(11.86)^2}{(5.2)^3} = \frac{140.6596}{140.608} = 1.000366978$
   c. $\frac{(1.88)^2}{(1.52)^3} = \frac{3.5344}{3.511808} = 1.006433154$

Worksheet 16.3A

1. Check for both the multiplication written out and the final answer. Students were told not to round.
   a. 7 • 10 • 10 • 10 • 10 = 70,000
   b. 7 • 10 • 10 = 700
   c. $7 \cdot \frac{1}{10} \cdot \frac{1}{10} \cdot \frac{1}{10} \cdot \frac{1}{10} = 0.0007$
   d. $7 \cdot \frac{1}{10} \cdot \frac{1}{10} = 0.07$

2. a. 4.5×10^2
   b. 7.24×10^3
   c. 4.5×10^{-2}
   d. 7.24×10^{-3}
   e. 5.9064×10^9
   f. 5.234×10^{-7}

3. a. $\frac{1}{6^2} = \frac{1}{36}$
   b. $\frac{1}{7^2} = \frac{1}{49}$
   c. $\frac{1}{3^3} = \frac{1}{27}$

Worksheet 16.3B

1. a. $\frac{1}{10^5} = 0.00001$
   b. 100,000

---

[2] [See more details in Don Batten, Ken Ham, Jonathan Sarfati, and Carl Wieland, *The Revised and Expanded Answers Book: The 20 Most-Asked Questions About Creation, Evolution, & the Book of Genesis Answered!* rev. ed. (Green Forest, AR: Master Books, 2000), p. 81, and Dr. Andrew A. Snelling, "Radiometric Dating: Problems with the Assumptions," *Answers Magazine* (September 2, 2009; last featured August 4, 2010), https://answersingenesis.org/geology/radiometric-dating/radiometric-dating-problems-with-the-assumptions/.]

2. a. 4.87×10^{24} kg
   b. 1.9885×10^{30} kg
   c. 1.082×10^{8} km
   d. 6.67408×10^{-11}
   e. $8.854187817 \times 10^{-12}$

3. a. 299,792,458 meters per second
   b. 602,214,085,700,000,000,000,000
   c. 0.00000005670367
   d. 0.0000000159
   e. 0.000000000000000000016

Worksheet 16.4

1. a. 1.41×10^{17}
   b. 4.44×10^{-11}
   c. 1.8×10^{9}
   d. 1.67×10^{-10}

2. $\frac{1}{15!} = 7.65 \times 10^{-13}$

3. a. 5.772×10^{-6}
   b. 0.000005772
   c. 2.67616×10^{-5}
   d. 0.0000267616
   e. 3.20238×10^{-5}
   f. 0.0000320238

4. a. $E = (1)(299{,}792{,}458)^2 = 8.987551787 \times 10^{16}$ joules
   b. $E = (45)(299{,}792{,}458)^2 = 4.044398304 \times 10^{18}$ joules

5. a. $\frac{3}{6^3} = \frac{3}{216} = \frac{1}{72}$
   b. 6^{-4}

Worksheet 16.5

1. a. $5x^2$
   b. $2x^3 + 5x^2$
   c. cannot be simplified
   d. $4y^3$

2. a. 5.69×10^{-4}
   b. 1.8725623×10^{11}
   c. 8.97×10^{-6}
   d. 1.542563×10^{13}

3. a. 3.5×10^{-15} m
   b. 4.2×10^{7} km
   c. 2.8×10^{-3} m

4.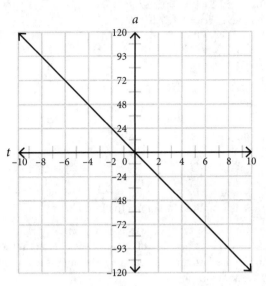

5. a. $y = -25x$
   b. Answer should be a meaning for the equation in 5a; one possibility is the relationship between altitude and time you're changing altitude at a rate of $-25 \frac{m}{sec}$.

6. a. $\frac{1}{3^5} = \frac{1}{243}$
   b. $\frac{1}{2^5} = \frac{1}{32}$

Worksheet 16.6

1. a. $(2 \cdot 2) \cdot (2 \cdot 2 \cdot 2 \cdot 2 \cdot 2)$
   b. $\frac{4 \cdot 4 \cdot 4}{4 \cdot 4}$

2. a. 2^7
   b. $4^1 = 4$

3. a. a^5
   b. $a^{3-2} = a^1 = a$
   or
   $\frac{a^{31}}{a^{2}} = a^1 = a$
   c. cannot be simplified
   d. v^9

4. a. $\frac{V}{B} = \frac{Bh}{B}$
   $\frac{V}{B} = h$ or $h = \frac{V}{B}$
   b. $\frac{89 \text{ ft}^3}{40 \text{ ft}^2} = h$
   $\frac{89 \text{ ft} \cdot \text{ft} \cdot \text{ft}}{40 \text{ ft} \cdot \text{ft}} = h$
   $2.23 \text{ ft} = h$
   c. $V = 40 \text{ ft}^2 \cdot 8 \text{ ft}$
   $V = 320 \text{ ft}^3$
   d. $4{,}000 \text{ ft}^3 \cdot \frac{1 \text{ yd}}{3 \text{ ft}} \cdot \frac{1 \text{ yd}}{3 \text{ ft}} \cdot \frac{1 \text{ yd}}{3 \text{ ft}} = \frac{4{,}000 \text{ yd}^3}{27} = 148.15 \text{ yd}^3$

5. $(5.97 \times 10^{24})(7.3 \times 10^{22}) = 4.36 \times 10^{47}$

6. a. $\frac{1}{81}$
   b. 0.0000025
   c. $7x^2$

Worksheet 16.7

1. a. $\frac{1}{8} = 0.125 = 12.5\%$
   b. $\frac{1}{8} \cdot \frac{1}{8} \cdot \frac{1}{8} = \frac{1}{512} = 0.002 = 0.2\%$
   c. independent event
   d. $100\% - 60\% = 40\%$

e. $\frac{2}{50} = 0.04 = 4\%$

f. $\frac{2}{50} \cdot \frac{1}{49} = 0.0008 = 0.08\%$

(There's a $\frac{2}{50}$ chance the first draw will be John's name and a $\frac{1}{49}$ chance the second will be John's name.)

g. dependent event

h. total combinations $= 10 \cdot 10 \cdot 10 \cdot 10 = 10^4 = 10{,}000$

probability $= \frac{1}{10{,}000} = 0.0001 = 0.01\%$

(There are 10,000 possible combinations, out of which we're finding the probability of the 1 correct combination.)

a.
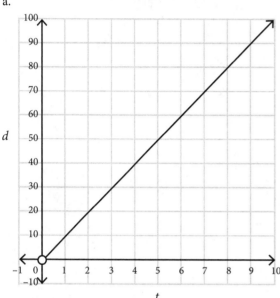

b.
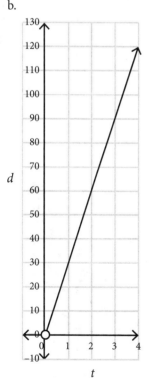

c.
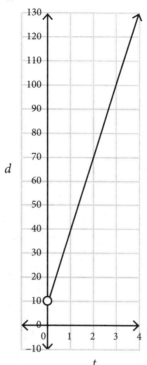

3.
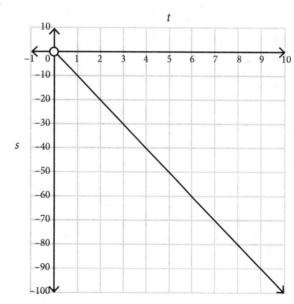

4.
a. one
b. Yes; for every value for time, there's only one value for growth.
c. No; there's *not* only one value for y for every value of x.
d. d and t
e. 30 and 10
f. $t > 0$
g. 30
h. 10
i. 0

5. Graph may vary in scale.

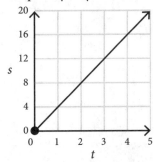

6. a. 10
   b. 5
   c. $y = 5x + 10$, where $x > 0$

7. a. 1
   b. $\frac{1}{4^3} = \frac{1}{64}$
   c. $4 + 5 \cdot 20 =$
   $4 + 100 = 104$
   d. $\frac{1}{125}$
   e. $2 \cdot 8 \cdot 1{,}296 = 20{,}736$
   f. $v^{2+6} = v^8$
   g. $v^{8-4} = v^4$ or $\frac{v^8}{v^4} = v^4$
   h. cannot be simplified
   i. $4x^2$
   j. cannot be simplified

8. a. $4(5)^8 = 4(390{,}625) = 1{,}562{,}500 = 1.56 \times 10^6$
   b. $15(8.03)^{25} = 6.22 \times 10^{23}$
   c. $0.000000209 = 2.09 \times 10^{-7}$
   d. 9.66×10^7

9. a. $x + -125 = 50$ (simplified exponent)
      $x = 175$ (added 125 to both sides)
   b. $x + \frac{1}{8} = 25$ (simplified exponent)
      $x = 24\frac{7}{8}$ or 24.88 (added $-\frac{1}{8}$ to both sides)

10. a. $24{,}873.6 \text{ mi} = 2(3.14)r$
       $24{,}873.6 \text{ mi} = 6.28r$
       $3{,}960.76 \text{ mi} = r$ (divided both sides by 6.28)
    b. $V = \frac{4}{3}(3.14)(3{,}960.76 \text{ mi})^3$
       $V = 2.60 \times 10^{11} \text{ mi}^3$

11. $P = 4(1 + 0.04)^{60}$
    $P = 42.08$ beetles
    $P = 42$ beetles   (rounded per instructions)

Worksheet 17.1

1. a. A square root is a way of concisely asking for the number that, times itself, will equal the number given.
   b. true
   c. a positive square root is meant

2. Check that both the prime factors are listed and the square roots.
   a. prime factors = $5 \cdot 5$
      square root = 5
   b. prime factors = $2 \cdot 2 \cdot 7 \cdot 7$
      square root = $2 \cdot 7 = 14$

Note: We found the square root by grouping the prime factors into the factor that, multiplied by itself, equals 196.
$(2 \cdot 7)(2 \cdot 7) = (14)(14) = 196$
   c. prime factors = $3 \cdot 3 \cdot 7 \cdot 7$
      square root = $3 \cdot 7 = 21$
   d. prime factors = $2 \cdot 2 \cdot 3 \cdot 3 \cdot 5 \cdot 5$
      square root = $2 \cdot 3 \cdot 5 = 30$
   e. prime factors = $11 \cdot 11$
      square root = 11

3. a. 3.997×10^2
   b. 0.0000267
   c. $5x^2$
   d. $4x^4$
   e. $y^{3-2} = y^1 = y$ or $\frac{y^3}{y^2} = y^1 = y$
   f. $\frac{1}{16}$
   g. $\frac{1}{8}$

Worksheet 17.2

1. Check that the square roots are both rewritten with exponents and solved.
   a. $\sqrt{7^2} = 7$
   b. $\sqrt{5^2} = 5$
   c. $\sqrt{9^2} = 9$
   d. $\sqrt{10^2} = 10$

2. a. 12
   b. 3.5
   c. y
   d. c

3. a. 64
   b. 21
   c. 101
   d. x

4. a. $(\sqrt{x})^2 = (9)^2$
      $x = 81$
   b. $(\sqrt{x})^2 = (4)^2$
      $x = 16$
   c. $(\sqrt{x})^2 = (2)^2$
      $x = 4$
   d. $(\sqrt{x})^2 = (5)^2$
      $x = 25$

5. a. $\sqrt{81} = 9$
      $9 = 9$
   b. $\sqrt{16} = 4$
      $4 = 4$
   c. $\sqrt{4} = 2$
      $2 = 2$
   d. $\sqrt{25} = 5$
      $5 = 5$

6. prime factors = $2 \cdot 2 \cdot 11 \cdot 11$
   square root = $2 \cdot 11 = 22$

7. a. 5.67×10^{-4}
   b. 0.00000042
   c. $42a^4$
   d. $7a^{2-2} = 7a^0 = 7(1) = 7$

or

$\frac{7a^2}{a^2} = 7$

Note: Any number raised to the zeroth power equals 1.

Worksheet 17.3

a. $y = 4$ (took the square root of both sides)
b. $v = 13$ (took the square root of both sides)
c. $s^2 = 256$ in^2
   $s = 16$ in (took the square root of both sides)

a. $4^2 = 16$
   $16 = 16$
b. $13^2 = 169$
   $169 = 169$
c. $(16\text{ in})^2 = 256$ in^2
   256 in$^2 = 256$ in^2

144 in$^2 = s^2$
12 in $= s$ (took the square root of both sides)

a. prime factors $= 2 \cdot 2 \cdot 2 \cdot 2 \cdot 2 \cdot 2 \cdot 3 \cdot 3$
   square root $= 2 \cdot 2 \cdot 2 \cdot 3 = 24$
b. $v = 60^2$ (squared both sides)
   $v = 3{,}600$
c. $x^2 = 16$ (divided both sides by 2)
   $x = 4$ (took the square root of both sides)

d. 2×10^{-8}

Worksheet 17.4

a. 9 and 10
b. 8 and 9

a. 21 and 22
b. 24 and 25

a. 20.49
b. 28.28
c. 35.57

a. $c = 27.93$
b. 108 in$^2 = s^2$
   10.39 in $= s$ (took the square root of both sides)
c. 674 m$^2 = s^2$
   25.96 m $= s$ (took the square root of both sides)

a. 5.678×10^{-6}
b. $x^2 = 64$
   $x = 8$ (took the square root of both sides)
c. $6x^2$
d. $x^{4+6} = x^{10}$
e. prime factors $= 5 \cdot 5 \cdot 7 \cdot 7$
   square root $= 5 \cdot 7 = 35$

Students should have written down one fact about the history of calculators.

Worksheet 17.5

1.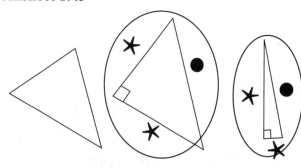

2. a. $(5\text{ in})^2 + (12\text{ in})^2 = c^2$
      25 in$^2 + 144$ in$^2 = c^2$
      169 in$^2 = c^2$
      $\sqrt{169\text{ in}^2} = \sqrt{c^2}$
      13 in $= c$
   b. $(12\text{ ft})^2 + (17\text{ ft})^2 = c^2$
      144 ft$^2 + 289$ ft$^2 = c^2$
      433 ft$^2 = c^2$
      $\sqrt{433\text{ ft}^2} = \sqrt{c^2}$
      20.81 ft $= c$
   c. $(2.5\text{ m})^2 + (4.5\text{ m})^2 = c^2$
      6.25 m$^2 + 20.25$ m$^2 = c^2$
      26.5 m$^2 = c^2$
      $\sqrt{26.5\text{ m}^2} = \sqrt{c^2}$
      5.15 m $= c$
   d. $(7\text{ in})^2 + (9\text{ in})^2 = c^2$
      49 in$^2 + 81$ in$^2 = c^2$
      130 in$^2 = c^2$
      $\sqrt{130\text{ in}^2} = \sqrt{c^2}$
      11.4 in $= c$
   e. $(6\text{ m})^2 + (10\text{ m})^2 = c^2$
      36 m$^2 + 100$ m$^2 = c^2$
      136 m$^2 = c^2$
      $\sqrt{136\text{ m}^2} = \sqrt{c^2}$
      11.66 m $= c$
   f. $(8\text{ m})^2 + (15\text{ m})^2 = c^2$
      64 m$^2 + 225$ m$^2 = c^2$
      289 m$^2 = c^2$
      $\sqrt{289\text{ m}^2} = \sqrt{c^2}$
      17 m $= c$

3. a. $(3\text{ mi})^2 + (5\text{ mi})^2 = c^2$
      9 mi$^2 + 25$ mi$^2 = c^2$
      34 mi$^2 = c^2$
      $\sqrt{34\text{ mi}^2} = \sqrt{c^2}$
      5.83 mi $= c$
   b. $(9\text{ mi})^2 + (2\text{ mi})^2 = c^2$
      81 mi$^2 + 4$ mi$^2 = c^2$
      85 mi$^2 = c^2$
      $\sqrt{85\text{ mi}^2} = \sqrt{c^2}$
      9.22 mi $= c$
   c. $(9\text{ mi} + 2\text{ mi}) - 9.22\text{ mi} = 11\text{ mi} - 9.22\text{ mi} = 1.78\text{ mi}$

4. $(90\text{ ft})^2 + (90\text{ ft})^2 = c^2$
   $8{,}100$ ft$^2 + 8{,}100$ ft$^2 = c^2$
   $16{,}200$ ft$^2 = c^2$
   $\sqrt{16{,}200\text{ ft}^2} = \sqrt{c^2}$
   127.28 ft $= c$

5. a. 5.79×10^{29}

b. 25 and 26
c. $5^{6+8} = 5^{14}$
d. $x^{6+8} = x^{14}$
e. prime factors = 2 • 2 • 2 • 2 • 3 • 3 • 3 • 3
   square root = 2 • 2 • 3 • 3 = 36

Worksheet 17.6

1. a. $x^2 = 130$ (added –25 to both sides)
   $x = 11.4$ (took the square root of both sides)
   b. $x^2 = 318$ (added 18 to both sides)
   $x = 17.83$ (took the square root of both sides)
   c. $y^2 = 821$ (added –58 to both sides)
   $y = 28.65$ (took the square root of both sides)
   d. $x^2 = 80$ (divided both sides by 5)
   $x = 8.94$

2. a. $(12 \text{ ft})^2 + b^2 = (20 \text{ ft})^2$
   $144 \text{ ft}^2 + b^2 = 400 \text{ ft}^2$
   $b^2 = 256 \text{ ft}^2$ (added –144 ft² to both sides)
   $\sqrt{b^2} = \sqrt{256 \text{ ft}^2}$
   $b = 16 \text{ ft}$
   b. $a^2 + (9 \text{ in})^2 = (15 \text{ in})^2$
   $a^2 + 81 \text{ in}^2 = 225 \text{ in}^2$
   $a^2 = 144 \text{ in}^2$ (added –81 in² to both sides)
   $\sqrt{a^2} = \sqrt{144 \text{ ft}^2}$
   $a = 12 \text{ ft}$

3. a. No; we don't know if the triangle is a right triangle.
   b. $(50 \text{ yd})^2 + (100 \text{ yd})^2 = c^2$
   $2,500 \text{ yd}^2 + 10,000 \text{ yd}^2 = c^2$
   $12,500 \text{ yd}^2 = c^2$
   $\sqrt{12,500 \text{ yd}^2} = \sqrt{c^2}$
   $111.8 \text{ yd} = c$
   c. $(5.6 \text{ ft})^2 + (5 \text{ ft})^2 = c^2$
   $31.36 \text{ ft}^2 + 25 \text{ ft}^2 = c^2$
   $56.36 \text{ ft}^2 = c^2$
   $\sqrt{56.36 \text{ ft}^2} = \sqrt{c^2}$
   $7.51 \text{ ft} = c$

4. a. $17.58(1.09)^{15} = 64.03$
   b. $5x^2 = 100$ (combined like terms)
   $x^2 = 20$ (divided both sides by 5)
   $x = 4.47$ (took the square root of both sides)
   c. 15 and 16
   d. $4^{5-3} = 4^2 = 16$
   or
   $\frac{4^5}{4^3} = 4^2 = 16$
   e. 2.33000042×10^2
   f. prime factors = 2 • 2 • 2 • 2 • 2 • 2 • 2 • 2 • 2 • 2
   square root = 2 • 2 • 2 • 2 • 2 = 32

Worksheet 17.7

1. a. $(5 \text{ ft})^2 + (10 \text{ ft})^2 = c^2$
   $25 \text{ ft}^2 + 100 \text{ ft}^2 = c^2$
   $125 \text{ ft}^2 = c^2$
   $\sqrt{125 \text{ ft}^2} = \sqrt{c^2}$
   $11.18 \text{ ft} = c$
   b. $(6.5 \text{ ft})^2 + (3 \text{ ft})^2 = c^2$
   $42.25 \text{ ft}^2 + 9 \text{ ft}^2 = c^2$
   $51.25 \text{ ft}^2 = c^2$
   $\sqrt{51.25 \text{ ft}^2} = \sqrt{c^2}$
   $7.16 \text{ ft} = c$
   c. no

2. a. $(4 \text{ ft})^2 + (6 \text{ ft})^2 = c^2$
   $16 \text{ ft}^2 + 36 \text{ ft}^2 = c^2$
   $52 \text{ ft}^2 = c^2$
   $\sqrt{52 \text{ ft}^2} = \sqrt{c^2}$
   $7.21 \text{ ft} = c$
   b. $(10.5 \text{ in})^2 + b^2 = (20.5 \text{ in})^2$
   $110.25 \text{ in}^2 + b^2 = 420.25 \text{ in}^2$
   $b^2 = 310 \text{ in}^2$ (added –110.25 in² to both sides)
   $\sqrt{b^2} = \sqrt{310 \text{ in}^2}$
   $b = 17.61 \text{ in}$
   c. No; we do not know if the triangle is a right triangle.

3. a. 2.6147×10^{-8}
   b. $8x^2 = 1,024$ (combined like terms)
   $x^2 = 128$ (divided both sides by 8)
   $x = 11.31$ (took the square root of both sides)
   c. prime factors = 2 • 2 • 2 • 2 • 5 • 5 • 5 • 5
   square root = 2 • 2 • 5 • 5 = 100
   d. 27 and 28
   e. $v^{4+2} = v^6$

Worksheet 17.8

1. a. the number that, times itself <u>6</u> times equals <u>50</u>
   b. 50
   c. 6
   d. $\sqrt{}$

2. Check for both prime factors and cubed root.
   a. prime factors = 2 • 2 • 2
   cubed root = 2
   b. prime factors = 2 • 2 • 2 • 2 • 2 • 2 • 2 • 2 • 2
   cubed root = 2 • 2 • 2 = 8
   Note: We found the cubed root by grouping the prime factors into the factor that, multiplied by itself 3 times, equals 512.
   (2 • 2 • 2)(2 • 2 • 2)(2 • 2 • 2) = (8)(8)(8) = 512
   c. prime factors = 2 • 2 • 2 • 3 • 3 • 3
   cubed root = 2 • 3 = 6
   Note: We found the cubed root by grouping the prime factors into the factor that, multiplied by itself 3 times, equals 216.
   (2 • 3)(2 • 3)(2 • 3) = (6)(6)(6) = 512

3. a. $850 \text{ m}^2 = s^2$
   $29.15 \text{ m} = s$ (took the square root of both sides)
   b. $(29.15 \text{ m})^2 + (29.15 \text{ m})^2 = c^2$
   $849.7225 \text{ m}^2 + 849.7225 \text{ m}^2 = c^2$
   $\sqrt{1,699.445 \text{ m}^2} = \sqrt{c^2}$
   41.22 m
   c. $343 \text{ ft}^3 = s^3$
   $7 \text{ ft} = s$ (took the cubed root of both sides)

$(42 \text{ in})^2 + (18.5 \text{ in})^2 = c^2$
$1{,}764 \text{ in}^2 + 342.25 \text{ in}^2 = c^2$
$2{,}106.25 \text{ in}^2 = c^2$
$\sqrt{2{,}106.25 \text{ in}^2} = \sqrt{c^2}$
$45.89 \text{ in} = c$

a. -4.42×10^{-5}
b. I need to know that the triangle is a right triangle.
c. $4x^{2+3} = 4x^5$
d. $\frac{4x^2}{x^3} = \frac{4}{x}$ or $4x^{-1}$
or
$4x^{2-3} = 4x^{-1}$ or $\frac{4}{x}$

a. $9x^3 + 6 = 1{,}131$ (combined like terms)
   $9x^3 = 1{,}125$ (added –6 to both sides)
   $x^3 = 125$ (divided both sides by 9)
   $x = 5$ (took the cubed root of both sides)

Worksheet 18.1

Note: If students need a review of finding missing numbers in proportions, review Lessons 5.1 and 5.2.

$\frac{2.5 \text{ ft}}{8 \text{ ft}} = \frac{x}{3 \text{ in}}$; $x = 0.94$ in

We've used x to stand for the missing angle in these problems, but the student could have used any symbol.
a. $85° + 45° + x = 180°$
   $130° + x = 180°$
   $x = 50°$ (added –130° to both sides)
b. $75° + 30° + x = 180°$
   $105° + x = 180°$
   $x = 75°$ (added –105° to both sides)
c. $90° + 45° + x = 180°$
   $135° + x = 180°$
   $x = 45°$ (added –135° to both sides)

No; the definition of a triangle is different in spherical geometry.

a. two
b.

c. We need to know that *one* more set of corresponding angles are congruent.
d. We know because of the AA similarity theorem. (Two triangles have to be similar if two sets of their corresponding angles are congruent. The picture shows two sets of corresponding congruent angles — the right angles and the other marked angles.)

e. $\frac{x}{6.53 \text{ ft}} = \frac{28.63 \text{ in}}{7.48 \text{ in}}$
   $x = 25$ ft

6. a. The triangle in 3c. (It has a 90°, or right, angle.)
   b.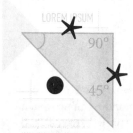

7. $(2 \text{ in})^2 + (3 \text{ in})^2 = c^2$
   $4 \text{ in}^2 + 9 \text{ in}^2 = c^2$
   $13 \text{ in}^2 = c^2$
   $\sqrt{13 \text{ in}^2} = \sqrt{c^2}$
   $3.61 \text{ in} = c$

8. *prime factors* $= 5 \cdot 5 \cdot 9 \cdot 9$
   square root $= 5 \cdot 9 = 45$

Worksheet 18.2

1. Check that tangents were found using the method shown.
   a. tangent of $60° = \frac{3.46 \text{ in}}{2 \text{ in}} = 1.73$
   b. 1.73
   (The dimensions don't matter — the ratio between the opposite and adjacent sides of any 60o angle in a right triangle will always be the same since all right triangles with a 60° angle are similar.)
   c. tangent of $30° = \frac{2 \text{ in}}{3.46 \text{ in}} = 0.58$

2. a. 5.67
   b. 3.27
   c. 0.70
   d. 0.27

3. a. $1 = \frac{x}{4 \text{ ft}}$
      $4 \text{ ft} = x$ (multiplied both sides by 4 ft)
   b. $0.36 = \frac{\text{opposite leg}}{\text{adjacent leg}}$
      $0.36 = \frac{\text{opposite leg}}{4 \text{ in}}$
      $1.44 \text{ in} = \text{opposite leg}$ (multiplied both sides by 4 in)

4. a. tangent of $55° = \frac{x}{20 \text{ ft}}$
      $1.428148007 = \frac{x}{20 \text{ ft}}$ (found the tangent of 55° on a calculator)
      $28.56 \text{ ft} = x$ (multiplied both sides by 20 ft)
      $29 \text{ ft} = x$ (rounded per instructions)
   b. *total height of house* $= 29$ ft $+ 6$ ft $= 35$ ft

5. Yes; the triangles have two sets of corresponding congruent angles (the 90° angles and the 30° angles.)

6. a. 25 and 26
   b. $(50 \text{ ft})^2 + b^2 = (78 \text{ ft})^2$
      $2{,}500 \text{ ft}^2 + b^2 = 6{,}084 \text{ ft}^2$
      $b^2 = 3{,}584 \text{ ft}^2$ (added –2,500 ft² to both sides)
      $\sqrt{b^2} = \sqrt{3{,}584}$
      $b = 59.87$ ft
   c. *prime factors* $= 2 \cdot 2 \cdot 3 \cdot 3 \cdot 3 \cdot 3 \cdot 3 \cdot 3$
      square root $= 2 \cdot 3 \cdot 3 \cdot 3 = 54$

Worksheet 18.3

1. a. $\frac{12 \text{ ft}}{13 \text{ ft}} = 0.92$
   b. $\frac{3 \text{ ft}}{5 \text{ ft}} = 0.6$
2. a. $\frac{5 \text{ ft}}{13 \text{ ft}} = 0.38$
   b. $\frac{4 \text{ ft}}{5 \text{ ft}} = 0.8$
3. a. $\frac{12 \text{ ft}}{5 \text{ ft}} = 2.4$
   b. $\frac{3 \text{ ft}}{4 \text{ ft}} = 0.75$
4. a. We know from the AA similarity theorem (or because they have two sets of corresponding angles that are congruent). (Two triangles have to be similar if two sets of their corresponding angles are congruent.)
   b. Yes; they both have a right angle marked.
   c. $\frac{12 \text{ in}}{46.36 \text{ in}} = 0.26$
   d. 0.26
   e. $\frac{44.78 \text{ in}}{46.36 \text{ in}} = 0.97$
   f. 0.97
5. a. 0.91
   b. 0.93
   c. 1
   d. 0.82
   e. 0.57
6. proportional and their corresponding angles are congruent
7. tangent of 65° = $\frac{5 \text{ ft}}{x}$
   $2.144506921 = \frac{5 \text{ ft}}{x}$ (found the tangent of 65° using the calculator)
   $(2.144506921)x = 5 \text{ ft}$ (multiplied both sides by x)
   $x = 2.33 \text{ ft}$ (divided both sides by 2.144506921)
8. a. $x = 3$ (divided both sides by 15)
   b. $16x = 45$ (combined like terms)
   $x = 2.81$ (divided both sides by 16)
   c. $-14x = 45$ (combined like terms)
   $x = -3.21$ (divided both sides by -14)
   d. $16x^2 = 45$ (combined like terms)
   $x^2 = 2.8125$ (divided both sides by 16)
   $x = 1.68$ (took the square root of both sides)
   e. prime factors = $5 \cdot 5 \cdot 11 \cdot 11$
   square root = $5 \cdot 11 = 55$
9. a. $(6.5 \text{ ft})^2 + b^2 = (8 \text{ ft})^2$
   $42.25 \text{ ft}^2 + b^2 = 64 \text{ ft}^2$
   $b^2 = 21.75 \text{ ft}^2$ (added -42.25 ft^2 to both sides)
   $\sqrt{b^2} = \sqrt{21.75 \text{ ft}^2}$
   $b = 4.66 \text{ ft}$
   b. 106 and 107

Worksheet 18.4

1. a. 0.77
   b. 0.64
   c. 1.19
   d. 0.26
   e. 0.97
   f. 3.73

2. a. $\cos(28°) = 0.88$
   b. $\tan(28°) = 0.53$
   c. $\sin(28°) = 0.47$
3. a. 45°
   b. false
   (In function notation, the parentheses enclose the input to the function.)
   c. Similar shapes have <u>proportional</u> sides. This means that the ratio between their corresponding sides will be <u>equal</u>
4. a. $slope = \frac{24}{4} = 6$
   b. $\tan(80.54°) = 6$
   The tangent and the slope are the same.
   Note: The small difference before you round to the second decimal place is due to using a rounded angle value — the actual angle value is more precise than 80.54°.
5. a. $\tan(55°) = \frac{x}{20 \text{ ft}}$
   $\tan(55°) \cdot 20 \text{ ft} = x$ (multiplied both sides by 20 ft)
   $1.428148007 \cdot 20 \text{ ft} = x$ (found the tangent of 55° on a calculator)
   $28.56 \text{ ft} = x$
   Note: Notice that we waited to find the tan(55°) on the calculator until the end. We could have found it sooner, but it's often helpful to wait to calculate its value until we've finished rearranging the equation.
   b. total height of light = $28.56 \text{ ft} + 2.48 \text{ ft} = 31.04 \text{ ft}$
6. $(4{,}000 \text{ ft})^2 + (3{,}000 \text{ ft})^2 = c^2$
   $16{,}000{,}000 \text{ ft}^2 + 9{,}000{,}000 \text{ ft}^2 = c^2$
   $25{,}000{,}000 \text{ ft}^2 = c^2$
   $\sqrt{25{,}000{,}000 \text{ ft}^2} = \sqrt{c^2}$
   $5{,}000 \text{ ft} = c$
7. a. 29 and 30
   b. 225 (squared both sides)
   c. prime factors = $7 \cdot 7 \cdot 7$
   cubed root = 7

Worksheet 18.5

1. a. 0
   b. 0.36
   c. −0.7
   d. 0
   e. −0.34
   f. −0.57
   g. −1
   h. −0.94
   i. 0.82
2. a. Answer should be a way describing sounds mathematically helps us; one possible answer is that it allows us to reproduce sounds digitally.
   b. 200°
3. a. 1
   b. 0
   c. yes
   (For every angle size, there's only one cosine value.)
4. Students were instructed to study for the quiz.

Worksheet 19.1

Winter: a, f
Spring/Summer/Fall: b, c, d, e
Brittany: a, b, c
William: a, c, d

1. a. an element of
   b. A
2. a. Boeing 787s
   b.

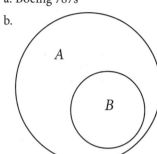

   yes
3. a. $\tan(70°) = \frac{x}{18.2 \text{ ft}}$
      $\tan(70°) \cdot 18.2 \text{ ft} = x$ (multiplied both sides by 18.2 ft)
      $2.747477419 \cdot 18.2 \text{ ft} = x$ (found the tangent of 70° on a calculator)
      $50 \text{ ft} = x$
      height of tree = 50 ft + 4.8 ft = 54.8 ft
   b. 0.52
   c. 59°
   d. 0.52
   e. The cosine of 59° tells us the ratio between the leg adjacent to a 59° angle and the hypotenuse in a right triangle.
   f. 17 and 18

Worksheet 19.2

1. a. {5 in, 8 in, 11 in}
   b. $x \in \{5, 7\}$
   c. $t \in \{20 \text{ min}, 25 \text{ min}, 30 \text{ min}\}$
2. a.

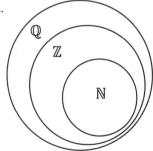

   b. Rational Numbers: Can be expressed as a ratio (i.e., division) of one integer to another
      Integers: Non-fractional numbers
      Natural Numbers: Integers 1 and greater (Some definitions include 0.)
3. a. true
   b. false
   c. true
   d. false
4. a. no
      (π is an irrational number.)
   b. yes
   c. no
5. $\tan(45°) = \frac{x}{50 \text{ ft}}$
   $\tan(45°) \cdot 50 \text{ ft} = x$ (multiplied both sides by 50 ft)
   $1 \cdot 50 \text{ ft} = x$ (found the tangent of 45° on a calculator)
   $50 \text{ ft} = x$
6. a. $\frac{15}{15.23} = 0.98$
   b. $\frac{2.64}{15.23} = 0.17$
   c. $\frac{15 \text{ ft}}{2.64 \text{ ft}} = 5.68$

Worksheet 19.3

1. "an ordered set of quantities."[3]
2. a. {2, 7(2), 14(2), 28(2), ...}
      {2, 14, 28, 56, ...}
   b. {3, 7(3), 14(3), 28(3), ...}
      {3, 21, 42, 84, ...}
   c. {5, 3(5), 6(5), 9(5), ...}
      {5, 15, 30, 45, ...}
   d. {5, 2(5), 3(5), 4(5), ...}
      {5, 10, 15, 20, ...}
   e. true
3. {49 Hz, 2(49 Hz), 3(49 Hz), 4(49 Hz), 5(49 Hz), ...}
   {49 Hz, 98 Hz, 147 Hz, 196 Hz, 245 Hz, ...}
4. a. yes
   b. Answer should be any sequence of integers.
5. a. yes
   b. no
   c. $x \in Z$
   d. 0.67
   e. sine of an angle = $\frac{\text{opposite leg}}{\text{hypotenuse}}$
      $\sin(53°) = \frac{x}{9 \text{ ft}}$
      $\sin(53°) \cdot 9 \text{ ft} = x$ (multiplied both sides by 9 ft)
      $0.79863551 \cdot 9 \text{ ft} = x$ (found the sine of 53° on the calculator)
      $7.19 \text{ ft} = x$
   f. false
      (They are similar, not congruent.)
   g. $\tan(30°) = 0.58$
   h. prime factors = $3 \cdot 3 \cdot 3 \cdot 5 \cdot 5 \cdot 5$
      cubed root = $3 \cdot 5 = 15$
6. Student should play the notes shown on the worksheet on a piano if possible.

Worksheet 19.4

1. a. difference
   b. ratio
   c. Yes; the common difference is 3.
   d. arithmetic sequence
   e. Yes; the common ratio is 3.
   f. geometric sequence
   g. There is not a common difference or ratio.

---

[3] [*The American Heritage Dictionary of the English Language*, 1980 new college ed., s.v., "sequence."]

h. neither
i. 14, 20
(The pattern is to subtract 2, then add 6. Since 6 was added to get to 16, it was time to subtract 2, getting us 14. Then we added 6 to get 20.)

2. a. {7(4), 14(4), 28(4), ...}
   {28, 56, 112, ...}
   b. $\frac{28s}{14s} = \frac{^2 28s}{14s} = 2$ $\frac{14s}{7s} = \frac{^2 14s}{7s} = 2$
   c. {7s, 14s, 28s, 56s ...}
   (We multiplied the previous element by the common ratio: 28s • 2 = 56s. Remember, multiplication can be done in any order, so even though we don't know the value of s, we can multiply the 28 and the 2 together.)

3. a. {6(3), 9(3), 12(3), ...}
   {18, 27, 36, ...}
   b. 12x − 9x = 3x   9x − 6x = 3x
   c. {6x, 9x, 12x, 15x ...}
   (We added the common difference of 3x to the previous element: 12x + 3x = 15x.)

4. {49 Hz, 2(49 Hz), 4(49 Hz), 8(49 Hz), 16(49 Hz), ...}
   {49 Hz, 98 Hz, 196 Hz, 392 Hz, 784 Hz, ...}

5. false

6. a. $\frac{5 \text{ in}}{5.96 \text{ in}} = 0.84$
   b. $\frac{3.25 \text{ in}}{5.96 \text{ in}} = 0.55$
   c. $\frac{3.25 \text{ in}}{5 \text{ in}} = 0.65$

7. a. no
   b. no
   c. $s \in \mathbb{Z}$
   d. sin(55°) = 0.82

Worksheet 19.5

1. Student should do the online experiment and write a short paragraph explaining the results.

2. Students were instructed to study for the quiz.

Worksheet 20.1

1. a. 0.04
   b. 0.006
   c. 0.0002
   d. 5

2. a. $P = \$400(1 + 0.06)^3$
   $P = \$476.41$
   b. $P = \$600(1 + 0.0025)^{60}$
   $P = \$696.97$

3. $476.41 − $400 = $76.41
   Note: Since the problem told us nothing was deposited or withdrawn, the difference between the initial balance (P_o) and ending balance (P) will be the amount earned in interest.

4. a. R • 150 pages = 40 pages
   R = 0.2667   (divided both sides by 150 pages)
   R = 26.67%

   b. 1.1 • 4.5 yd = 4.95 yd, which rounds to 5 yd
   Note: We could also have found 10% of 4.5 yd, and then added that amount to 4.5 yd. Multiplying by 1.1 is a faster way to find 110%.
   c. 0.25 • B = $350
   B = $1,400   (divided both sides by 0.25)

5. a. {5, 6(5), 36(5), ...}
   {5, 30, 180, ...}
   b. $\frac{36p}{6p} = 6$ $\frac{6p}{p} = 6$
   c. geometric
   d. {p, 6p, 36p, 216p,...}
   (We found the value by multiplying the previous element by the common ratio: 36p • 6 = 216p.)

Worksheet 20.2

1. a. 6 • 12 = 72
   (multiplied 12, the number of periods in a year, by 6, the number of years)
   b. 6 • 365 = 2,190
   (multiplied 365, the number of periods in a year, by 6, the number of years)

2. a. $\frac{0.03}{12} = 0.0025$
   (divided the annual rate of 3% by 12, the number of periods in a year)
   b. $\frac{0.03}{365} = 0.000082192$
   (divided the annual rate of 3% by 365, the number of periods in a year)

3. a. $P = \$10,000(1 + 0.0025)^{72}$
   $P = \$11,969.48$
   b. $P = \$10,000(1 + 0.000082192)^{2,190}$
   $P = \$11,972.09$

4. *number of periods* = 3 • 365 = 1,095
   (multiplied 365, the number of periods in a year, by 3, the number of years)
   rate per period = $\frac{0.025}{365} = 0.000068493$
   (divided the annual rate of 2.5% by 365, the number of periods in a year)
   $P = \$500(1 + 0.000068493)^{1,095}$
   $P = \$538.94$

5. a. $d = \frac{1 \text{ mi}}{20 \text{ min}} \cdot 240 \text{ min}$
   d = 12 mi
   Note: We converted 4 hours to 240 minutes before solving. Students could have converted $\frac{1 \text{ mi}}{20 \text{ min}}$ to miles per hour instead. The important thing was to get the units the same so they would cancel out.
   b. 0.5 • 4 yd = 2 yd
   2 yd • $\frac{36 \text{ in}}{1 \text{ yd}}$ = 72 in

6. {2, 4(2), 7(2), ...}
   {2, 8, 14, ...}
   b. 7p − 4p = 3p   4p − p = 3p
   c. arithmetic sequence
   d. {p, 4p, 7p, 10p, ...}
   (We found the value by adding the common difference to the previous element: 7p + 3p = 10p.)

Worksheet 20.3

a. 0.04 • $10,000 = $400
b. 0.026 • $3,000 = $78

a. $P = \$400t + \$10,000$
b. *the interest earned each year*
c. *the initial investment*

compound interest
(In compound interest, the interest continues to increase the balance off which the interest is calculated the next period.)

interest earned at an APY of 2.2%:
0.022 • $5,000 = $110
interest earned at an APY of 1.5%:
0.015 • $5,000 = $75
additional earnings at an APY of 2.2%:
$110 − $75 = $35

a. $R \cdot 36 = 1$
   $R = 0.0278$ (divided both sides by 36)
   $R = 2.78\%$ (converted to a percent)
b. $0.25 \cdot B = \$145$
   $B = \$580$ (divided both sides by 0.25)
c. cost of 4-lb item after 12% coupon:
   0.88 • $4.50 = $3.96
   amount per pound for 4-lb item:
   $\frac{\$3.96}{4} = \$0.99$
   amount per pound for 3.5-lb item:
   $\frac{\$3.75}{3.5} = \$1.07$
   The 4-lb item is the better price per pound.
   Note: We could also have found the cost of the 4-lb item by finding 12% of $4.50, and then subtracting that from $4.50 to find the price after the coupon.
d. converting to square feet:
   $\frac{1}{18 \text{ ac}} \cdot \frac{43,560 \text{ ft}^2}{1 \text{ ac}} = 2,420 \text{ ft}^2$
   $A = \ell w$
   $2,420 \text{ ft}^2 = \ell \cdot 40 \text{ ft}$
   $60.5 \text{ ft} = \ell$ (divided both sides by 40 ft)

a. geometric sequence
   (The common ratio is 2.)
b. arithmetic sequence
   (The common difference is −2.)
c. {$x, 2x, 3x, 4x, \ldots$}
d. no
   (−5 is not a natural number.)

Worksheet 20.4

a. Answers will vary. One would be that a budget can help us live within the income God has provided.
b. $1,200 − $800 = $400
c. $\frac{\$450}{12} = \$37.50$
d. $\frac{\$5,000}{12} = \$416.67$
e. 4.33 • $25 = $108.25
f. $\frac{\$130 + \$150 + \$99 + \$111}{4} = \frac{\$490}{4} = \$122.50$

2.

Hypothetical Vacation Budget
Transportation
Total for Plan A = $450 + 2($25) + $55 = $555
Total for Plan B = $0.50(700) + $15 = $365
Lodging
Total for Plan A = 3($70) = $210
Total for Plan B = 3($15) = $45
Meals
Total for Plan A = 5($6 + $8 + $10) = $120
Total for Plan B = $4 + $4 + $10 + $10 + $30 = $58
Activities
Total for Plan A = $25 + $50 + $10 = $85
Total for Plan B = $5
GRAND TOTAL
Grand Total for Plan A = $555 + $210 + $120 + $85 = $970
Grand Total for Plan B = $365 + $45 + $58 + $5 = $473

3. a. $0.075 \cdot \$60,000 = P$
      $\$4,500 = P$
   b. $0.05 \cdot B = \$3,500$
      $B = \$70,000$ (divided both sides by 0.05)
   c. $R \cdot \$65,000 = \$6,500$
      $R = 0.1$ (divided both sides by $65,000)
      $R = 10\%$ (converted to a percent)
   d. $4,500 − $150 = $4,350
   e. weekly earnings:
      0.04 • $1,000 = $40
      difference from $400 weekly salary:
      $400 − $40 = $360
      amount less per year:
      52 • $360 = $18,720

4. a. neither
   b. 5, 3
      (The pattern is to subtract 2, and then increase 1. Since 2 was subtracted from 6 to get 4, we increased 4 by 1 to find the next element (5), and then subtracted 2 from that to get 3.)

Worksheet 20.5

1. a. 15 and 16
   b. *prime factors* = 2 • 2 • 2 • 5 • 5 • 5
      cubed root = 2 • 5 = 10
   c. *prime factors* = 2 • 2 • 3 • 3 • 7 • 7
      square root = 2 • 3 • 7 = 42

2. a. $x = 121$ (squared both sides)
   b. $156.25 \text{ ft}^2 = s^2$
      $12.5 \text{ ft} = s$ (took the square root of both sides)
   c. $a^2 = 421$ (added −79 to both sides)
      $a = 20.52$ (took the square root of both sides)

3. a. Yes; we know because of the AA similarity theorem (or because they have two sets of corresponding angles that are congruent).
      (Two triangles have to be similar if two sets of their corresponding angles are congruent. In all right triangles

with a 40° angle, both the 40° angles and the 90° angles are congruent, so the triangles are similar.)
b. yes
(All right triangles with 40° angles are similar, so the ratio between their corresponding sides will be the same.)
c. 0.64

4. a.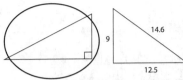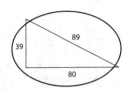

Note: We know the triangle on the far right is truly a right triangle because $39^2 + 80^2 = 89^2$. The middle triangle is not a right triangle as $12.5^2 + 9^2$ does *not* equal 14.6^2. We know the triangle on the left is a right triangle because the right angle is marked.

b. $sine = \frac{opposite\ leg}{hypotenuse} = \frac{1\ in}{2.28\ in} = 0.44$
c. $tangent = \frac{opposite\ leg}{adjacent\ leg} = \frac{1\ in}{2.05\ in} = 0.49$
d. $cosine = \frac{adjacent\ leg}{hypotenuse} = \frac{2.05\ in}{2.28\ in} = 0.9$
e. $tangent = \frac{opposite\ leg}{adjacent\ leg}$

$\tan(78°) = \frac{a}{7\ ft}$
$\tan(78°) \cdot 7\ ft = a$ (multiplied both sides by 7 ft)
$4.70463011 \cdot 7\ ft = a$ (found tan(78°) on a calculator)
$32.93\ ft = a$

f. $(32.93\ ft)^2 + (7\ ft)^2 = c^2$
$1,084.3849\ ft^2 + 49\ ft^2 = c^2$
$1,133.3849\ ft^2 = c^2$
$\sqrt{1,133.3849\ ft^2} = \sqrt{c^2}$
$33.67\ ft = c$

5. a. no
b. yes
c. $\{4, 4 + 3, 4 + 6, \ldots\}$
$\{4, 7, 10, \ldots\}$
d. $(x + 6) - (x + 3) = \underline{3}$ $(x + 3) - (x) = \underline{3}$
Note: We used the distributive property to remove the parentheses from $(x + 6) - (x + 3)$:
$x + 6 + -1(x + 3) =$
$x + 6 + -x + -3 = 3$
e. $\{x, x + 3, x + 6, \underline{x + 9}, \ldots\}$
(We found the value by adding the common difference to the previous element: $x + 6 + 3 = x + 9$.)
f. arithmetic sequence
g. $\{3, 3^2, 3^3, 3^4, \ldots\}$
$\{3, 9, 27, 81, \ldots\}$
h. $\frac{x^4}{x^3} = \underline{x^1\ or\ x}$ $\frac{x^2}{x} = \underline{x^1\ or\ x}$
i. $\{x, x^2, x^3, x^4, \underline{x^5}, \ldots\}$
(We found the value by multiplying the previous element by the common ratio: $x^4 \cdot x = x^5$.)
j. geometric sequence

6. a. *number of periods* $= 5 \cdot 12 = 60$
(multiplied 12, the number of periods in a year, by 5, the number of years)
rate per period $= \frac{0.0325}{12} = 0.002708333$
(divided the annual rate of 3.25% by 12, the number of periods in a year)
$P = \$29,000(1 + 0.00270833)^{60}$

$P = \$34,109.51$
b. The money invested at 5% compound interest.
c. finding 110% of previous year's budget to get new year budget:
$1.10 \cdot \$400 = \$440$
dividing new yearly budget by 12 to find monthly budget:
$\frac{\$440}{12} = \$36.67$
Note: We could have also found 10% of $400 and added that to $400 in order to find last year's budget plus 10%. Finding 110% was simply a faster way to do the same thing.
d. discount with 15% off coupon:
$0.15 \cdot \$45 = \$6.75$
discount with $5 off coupon:
$\$5$
difference:
$\$6.75 - \$5.00 = \$1.75$
The 15%-off coupon will result in saving $1.75 more.
e. $d = st$
$1.5\ mi = s(20\ min)$
$\frac{1.5\ mi}{20\ min} = s$ (divided both sides by 20 min)
converting to miles per hour:
$\frac{1.5\ mi}{20\ min} \cdot \frac{60\ min}{1\ hr} = 4.5\ \frac{mi}{hr}$
You would have to travel $4.5\ \frac{mi}{hr}$.

Worksheet 21.1

1. Student should begin end-of-the-year project. The project will be due on Test 5 (the final test).

2. a. $x = 5$ (divided both sides by $3)
b. $x = \$210$ (added $90 to both sides)
c. $x = -500$ (multiplied both sides by –5)
d. $\frac{5}{5}x - \frac{4}{5}x = 120$
$\frac{1}{5}x = 120$ (combined like terms)
$x = 600$ (divided both sides by $\frac{1}{5}$ by multiplying them by $\frac{5}{1}$)
e. $x = \$2,500$ (divided both sides by $\frac{1}{10}$ by multiplying them by $\frac{10}{1}$)
f. $\frac{1}{60}x = 40\ hr$
$x = 2,400\ hr$ (divided both sides by $\frac{1}{60}$ by multiplying them by $\frac{60}{1}$)
g. $\frac{2,400\ hr}{\frac{8\ hr}{day}} = {}^{300}2,400\ hr \cdot \frac{day}{8\ hr} = 300\ days$
h. $\frac{3}{3}x - \frac{2}{3}x = 67$
$\frac{1}{3}x = 67$ (combined like terms)
$x = 201$ (divided both sides by $\frac{1}{3}$ by multiplying them by $\frac{3}{1}$)
i. $5x = 45$ (combined like terms)
$x = 9$ (divided both sides by 5)
j. $8 + -1(2 + x) = 20$
$8 + -2 + -x = 20$
$6 + -x = 20$
$-x = 14$ (added –6 to both sides)

$x = -14$ (multiplied both sides by –1)

k. $6 + 2x + 2(5) = 86$
$6 + 2x + 10 = 86$
$16 + 2x = 86$
$2x = 70$ (added –16 to both sides)
$x = 35$ (divided both sides by 2)

a. $12{,}000 \text{ in}^3 = (400 \text{ in}^2)(h)$
$30 \text{ in} = h$ (divided both sides by 400 in²)

b. $A = \frac{1}{2}bh$
$18 \text{ in}^2 = \frac{1}{2} \cdot 6 \text{ in} \cdot h$
$18 \text{ in}^2 = 3 \text{ in} \cdot h$
$6 \text{ in} = h$ (divided both sides by 3 in)

a. $10 \text{ mi} = s(2 \text{ hr})$
$\frac{\cancel{10}^5 \text{ mi}}{\cancel{2}\text{ hr}} = \frac{s(\cancel{2}\text{ hr})}{\cancel{2}\text{ hr}}$
$5 \frac{\text{mi}}{\text{hr}} = s$

b. $12 \text{ mi} = (\frac{6.5 \text{ mi}}{1 \text{ hr}})t$
$12 \text{ mi} \cdot \frac{1 \text{ hr}}{6.5 \text{ mi}} = (\frac{\cancel{6.5 \text{ mi}}}{\cancel{1 \text{ hr}}})t \cdot \frac{\cancel{1 \text{ hr}}}{\cancel{6.5 \text{ mi}}}$
$1.85 \text{ hr} = t$
Converting fractional portion to minutes:
$0.85 \cancel{\text{ hr}} \cdot \frac{60 \text{ min}}{1 \cancel{\text{ hr}}} = 51 \text{ min}$
$1 \text{ hr}, 51 \text{ min} = t$

c. $d = (\frac{50 \text{ mi}}{60 \text{ min}})(25 \text{ min})$
$d = (\frac{50 \text{ mi}}{60 \cancel{\text{ min}}})(25 \cancel{\text{ min}})$
$d = 20.83 \text{ mi}$

Note: Notice that we wrote the speed as $\frac{50 \text{ mi}}{60 \text{ min}}$ instead of $\frac{50 \text{ mi}}{1 \text{ hr}}$ so the units would cancel out.

Worksheet 21.2

a.

Ages of Lawful Permanent Residents Who Were Naturalized Between 1973–1975	Frequency	Relative Frequency
18–24	130,675	28.09%
25–34	197,111	42.37%
35–44	78,160	16.8%
45+	59,214	12.73%

Note: Due to rounding, the relative frequencies only total 99.99%. The unrounded values would total 100%.

The relative frequencies were obtained by dividing the value in the frequency column by the total number of data points (in this case, 465,160).

b. Answer should be at least one reason to question conclusion given. *Example*: The proposed conclusion used the word "people," but the statistic was not about "people" in general, but rather lawful permanent residents. Also, the conclusion was a very broad one that would apply to all years, but the data was only for three years back in the 1970s. Circumstances could have changed, affecting the number of lawful permanent residents who naturalize in each age group. We could only conclude that more lawful permanent residents naturalized for the years 1973–1975.

c. $average = \frac{0.5 + 1.9 + 2.4 + 2.9 + 3.3 + 3.5 + 3.5 + 5.5 + 7.5 + 8}{10} =$

$\frac{39}{10} = 3.9$ mph

d. $mode = 3.5$ mph

e. 0.5, 1.9, 2.4, 2.9, ③.3, 3.5, 3.5, 5.5, 7.5, 8
$median = \frac{3.3 + 3.5}{2} = 3.4$ mph

2. a. $\frac{1}{2} \cdot \frac{1}{2} \cdot \frac{1}{2} = \frac{1}{8} = 0.125 = 12.5\%$

b. 1:7
Note: We saw in 2a that there are 8 total outcomes, 1 of which produces the event. Odds compare the outcomes that produce the event with the outcomes that do not produce the event, rather than with the total outcomes. The 7 was found by subtracting 1 (the outcomes that produce the event) from 8 (the total outcomes).

c. $\frac{3}{20} = 0.15 = 15\%$

d. $\frac{3}{20} \cdot \frac{2}{19} \cdot \frac{1}{18} = \frac{6}{6{,}840} = 0.0009 = 0.09\%$

e. $\frac{3}{20} \cdot \frac{3}{20} \cdot \frac{3}{20} = \frac{27}{8{,}000} = 0.0034 = 0.34\%$

3. a. 0.71

b. $\sin(57.55°) = \frac{s}{2.69 \text{ ft}}$
$\sin(57.55°) \cdot 2.69 \text{ ft} = s$ (multiplied both sides by 2.69 ft)
$0.843860007 \cdot 2.69 \text{ ft} = s$ (found the sin(57.55°) on a calculator)
$2.27 \text{ ft} = s$

c. $cosine \text{ of } angle = \frac{2.1 \text{ in}}{2.37 \text{ in}} = 0.89$

4. a. $\frac{0.054}{365} = 0.000147945$
(divided the annual rate of 5.4% by 365, the number of periods in a year)

b. $R \cdot \$55.53 = \$8.33$
$R = 0.15$ (divided both sides by $55.53)
$R = 15\%$ (converted to a percent)

c. $\frac{\$532}{6} = \$88.67$

5. Students should continue to work on the end-of-year project assigned in Worksheet 21.1.

Worksheet 21.3A

1. a. 23 and 24
b. *prime factors* $= 7 \cdot 7 \cdot 7$
cubed root $= 7$
c. $3f$
d. $-2x$
e. s^5

2. a. $x^2 = 226$ (added –89 to both sides)
$x = 15.03$ (took the square root of both sides)

b. $60(7.015)^7 = 50{,}158{,}550.54$

c. 5.015855054×10^7

d. $A = s^2$
$289 \text{ in}^2 = s^2$
$17 \text{ in} = s$ (took the square root of both sides)

e. 0.98

f. $x < 81$ (added –5 to both sides)
g. $x < 30$ (divided both sides by 6)
h. $x > -30$ (divided both sides by –6 and changed the direction of the sign)

3. a. $0.05 \cdot B = \$450$

$B = \$9,000$ (divided both sides by 0.05)

b. $\cos(45.1°) = \frac{s}{17}$
$\cos(45.1°) \cdot 17 = s$ (multiplied both sides by 17)
$12 = s$

c. $\{4, 4 - \frac{1}{2}, 4 - 1, 4 - 1\frac{1}{2}, \ldots\}$
$\{4, 3\frac{1}{2}, 3, 2\frac{1}{2}, \ldots\}$

d.
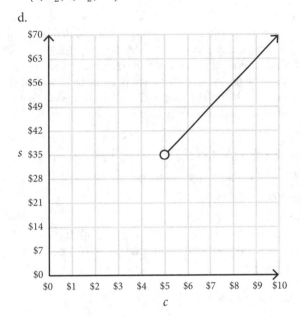

4. Students were told to solve each problem using a proportion and cross multiplication.

a. $\frac{200 \text{ ft}}{85 \text{ ft}} = \frac{10 \text{ in}}{x}$
$200 \text{ ft} \cdot x = 85 \text{ ft} \cdot 10 \text{ in}$ (cross multiplied)
$200 \text{ ft} \cdot x = 850 \text{ ft} \cdot \text{in}$
$4.25 \text{ in} = x$ (divided both sides by 200 ft)

b. $\frac{14 \text{ ft}}{20 \text{ ft}} = \frac{3 \text{ in}}{x}$
$14 \text{ ft} \cdot x = 20 \text{ ft} \cdot 3 \text{ in}$ (cross multiplied)
$14 \text{ ft} \cdot x = 60 \text{ ft} \cdot \text{in}$
$x = 4.29 \text{ in}$ (divided both sides by 14 ft)

c. $\frac{1 \text{ degree}}{60 \text{ arcminutes}} = \frac{x}{8{,}090 \text{ arcminutes}}$
$1 \text{ degree} \cdot 8{,}090 \text{ arcminutes} = 60 \text{ arcminutes} \cdot x$
$134.83 \text{ degrees} = x$ (divided both sides by 60 archminutes)

5. Students should continue to work on the end-of-year project assigned in Worksheet 21.1.

Worksheet 21.3B

1. a. Graph may vary in scale.

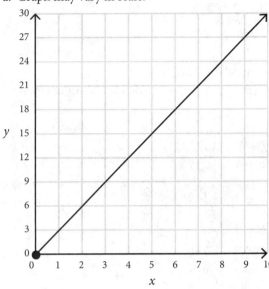

b. $y = 56 \frac{\text{mi}}{\text{hr}} + x$ (added s_o to both sides)
c. $x = 27\frac{7}{8}$ (added $7\frac{7}{8}$ to both sides)
d. $100 + -8 + -4x = 20$
$92 + -4x = 20$
$-4x = -72$ (added −92 to both sides)
$x = 18$ (divided both sides by −4)
e. $R \cdot 87 = 25$
$R = 0.2874$ (divided both sides by 87)
$R = 28.74\%$ (converted to a percent)
f. 0.00000264
g. 2.5×10^{-5}
h. $x > -50$ (divided both sides by −2 and changed the direction of the sign)
i. prime factors = $3 \cdot 3 \cdot 11 \cdot 11$
square root = $3 \cdot 11 = 33$
j. no
(There's *not* only one value for y for every value of x.)

2. $(9 \text{ ft})^2 + (12 \text{ ft})^2 = c^2$
$81 \text{ ft}^2 + 144 \text{ ft}^2 = c^2$
$225 \text{ ft}^2 = c^2$
$15 \text{ ft} = c$ (took the square root of both sides)

3. a. $0.7A = 700$ (multiplied both sides by A)
$A = 1{,}000$ (divided both sides by 0.7)
b. $5.4 = F$ (multiplied both sides by 60)

4. Students should continue to work on the end-of-year project assigned in Worksheet 21.1.

Worksheet 21.3C

1. a. $6y^2 + 2y$ (combined like terms)
b. 8^{-3}
c. $100\% - 30\% = 70\%$
d. 29 and 30

2. a. *amount of shrinkage* = $0.031 \cdot 2.5 \text{ ft} = 0.0775 \text{ ft}$
finished distance across the grain =
$2.5 \text{ ft} - 0.0775 \text{ ft} = 2.42 \text{ ft}$

Note: We could have also found the answer by subtracting 3.1% from 100%, getting 96.9%, and then finding 96.9% of 2.5 ft.

b. $\frac{1.75 \text{ barrels}}{50 \text{ yd}^2} = \frac{x}{600 \text{ yd}^2}$
21 barrels = x

a. $200 \cdot 28 = r(14)$
$5,600 = 14r$
$400 = r$ (divided both sides by 14)

b. $28 \cdot 100 = r(8)$
$2,800 = r(8)$
$350 = r$ (divided both sides by 8)

Students should continue to work on the end-of-year project assigned in Worksheet 21.1.

Answers to Quizzes

Quiz 1 (Chapters 1 and 2)

1. a. $7 + 8.2(1.5 - 1.25) - 8 =$
   $7 + 8.2(0.25) - 8 =$
   $7 + 2.05 - 8 =$
   $9.05 - 8 = 1.05$
   b. -8
   c. 9
   d. $\frac{1}{3\cancel{9}} \cdot \frac{\cancel{3}}{2} = \frac{1}{6}$
   e. $\frac{5}{2\cancel{2}} \cdot \frac{3}{\cancel{10}_2} = \frac{3}{4}$
   f. $2\frac{3}{9} + 5\frac{6}{9} = 7\frac{9}{9} = 8$
   g. Check to make sure problem was solved using the distributive property.
   $5(7 + 8) =$
   $5(7) + 5(8) =$
   $35 + 40 = 75$
   h. -2

2. a. $\frac{17}{209}$
   (The ft canceled out.)
   b. $8 = 2 \cdot 2 \cdot 2$
   $88 = 2 \cdot 2 \cdot 2 \cdot 11$
   c. 8
   d. $\frac{55}{10}$
   e. 0.34

3. a. finding the square feet needed:
   $4 \text{ ft} \cdot 60 + 4 \text{ ft} \cdot 160 \text{ ft} =$
   $240 \text{ ft}^2 + 640 \text{ ft}^2 = 880 \text{ ft}^2$
   finding the cost:
   $880 \text{ ft}^2 \cdot \frac{\$2.50}{1 \text{ ft}^2} = \$2,200$
   b. $V = (24 \text{ in} \cdot 42 \text{ in})(8 \text{ in}) = 8,064 \text{ in}^2$

4. a. the opposite of
   b. true

5. a. $15 \cdot \$62.54 = \$938.10$
   b. $5\ °C - 63\ °C = -58\ °C$
   c. *expenses* = $\$30 + \$22 + \$16 + \$2.75 + \$27 = \$97.75$
   income = $(240 \cdot \$2) + \$5 = \$485$
   profit = $\$485 - \$97.75 = \$387.25$

Quiz 2 (Chapter 3)

1. Check to make sure students showed how they obtained the answer by adding, subtracting (i.e., adding a negative number), multiplying, or dividing the same amount to both sides, as shown in 1a.
   a. $\frac{x \cdot \cancel{12}}{\cancel{12}} = \frac{480}{\cancel{12}}^{40}$
   $x = 40$
   b. $x = 49$ (multiplied both sides by 7)
   c. $x = 101$ (added 87 to both sides)
   d. $x = 3$ (divided both sides by 42)
   e. $x = 115$ (added -99 to both sides)

2. a. $800 \text{ mi} = s \cdot 20 \text{ hr}$
   $40 \frac{\text{mi}}{\text{hr}} = s$ (divided both sides by 20 hr)
   b. $-1,000 \text{ ft} = r \cdot 6 \text{ min} + 0 \text{ ft}$

$-1,000 \text{ ft} = r \cdot 6 \text{ min}$
$-166.67 \frac{\text{ft}}{\text{min}} = r$

3. a. $37 \text{ ft} + 37.5 \text{ ft} + 85.5 \text{ ft} + x + 51 \text{ ft} + 37 \text{ ft} + 37 \text{ ft} + 37 \text{ ft} = 392 \text{ ft}$
   $322 \text{ ft} + x = 392 \text{ ft}$
   $x = 70 \text{ ft}$ (added -322 ft to both sides)
   b. $x + 52 \text{ m} + 52 \text{ m} + 52 \text{ m} + 42 \text{ m} = 265 \text{ m}$
   $x + 198 \text{ m} = 265 \text{ m}$
   $x = 67 \text{ m}$ (added -198 m to both sides)

4. $A = l \cdot w$
   $55.5 \text{ ft}^2 = l \cdot 5 \text{ ft}$
   $\frac{55.5 \text{ ft}^2}{5 \text{ ft}} = \frac{l \cdot 5 \text{ ft}}{5 \text{ ft}}$
   $11.1 \text{ ft} = l$

5. yes

Quiz 3 (Chapter 4)

1. Check to make sure students showed how they obtained the answer by adding, subtracting (i.e., adding a negative number), multiplying, or dividing the same amount to both sides, as shown in 1a.
   a. $x + -\frac{1}{3} = 2\frac{2}{3} + -\frac{1}{3}$
   $x = 2\frac{1}{3}$
   b. $x = 6\frac{1}{2} + \frac{5}{6}$ (added $\frac{5}{6}$ to both sides)
   $x = 6\frac{3}{6} + \frac{5}{6}$
   $x = 7\frac{2}{6}$
   $x = 7\frac{1}{3}$
   c. $x = \$3$ (divided both sides by $\frac{2}{3}$ by multiplying them by $\frac{3}{2}$)
   d. $x = 264$ (divided both sides by $\frac{1}{3}$ by multiplying them by $\frac{3}{1}$)
   e. $80 = 20 \cdot x$ (multiplied both sides by x)
   $4 = x$ (divided both sides by 20)
   f. $x + \frac{1}{2} = 15$
   $x = 14\frac{1}{2}$ (added $-\frac{1}{2}$ to both sides)

2. $V = \frac{1}{3} \cdot B \cdot h$
   $V = \frac{1}{3}(35.4 \text{ m} \cdot 35.4 \text{ m})(21.6 \text{ m})$
   $V = 9,022.75 \text{ m}^3$

Quiz 4 (Chapter 5)

1. Check to see that cross multiplication was used, as shown in 1a.
   a. $\frac{3 \text{ notes}}{1 \text{ measure}} = \frac{x}{32 \text{ measures}}$
   $(3 \text{ notes})(32 \text{ measures}) = (1 \text{ measure})(x)$
   $96 \text{ notes} = x$ (divided both sides by 1 measure)
   b. $\frac{2.5 \text{ lb}}{1 \text{ gal}} = \frac{x}{100 \text{ gal}}$; $x = 250$ lb
   c. $\frac{6 \text{ ft}}{10 \text{ ft}} = \frac{w}{15 \text{ ft}}$; $w = 9$ ft

2. a. $207,360 \text{ in}^3 \cdot \frac{1 \text{ ft}}{12 \text{ in}} \cdot \frac{1 \text{ ft}}{12 \text{ in}} \cdot \frac{1 \text{ ft}}{12 \text{ in}} = 120 \text{ ft}^2$
   b. $4,620 \text{ in}^3 \cdot \frac{1 \text{ gal}}{231 \text{ in}^3} = 20$ gal

3. a. $5,659 \text{ mi} = \frac{400 \text{ mi}}{1 \text{ hr}} \cdot t$
   $5,659 \text{ mi} \cdot \frac{1 \text{ hr}}{400 \text{ mi}} = \frac{400 \text{ mi}}{1 \text{ hr}} \cdot t \cdot \frac{1 \text{ hr}}{400 \text{ mi}}$
   $14.15 \text{ hr} = t$

Converting the fractional portion to minutes:
$0.15 \text{ hr} \cdot \frac{60 \text{ mi}}{1 \text{ hr}} = 9$ min
14 hr, 9 min $= t$

b. $6,862 \text{ mi} = \frac{500 \text{ mi}}{1 \text{ hr}} \cdot t$
$6,862 \text{ mi} \cdot \frac{1 \text{ hr}}{500 \text{ mi}} = \frac{500 \text{ mi}}{1 \text{ hr}} \cdot t \cdot \frac{1 \text{ hr}}{500 \text{ mi}}$
$13.72 \text{ hr} = t$

Converting the fractional portion to minutes:
$0.72 \text{ hr} \cdot \frac{60 \text{ min}}{1 \text{ hr}} = 43.2$
13 hr, 43 min $= t$ (rounded per instructions)

c. $a = -0.75 \frac{\text{ft}}{\text{sec}} \cdot 8 \text{ min} + 0 \text{ ft}$
Converting $\frac{\text{ft}}{\text{sec}}$ to $\frac{\text{ft}}{\text{min}}$:
$-0.75 \frac{\text{ft}}{\text{sec}} \cdot \frac{60 \text{ sec}}{1 \text{ min}} = -45 \frac{\text{ft}}{\text{min}}$
$a = -45 \frac{\text{ft}}{\text{min}} \cdot 8 \text{ min} + 0 \text{ ft}$
$a = -360$ ft

4. a. $\frac{F_1}{100 \text{ lb}} = \frac{0.25 \text{ ft}}{3 \text{ ft}}$; $F_1 = 8.33$ lb
   b. $\frac{F_1}{100 \text{ lb}} = \frac{0.25 \text{ ft}}{2 \text{ ft}}$; $F_1 = 12.5$ lb

Bonus: Answer should be one lesson we can learn from the life of Archimedes. See Lesson 5.6 in the *Student Textbook* for ideas.

Quiz 5 (Chapter 6)

1. a. $1.4 \cdot \$2 = P$
   $\$2.80 = P$
   b. $R \cdot \$15,000 = \$7,000$
   $R = 0.4667$ (divided both sides by $15,000)
   $R = 46.67\%$ (converted to a percent)
   c. $R \cdot 25 = 8$
   $R = 0.32$ (divided both sides by 25)
   $R = 32\%$ (converted to a percent)
   d. $100\% - 32\% = 68\%$
   e. $0.58 \cdot B = \$10,530$
   $B = \$18,155.17$ (divided both sides by 0.58)
   f. $0.22 \cdot 2,400 \text{ mg} = 528$ mg

2. $\frac{A}{l} = w$ (divided both sides by l)
   $w = \frac{A}{l}$ (swapped the entire sides of the equation)

3. a. true
   b. Answer should be a fact from Newton's life. See Lesson 6.5 in the *Student Textbook*.

Quiz 6 (Chapter 7)

1. a. 5
   b. $5y$
   c. They mean the same thing because multiplying by 1 doesn't change the value of a quantity (the identity property of multiplication).

2. a. $\frac{5}{7}x + \frac{2}{7}x = 5$
   $\frac{7}{7}x = 5$ (combined like terms)
   $x = \frac{25}{7} = 3\frac{4}{7}$ (divided both sides by $\frac{7}{5}$ by multiplying them by $\frac{5}{7}$)
   b. $3x = 18$ (combined like terms)
   $x = 6$ (divided both sides by 3)
   c. $10x = 190$ (combined like terms)

$x = 19$ (divided both sides by 10)
d. $7x = 80$ (combined like terms)
$x = 11.43$ (divided both sides by 7)

$R \cdot 160 = 30$
$R = 0.1875$ (divided both sides by 160)
$R = 18.75\%$ (converted to a percent)

nus: solid gold

uiz 7 (Chapter 8)

a. $-x = -20$ (added –106 to both sides)
$x = 20$ (multiplied both sides by –1)

$x - -6 = 108$
$x + 6 = 108$
$x = 102$ (added –6 to both sides)

$(-3)(-6) = 18$

$2x = 89$ (combined like terms)
$x = 44.5$ (divided both sides by 2)

$3x = 135$ (combined like terms)
$x = 45$ (divided both sides by 3)

$-x = -22.64$ (added –85.42 to both sides)
$x = 22.64$ (multiplied both sides by –1)
$2x = 40$ (added $-x$ to both sides)
$x = 20$ (divided both sides by 2)

opposite

Answer should be a word problem for one of the problems on the quiz. See similar problems throughout Chapter 8 for ideas.

uiz 8 (Chapter 9)

Check both answer and that problem was set up using parentheses: $0.08(\$7 - \$2.50) = \$0.36$

a. $3(\frac{2}{3}) + 3x = 8$
$2 + 3x = 8$
$3x = 6$ (added –2 to both sides)
$x = 2$ (divided both sides by 3)

b. $1.08(\$78 + -x) = \$75$
$1.08(\$78) + -1.08x = \$75$
$\$84.24 + -1.08x = \$75$
$-1.08x = -9.24$ (added –$84.24 to both sides)
$x = \$8.56$ (divided both sides by –1.08)

c. $-5(8 + -x) = -20$
$-5(8) + -5(-x) = -20$
$-40 + 5x = -20$
$5x = 20$ (added 40 to both sides)
$x = 4$ (divided both sides by 5)

d. $\$800 + -1(\$4 + x) = \$795.75$
$\$800 + -1(\$4) + -1x = \$795.75$
$\$800 + -\$4 + -x = \$795.75$
$\$796 + -x = \$795.75$
$-x = -\$0.25$ (added –$796 to both sides)
$x = \$0.25$ (multiplied both sides by –1)

$2[3(20)] =$
$2[60] =$
120

the number of lessons completed each day

Quiz 9 (Chapter 10)

1. a. $x \geq 60 \frac{mg}{dL}$
   b. $x > \$50$

2. a.

   b.

3. a. $x + 5 > 20$
   b. $-4x \leq -16$
   c. $x - 6 < 25$
   d. $80x \geq 1{,}600$

4. a. $x > 15$ (added –5 to both sides)
   b. $x \geq 4$ (divided both sides by –4 and changed the direction of the sign)
   c. $x < 31$ (added 6 to both sides)
   d. $x \geq 20$ (divided both sides by 80)

Quiz 10 (Chapter 11)

Check analysis submitted for understanding of statistics.

Quiz 11 (Chapter 12)

1. a. $\frac{15{,}000}{30{,}000} = 0.5 = 50\%$
   b. $\frac{15{,}000}{30{,}000} \cdot \frac{15{,}000}{30{,}000} = 0.25 = 25\%$
   c. $100\% - 95\% = 5\%$

2. a. $\frac{3}{12} = 0.25 = 25\%$
   b. $\frac{4}{30} = 0.1333 = 13.33\%$
   c. $4:26$
   d. $\frac{4}{30} \cdot \frac{3}{29} = \frac{12}{870} = 0.0138 = 1.38\%$

3. $10 \cdot 10 \cdot 10 \cdot 10 = 10{,}000$

Bonus: Answer should be three different ways probability applies not mentioned on the quiz. Possibilities include the weather, insurance, games, genetics, and atoms.

Quiz 12 (Chapter 13)

1. a. constant
   b. one
   c. y could have multiple values.
   d. no

2. a. T or the total earnings
   b. $\underline{T}$ as a function of $\underline{B}$
   c. B or Job B
   d. $\underline{B}$ as a function of $\underline{T}$

3. a.

s (input, in $\frac{mi}{hr}$)	$d = s(5 \text{ hr})$, where $s \geq 0$	d (output, in mi)
15	$d = (15)(5)$	75
45	$d = (45)(5)$	225
60	$d = (60)(5)$	300

   b.
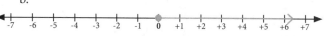

Quiz 13 (Chapter 14)

1. a.

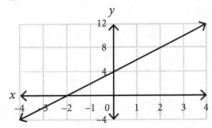

   b.

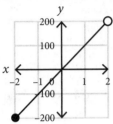

2. a. 2
   b. 100
   c. 2
   d. 0
   e. There should be a box around "where $-2 \le x < 2$" in problem 1b.

3. a. $y = 12x$
   b. $y = 5x + 10$

4. a. false
      (It is the value at which the line intercepts the vertical axis.)
   b. true
   c. true
      (For every value for x, there's only one value for y.)

5.

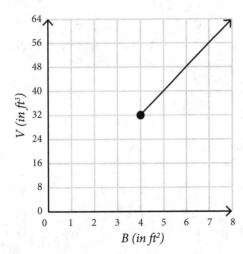

Bonus: Answer should be student's thoughts on statement and Descartes' philosophy. The text pointed out that Descartes' thinking, not God's Word, was his starting point.

Quiz 14 (Chapter 15)

1. a. $16 + 4(27 − 2) =$
       $16 + 4(25) =$
       $16 + 100 = 116$

   b. $9^4 + 5 =$
       $6,561 + 5 = 6,566$
   c. x^5
   d. $3x$

2. a. $A = (7.6 \text{ ft})^2 = 57.76 \text{ ft}^2$
   b. $V = 30 \text{ in} \cdot 20 \text{ in} \cdot 4 \text{ in} = 2,400 \text{ in}^3$
   c. $V = (4 \text{ m})^3 = 64 \text{ m}^3$

3. a. $P = (10)(1 + 0.05)^{20}$
      $P = 26.53$ bacteria
      $P = 27$ bacteria   (rounded per instructions)
   b. $P = (15 \text{ mg})(1 − 0.01)^{24}$
      $P = 11.79$ mg

Bonus: Answer should be an explanation of why we find suffering and death in the world (see Lesson 15.8 in the *Student Textbook*).

Quiz 15 (Chapter 16)

1. a. $\frac{1}{5^2} = \frac{1}{25}$
   b. $\frac{1}{3^4}$

2. a. 5.6247×10^{-6}
   b. 5.264158×10^8
   c. $5,620,000,000,000,000$
   d. 0.0000000312

3. a. x^9
   b. x^3
   c. $3x^5$
   d. 1×10^3
   e. 8×10^6

Bonus: Rhetorical algebra used words and syncopated algebra used symbols.

Quiz 16 (Chapter 17)

1. a. *prime factors* = $2 \cdot 2 \cdot 3 \cdot 3 \cdot 3 \cdot 3$
      square root = $2 \cdot 3 \cdot 3 = 18$
   b. *prime factors* = $2 \cdot 2 \cdot 2 \cdot 2 \cdot 2 \cdot 2$
      cubed root = $2 \cdot 2 = 4$
   c. $x = 58,081$ (squared both sides)
   d. $456 \text{ in}^2 = s^2$
      $21.35 \text{ in} = s$ (took the square root of both sides)

2. a. $(16.3 \text{ ft})^2 + (12.5 \text{ ft})^2 = c^2$
      $265.69 \text{ ft}^2 + 156.25 \text{ ft}^2 = c^2$
      $421.94 \text{ ft}^2 = c^2$
      $\sqrt{421.94 \text{ ft}^2} = \sqrt{c^2}$
      $20.54 \text{ ft} = c$
   b. $a^2 + (0.7 \text{ in})^2 = (1.4 \text{ in})^2$
      $a^2 + 0.49 \text{ in}^2 = 1.96 \text{ in}^2$
      $a^2 = 1.47 \text{ in}^2$ (added −0.49 in² to both sides)
      $\sqrt{a^2} = \sqrt{1.47 \text{ in}^2}$
      $a = 1.21 \text{ in}$
   c. not enough information
      (We don't know if the triangle is a right triangle.)

3. a. $(12 \text{ in})^2 + (5 \text{ in})^2 = c^2$
      $144 \text{ in}^2 + 25 \text{ in}^2 = c^2$
      $169 \text{ in}^2 = c^2$
      $\sqrt{169 \text{ in}^2} = \sqrt{c^2}$

13 in = c
b. yes

$(250 \text{ yd})^2 + (325 \text{ yd})^2 = c^2$
$62,500 \text{ yd}^2 + 105,625 \text{ yd}^2 = c^2$
$168,125 \text{ yd}^2 = c^2$
$\sqrt{168,125 \text{ yd}^2} = \sqrt{c^2}$
410.03 yd = c

Bonus: The Pythagoreans believed everything (including fractions) could be reduced one way or another to whole numbers. Yet when we apply the Pythagorean theorem, we encounter numbers (such as the $\sqrt{2}$) that can't be described using whole numbers alone.

Quiz 17 (Chapter 18)

a. $\frac{5 \text{ ft}}{7.7 \text{ ft}} = 0.65$
b. $\frac{5 \text{ ft}}{9.18 \text{ ft}} = 0.54$
c. $\frac{7.7 \text{ ft}}{9.18 \text{ ft}} = 0.84$

a. 90° *or* right
b. proportional
c. sin(40°) = 0.64

a. 0.27
b. 0.62

$\tan(20°) = \frac{x}{10.3 \text{ in}}$
$\tan(20°) \cdot 10.3 \text{ in} = x$ (multiplied both sides by 10.3 in)
3.75 in = x

Quiz 18 (Chapter 19)

a. 57 ∈ C
b. yes
(According to the Venn diagram, all the elements of C are also elements of E.)

a. yes
b. yes
c. x ∈ ℕ

a. {3, 4(3), 8(3), 12(3), 16(3), ...}
   {3, 12, 24, 36, 48, ...}
b. Yes; the common ratio is 3.
c. geometric sequence
d. 189, 567
   (Each number in the sequence is 3 times the one before it.)

Quiz 19 (Chapter 20)

a. *number of periods* = 10 • 12 = 120
   (multiplied 12, the number of periods in a year, by 10, the number of years)
b. *rate per period* = $\frac{0.033}{12}$ = 0.00275
   (divided the annual rate of 3.3% by 12, the number of periods in a year)
c. $P = \$700(1 + 0.00275)^{120}$
   P = \$973.24
d. 0.05 • \$6,000 = \$300

a. $\frac{\$700}{3}$ = \$233.33
b. 4.33 • \$450 = \$1,948.50

3. a. 0.4 • 10 gal = 4 gal
   4 gal • $\frac{16 \text{ c}}{1 \text{ gal}}$ = 64 c
   b. R • \$1,200 = \$500
   R = 0.4167   (divided both sides by \$1,200)
   R = 41.67%   (converted to a percent)

Bonus: Answer should be a truth from Scripture to keep in mind while working with money. Possibilities include not to lay up treasures on earth, that treasure here is temporary, that we can't serve God and money, and to seek the Lord rather than wealth.

Answer to Tests

Test 1 (Chapters 1–5)

1. On 1a and 1b, students should show how they obtained their answer using cross multiplication.

   a. $\frac{250 \text{ words}}{1 \text{ min}} = \frac{2{,}000 \text{ words}}{x}$

   250 words • x = 1 min • 2,000 words
                         (cross multiplied)

   x = 8 min   (divided both sides by 250 words)

   b. $\frac{90 \text{ strokes}}{1 \text{ min}} = \frac{x}{60 \text{ min}}$

   90 strokes • 60 min = 1 min • x
                         (cross multiplied)

   5,400 strokes • min = 1 min • x
   5,400 strokes = x (divided both sides by 1 min)

   c. 5 mi • $\frac{1.609344 \text{ km}}{1 \text{ mi}}$ • $\frac{1{,}000 \text{ m}}{1 \text{ km}}$ = 8,046.72 m

   d. 85 ft² • $\frac{1 \text{ yd}}{3 \text{ ft}}$ • $\frac{1 \text{ yd}}{3 \text{ ft}}$ = 9.44 yd²

   e. x = 65   (divided both sides by $\frac{4}{5}$ by multiplying them by $\frac{5}{4}$)

   f. 400 mi = s • 8 hr
   50 $\frac{\text{mi}}{\text{hr}}$ = s (divided both sides by 8 hr)

   g. $V = B \cdot h$
   Volume of each cylinder = (3.14 • 6 ft • 6 ft)(32 ft) = 3,617.28 ft³
   Volume of all 4 cylinders = 4 • 3,617.28 ft³ = 14,469.12 ft³
   Bushels in all 4 cylinders = 14,469.12 ft3 • 12 in/1 ft • 12 in/1 ft • 12 in/1 ft • 1 bushel/2,150.42 in • 1 bushel/2,150.42 in • 1 bushel/2,150.42 inches = 3,875.62 bushels

   h. 80 in² = 5.5 in • w
   14.55 in = w (divided both sides by 5.5 in)

2. a. 6 • $\frac{4}{1}$ = 24
   b. 7
   c. –4
   d. 17

3. a. x = 18.6   (added –6 to both sides)
   b. x = 7.78   (divided both sides by 4.5)
   c. 25 = 5x (multiplied both sides by x)
      5 = x (divided both sides by 5)
   d. x = 40   (added 8 to both sides)

Test 2 (Chapters 6–11)

1. a. average = $\frac{45 + 31 + 35 + 41 + 28 + 40}{6}$ = 36.67 people, which rounds to 37 people

   b. 2 data points   2 data points
      28 + 31 + ⟨35 + 40⟩ + 41 + 45

   median = $\frac{35 + 40}{2}$ = 37.5, which rounds to 38 people

   c. $t - e = r$ or $t + -e = r$ (added –e to both sides)
      $r = t - e$ or $r = t + -e$ (swapped the entire sides of the equation)

   d. $x \geq \$6{,}000$

   e. 6x + 3x = $495
      9x = $495   (combined like terms)
      x = $55   (divided both sides by 9)

   f. R • 55 = 44
      R = 0.8   (divided both sides by 52)
      R = 80%   (converted to a percent)

   g. 0.025 • B = 55 people
      B = 2,200 people   (divided both sides by 0.025)

2. a. 4x = 48   (combined like terms)
      x = 12   (divided both sides by 4)

   b. 22 + –2(5) + –2x = 22
      12 + –2x = 22
      –2x = 10   (added –12 to both sides)
      x = –5   (divided both sides by –2)

   c. x < $60   (added –$5 to both sides)

   d. $\frac{4}{4}x + \frac{1}{4}x = 8$
      $\frac{5}{4}x = 8$ (combined like terms)
      $x = \frac{32}{5} = 6\frac{2}{5}$ (divided both sides by $\frac{5}{4}$ by multiplying them by $\frac{4}{5}$)

   e. x > –26   (divided both sides by –4 and changed the direction of the sign)

   f. 50 + –1(1 + x) = 2
      50 + –1 + –x = 2
      49 + –x = 2
      –x = –47   (added –49 to both sides)
      x = 47   (multiplied both sides by –1)

   g. x > 2   (divided both sides by 5)

3. a. x > –105
   b.
   c. 0.055 • $78.50 = $4.32
   d. 0.06 • B = 5.04
      B = 84   (divided both sides by 0.06)

Test 3 (Chapter 12–16)

1. a. $\frac{1}{4}$ = 0.25 = 25%
   b. $\frac{1}{4} \cdot \frac{1}{4} = \frac{1}{16}$ = 0.0625 = 6.25%
   c. 5 • 5 • 5 • 5 = 5⁴ = 625

2. a.
   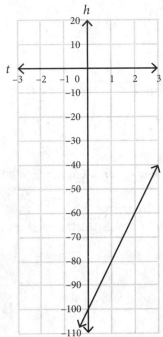

PAGE 418 | PRINCIPLES OF MATHEMATICS 2

b.

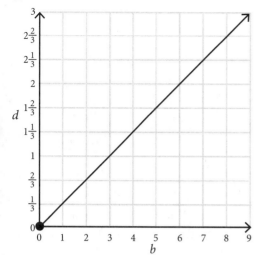

a. one
b. yes
   (For every value for x, there's only one value for y.)

a. 0.06
b. 0
c. $P = 0.06B$, where $B \geq 0$
d. P as a function of B

a. $(8)^2 = 64$
b. $\frac{1}{5^2} = \frac{1}{25}$
c. $16(0.44)^6 = 0.12$
d. $6x^2$

a. 4.35×10^{-3}
b. 1.42325×10^{11}

$V = \frac{4}{3}(3.14)(4.1 \text{ in})^3$
$V = 288.55 \text{ in}^3$

Test 4 (Chapter 17–21)

a. 22 and 23
b. prime factors = 2 • 2 • 2 • 2 • 11 • 11
   square root = 2 • 2 • 11 = 44
c. prime factors = 3 • 3 • 3 • 3 • 3 • 3
   cubed root = 3 • 3 = 9

a. $x^2 = 7{,}396$ (squared both sides)
b. 78 in² = s²
   8.83 in = s (took the square root of both sides)
c. 0.27

a. $(15 \text{ ft})^2 + (8 \text{ ft})^2 = c^2$
   225 ft² + 64 ft² = c²
   289 ft² = c²
   17 ft = c (took the square root of both sides)
b. $h^2 + (3.5 \text{ ft})^2 = (5 \text{ ft})^2$
   $h^2 + 12.25 \text{ ft}^2 = 25 \text{ ft}^2$
   $h^2 = 12.75 \text{ ft}^2$ (added –12.25 ft² to both sides)
   $h = 3.57 \text{ ft}$ (took the square root of both sides)
c. cosine = $\frac{3.5 \text{ ft}}{5 \text{ ft}} = 0.7$
d. $\sin(45°) = \frac{h}{8 \text{ ft}}$

$\sin(45°) \cdot 8 \text{ ft} = h$ (multiplied both sides by 8 ft)
$0.707106781 \cdot 8 \text{ ft} = h$ (found the value of sin(45°) on a calculator)
5.66 ft = h
e. cos(35°) = 0.82

4. a. no
   b. $3x - 2x = \underline{x}$ $2x - x = \underline{x}$
   c. arithmetic sequence
   d. {x, 2x, 3x, $\underline{4x}$, ...}
      (We added the common difference of x to the previous element: 3x + x = 4x)
   e. {3, $\frac{1}{2}$(3), $\frac{1}{4}$(3), $\frac{1}{8}$(3), ...}
      {3, $1\frac{1}{2}$, $\frac{3}{4}$, $\frac{3}{8}$, ...}
   f. {2, 5, 3, 5, $\underline{4}$, $\underline{5}$, ...}
      (The pattern is to alternate between increasing by 1 and the number 5.)

5. a. *number of months in 5 years* = 5 • 12 = 60
      (multiplied 12, the number of periods in a year, by 5, the number of years)
   b. *monthly rate* = $\frac{0.025}{12}$ = 0.002083333
      (divided the annual rate of 2.5% by 12, the number of periods in a year)
   c. $P = \$15{,}000(1 + 0.002083333)^{60}$
      $P = \$16{,}995.02$
   d. $\frac{\$60{,}000}{12} = \$5{,}000$
   e. $0.1 \cdot \$30{,}000 = \$3{,}000$
      $\frac{\$3{,}000}{12} = \$250$

Test 5 (Chapter 1–21)

1. a. $R \cdot 144 = 23$
      $R = 0.1597$ (divided both sides by 144)
      $R = 15.97\%$ (converted to a percent)
   b. $x = \$750{,}000$ (divided both sides by $\frac{1}{50}$ by multiplying them by $\frac{50}{1}$)
   c. $R \cdot \$50 = \$6$
      $R = 0.12$ (divided both sides by $50)
      $R = 12\%$ (converted to a percent)
   d. $5(\$6 + -x) = \$120$
      $5(\$6) + -5x = \$120$
      $\$30 - 5x = \$20$
      $-5x = -\$10$ (added –$30 to both sides)
      $x = \$2$ (divided both sides by –5)
   e. $x = \$140$ (divided both sides by $\frac{1}{4}$ by multiplying them by $\frac{4}{1}$)
   f. 495 mi = s(9 hr)
      $55 \frac{\text{mi}}{\text{hr}} = s$ (divided both sides by 9 hr)
   g. $5 \text{ mi} = \frac{65 \text{ mi}}{60 \text{ min}} \cdot t$
      4.62 min = t (divided both sides by $\frac{65 \text{ mi}}{60 \text{ min}}$ by multiplying them by $\frac{60 \text{ min}}{65 \text{ mi}}$)
      5 min = t (rounded per instructions)
      Note: Students may have solved a different way; look for correct answer.
   h. $\frac{1}{4} \cdot \$80 = \$20$

2. a. $A = \ell w$
      80 ft² = ℓ • 8 ft

      10 ft = ℓ (divided both sides by 8 ft)
   b. $(15 \text{ ft})^2 + (20 \text{ ft})^2 = c^2$
      $225 \text{ ft}^2 + 400 \text{ ft}^2 = c^2$
      $625 \text{ ft}^2 = c^2$
      $\sqrt{625 \text{ ft}^2} = \sqrt{c^2}$
      25 ft = c
   c. 1
   d. $\frac{0.5}{1.3} = 0.38$
   e. $89 \text{ ft}^2 = s^2$
      9.43 = s   (took the square root of both sides)
   f. $\frac{40 \text{ ft}}{50 \text{ ft}} = \frac{0.2 \text{ ft}}{x}$
      x = 0.25 ft

3. a.

b (input)	p (output)
−600	−300
0	0
600	300

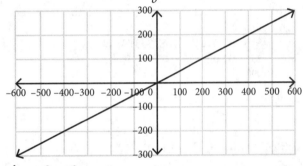

   b. $y = 2x - 6$

4. a. $\frac{1}{6} \cdot \frac{1}{6} \cdot \frac{1}{6} \cdot \frac{1}{6} = \frac{1}{1,296} = 0.00077 = 0.08\%$
   b. $average = \frac{3 \text{ in} + 4 \text{ in} + 2.5 \text{ in} + 0 \text{ in} + 8.8 \text{ in} + 0 \text{ in} + 0.5 \text{ in}}{7} =$
      $\frac{18.8}{7} = 2.69$ in
   c. No; a week's worth of data is not enough data from which to draw a conclusion.
   d. mode = 0 in
   e. 0 in, 0 in, 0.5 in, (2.5 in), 3 in, 4 in, 8.8 in
      median = 2.5 in

5. a. 0.0000000000256
   b. $5(3.03)^{15} = 83,293,177.85$
   c. {2, 4(2), 8(2), 24(2), . . .}
      {2, 8, 16, 48,…}
   d. 3y = 9   (combined like terms)
      y = 3   (divided both sides by 3)
   e. $4(3)^2 = 4(9) = 36$
   f. x < 16   (divided both sides by 4)
   g. prime factors = $2 \cdot 2 \cdot 2 \cdot 2 \cdot 7 \cdot 7$
      square root = $2 \cdot 2 \cdot 7 = 28$

6. $V = \frac{1}{3}(3.14 \cdot 6 \text{ in} \cdot 6 \text{ in})(28 \text{ in})$
   $V = 1,055.04 \text{ in}^3$

7. Students should submit end-of-year project assigned on Worksheet 21.1. Use your own judgment in grading.

General Instructions for Students

(To be given to the student on Day 1.)

Worksheets, Quizzes, and Tests

Review — If at any point you hit a concept that does not make sense, back up and review the preceding concepts. Be sure to take advantage of the reference notebook you'll be instructed to start in Worksheet 1.1.

Calculator — Anytime you see a (🖩) or when instructed to on a quiz or test, you are permitted to use a calculator to solve the problem. Unless instructed otherwise by your parent/teacher, all other problems should be solved without the use of a calculator, as you won't always have a calculator with you when you need to solve a problem in real life.

Showing Your Work — When solving many problems, you will be instructed to show your work. Even if you could solve some of the problems mentally, showing your work will help you master the skills so you'll be prepared to apply them to more advanced problems later.

Word Problems — You should write down enough steps that it's obvious how you solved a word problem. While writing down steps may seem like busy work on simple problems, forming the habit of organizing your steps on paper from the beginning will greatly help you avoid mistakes on in-depth problems involving numerous steps.

Units of Measure — If a unit of measure (such as dollars, feet, etc.) is given in a problem, you should always include it in your answer.

Rounding — Unless otherwise instructed, answers should be rounded to two decimal places. When using a calculator, do not round until your final answer. When answers are written as a percent, the percent should be rounded to two decimal places.

   Example: 4.567 rounds to 4.57

   Example: 26.3574% rounds to 26.36%

Fractions — Fractional answers should be in lowest terms unless otherwise specified. This includes rewriting improper fractions as mixed numbers.

If a problem is given with a fraction in it, list any partial quantities in your answer as a fraction. There is an exception to this: if the problem includes both fractions and decimals, you may give your answer in either notation, unless otherwise specified.

Pi (π) — The symbol π stands for the ratio between the circumference and diameter of a circle. It is an irrational number that begins 3.14159265358979323846264338327950288419716939937510582097494 4592307816406286 . . . and continues on and on. Since we can't precisely calculate the value, we have to approximate it when solving problems involving π. While many calculators have a π button you can use in solving problems to get a more accurate value for π, in this course, **use the rounded value of 3.14 for π**.

Quizzes and Tests — When you are told you can consult reference sheets for quizzes and tests, you are allowed to consult any reference sheet (p. 423-433) even if fewer page numbers are listed.

Study Days

The study days built into the schedule are designed to give you a chance to study on your own! While you c
study different ways, here are a few suggestions:

- Start by looking at chapter synopsis (or synopses) for the chapter(s) you're studying. Review any concept
listed there you may have forgotten. Look at the worksheets for the chapter(s), especially at problems you
got wrong. Do you know how to solve them now? When studying for a test, also go back over the quizze
for the chapters covered on the test.

- Review any concepts you know were more challenging for you.

- Look at any notes you've taken. Review any flashcards you've made (or make some if you've not made an
yet).

Reference Sheets

Please tear these pages out and place in your math notebook, along with blank paper on which to add your own notes.

Polygon

(Closed, two-dimensional figure with straight lines)

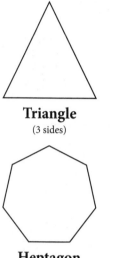
Triangle
(3 sides)

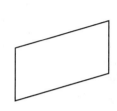
Quadrilateral
(4 sides)

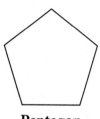
Pentagon
(5 sides)

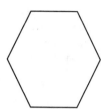
Hexagon
(6 sides)

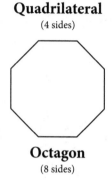
Heptagon
(7 sides)

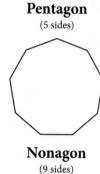
Octagon
(8 sides)

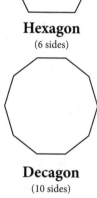
Nonagon
(9 sides)

Decagon
(10 sides)

Regular Polygon

(All sides are equal; all edges would touch a circle drawn around the figure, as all angles are the same.)

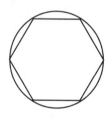 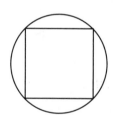 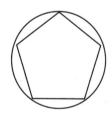

Irregular Polygon

(Polygons that are not regular.)

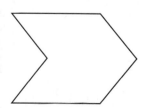 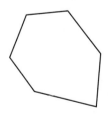  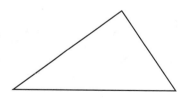

Specific Quadrilaterals

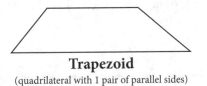

Trapezoid
(quadrilateral with 1 pair of parallel sides)

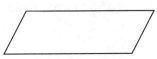

Parallelogram
(quadrilateral with both pairs of opposite sides parallel)

Some books define a trapezoid as a quadrilateral with 1, and only 1, pair of parallel sides, while others as a quadrilateral with 1 (or more) pair of parallel sides. Likewise, some define a rhombus/diamond differently than listed here. Always remember that definitions can — and do — vary!

Rhombus/Diamond
(parallelogram with equal-length sides)

Rectangle
(parallelogram with right angles)

Square
(parallelogram with equal-length sides *and* right angle)

Triangles Categorized by Length of Sides

Isosceles
(two equal sides)

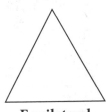

Equilateral
(all equal sides)

Scalene
(no equal sides)

Triangles Categorized by Angles

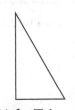

Right Triangle
(a right angle)

Acute Triangle
(all acute angles)

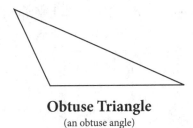

Obtuse Triangle
(an obtuse angle)

Circle

(closed two-dimensional figure; each part of the edge is equally distant from the center)

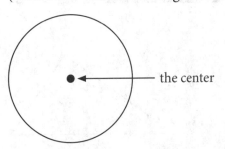

Prism

(A solid with two bases that are parallel polygons, and faces [sides] that are parallelograms; the prism is named after the shape of the bases.)

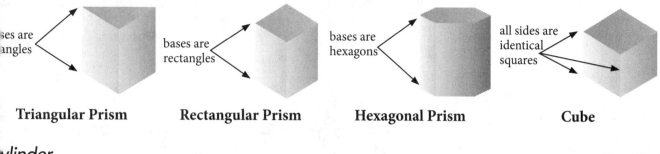

bases are triangles — **Triangular Prism**

bases are rectangles — **Rectangular Prism**

bases are hexagons — **Hexagonal Prism**

all sides are identical squares — **Cube**

Cylinder

(A solid with two bases that are equal parallel circles, having an equal diameter in any parallel plane between them.)

Prism and cylinder definitions were based on *Ray's New Higher Arithmetic*, Revised (Cincinnati: Van Antwerp, Bragg & Co., 1880), p. 390.

Formulas

Shape Name	Type of Shape	Perimeter	Area
Polygons		P = sum of the lengths of each side or $P = s_1 + s_2 \ldots s_n$	View as multiple triangles or other shapes.
Regular Polygon		P = (number of sides) • (length of a side) or $P = n \cdot s$ or $P = n(s)$ or $P = ns$	View as multiple triangles or other shapes.
Rectangle		$P = (2 \cdot length) + (2 \cdot width)$ or $P = 2 \cdot \ell + 2 \cdot w$ or $P = 2(\ell) + 2(w)$ or $P = 2\ell + 2w$	$A = length \cdot width$ or $A = \ell \cdot w$ or $A = \ell(w)$ or $A = \ell w$
Square		$P = 4 \cdot side$ or $P = 4 \cdot s$ or $P = 4(s)$ or $P = 4s$	$A = side \cdot side$ or $A = s \cdot s$ or $A = s(s)$ or $A = s^2$
Parallelogram		$P = (2 \cdot base) + (2 \cdot side)$ or $P = 2 \cdot b + 2 \cdot s$ or $P = 2(b) + 2(s)$ or $P = 2b + 2s$	$A = base \cdot height$ or $A = b \cdot h$ or $A = b(h)$ or $A = bh$
Triangle		Perimeter = sum of the lengths of each side or $P = s_1 + s_2 + s_3$	$A = \frac{1}{2} \cdot base \cdot height$ or $A = \frac{base \cdot height}{2}$ $A = \frac{1}{2} \cdot b \cdot h$ or $A = \frac{1}{2}bh$ or $A = \frac{b \cdot h}{2}$ or $A = \frac{bh}{2}$

A = Area
B = area of the base
b = base
C = circumference
d = diameter

h = height
ℓ = length
n = number of sides
P = Perimeter
π = 3.14

r = radius
s = side
V = Volume
w = width (or height)

Shape Name	Type of Shape	Circumference	Area
Circle		*Circumference = π • diameter* or $C = \pi \cdot d$ or $C = \pi(d)$ or $C = \pi d$ *Circumference = 2 • π • radius* or $C = 2 \cdot \pi \cdot r$ or $C = 2(\pi)(r)$ or $C = 2\pi r$	*Area = π • radius • radius* or $A = \pi \cdot r^2$ or $A = \pi(r^2)$ or $A = \pi r^2$
		diameter = 2 • radius or $d = 2 \cdot r$ or $d = 2r$ radius = $\frac{1}{2}$ • diameter or $r = \frac{1}{2} \cdot d$ or $r = \frac{1}{2}d$	

Shape Name	Type of Shape	Volume	Area
Prism		*Volume = area of base • height* or $V = B \cdot h$ or $V = Bh$	Total surface area = area of all the sides (i.e., surfaces) of a solid object
Cylinder		*Volume = area of base • height* or $V = B \cdot h$ or $V = Bh$	did not cover
Pyramid		*Volume* = $\frac{1}{3}$ • *area of base • height* or $V = \frac{1}{3} \cdot B \cdot h$ or $V = \frac{1}{3}Bh$	did not cover
Sphere		*Volume* = $\frac{4}{3}$ • π • *radius³* or $V = \frac{4}{3} \cdot \pi \cdot r^3$ or $V = \frac{4}{3}\pi r^3$	did not cover

A = Area
B = area of the base
b = base
C = circumference
d = diameter

h = height
ℓ = length
n = number of sides
P = Perimeter
π = 3.14

r = radius
s = side
V = Volume
w = width (or height)

PRINCIPLES OF MATHEMATICS 2 | PAGE 427

Units of Measure

Distance

Distance – U.S. Customary
12 inches (in) = 1 foot (ft)
3 feet / 36 inches = 1 yard (yd)
1,760 yard / 5,280 feet = 1 mile (mi)

Distance – Metric/SI
10 millimeters (mm) = 1 centimeter (cm)
10 centimeters = 1 decimeter (dm)
10 decimeters / 100 centimeters / 1,000 millimeters = 1 meter (m)
10 meters = 1 decameters (dam)
10 decameters = 1 hectometer (hm)
10 hectometers / 1,000 meters = 1 kilometer (km)

Conversion Between Systems
1 inches (in) = 2.54 centimeter (cm)
1 foot (ft) = 30.48 centimeter (cm)
1 yard (yd) = 0.9144 meter (m)
1 mile (mi) = 1.609344 kilometer (km)

Time

60 seconds (s) = 1 minute (min)
60 minutes = 1 hour (hr)
24 hours = 1 day (d)
7 days = 1 week (wk)
365 days = 1 year (yr *or* y)

Liquid Capacity

U.S. Customary
3 teaspoons (tsp) = 1 tablespoon (Tbsp)
16 tablespoons = 1 cup (c)
2 cups = 1 pint (pt)
2 pints = 1 quart (qt)
4 quarts = 1 gallon (gal)

2 tablespoons (Tbsp) ≈ 1 fluid ounce (fl oz)
8 fl oz = 1 cup (c)
16 fl oz = 1 pint (pt)
32 fl oz = 1 quart (qt)
128 fl oz = 1 gallon (gal)

Conversion Between Systems
1 teaspoon ≈ 5 milliliters
1 gallon = 3.78541 liters

1 pint = 28.875 in^3
1 quart = 57.75 in^3
1 gallon = 231 in^3

Metric
10 milliliters (ml *or* mL) = 1 centiliter (cl *or* cL)
10 centiliter / 100 milliliter = 1 deciliter (dl *or* dL)
10 deciliter / 100 centiliter / 1,000 milliliter = 1 liter (*l or* L)
10 liters = 1 dekaliter (dal *or* daL)
10 dekaliter = 1 hectoliter (hl *or* hL)
10 hectoliter / 1,000 liters = 1 kiloliter (kl *or* kL)

Dry Capacity

U.S. Customary
2 pints (pt) = 1 quart (qt)
8 quart = 1 peck (pk)
4 peck = 1 bushel (bu) / 32 quarts (qt)

Conversion Between Systems
1 quart = 67.2006 inches^3
1 bushel = 2,150.42 inches^3

Note: The pint and quart here represent a larger capacity than the ones measuring liquid—they should not be used interchangeably. Unless the problem specifically states otherwise, you can assume pint and quart in this course refer to the liquid units.

Mass

U.S. Customary
16 ounces (oz) = 1 pound (lb)
2,000 pounds = 1 ton (called a "short ton")

Conversion Between Systems
1 ounce = 28.3495 grams
1 pound = 453.592 grams
1 U.S. ton (called a short ton) = 0.907185 metric tons

Note: These ounces are different than the fluid ounces listed under liquid capacity.

Metric
10 milligrams (mg) = 1 centigram (cg)
10 centigrams / 100 milligrams = 1 decigram (dg)
10 decigrams / 100 centigrams / 1,000 milligrams = 1 gram (g)
10 grams = 1 dekagram (dag)
10 dekagrams = 1 hectogram (hg)
10 hectograms / 1,000 grams = 1 kilogram (kg)

For more unit details, see the official standards given in Tina Butcher, Linda Crown, Rick Harshman, and Juana Williams, eds. *NIST Handbook 44: 97th National Conference on Weights and Measures 2012*, 2013 ed. (Washington: U. S. Department of Commerce, 2012), Appendix C. Found on http://www.nist.gov/pml/wmd/pubs/h44-13.cfm, accessed 10/6/2014.

Important Mathematical Relationships

Distance Problems See Lessons 3.5, 3.7, and 5.3.

$$d = s \cdot t \text{ or } d = st$$
$$\text{distance} = \text{speed} \cdot \text{time}$$

Altitude (or Height) Problems See Lesson 3.7.

$$a = r \cdot t + a_i$$
altitude (or height) = rate of change in altitude (or height) • time + initial altitude (or height)

Percent Problems See Lesson 6.3.

$$R \cdot B = P \text{ or } RB = P$$
$$\text{Rate} \cdot \text{Base} = \text{Percentage}$$
Think: The rate *of* the base *equals* the percentage.

Probability See Chapter 12.

$$\text{probability of an event} = \frac{\text{outcomes that produce event}}{\text{total possible outcomes}}$$

$$\text{odds for} = \frac{\text{outcomes that produce event}}{\text{outcomes that do not produce event}}$$

$$\text{odds against} = \frac{\text{outcomes that do not produce event}}{\text{outcomes that produce event}}$$

Pythagorean Theorem See Lessons 17.5–17.7.

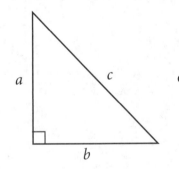 or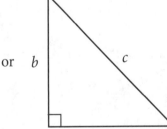

$$a^2 + b^2 = c^2$$

where c stands for the length of the hypotenuse of a right triangle, and a and b stand for the length of the two legs of the same right triangle

Trigonometry See Chapter 18.

Tangent of an angle — The ratio between the opposite and adjacent leg of either non-right angle in a right triangle.

$$\text{tangent of an angle} = \frac{\text{opposite leg}}{\text{adjacent leg}}$$

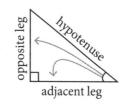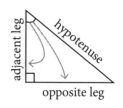

Sine of an angle — The ratio between the opposite leg of either non-right angle in a right triangle and the hypotenuse.

$$\text{sine of an angle} = \frac{\text{opposite leg}}{\text{hypotenuse}}$$

Cosine of an angle — The ratio between the adjacent leg of either non-right angle in a right triangle and the hypotenuse.

$$\text{cosine of an angle} = \frac{\text{adjacent leg}}{\text{hypotenuse}}$$

Exponential Growth and Decay
(Applies to Compound Interest Too) See Lessons 15.5–15.7 and Lessons 20.1–20.2.

$$P = P_0(1 + r)^t$$

where
P = final amount after growth or decay
P_0 = initial amount before growth or decay
r = rate of growth or decay over a specified period of time
t = the number of specified periods of time that have passed

Mathematical Relationships See Lesson 13.2–13.5 and 14.1 for an explanation.
Important Terms

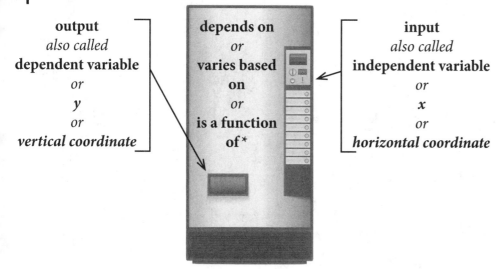

output
also called
dependent variable
or
y
or
vertical coordinate

depends on
or
varies based on
or
is a function of *

input
also called
independent variable
or
x
or
horizontal coordinate

*The term *is a function of* is only used if we know there's only one output for every input.

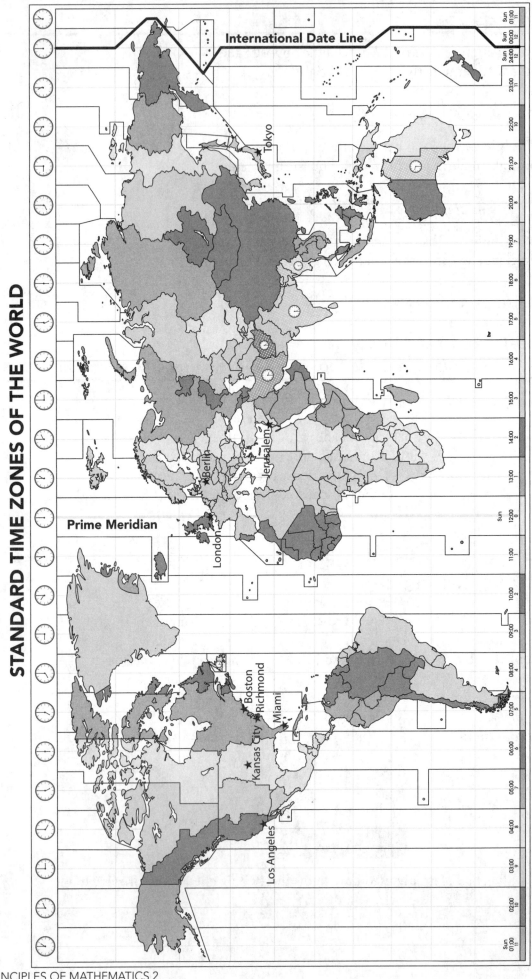